Nonlinear Dynamics and Economics presents some of the recent developments in non-linear economic dynamics along with related research from associated fields, including mathematics, statistics, biology, and physics. This volume comprises the tenth in the *International Symposia in Economic Theory and Econometrics* series under the general editorship of William Barnett. This proceedings volume includes revisions of the most important papers presented at a conference held at the European University Institute in Florence on July 6–17, 1992, along with revisions of the related, invited papers presented at the annual meetings of the American Statistical Association held in San Francisco on August 8–12, 1993.

The organizers of the Florence conference were Mark Salmon at the European University Institute in Florence, Alan Kirman of the Université d'Aix–Marseille III, and David Rand and Robert Mackay from the Mathematics Department at Warwick University in England. The joint proceedings arrangement between sessions of the annual meetings of the American Statistical Association and the Florence conference was made possible by the fact that William Barnett was Program Chair for the American Statistical Association in Business and Economic Statistics during the year 1993.

Funding for the Florence conference came from a grant from the European Science Foundation through the Centre for Economic Policy Research in London and the European University Institute in Florence. The proceedings volumes from conferences in this series are sponsored by the IC^2 Institute at the University of Texas at Austin and are cosponsored by the RGK Foundation.

Nonlinear dynamics and economics

International Symposia in Economic Theory and Econometrics

Editor
William A. Barnett, Washington University in St. Louis

Other books in the series

William A. Barnett and A. Ronald Gallant
New approaches to modeling, specification selection, and econometric inference

William A. Barnett and Kenneth J. Singleton
New approaches to monetary economics

William A. Barnett, Ernst R. Berndt, and Halbert White
Dynamic econometric modeling

William A. Barnett, John Geweke, and Karl Shell
Economic complexity

William A. Barnett, James Powell, and George E. Tauchen
Nonparametric and semiparametric methods in econometrics and statistics

William A. Barnett, Bernard Cornet, Claude d'Aspremont,
Jean J. Gabszewicz and Andreu Mas-Colell
Equilibrium theory and applications

William A. Barnett, Melvin J. Hinich, and Norman J. Schofield
Political economy: Institutions, competition and representation

William A. Barnett, Hervé Moulin, Maurice Salles, and Norman J. Schofield
Social choice, welfare, and ethics

William A. Barnett, Giancarlo Gandalfo, and Claude Hillinger
Dynamic disequilibrium modeling

Nonlinear dynamics and economics

Proceedings of the Tenth International Symposium
in Economic Theory and Econometrics

Edited by

WILLIAM A. BARNETT
Washington University in St. Louis

ALAN P. KIRMAN
Université d'Aix–Marseille III

MARK SALMON
European University Institute

CAMBRIDGE
UNIVERSITY PRESS

CAMBRIDGE UNIVERSITY PRESS
Cambridge, New York, Melbourne, Madrid, Cape Town,
Singapore, São Paulo, Delhi, Mexico City

Cambridge University Press
The Edinburgh Building, Cambridge CB2 8RU, UK

Published in the United States of America by Cambridge University Press, New York

www.cambridge.org
Information on this title: www.cambridge.org/9780521471411

First published 1996

A catalogue record for this publication is available from the British Library

Library of Congress Cataloguing in Publication Data
International Symposium in Economic Theory and Econometrics
    (10th: 1992, Florence, Italy)
    Nonlinear dynamics and economics: proceedings of the Tenth
International Symposium in Economic Theory and Econometrics
/ edited by William A. Barnett, Alan P. Kirman, and Mark Salmon.
p.   cm. – (International symposia in economic theory and
econometrics)
    Papers presented at a conference held at the European University
in Florence, Italy, July 6–17, 1992 and invited papers presented at
the annual meeting of the American Statistical Association in
San Francisco Aug. 8–12, 1993.
ISBN 0-521-47141-9
1. Statics and dynamics (Social sciences) – Congresses. 2. Economics,
Mathematical – Congresses. 3. Chaotic behavior in systems – Congresses.
4. Differential equations. Nonlinear–Congresses. I. Barnett, William A.
II. Kirman, A. P. III. Salmon, Mark. IV. American Statistical Association.
V. Title. VI. Series.   96-5301
HB145.I59   1992   CIP
330'.01'51 – dc20

ISBN 978-0-521-47141-1 Hardback

Contents

Series editor's introduction   *vii*
Contributors   *x*

I   Instability in economic theory

1   Chaotic dynamics in overlapping generations models with
    production   3
    Alfredo Medio and Giorgio Negroni

2   Evolutionary chaos: Growth fluctuations in a Schumpeterian
    model of creative destruction   45
    Gerald Silverberg and Doris Lehnert

II   Nonlinearity in financial markets

3   Detection of nonlinearity in foreign-exchange data   77
    Paolo Guarda and Mark Salmon

4   Chaos and nonlinear dynamics in futures markets   113
    Apostolos Serletis and Paul Dormaar

5   Continuous-time chaos in stock market dynamics   133
    Kehong Wen

III   Tests for nonlinearity and chaos

6   An experimental design to compare tests of nonlinearity and
    chaos   163
    William A. Barnett, A. Ronald Gallant, Melvin J. Hinich,
    Jochen A. Jungeilges, Daniel T. Kaplan, and Mark J. Jensen

v

7   Testing time series for nonlinearities: The BDS approach   191
     W. D. Dechert

8   Searching for nonlinearity in mean and variance   201
     Ted Jaditz and Chera L. Sayers

9   Operational characteristics of White's test for neglected
     nonlinearities   219
     J. A. Jungeilges

10   Time series, stochastic and chaotic   267
     Thomas J. Taylor

11   Linearity testing and nonlinear modeling of economic time
     series   281
     Timo Teräsvirta

IV   Frequency domain methods and nonlinear business cycles

12   The importance of being nonlinear: A frequency-domain
     approach to nonlinear model identification and estimation   297
     Richard Ashley and Douglas Patterson

13   Trends, shocks, persistent cycles in evolving economy:
     Business-cycle measurement in time-frequency
     representation   307
     Ping Chen

14   International evidence of business-cycle nonlinearity   333
     Philip Rothman

V   Nonlinear prediction and forecasting

15   Local Lyapunov exponents: Predictability depends on where
     you are   345
     Barbara A. Bailey

16   Forecasting realignments: The case of the French franc in
     the exchange-rate mechanism   361
     Bruce Mizrach

17   Daily returns in international stock markets: Predictability,
     nonlinearity, and transaction costs   369
     Steve Stachell and Allan Timmermann

18   Nonparametric forecasts of gold rates of return   393
     Thanasis Stengos

Series editor's introduction

This volume is the tenth in a series, called *International Symposia in Economic Theory and Econometrics*. The proceedings series is under the general editorship of William Barnett. Individual volumes in the series generally have co-editors, who differ for each volume, since the topics of the conferences change each year. The Cambridge University Press monograph series that publishes the proceedings of the conferences is sponsored by the IC^2 Institute at the University of Texas at Austin and are cosponsored by the RGK Foundation.[1]

Much of this volume comprises the proceedings of the conference, "Nonlinear Dynamics and Economics," held at the European University Institute in Florence, Italy, on July 6–17, 1992. This volume includes the most important refereed papers presented at the conference, as well as related, invited papers presented at the annual meetings of the American Statistical Association held in San Francisco on August 8–12, 1993. This unusual joint arrangement between sessions of the annual meetings of the American Statistical Association and the Florence conference was made possible by the fact that William Barnett was Program Chair for the American Statistical Association in Business and Economic Statistics during the year 1993.

The purpose of the Florence conference was to bring together mathematicians, economists, statisticians, biologists, and physicists who are interested in nonlinear dynamics and chaos to see what cross fertilization could be achieved. The interdisciplinary nature of the conference is evident from many of the papers, although the primary area of application of the research published in this volume is economics.

The volume is divided topically into five parts: Part I concerns instability in economic theory; part II, nonlinearity in financial markets; part III, tests for nonlinearity and chaos; part IV, frequency domain methods and nonlinear business cycles; and part V, nonlinear prediction and forecasting. The organizers

---

IC^2 stands for Innovation, Creativity, and Capital

of the Florence conference thankfully acknowledge financial support from a grant from the European Science Foundation through the Centre for Economic Policy Research in London and the European University Institute in Florence.

The first conference in this Cambridge series was co-organized by William Barnett and Ronald Gallant, who also co-edited that proceedings volume. That volume appeared as the volume 30, October/November 1985 edition of the *Journal of Econometrics* and has been reprinted in this Cambridge University Press monograph series as a volume entitled *New approaches to modeling, specification selection, and econometric inference.*

Beginning with the second symposium in the series, the proceedings of the symposia appear exclusively as volumes in this Cambridge University Press monograph series. The co-organizers of the second symposium and coeditors of its proceedings volume were William Barnett and Kenneth Singleton. The topic (and volume title) was *New approaches to monetary economics.* The co-organizers of the third symposium, which was on *Dynamic econometric modeling,* were William Barnett and Ernst Berndt; and the co-editors of that proceedings volume were William Barnett, Ernst Berndt, and Halbert White. The co-organizers of the fourth symposium and co-editors of its proceedings volume, which was entitled *Economic complexity: Chaos, sunspots, bubbles and nonlinearity,* were William Barnett, John Geweke, and Karl Shell. The co-organizers of the fifth symposium and co-editors of its proceedings volume, which was on *Nonparametric and semiparametric methods in econometrics and statistics,* were William Barnett, James Powell, and George Tauchen. The co-organizers and proceedings co-editors of the sixth symposium, which was on *Equilibrium theory and applications,* were William Barnett, Bernard Cornet, Claude d'Aspremont, Jean Gabszewicz, and Andreu Mas-Colell. The co-organizers of the seventh symposium, which was on *Political economy,* were William Barnett, Melvin Hinich, Douglass North, Howard Rosenthal, and Norman Schofield. The co-editors of that proceedings volume were William Barnett, Melvin Hinich, and Norman Schofield.

The eighth symposium was part of a large-scale conference on *Social choice, welfare, and ethics.* That conference was held in Caen, France, on June 9–12, 1993. The organizers of the conference were Maurice Salles and Hervé Moulin. The co-editors of that proceedings volume were William Barnett, Hervé Moulin, Maurice Salles, and Normal Schofield. The ninth volume in the series was on *Dynamic disequilibrium modeling: Theory and applications,* and was organized by Claude Hillinger at the University of Munich, Giancarlo Gandolfo at the University of Rome "La Sapienza," A. R. Bergstrom at the University of Essex, and P. C. B. Phillips at Yale University. The co-editors of the proceedings volume were William Barnett, Giancarlo Gandolfo, and Claude Hillinger.

The organizers of the Florence conference, which produced part of this tenth volume, were Mark Salmon and Alan Kirman at the European University

Institute in Florence, and David Rand and Robert MacKay from the Mathematics Department at Warwick University in England, while the organizer of the invited American Statistical Association sessions, which produced some of the papers in the volume, was William Barnett. Although the dates of the Florence conference preceded those of the eighth and ninth conferences in the series, the delayed sequencing of this proceedings volume within the series resulted from the lengthy refereeing procedure adopted for this volume, and from the merging of some of the papers from the Florence conference with some of the invited papers presented at the American Statistical Association meetings held in San Francisco on August 8–12, 1993.

The intention of the volumes in this proceedings series to provide **refereed** journal-quality collections of research papers of unusual importance in areas of currently highly visible activity within the economics profession. Because of the refereeing requirements associated with the editing of the proceedings, the volumes in the series do not necessarily contain all of the papers presented at the corresponding symposia.

William A. Barnett
Washington University in St. Louis

Contributors

Richard Ashley
Department of Economics
Virginia Tech

Barbara A. Bailey
Department of Statistics
North Carolina State University

William A. Barnett
Department of Economics
Washington University in St. Louis

Ping Chen
Center for Studies in Statistical
    Mechanics and Complex Systems
University of Texas at Austin

W. D. Dechert
Department of Economics
University of Wisconsin

Paul Dormaar
Department of Economics
University of Calgary

A. Ronald Gallant
Department of Economics
University of North Carolina at
    Chapel Hill

Paolo Guardo
Department of Economics
European University Institute

Melvin Hinich
Department of Government
University of Texas at Austin

Ted Jaditz
Bureau of Labor Statistics
Department of Labor

Mark J. Jensen
Department of Economics
Southern Illinois University at
    Carbondale

Jochen Jungeilges
Department of Economics
University of Osnabrück

Daniel Kaplan
Department of Physiology
McGill University

Doris Lehnert
Institute for Social Research
University of Stuttgart

Alfredo Medio
Department of Economics
University of Venice

Bruce Mizrach
Department of Economics
Rutgers University

Giorgio Negroni
Department of Economics
Catholic University of Milan and
    University of Pavia

Douglas Patterson
Department of Finance
Virginia Tech

Philip Rothman
Department of Economics
East Carolina University

Mark Salmon
Department of Economics
European University Institute

Steve Satchell
Birkbeck College
University of London

Chera Sayers
Department of Economics
University of Houston

Apostolos Serletis
Department of Economics
University of Calgary

Gerald Silverberg
ILASA

Thanasis Stengos
Department of Economics
University of Guelph

Thomas J. Taylor
Department of Mathematics
Arizona State University

Timo Teräsvirta
Stockholm School of Economics

Allan Timmermann
Birkbeck College
University of London

Kehong Wen
Haas School of Business
University of California at Berkeleyx

PART I

Instability in economic theory

CHAPTER 1

Chaotic dynamics in overlapping generations models with production

Alfredo Medio and Giorgio Negroni

1   Introduction

Over the past decade there has been an increasing interest in the possibility of cyclical and chaotic behavior in perfectly competitive economies. Particular attention has been given to the overlapping generations (OLG) models, with or without production [see, e.g., the contributions of Benhabib and Day (1982), Grandmont (1985), Reichlin (1986), Benhabib and Laroque (1988) and Jullien (1988)].

In this paper we are concerned with the possibility of chaotic dynamics in a two-periods OLG model with production. To the best of our knowledge, in this class of models complex behavior has been found only in the case of *backward perfect foresight*[1] (see e.g., Medio (1992) for the case of a nonmonetary economic with a Leontief technology, and Jullien (1988) for the case of a monetary economy with a production technology that allows for some substitution between factors).

As Woodford (1990) pointed out, this is a rather disturbing occurrence but, as we prove here, it is by no means the only possibility. In fact, in Medio's model, economic agents only work when young and consume only when old, whereas Jullien assumes an exogenously given labor supply. If we modify these restrictive assumptions by endogenizing labor-supply decisions and allowing agents to consume *also* when young, then it is not too hard to overcome the difficulty and to prove the existence of chaotic forward dynamics. As we show in Section 2, the possibility of defining forward dynamics crucially depends on the choice of the utility function for consumption in the second period, whereas the occurrence of complex dynamics also depends on the interaction of the utility function for consumption in the first period and the production function.

---

[1] See Benhabib and Day (1982) for the possibility of chaotic dynamics with forward perfect foresight in a pure consumption economy.

3

We consider two classes of utility functions for the first period, labeled CARA and CRRA.[2] Forward dynamics requires that utility function for the second period be always of the CRRA type.

We also consider the two classes of technologies: the linear Leontief and the CES. Combining the technologies and the first-period utility functions, we get four kinds of economies, which we label CARAL(Leontief), CRRAL(Leontief), CARACES, and CRRACES. We prove that each of them admits some combinations of parameters that generate cyclical or chaotic evolutions.

The paper is organized as follows: in Section 2, we discuss the origin of backward perfect foresight in OLG models with production of the traditional type. In Section 3, we introduce our model of intertemporal choice, and in Section 4, we consider the production side of the model in the case of a Leontief technology. In Sections 5 and 6, we present our results, respectively, for CRRAL and CARAL economies. In Section 7, we introduce a CES technology; in Sections 8 and 9, respectively, we analyze the CRRACES and the CARACES economies. We present analytical results whenever it is possible and numerical simulations of the more interesting occurrences. Some economic explanations of complex dynamics are left to Section 10.

2   Backward and forward dynamics: Some preliminary results

In the simpler and most common variation of the OLG model, agents live for two period: they work when young and consume when old. Let w_t and R_{t+1} be, respectively, the real wage rate and the real interest rate; also let $u(c_{t+1})$ and $v(l_t)$ denote the utility of consumption in the second period and the disutility of labor in the first period, respectively. The problem faced by the young (representative) agent at the beginning of period t is thus to choose c_{t+1} and l_t that maximize $[u(c_{t+1}) - v(l_t)]$ subject to the constraints: $k_t = w_t l_t$ and $c_{t+1} = R_{t+1}k_t$.

In this case, from the first-order conditions we get

$$w_t R_{t+1} u'(c_{t+1}) - v'(l_t) = 0.$$

Note, that the first-order conditions may be written as $c_{t+1}u'(c_{t+1}) - l_t v'(l_t) = 0$ from which, putting $\mathcal{U}(c_{t+1}) = c_{t+1}u'(c_{t+1})$ and $\mathcal{V}(l_t) = l_t v'(l_t)$, we obtain $\mathcal{U}(c_{t+1}) - \mathcal{V}(l_t) = 0$. Now, this equation implicitly defines forward perfect

---

[2] CRRA stands for constant relative risk aversion and has the general functional for $u(c) = \alpha^{-1}c^\alpha$, $0 < \alpha < 1$; CARA stands for constant absolute risk aversion and has the form $u(c) = -re^{-c}$, $r > 0$.

foresight dynamics if $\mathcal{U}$ is invertible. If we denote the relative degrees of risk aversion pertaining to the consumption and labor-supply functions by $\rho_2 = -c_{t+1}u''(c_{t+1})/u'(c_{t+1}) > 0$, and $\rho_l = l_t v''(l_t)/v'(l_t) > 0$ respectively, we see that because $\mathcal{U}'(c_{t+1}) = u'[1 - \rho_2]$ and $\mathcal{V}'(l_t) = v'[1 + \rho_l]$, $\mathcal{U}$ is invertible if the sign of $1 - \rho_2$ does not change. This condition, in turn, implies that saving is a monotonic function of the real interest rate.[3]

Reichlin (1986) assumed precisely this condition, and showed that, in the case of a Leontief technology, for $\rho_2 < 1$ the stationary state loses its stability through a Neimark[4] bifurcation when $b \geq 2$, where b represents the output-capital ratio. On the other hand, Reichlin also showed that, with a production technology with variable proportions, a Neimark bifurcation is possible, provided that the elasticity substitution between capital and labor at the steady state is less that the share of capital income.

Medio (1992) used the same framework as Reichlin to prove the existence of backward perfect-foresight chaotic dynamics, for the case of a Leontief technology. The author here assumed a utility function of the CARA type for second-period consumption, and a disutility function of the CRRA type for current labor supply.

3   Forward dynamics: The basic model

Let us consider an economy composed of two overlapping generations. The members of each generation live for two periods (youth and old age) and work only when young, but consume in both periods of life. To simplify the analysis, we consider a real economy in which there is only one commodity (e.g., corn) that can be consumed or used in the production process.

Let us assume that the overall utility function is time separable. The utility derived from consumption in the first and second period, and the disutility of labor in the first period, are denoted by $u_1(c_t)$, $u_2(c_{t+1})$, and $v(l_t)$, respectively. We further assume that the functions u_1, u_2 and v are continuous on $[0, +\infty)$ and that, for $c, l > 0$, they satisfy the following conditions: $u_i'(c) > 0$, $u_i''(c) < 0$, for $i = 1, 2$, and $v'(l) > 0$, $v''(l) > 0$.

---

[3] On the other hand, because $\mathcal{V}' = v'(1 + \rho_l) > 0$ always, it follows that it is always possible to derive backward solutions. Indicating with s_t the young agent's saving at the beginning of period t, from the budget constraint we get: $c_{t+1} = R_{t+1}s_t$ and $l_t = s_t/w_t$. Substituting these variables into the first-order conditions, we get $\phi(s_t, R_{t+1}, w_t) = 0$. Now because $\partial\phi/\partial R_{t+1} = w_t(u' + R_{t+1}s_t u'')$, and $\partial\phi/\partial w_t = R_{t+1}u' + s_t v'' w_t^{-2}$, it can be seen immediately that $\partial\phi/\partial w_t > 0$, always; on the contrary, $\partial\phi/\partial R_{t+1}$ is positive if $u' + c_{t+1}u'' > 0$, that is if $1 > \rho_2$

[4] We use the term Neimark bifurcation instead of Hopf bifurcation for discrete-time dynamical systems, because the basic results in this area were not found by Hopf but by Neimark (and Sarker). Moreover, using the same name for two totally different phenomena is confusing. A broad definition of this bifurcation, and some references, are given in Section 5.

The problem faced by the young (representative) agent at the beginning of period t is to choose c_t, c_{t+1}, and l_t that solve the following program:

$$\max \quad [u_1(c_t) + u_2(c_{t+1}) - v(l_t)]$$
$$\text{s.t.} \quad s_t k_t \le w_t l_t - c_t$$
$$c_{t+1} \le R_{t+1} k_t$$
$$c_t, c_{t+1}, k_t, l_t > 0.$$

The first-order conditions are:

$$u_1'(c_t) - R_{t+1} u_2'(c_{t+1}) = 0 \tag{1.1}$$

$$u_2'(c_{t+1}) R_{t+1} w_t - v'(l_t) = 0 \tag{1.2}$$

$$c_{t+1} = R_{t+1}(w_t l_t - c_t). \tag{1.3}$$

Solving equation (1.3) for $R_{t+1} w_t$, and substituting into equation (1.2) we get the following equation:

$$u_2'(c_{t+1})c_{t+1} + u_2'(c_{t+1})R_{t+1} c_t - v'(l_t)l_t = 0. \tag{1.4}$$

From equation (1.1) we also get $R_{t+1} = u_1'(c_t)/u_2'(c_{t+1})$. Substituting this expression into equation (1.4), we get

$$u_1'(c_t)c_t + u_2'(c_{t+1})c_{t+1} - v'(l_t)l_t = 0.$$

Let us now define the following new functions: $\mathcal{U}_1(c_t) \equiv u_1'(c_t)c_t$, $\mathcal{U}_2(c_{t+1}) \equiv u_2'(c_{t+1})c_{t+1}$, and $\mathcal{V}(l_t) \equiv v'(l_t)l_t$. Then we have

$$\frac{\partial \mathcal{U}_1(c_t)}{\partial c_t} = u_1'(c_t)[1 - \rho_1],$$

$$\frac{\partial \mathcal{U}_2(c_{t+1})}{\partial c_{t+1}} = u_2'(c_{t+1})[1 - \rho_2],$$

$$\frac{\partial \mathcal{V}(l_t)}{\partial l_t} = v'(l_t)[1 + \rho_l],$$

where $\rho_j (j = 1, 2, l)$ are the degrees of relative risk adversion associated with the relevant (dis)utility functions, as defined above. Using the new functions, the dynamical system derived from the consumer's choice is implicitly defined by the following equation:

$$\mathcal{U}_1(c_t) + \mathcal{U}_2(c_{t+1}) - \mathcal{V}(l_t) = 0. \tag{1.5}$$

To get forward dynamics, we need $\mathcal{U}_2(c_{t+1})$ to be invertible in the relevant domain; this, in turn, requires that over the domain, the sign of $(1 - \rho_2)$ does not change. When this condition is satisfied, we have

$$c_{t+1} = \mathcal{U}_2^{-1}[\mathcal{V}(l_t) - \mathcal{U}_1(c_t)] = h(l_t, c_t). \tag{1.6}$$

In the sequel of the paper we consider the following utility functions:

$$u_1(c_t) = -re^{-c_t} \quad r > 0 \tag{1.7a}$$

$$u_1(c_t) = \frac{1}{\theta}c_t^\theta \quad 0 < \theta < 1 \tag{1.7b}$$

$$u_2(c_{t+1}) = \frac{1}{\alpha}c_{t+1}^\alpha \quad 0 < \alpha < 1 \tag{1.7c}$$

$$v(l_t) = \frac{1}{\gamma}l_t^\gamma \quad \gamma > 1. \tag{1.7d}$$

Note that equations (1.7b–d) are utility functions of the CRRA type, whose coefficients of relative risk adversion are, respectively, $\rho_1 = 1 - \theta$, $\rho_2 = 1 - \alpha$, and $\rho_l = \gamma - 1$, and therefore independent of c_t, whereas utility function (7.1a) is of the CARA type, with $\rho_1 = f(c_t) = c_t$. In what follows, we use the labels CARA or CRRA when in the dynamical equation (1.6) there appears a function of type (1.7a) or (1.7b), respectively.

3.1 Saving function

Let us now consider equation (1.4). From this we wish to derive the agent's saving function. Let $s_t = w_t l_t - c_t$ denote the saving of the young agent in period t. From this definition and from the budget constraints we get

$$u_1'(w_t l_t - s_t)[w_t l_t - s_t] + u_2'(R_{t+1}s_t)R_{t+1}s_t - v'[(s_t + c_t)/w_t][(s_t + c_t)/w_t] = 0.$$

In general terms, this equation can be written as $\phi(s_t, R_{t+1}, w_t, l_t, c_t) = 0$. Provided that $\partial\phi/\partial s_t \neq 0$, this equation implicitly defines a saving function: $s_t = g(R_{t+1}, w_t, l_t, c_t)$.

The elasticity of saving with respect to the interest rate is

$$\frac{\partial s_t}{\partial R_{t+1}} \frac{R_{t+1}}{s_t} = \frac{1 - \rho_2}{1 + \rho_2 + \rho_l - \rho_1}. \tag{1.8}$$

Note that had we not introduced the possibility of consumption in the first period, the elasticity of saving with respect to the interest rate would have been $(1 - \rho_2)(\rho_2 + \rho_l)^{-1}$, as in Reichlin (1986). Thus, for a given value of ρ_2 we may get a value of the elasticity of saving with respect to the interest rate higher (or lower) than that of the Reichlin's model, depending on the values of ρ_1 and ρ_l.[5]

---

[5] In Reichlin's model, saving is an increasing function of the interest rate if $\rho_2 < 1$. In the CRRA case, saving is always an increasing function of R; in the CARA case, however, saving is positively or negatively related to R, according to whether c_t is smaller or larger than $1 + \gamma - \alpha$.

Using the functional forms (1.7), the elasticity of saving with respect to the real interest rate becomes

$$\frac{\partial s_t}{\partial R_{t+1}} \frac{R_{t+1}}{s_t} = \frac{\alpha}{1 + \gamma - \alpha - c_t}$$

for the CARA case, and

$$\frac{\partial s_t}{\partial R_{t+1}} \frac{R_{t+1}}{s_t} = \frac{\alpha}{\gamma - \alpha + \theta}$$

for the CARA case.

Making use of equations (1.7a,c,d), equation (1.6) becomes

$$c_{t+1} = [l_t^\gamma - rc_t e^{-c_t}]^{1/\alpha}. \tag{1.9a}$$

If instead we use equations (1.7b–d), we get

$$c_{t+1} = [l_t^\gamma - c_t^\theta]^{1/\alpha}. \tag{1.9b}$$

Equation (1.9a), or (1.9b), represents the optimal evolution of consumption, derived from consumer's intertemporal choice of consumption and leisure only. It is, so to speak, the first half of our dynamical system, to complete which we need a second equation that takes the technology side of the system into account.

4   Leontief technology

Let us turn to the production side of the economy. As mentioned before, we consider two different production technologies: linear Leontief and CES.

In the former case, we assume that output in period t, x_t, is produced by current labor and capital invested in the previous period; thus,

$$x_t = \min[al_t, bk_{t-1}], \tag{1.10}$$

where $b > 1$ (to ensure variability of the economy). In this kind of economy, we get $R_t = b(1 - w_t)$. Also, the equilibrium condition in the product market yields

$$x_t = k_t + c_t. \tag{1.11}$$

For simplicity, in what follows we put $a = 1$. From the assumption of full employment of capital, we have $x_t = bk_{t-1}$ and, taking into account the equilibrium condition (1.11), we obtain $x_t = b(x_{t-1} - c_{t-1})$. From the assumption of full employment of labor, and remembering that $a = 1$, we have $x_t = l_t$. Hence, moving forward one period, we obtain the second dynamical equation of the model:

$$l_{t+1} = b(l_t - c_t). \tag{1.12}$$

Equations (1.9) and (1.12) represent the evolution of the system that is compatible with intertemporal optimization and equilibrium conditions in a Leontief economy.

5 Chaotic dynamics in a CRRAL economy

Let us now consider the simpler case in which both the utility functions for first- and second-period consumption are of a CRRA type (the labor disutility function is of this type throughout the paper). In this case, we have the following dynamical system:

$$c_{t+1} = (l_t^\gamma - c_t^\theta)^{1/\alpha} \tag{1.13a}$$

$$l_{t+1} = b(l_t - c_t), \tag{1.13b}$$

where $\gamma > 1$, $b > 1$, and $0 < (\alpha, \theta) < 1$.

The system (1.13a,b) has two equilibria. The first, a trivial one, is $E_1 : (\bar{l} = 0, \bar{c} = 0)$. The second equilibrium cannot be computed explicitly, but we can show that it is unique and strictly positive (In what follows, we assume that $\alpha \geq \theta$. All of the relevant results could be proved analogously for $\alpha < \theta$).

Lemma 1.1: *System (1.13a, b) has a unique positive equilibrium at E_2 : $(\bar{c} > 1, \bar{l} > 1)$.*

Proof: From equation (1.13b), we get $\bar{l} = b(b-1)^{-1}\bar{c}$. From equation (1.13a), we get $1 + \bar{c}^{\theta-\alpha} = \psi\bar{c}^{\gamma-\alpha}$, where $\psi \equiv b^\gamma(b-1)^{-\gamma}$. Let us call the left-hand side and the right-hand side of this equation $f(c)$ and $g(c)$, respectively. Observe that, having assumed $\alpha > \theta$, it follows that $\lim_{c \to 0} f(c) = \infty$, and $\lim_{c \to \infty} f(c) = 1$; note also that $f'(c) < 0$ and $f''(c) > 0$. Regarding $g(c)$, we have $g(0) = 0$, $\lim_{c \to \infty} g(c) = \infty$ and $g'(c) > 0$. It follows that $f(c) = g(c)$ has a unique solution and this solution is in the first orthant of the (c, l) plane. $\square$

The content of Lemma 1.1 is represented in Figure 1.1

Let us now analyze the local stability of E_1. Evaluating the Jacobian matrix at E_1, we get

$$J_1 = \begin{bmatrix} 0 & 0 \\ -b & b \end{bmatrix}$$

when $\theta < \alpha$. In this case, from inspection of J_1 we see that the eigenvalues are respectively 0 and $b > 1$. Therefore, E_1 is locally unstable and it is not possible to find oscillatory motion around it. (Note that when $\theta > \alpha$, the first eigenvalue is equal to $-\infty$, whereas the second in still equal to $b > 1$).

Let us now consider local stability of E_2. Evaluating the Jacobian matrix at E_2, we get

$$J_2 = \begin{bmatrix} -\frac{\theta}{\alpha}c^{\theta-\alpha} & \frac{\gamma}{\alpha}\left(\frac{b}{b-1}\right)^{\gamma-1}c^{\gamma-\alpha} \\ -b & b \end{bmatrix}.$$

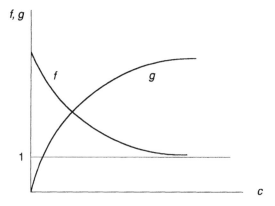

Figure 1.1.

Therefore, we have

$$\text{Tr } J_2 = -\frac{\theta}{\alpha}c^{\theta-\alpha} + b,$$

$$\text{Det } J_2 = (b-1)\frac{\gamma}{\alpha} + [\gamma(b-1) - b\theta]\frac{c^{\theta-\alpha}}{\alpha}.$$

Keeping in mind that stability of equilibrium requires that the following conditions be met

(i) $1 + \text{Tr } J_2 + \text{Det } J_2 > 0,$
(ii) $1 - \text{Tr } J_2 + \text{Det } J_2 > 0,$ (1.13c)
(iii) $1 - \text{Det } J_2 > 0,$

we can now state the following result:

Proposition 1.1: *Let us consider the equilibrium E_2, of the dynamical system (1.13a,b); E_2 is a stable equilibrium for sufficiently small γ, sufficiently large α, or sufficiently small b.*

Proof: For simplicity, we prove the proposition assuming $\alpha = \theta$, but the result extends in an obvious manner to the case $\alpha > \theta$. In this case, the set of inequalities (1.13c) that governs the stability conditions becomes: (i) $2\gamma(b-1)\alpha^{-1} > 0$; (ii) $2(b-1)(\gamma - \alpha)\alpha^{-1} > 0$; (iii) $2\gamma(b-1)\alpha^{-1} - b - 1 < 0$. Notice that the first two inequalities are always satisfied, because γ and b are both larger than one. The third inequality is obviously satisfied if γ is small, α is large, or b is near 1. Therefore, low productivity, low elasticity of consumption utility function, and high elasticity of labor utility function work for stability.   □

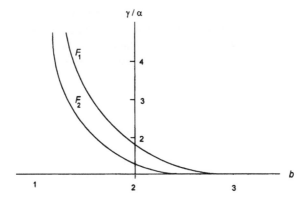

Figure 1.2.

Proposition 1 is illustrated in Figure 1.2. The curve $F_1(b, \gamma, \alpha)$ is defined by the equation $1 + \mathrm{Tr}J_2 + \mathrm{Det}J_2 = 0$, that is, the equation $\gamma/\alpha = [2(b - 1)]^{-1}(1 + b)$ and is the locus of points corresponding to the stability boundary for E_2 (southwest, stable; northeast, unstable). The curve $F_2(b, \gamma, \alpha)$ is defined by the equation $(\mathrm{Tr}J_2)^2 = 4\mathrm{Det}J_2$, that is, $\gamma/\alpha = [8(b - 1)]^{-1}(1 + b)^2$, and is the locus of points corresponding to the flutter boundary, southwest of which the eigenvalues of J_2 are real, northeast of which they are complex conjugate.

Before discussing loss of stability and local bifurcations, we need to recapitulate some elementary notions in bifurcation theory. Only very broad definitions suffice here. The interested reader will find more rigorous definitions and theorems, for example, in Guckenheimer and Holmes (1983) and Devaney (1989); see also Medio (1992).

Definition 1 (Flip bifurcation): For a μ-family of discrete dynamical systems, or maps, a stable fixed (or equilibrium) point loses its stability through a flip bifurcation when, changing the bifurcation parameter μ, one of the (real) eigenvalues of the Jacobian matrix at equilibrium crosses the unit circle through -1, all of the (moduli of the) other eigenvalues remaining inside the circle.[6] The loss of stability of the equilibrium point leads to the emergence of a 2-cycle (which may be stable or unstable according to whether the bifurcation is super- or subcritical). Subsequent flip bifurcations may lead to period $4, 8, \cdots 2^n$ cycles and possibly to a cascade of bifurcations and chaos. This is known as the period-doubling route to chaos. Reverse flip bifurcations are also possible, leading to simpler dynamics.

---

[6] This, of course, corresponds to violation of stability condition (ii).

Definition 2 (Saddle-node bifurcation): For a μ-family of systems, as above, a stable fixed point loses its stability through a saddle-node (or fold) bifurcation when, changing μ, one of the (real) eigenvalues of the Jacobian matrix goes through $+1$. The bifurcation may lead to the appearance or disappearance of a pair of equilibria.[7]

Definition 3 (Neimark bifurcation): For a μ-family of maps of $\mathcal{R}^2$, a stable equilibrium point loses its stability through a Neimark bifurcation when, changing the bifurcation parameter μ, the modulus of a pair of (complex conjugate) eigenvalues of the Jacobian matrix crosses the unit circle, all of the other eigenvalues remaining inside the circle. Under certain, rather general, nonresonance conditions, which we assume to hold here, loss of stability of the equilibrium point leads to the emergence of an invariant circle on which the dynamics of the system may be periodic or quasiperiodic. Increasing (or decreasing) the bifurcation parameter beyond its bifurcation value, may lead to more complex dynamics, through a so-called quasiperiodic route to chaos, whose details are not yet entirely understood. Neimark bifurcations of iterates of a map are also possible, leading to multiple invariant circles and, possibly, to chaos.[8]

The considerations developed above, and a quick inspection of Figure 1.2, indicate that, for equations (1.13a,b), no flip bifurcation is possible. When we start from a stable configuration of parameters and increase b or γ (or decrease α), we must necessarily first cross the flutter boundary, F_2, and then the stability boundary, F_1. Thus, loss of stability in this case only takes place through a Neimark bifurcation, as was the case in Reichlin's (1986) model. We shall show, however, that besides the periodic behavior discussed by that author, other, more complex dynamics of the system are possible.

The global behavior of the CRRAL economy is analyzed numerically, with the usual caveats regarding the effects of computing approximation. Following the indications implicit in Figure 1.2, we have studied the changes occurring in the dynamics of the system as the parameters γ, $z = 1 - \alpha$, and b are increased past their bifurcation values. The results are shown in the bifurcation diagrams of Figures 1.3–1.5.

Over the relevant parameter intervals, we observe the following scenarios:

(i)   Neimark bifurcations with appearance of invariant circles and periodic or quasiperiodic dynamics, large periodic (mode-locking) windows;

---

[7] This corresponds to violation of stability condition (i).

[8] This corresponds to violation of stability condition (iii). It also can be shown that if conditions (i) and (ii) are verified and condition (iii) is violated, it must be true that $(\mathrm{Tr}\ J_2)^2 < 4\ \mathrm{Det}\ J_2$ and, therefore, the two eigenvalues of the matrix J_2 are complex conjugate.

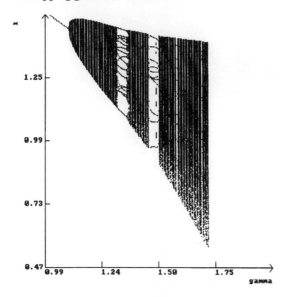

Figure 1.3. CRRAL Model. Gamma-bifurcation diagram.
$\gamma = (1, 2)$; $\alpha = \theta = 0.2$; $b = 1.2$.

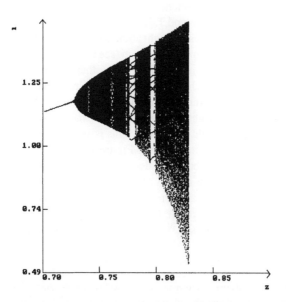

Figure 1.4. CRRAL Model. Alpha-bifurcation diagram.
$\gamma = 1.8$; $z = 1 - \alpha = (1 - \theta) = (0.7, 1)$; $b = 1.2$.

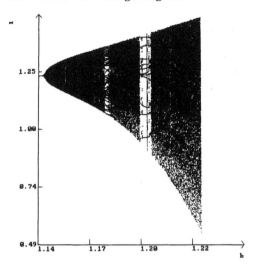

Figure 1.5. CRRAL Model. B-bifurcation diagram.
$\gamma = 1.5$; $\alpha = \theta = 0.2$; $b = (1.14, 1.25)$.

(ii) fractal-torus[9] phenomena with invariant circles containing regions where the circles are stretched, folded, and compressed back (see, in particular, Figures 1.6 and 1.7).

(iii) Multiple invariant circles, brought about by Neimark bifurcations of iterates of the original map of the system (see Figures 1.8–1.10). In these cases, the dynamics from one circle to another are periodic (and thus easily predictable), but the dynamics on each circle, may be periodic or quasiperiodic. Moreover, these circles too may break, leading to multiple fractal tori on which the dynamics are chaotic (see Figure 1.11).

(iv) Fully developed chaotic dynamics. This is sometimes brought about by linking separate fractal tori (see Figure 1.12).

(v) The different types of behavior do not follow one another in any obvious order, nor is the degree of complexity monotonically dependent on the relevant parameter. Sometimes the change of behavior is gradual, and therefore there are forewarnings of complex or chaotic behavior, but crises,[10] – sudden appearance or disappearance of

[9] We use here and elsewhere the term torus, interpreting the dynamics of a two-dimensional map on the plane as a Poincare map of a differential system of higher dimension.

[10] The phenomenon that we call crisis is known in the dynamical system literature as interior crisis or catastrophe or intermittency. It implies a sudden change of the size and/or qualitative properties of the attractor of a system when a parameter is slightly changed. A more detailed analysis can be found, for example, in Medio (1992) and in the literature quoted there.

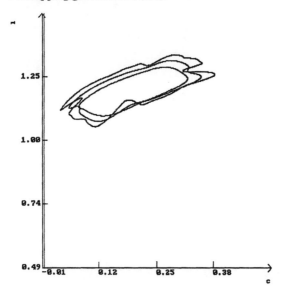

Figure 1.6. CRRAL Model. Torus breaking.
$z = 1 - \alpha = 0.75/6/7$; $\gamma = 1.5$; $b = 1.2$.

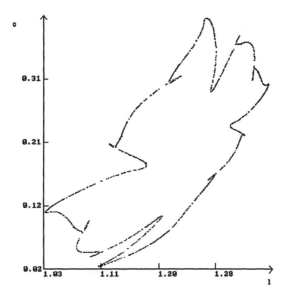

Figure 1.7. CRRAL Model. Torus breaking.
$\gamma = 1.5$; $1 - \alpha = 0.7757$; $b = 1.2$.

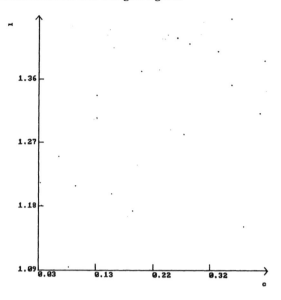

Figure 1.8. CRRAL Model. Multitorus route to chaos.
(a) $\gamma = 1.35$; $\alpha = 0.2$; $b = 1.2$.

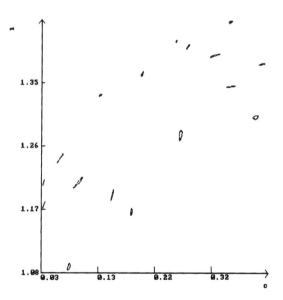

Figure 1.9. CRRAL Model. Multitorus route to chaos.
(b) $\gamma = 1.36$; $\alpha = 0.2$; $b = 1.2$.

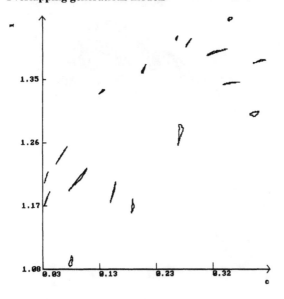

Figure 1.10. CRRAL Model. Multitorus route to chaos. (c) As Fig. 8, with $\gamma = 1.3622$.

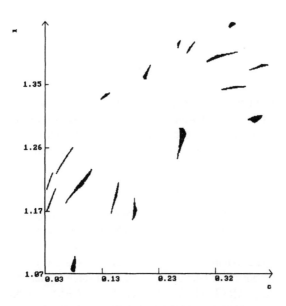

Figure 1.11. CRRAL Model. Multitorus route to chaos. (d) As Fig. 8,with $\gamma = 1.364$.

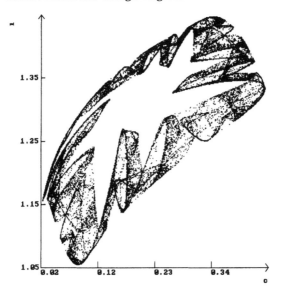

Figure 1.12. CRRAL Model. Multitorus route to chaos (e) As Fig. 8, with $\gamma = 1.3738$.

(periodic, quasiperiodic, or chaotic) attractors – are also observable. The dynamics exhibit the so-called sensitive dependence on parameters, that is, slight changes in the parameters bring about important qualitative changes in the dynamics.

(vi) In none of the cases investigated here, are the attractors globally stable (not even globally stable for positive initial conditions of the variables). The size of the basin of attraction varies from case to case. Also, when the relevant parameters become unduly large (or small), the system explodes, that is, the positivity constraints on the (consumption, labor, and capital) variables are violated.

(vii) Not all of the dynamical occurrences described above are necessarily encountered as we increase or decrease the relevant bifurcation parameter. In certain areas of the parameter space, the system explodes before complex behavior can be produced, and the bifurcation diagram consequently may be rather dull, including only periodic and quasiperiodic dynamics (see Figure 1.13). Most of the occurrences described above also take place in the other three models discussed in this article (CARAL, CRRACES, and CARACES). In what follows, therefore, we do not repeat their description in detail every time, but concentrate mainly on the distinguishing features of each model.

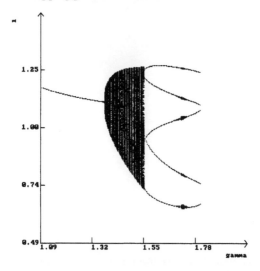

Figure 1.13. CRRAL Model. "Dull" bifurcation diagram.
$\alpha = 0.65; b = 1.5; \gamma = (1.1, 2)$.

6 Chaotic dynamics in a CARAL economy

We now tackle the more difficult case involving a CARA utility function for first-period consumption, where the labor disutility function and Leontief technology are the same as before. The evolution of the economy in this case is described by the following dynamical system:

$$c_{t+1} = [l_t^\gamma - rc_t e^{-c_t}]^{1/\alpha} \tag{1.14a}$$

$$l_{t+1} = b(l_t - c_t), \tag{1.14b}$$

where $\gamma > 1, 0 < \alpha < 1, b > 1$, and $r > 0$.

This system has two equilibria: the first is trivial, E_1:$(\bar{l} = 0, \bar{c} = 0)$. The second equilibrium, E_2, cannot be computed explicitly; nevertheless we can state the following result, which ensures the uniqueness of E_2 and the positiveness of the state variables at E_2:

Lemma 1.2: *System (1.14a,b) has a unique positive equilibrium $E_2 : 0 < \bar{c} > \psi^{1/(\alpha-\gamma)} < 1, \bar{l} > 1 > \psi^{\alpha/\gamma(\alpha-\gamma)}$.*

Proof: From equation (1.14b), we get $\bar{l} = b(b-1)^{-1}\bar{c}$. Let us now define $\psi = b^\gamma(b-1)^{-\gamma} > 1$. From equation (1.14b), we get $\psi\bar{c}^{\gamma-1} - \bar{c}^{\alpha-1} = re^{-\bar{c}}$. Let us set $f(c)$ and $g(c)$, respectively, equal to the left-hand side and right-hand side of this equation. These functions are continuous and, as c goes from

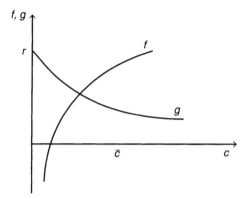

Figure 1.14.

0 to ∞, $f(c)$ increases monotonically from $-\infty$ to $+\infty$ and $g(c)$ decreases monotonically from r to 0. Therefore $f(c) = g(c)$ has a unique solution for $c > 0$. From this, the statement of the lemma promptly follows.   □

The content of Lemma 1.2 is represented in Figure 1.14.

Before discussing the stability properties of the system, we present an overview of its dynamics, considering the phase diagram for the dynamical system as represented by equations (1.14a, b). Letting $c_{t+1} = c_t = c$ and $l_{t+1} = l_t = l$, from equation (1.14a) we get $l = F(c) = [c^\alpha + rce^{-c}]^{1/\gamma}$; from equation (1.14b), we get $l = b(b-1)^{-1}c$. Note that $F(0) = 0$ and $\lim_{c \to \infty} F(c) = \infty$. Also note that $F'(c) = \alpha c^{\alpha-1} + r(1-c)e^{-c}$ from which we can see that $F'(0) = +\infty$. Finally, the meaningful dynamics (i.e., those that do not violate the constraints $c, l > 0$) are defined only in the region of the phase space lying above the 45-deg line. All of this is depicted in Figure 1.15.

Let us now turn to the study of the (local) stability of E_1. Evaluating the Jacobian matrix at this equilibrium, we get

$$J_1 = \begin{bmatrix} 0 & 0 \\ -b & b \end{bmatrix}.$$

From inspection of J_1, we immediately see that the two eigenvalues are 0 and b, which is greater than 1. Therefore, E_1 is always locally unstable and there is no oscillatory motion near it.

Let us now turn to the local stability of E_2. Evaluating the Jacobian matrix at this equilibrium, we get

$$J_2 = \begin{bmatrix} f_1(\bar{c}) & f_2(\bar{c}) \\ -b & b \end{bmatrix},$$

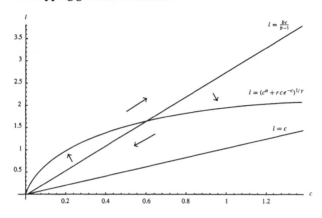

Figure 1.15.

where

$$\partial c_{t+1}/\partial c_t = (\psi \bar{c}^{\gamma-\alpha} - 1)(\bar{c} - 1)\alpha^{-1} \equiv f_1(\bar{c}) \tag{1.15}$$

$$\partial c_{t+1}/\partial l_t = \gamma \bar{c}^{\gamma-\alpha}[b/(b-1)]^{\gamma-1}\alpha^{-1} \equiv f_2(\bar{c}). \tag{1.16}$$

Note that, in this case, we could not represent the equilibrium value of c as an explicit function of the parameters α, γ, b, and r. However, considering the functions $f(c)$ and $g(c)$ (see Proof of Lemma 1.2, above) and Figure 1.14, we can easily see that the (positive) equilibrium value of c, $\bar{c}$, increases monotonically from $(0 < \psi^{1/(\alpha-\gamma)} < 1)$ to $+\infty$ as r varies from 0 to $+\infty$ (for $r = 0$, the two equilibria E_1 and E_2 coalesce). As b goes from 1 to $+\infty$, $\bar{c}$ varies monotonically from 0 to a finite value $\hat{c} > 1$, which depends or r. It can also be ascertained that $\bar{c}$ increases or decreases with α and γ according to whether $\bar{c} < 1$ or $\bar{c} > 1$. Unless we indicate differently, in what follows we fix α and γ and concentrate on the effects of changing the parameters b (productivity coefficient) and r [steepness of the derived utility function $\mathcal{U}_1(c_t)$].

In view of the complicated forms of the functions involved, and the large number of parameters, a detailed study of stability conditions would be cumbersome or even impossible. It is not too difficult, however, to give a broad picture of the local bifurcations occurring in the system under investigation, which will provide guidance for the numerical simulations that follow. For this purpose, let us first consider the question of stability of equilibrium E_2. By making use of the functions f_1 and f_2 defined above, conditions (1.13c) governing stability of equilibrium can be rewritten thus:

(i) $1 + b + f_1 + b(f_1 + f_2) > 0,$

(ii) $1 - b - f_1 + b(f_1 + f_2) > 0,$ $\qquad\qquad$ (1.13d)

(iii) $1 - b(f_1 + f_2) > 0.$

Condition (ii) is always verified for $b > 1$. We can promptly see that, if $r = 0$ $(c = \psi^{1/(\alpha-\gamma)})$, $[1 - b - f_1 + b(f_1 + f_2)] \equiv G(c) = (b-1)(1 - \gamma\alpha^{-1}) > 0$. On the other hand, it can be verified that, if $b > 1$, $G'(c) > 0$ and therefore $G(c) > 0$ for $c > \psi^{1/(\alpha-\gamma)}(r > 0)$.

We then concentrate on conditions (i) and (ii) and provide a rather heuristic argument to prove the existence of stable equilibria and discuss the loss of stability occurring when the parameters are changed.[11] We then can state the following proposition.

Proposition 1.2: *For the system (1.14a, b) there exist configurations of the parameters α, γ, b, and r such that conditions (i)–(iii) hold and the equilibrium E_2 is stable.*

Proof: See Appendix A.   □

Having established the existence of stable configurations of parameters, we now want to investigate the possibility that these conditions are violated and bifurcations occur. We now state the following:

Proposition 1.3: *Equilibrium E_2 can lose its stability through a flip or a Neimark bifurcation.*

Proof: See Appendix A.   □

Proposition 1.3 indicates that, in principle, the dynamics of the CARAL model may follow both a period-doubling and a quasiperiodic route to cycles and chaos, a situation that is little known in general and, to the best of our knowledge, has never been encountered in economic models. The possible occurrence of both flip and Neimark bifurcations suggests that the model under investigation may have a dynamical configurations richer than that of CRRAL model. The following numerical simulations confirm this expectation. We only discuss here the bifurcation scenarios obtained by changing the parameter b (productivity coefficient) and r [the steepness of the derived utility function $\mathcal{U}_1(c_t)$].[12]

Figure 1.16 shows an aborted flip bifurcation: increasing b, we move from stable equilibrium to a period-2 cycle and back to a stable equilibrium. For still higher values of b, we have a Neimark bifurcation, whose enlargement is shown in Figure 1.17. Increasing further the productivity level, we have a

---

[11] For this purpose, we can make use of Figures A1.1, A1.2, and A1.3 in the appendix, which show the dependence of f_1 and f_2 on the parameters of the system. The proofs of Propositions 1.2 and 1.3 are in the appendix, also.

[12] We have omitted the discussion of the γ-bifurcation diagram because all its interesting features also appear in the r-bifurcation.

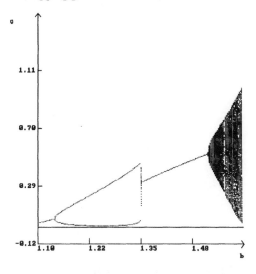

Figure 1.16. CARAL Model. Flip-Neimark bifurcations.
$\gamma = 1.2; r = 3; \alpha = 0.48; b = (1.1, 1.6)$.

beautiful sequence of increasingly complex dynamics, which we could label multitorus route to chaos. This is illustrated in Figures 1.18 through 1.22, showing, respectively, a period-9 cycle; nine invariant circles brought about by a Neimark bifurcation of the 9th iterate of the map of the system; a period-9 chaos produced by the breaking of the invariant circles and the appearance of nine chaotic islands; the linking of the islands in a single chaotic attractor, with quite evident remnants of 9-periodicity; and a fully developed chaotic attractor.

We now turn to the even more complex dynamical configurations brought about by changes in the parameter r. Note first that r is the crucial bifurcation parameter in the OLG models without production, briefly mentioned at the beginning of the paper. In those models, however, complexity arises invariably by increasing r and going through a period-doubling route. As we show in our model, the bifurcation scenarios related to changes in r are much more complicated.

Figures 1.23 through 1.27 show a, by now, familiar sequence of the multitorus route to chaos. We call the reader's attention only to the typical configurations of the chaotic attractor of Figure 1.27, where the fractal structure (presumably attributable to the so-called homoclinic tangles) is very evident. A different route to chaos is instead illustrated in Figure 1.28, where a sequence of flip bifurcations is evident, followed by a apparent crisis (a sudden increase in size of the attractor). For large values of r, the behavior is chaotic (Figure 1.29). A surprising complication is shown in Figure 1.30. Starting again from a value of r corresponding to a stable equilibrium and decreasing it, we have a loss of

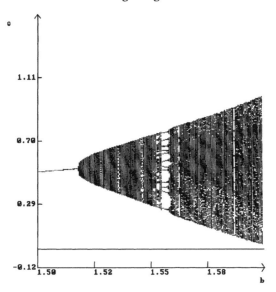

Figure 1.17. CARAL Model. Neimark bifurcation (enlargement). Enlarged right side of Fig. 16.

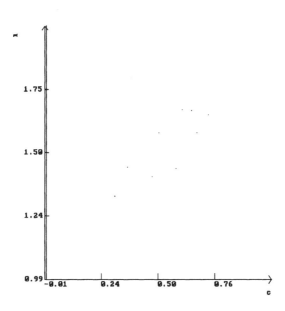

Figure 1.18. CARAL Model. Multitorus route to chaos I (induced by high productivity). (a) $\gamma = 1.2$; $\alpha = 0.49$; $b = 1.558$; $r = 3$.

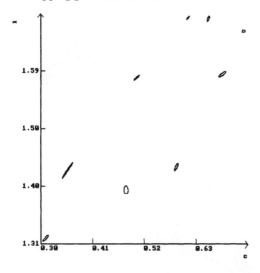

Figure 1.19. CARAL Model. Multitorus route to chaos I (induced by high productivity). (b) As Fig. 18, with $b = 1.55$.

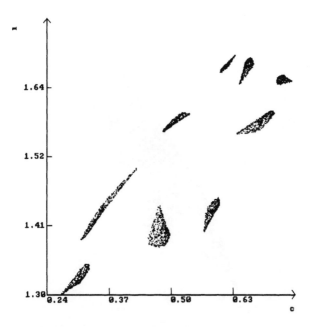

Figure 1.20. CARAL Model. Multitorus route to chaos I (induced by high productivity). (c) As Fig. 18, with $b = 1.55995$.

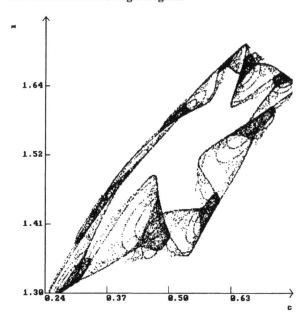

Figure 1.21. CARAL Model. Multitorus route to chaos I (induced by high productivity). (d) As Fig. 18, with $b = 1.56095$.

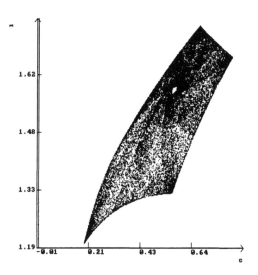

Figure 1.22. CARAL Model. Multitorus route to chaos I (induced by high productivity). (e) As Fig. 18, with $b = 1.57$.

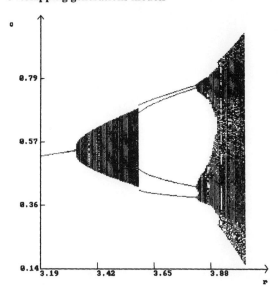

Figure 1.23. CARAL Model. Neimark r-bifurcation.
$\gamma = 1.2$; $r = (3.2, 4.1)$; $\alpha = 0.48$; $b = 1.5$.

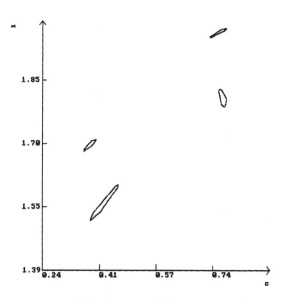

Figure 1.24. CARAL Model. Multitorus route to chaos II (induced by "steep"
derived utility function). (a) $\gamma = 1.2$; $r = 3.84$; $\alpha = 0.48$; $b = 1.5$.

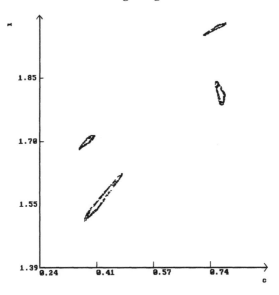

Figure 1.25. CARAL Model. Multitorus route to chaos II (induced by "steep" derived utility function). (b) As Fig. 24, with $r = 3.851$.

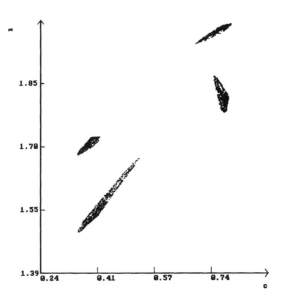

Figure 1.26. CARAL Model. Multitorus route to chaos II (induced by "steep" derived utility function). (b) As Fig. 24, with $r = 3.86$.

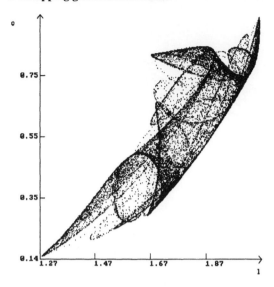

Figure 1.27. CARAL Model. Chaotic attractor I.
$\gamma = 1.2; r = 4.01; \alpha = 0.48; b = 1.5.$

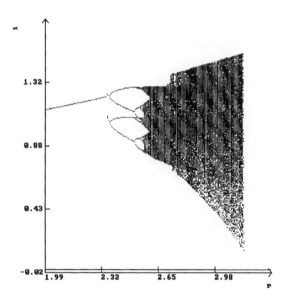

Figure 1.28. CARAL Model. Period doubling route to chaos.
$\gamma = 1.2; r = (2, 3.3); \alpha = 0.21; b = 1.3.$

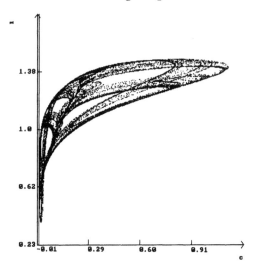

Figure 1.29. CARAL Model. Chaotic attractor.
$\gamma = 1.2; r = 3; \alpha = 0.21; b = 1.3.$

stability through a Neimark bifurcation with the known consequences. Thus, the effect of r on stability is not monotonic – a further instance of the fact that, in nonlinear models, simple statements on the (stabilizing or destabilizing) role of parameters are seldom appropriate.

7   CES technology

The cyclical and chaotic dynamical behaviors discussed so far occurred in economies in which technology allowed no factor substitution. One might wonder whether dropping this rather drastic assumption could lead to the elimination of some (or all) of the dynamical complexities. After all, intuitively, substitution should work for smoother, more stable dynamics. We know already, however, (Reichlin 1986) that low (but positive) substitution is compatible with cyclical behavior. To study this problem further, we consider the case of a production technology that allows for factor substitution when the factor prices change. We specifically consider the case of a CES production function, defined as follows:

$$f(n_t) = a[\delta n_t^{-\beta} + 1 - \delta]^{-1/\beta}, \qquad (1.17)$$

where $a > 0$ is a scale factor; $-1 < \beta < \infty; 0 < \delta < 1$ is a distribution factor; the elasticity of substitution is given by $\sigma = (1 + \beta)^{-1}$; n represents the labor/capital ratio. Under the hypothesis that the production process uses

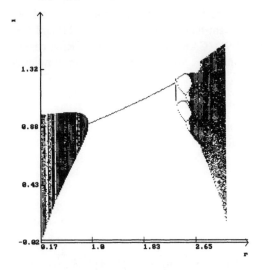

Figure 1.30. CARAL Model. Neimark and flip r-bifurcations.
$\gamma = 1.2; r = (0.2, 3.45); \alpha = 0.21; b = 1.3.$

current labor and previous period capital, we get

$$l_t = n_{t-1} k_{t-1}. \tag{1.18}$$

From the first-order conditions of profit maximization, we get $w_t = f'(n_{t-1})$ and $R_{t+1} = f(n_{t-1}) - n_{t-1} f'(n_{t-1})$. These conditions read

$$w_t = a\delta n_{t-1}^{-(1+\beta)} \left(\delta n_{t-1}^{-\beta} + 1 - \delta\right)^{-(1+\beta)/\beta} \tag{1.19}$$

$$R_{t+1} = a(1 - \delta)\left(\delta n_{t-1}^{-\beta} + 1 - \delta\right)^{-(1+\beta)/\beta}. \tag{1.20}$$

We also know from the consumer's budget constraint that

$$c_{t+1} = R_{t+1}(w_t l_t - c_t). \tag{1.21}$$

Moreover, because we are concerned with equilibrium analysis, we set the equilibrium condition of the commodity market as follows:

$$k_t = w_t l_t - c_t. \tag{1.22}$$

From equations (1.18) through (1.22), we derive the following equations:

$$c_{t+1} = a(1 - \delta)k_t \left(\delta n_t^{-\beta} + 1 - \delta\right)^{-(1+\beta)/\beta} \tag{1.23}$$

$$k_t = f(n_{t-1})k_{t-1}, \tag{1.24}$$

where

$$f(n_{t-1}) = a\left(\delta n_{t-1}^{-\beta} + 1 - \delta\right)^{-(1+\beta)/\beta} \left[\delta\left(n_{t-1}^{-\beta} + 1\right) - 1\right]k_{t-1}. \tag{1.25}$$

Equation (1.24) is thus the first half of our dynamical model. To complete it, we have to equate the right-hand side of equation (1.23) and the right-hand side of either equation (1.9a) (CARA case), or (1.9b) (CRRA case), and derive n_t as a function of n_{t-1} and k_{t-1}. We start from the latter, simpler case.

8   Chaotic dynamics in a CRRACES economy

To derive the dynamics in this case, we equate equations (1.23) and (1.9b) (putting $\alpha = \theta$), and obtain

$$n_t = g_1(k_{t-1}, n_{t-1}) \tag{1.26}$$

where

$$
\begin{aligned}
g_1(k_{t-1}, n_{t-1}) = \phi \left(n_{t-1}^\gamma k_{t-1}^\gamma - \alpha c_t^\alpha \right)^{\alpha(1+\beta)} \Big\{ \left[a^2(1-\delta) \right]^{\frac{\beta}{1+\beta}} \\
\times \left[\delta n_{t-1}^\beta + 1 + \delta \right]^{-1} \times \left[\delta \left(n_{t-1}^\beta + 1 \right) - 1 \right]^{\frac{\beta}{1+\beta}} k_{t-1}^{\frac{\beta}{1+\beta}} \\
+ \omega \left[n_{t-1}^\gamma k_{t-1}^\gamma - c_t^\alpha \right]^{\frac{\beta}{\alpha(1+\beta)}} \Big\}^{\frac{-1}{\beta}} .
\end{aligned}
\tag{1.27}
$$

and where $\phi = \delta^{\frac{1}{\beta}}(\alpha)^{\frac{-1}{1+\beta}}$, $\omega = (\delta - 1)(\alpha)^{\frac{\beta}{\alpha(1+\beta)}}$. The dynamics in a CRRACES economy are thus generated by equations (1.24) and (1.26). Note that c_t in equation (1.27) is defined by equation (1.23).

System (1.24)–(1.9b) has one equilibrium, E_1, with $k = 0$ (which, in turn, implies $l = 0$, and $c = 0$) and with any value of n for which the relevant functions of n are finite. Apart from E_1, there may generically be either zero, or two values of n that satisfy equation (1.24).[13] It also can be shown that, for any given $\bar{n}$, there exists only one value of k that satisfies equation (1.11).

Equations (1.24) and (1.9b) are rather formidable, and there is little hope, we believe, of finding any further analytical result. The dynamical behavior of the system has therefore been investigated numerically. So that we do not overburden the presentation, we consider here only the evolution of the global dynamics of the system in relation to a single parameter – the elasticity of substitution between the two factors. In this way, we concentrate on the crucial difference between the Leontief and the CES technologies (i.e., the possibility of substitution between capital and labor), without omitting any of the interesting types of behavior occurring in the CRRACES model.

[13] This can be seen by setting the right-hand side of equation (1.29) equal to one, that is,

$$a \left(\delta n^{-\beta} + 1 - \delta \right)^{(1+\beta)/\beta} = \left[\delta \left(n^{-\beta} + 1 \right) - 1 \right] \kappa$$

(in equilibrium analysis $\kappa_{t+1} = \kappa_t$ and $n_{t+1} = n_t$, $\forall t$) and solving for n graphically.

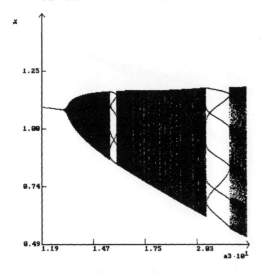

Figure 1.31. CRRACES Model. Beta-bifurcation I.
$a = 1.5; a_5 = 0.48; a_2 = 2; a_3 = (12, 23); a_4 = 0.2.$

The main results can be summarized with the help of Figures 1.31[14] through 1.37. The first of these contains (part of) a bifurcation diagram depending on the parameter $a3(\equiv \beta)$ which, as we have seen above, is inversely related to the elasticity of substitution σ. The diagram suggests the, by now, usual scenario ensuing from a Neimark bifurcation: periodic/quasiperiodic alternation, mode-locking windows, multiple tori, fractal tori, crisis, and chaos. Figure 1.32 shows a case of fully developed chaotic attractor, where the typical fractal structure and homoclinic tangles are quite evident. Note that periodic/quasiperiodic behavior can been observed with a value of the elasticity of substitution σ as high as 0.1, and chaotic behavior at $\sigma = 0.05$. Thus, the occurrence of chaotic dynamics occurring in economies with Leontief technology cannot be explained in terms of fixity of proportions only.

9   Chaotic dynamics in a CARACES economy

Let us now derive the dynamics of our economy, in the more complex case in which the utility function for second-period consumption is of the CARA type. Remember that, in this case, the evolution of c_{t+1} is given by equation (1.9a). Because the evolution of c_{t+1} implied by intertemporal optimization must be

---

[14] To facilitate the coding of the program used for generating the Figures that follow, notation has sometimes been changed, according to the following "table of conversion" (from Figures to text): $a_1 = \alpha; a_2 = \gamma; a_3 = \beta; a_4 = \delta; a_5 = 1 - a_1; h = c.$

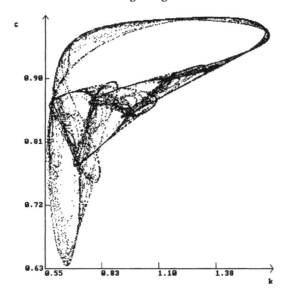

Figure 1.32. CRRACES Model. Chaotic attractor I.
$a = 1.4; a_5 = 1 - a_1 = 0.77; a_2 = 1.1; a_3 = 28; a_4 = 0.6.$

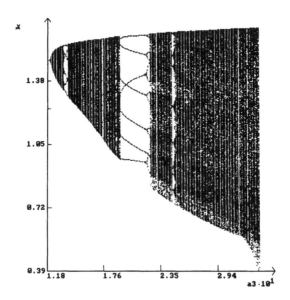

Figure 1.33. CRRACES Model. Beta-bifurcation II.
$a = 1.4; a_5 = 1 - a_1 = 0.77; a_2 = 1.1; a_3 = (12, 35); a_4 = 0.55.$

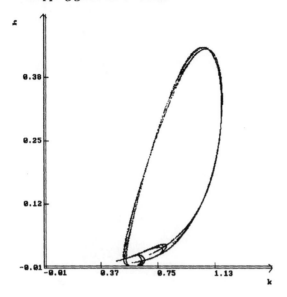

Figure 1.34. CRRACES Model. Torus breaking and chaos. (a) As Fig. 31 with $a_3 = 23.05$.

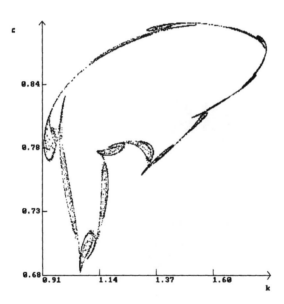

Figure 1.35. CRRACES Model. Torus breaking and chaos.
(b) $a = 1.45$; $a_5 = 0.772$; $a_1 = 0.228$; $a_3 = 20$; $a_4 = 0.2$; $a_2 = 1.1$.

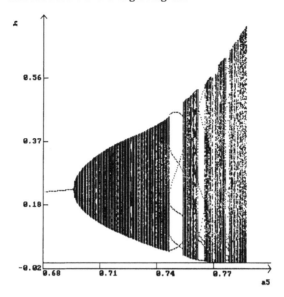

Figure 1.36. CRRACES Model. Bifurcation diagram for changing parameters. (a) $a = 1.45$; $a_5 = (0.68, 0.8)$; $a_3 = 20$; $a_4 = 0.4$; $a_2 = 1.1$.

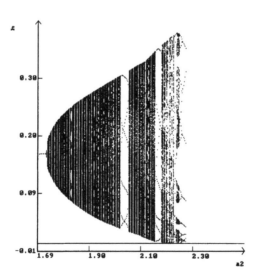

Figure 1.37. CRRACES Model. Bifurcation diagram for changing parameters. (b) $a = 1.5$; $a_5 = 0.52$; $a_3 = 20$; $a_4 = 0.2$; $a_2 = (1.7.2.5)$.

compatible with the evolution implied by market clearing, equations (1.23) and (1.9a) must be equated. Then, taking equation (1.18) into account, we get the following difference equation for n_t:

$$n_t = g(k_{t-1}, n_{t-1}), \tag{1.28}$$

where

$$g(k_{t-1}, n_{t-1}) =$$

$$\delta^{\frac{1}{\beta}}\left(\left\{\frac{a^2(1-\delta)[\delta(n_{t-1}^{\beta}+1)-1][\delta n_{t-1}^{-\beta}+1-\delta]^{\frac{-(1+\beta)}{\beta}}k_{t-1}}{[(n_{t-1}k_{t-1})^{\gamma}-rc_te^{-c_t}]^{\frac{1}{\alpha}}}\right\}^{\frac{\beta}{1+\beta}}\right.$$

$$\left.+(1-\delta)\cdot\right)^{\frac{-1}{\beta}} \tag{1.29}$$

and where c_t is derived from equation (1.23), shifting the time index one period backward. Using the substitution, equation (1.28) defines n_t, once n_{t-1} and k_{t-1} are known.

In this case, the dynamics of the economy are generated by the dynamical system defined by equations (1.24) and (1.28). Again c_{t+1} is derived by equation (1.23) from the knowledge of n_t and k_t.

We have already commented on existence (and number) of equilibria. The difficulty of finding detailed analytical results is even greater here than in the CRRACES model, but the numerical results are extremely interesting and we have found that the complexity of behavior of the CARACES model is as great as that of the corresponding CARAL one, in spite of the presence of substitution between factors.

We again concentrate the discussion of numerical simulations on the effects of changing the elasticity of substitution. As in the CARAL model, we have complex scenarios involving combinations of flip and Neimark bifurcations. A particularly intriguing example of this, which somewhat summarizes our findings, is shown in Figure 1.38, where increasing the parameter $a3(\equiv\beta)$ – and therefore decreasing σ – we have the following sequence of dynamical phenomena: a Neimark bifurcation with an interval of periodic/aperiodic dynamics; a crisis leading to a period-4 cycle; a flip bifurcation (of the 4th iterate of the map) with subsequent period-doubling sequence, leading to a fully developed chaos (see Figure 1.39 where fractal structure and homoclinic tangles are evident). For even larger values of $a3$ (smaller values of the degree of substitution), a crisis occurs with consequent disappearance of the chaotic attractor, which is replaced by a period-5 cycle. A large periodic window follows and for a value of σ of approximately 1%, we have an aborted Neimark bifurcation and an explosion of the system out of the admissible region.

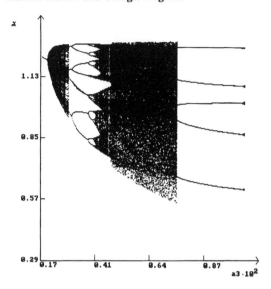

Figure 1.38. CRRACES Model. Bifurcations, crises and chaos with changing degree of factor substitution. $a = 1.5; b = 5; a_5 = 0.48; a_2 = 2.2; a_4 = 0.2; a_3 = (18, 110)$.

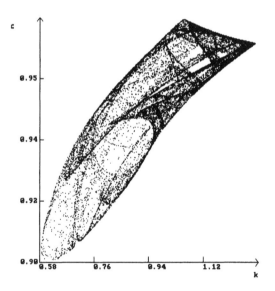

Figure 1.39. CRRACES Model. Chaotic attractor.
$a = 1.5; b = 5; a_5 = 0.48; a_2 = 2.2; a_3 = 68; a_4 = 0.2$.

10 Conclusions: Some economic explanations of complex dynamics

To investigate the origin of cyclical and chaotic behavior in our model, it is useful to trace out the complete sequence of substitution effects arising from consumer's optimal choice. By considering equation (1.4) we can derive the following expressions:

$$\frac{\partial c_{t+1}}{\partial l_t} = \frac{v'}{u_2'} \frac{1+\rho_l}{1-\rho_2} = R_{t+1} w_t \frac{1+\rho_l}{1-\rho_2} \tag{1.30}$$

$$\frac{\partial c_{t+1}}{\partial c_t} = -\frac{u_1'}{u_2'} \frac{1-\rho_1}{1-\rho_2} = -R_{t+1} \frac{1-\rho_1}{1-\rho_2} \tag{1.31}$$

$$\frac{\partial c_t}{\partial l_t} = \frac{v'}{u_2'} \frac{1+\rho_l}{1-\rho_1} = w_t \frac{1+\rho_l}{1-\rho_1}. \tag{1.32}$$

When $u_1(c_t)$ is of CARA type, equations (1.30)–(1.32) become:

$$\frac{\partial c_{t+1}}{\partial l_t} = R_{t+1} w_t \frac{\gamma}{\alpha} \tag{1.30a}$$

$$\frac{\partial c_{t+1}}{\partial c_t} = -R_{t+1} \frac{1-c_t}{\alpha} \tag{1.31a}$$

$$\frac{\partial c_t}{\partial l_t} = w_t \frac{\gamma}{1-c_t}. \tag{1.32a}$$

When $u_1(c_t)$ is of CRRA type, we get instead

$$\frac{\partial c_{t+1}}{\partial l_t} = R_{t+1} w_t \frac{\gamma}{\alpha} \tag{1.30b}$$

$$\frac{\partial c_{t+1}}{\partial c_t} = -R_{t+1} \frac{\theta}{\alpha} \tag{1.31b}$$

$$\frac{\partial c_t}{\partial l_t} = w_t \frac{\gamma}{\theta}. \tag{1.32b}$$

Note that Rw is the relative price of leisure in terms of next-period consumption, R is the relative price of current consumption in terms of next-period consumption, and w is the relative price of leisure in terms of current consumption.

Let us assume $\rho_2 < 1$. Then, from equation (1.30) we get $\partial c_{t+1}/\partial l_t > 0$ always, meaning that next-period consumption and current leisure are substitutes. From equation (1.31), we have $\partial c_{t+1}/\partial c_t > 0$ if $\rho_1 > 1$; this means that when $\rho_1 < 1$, substitution effect dominates, whereas income effect becomes predominant when $\rho_1 > 1$. Note also that when $\rho_1 < 1$, we have $\partial c_t/\partial l_t > 0$, indicating that current consumption and current leisure are substitute.

As we have seen from the simulations, on the (periodic, quasiperiodic, or chaotic) attractors, current consumption is, in most cases, less than one, so that saving is an increasing function of the real interest rate. The source of chaotic dynamics thus relies on the interrelations between the effects represented by equations (1.30)–(1.32). Let us now consider these effects.

As in Reichlin's model, during a boom, R_t falls and w_t increases. This can be seen as follows. From full employment of labor and from equilibrium in the commodity market, we get $c_t = -k_t + bk_{t-1}$. From the budget constraint of the young consumer, and from the equilibrium between saving and investment, we get $c_{t+1} = R_{t+1}k_t$. Moving the time indexes one period backward in the latter equation, and equating it with the former one, we get $b = R_t + k_t / k_{t-1}$. Therefore, during a boom, k_t / k_{t-1} increases and R_t declines, because b is fixed; the opposite holds during a recession. Note that in the case of a Leontief technology, we get $R_t = b(1 - w_t)$; hence, if the real interest rate falls during a boom, the real wage increases.

In Reichlin's model the force generating cyclical behavior is represented by equation (1.30) (future consumption/current leisure substitution). In fact, during a boom, $w_t R_{t+1}$ falls, meaning that the relative price of leisure in terms of next-period consumption falls, making c_{t+1} more expensive. For very low R_{t+1}, the substitution of current leisure for c_{t+1} is large enough to reduce the supply of labor, which, in turn, reduces saving and output, eventually reversing the cycle. Note, however, that in Reichlin's model we do not get chaotic dynamics: Equation (1.30) alone is not enough to generate forward complex behavior. However, as Medio (1992) shows, this mechanism can very well generate backward chaotic paths, if a utility function of the CARA type is used.

In our model, in addition to this mechanism the forces represented by equations (1.31) and (1.32) are also at work. Let us suppose that $u_1(c_t)$ is of CARA type. We first consider equation (1.31a) (future/current consumption substitution, or income effect), and suppose that $c_t < 1$. This mechanism essentially works in the same direction as the preceding one. In fact, the fall of R_{t+1} during a boom reduces the relative price of current consumption with respect to future consumption. This means that c_{t+1} is substituted for c_t, thus reducing saving and slowing down the accumulation of capital. Note that this second mechanism is the stronger, the smaller is α. The joint effect of equations (1.30) and (1.31) is thus likely to make the booms shorter.

Finally, let us consider the role of equation (1.32a) (current consumption/ current labor substitution). The mechanism introduces a force that may counterbalance the effect of the other two. In fact, during a boom, a larger w_t corresponds to a higher price of leisure in terms of current consumption. Because we are considering the case $c_t < 1$, this induces the agent to substitute leisure for current consumption. The reduction of leisure, that is the increase of labor supply, leads to greater output and saving, thus stimulating the boom. The increase in current consumption works exactly in the opposite direction.

If the increase in labor supply outweighs the increase in current consumption, the mechanism represented by equation (1.32a) introduces a force that keeps the boom alive. However, as the economy grows and consumption approaches 1, effect (1.31a) tends to become negligible, whereas effect (1.32a) becomes very large. This means that c increases much faster than l, thus terminating the boom. The dialectics between these forces seem to be at the origin of the chaotic behavior observed in the CARAL model. Analogous considerations hold for the CRRAL model.[15]

Let us recapitulate the main results of our investigations so far.

(i)   Introducing production into OLG models enormously increases the potential complexity of their dynamics. Periodic, aperiodic, and chaotic behaviors occur in many possible combinations. Chaotic attractors can be generated through different types of transition: period-doubling, quasiperiodicity, intermittency (or interior crisis) routes to chaos.

(ii)   Bifurcations leading to cycles and chaos may depend on a variety of parameters, such as elasticities of utility functions, productivity coefficients, elasticity of substitutions between factors.

(iii)   The effect of variations of parameters on stability as well as on the degree of complexity of the dynamics of the system need not be monotonic. As we have seen in the discussion of the CARAL model, for example, loss of equilibrium stability and the ensuing periodic or complex dynamics may be obtained both by increasing and decreasing the parameter r.

(iv)   In OLG models without production, a necessary condition for cycles and chaos to occur was the existence of an inverse relation (over a certain interval) between saving and the interest rate. In the models analyzed here, such an inverse relation almost never plays a significant role.[16]

(v)   As the numerical exercise of this paper have shown, complexity should not be taken as a single property of a dynamical system (chaos) that is or is not present. On the contrary, it should be recognized that complexity includes a rather large set of different classes of dynamical behavior: some classes are better understood than others, some of them are universal, and others are model specific.

[15] Note that the same mechanism is responsible for cycles and chaos in the case of a CES technology. In this case however, we need a relatively low elasticity of substitution between factors. In fact, only in this circumstance can we have R falling and w increasing during a boom, a condition that is required for the mechanism represented by the equations (1.30)–(1.32) to be activated. Our findings confirm thus the results of Reichlin (1986) and Benhabib and Laroque (1988).

[16] An inverse relation between saving and the rate of interest is possible in the models of the CARA type whenever consumption c is greater than one. However, as we have already stated, in virtually all cases discussed in this paper, the consumption coordinate of attractors is within the interval $0 < c < 1$.

(vi) In the economic literature, the discussion of chaos has most often taken place with a mathematical rather than physical approach. By this we mean that in most cases the authors have attempted to prove analytically that a certain abstract property called chaos (not necessarily the same in every case) was present. This has necessarily restricted the models to be considered to extremely simple and abstract ones, usually some adaptations of one of the very few dynamical systems investigated in the mathematical literature and amenable to full analytical treatment. Useful though such exercises might have been from a pedagogic point of view, they have a limited significance for an understanding of chaotic systems originating directly from economic problems. Given the state of the art, global information on the dynamics of the vast majority of nonlinear dynamical systems can be obtained only by combining the few analytical results supplied by dynamical system theory and carefully organized numerical simulations. In this paper we have attempted to provide a contribution in this direction.

11   Appendix

Proof: [Proof of Proposition 1.2]. From equations (1.15) and (1.16) and the equilibrium condition of Lemma 1.2, we see that, for $b > 1$, we can find corresponding values of $r \in (0, +\infty)$ such that c takes any preassigned value $\psi^{1/(\alpha-\gamma)} < c < \infty$. Thus we can study equilibrium conditions changing b and keeping the value of c fixed (by changing r appropriately). Suppose this value – call it $\hat{c}$ – is chosen greater than, but close to $\psi^{1/(\alpha-\gamma)}$, and consider the quantity $f_1(\hat{c}) + f_2(\hat{c})$, which we assume to be positive [this will be true if c is sufficiently close to $\psi^{1/(\alpha-\gamma)}$]. If we then decrease b, $f_1(c_0) < 0$ will decrease [i.e., $|f_1(c_0)|$ will increase] and $f_2(c_0) > 0$ will increase. As $b \to 1$, $|f_1|$ and f_2 will both tend to infinity, but – as can be seen from the definitions (1.15) and (1.16) – $|f_1| \to +\infty$ with $\psi \equiv [b(b-1)^{-1}]^\gamma$, whereas $f_2 \to +\infty$ with $[b(b-1)^{-1}]^{\gamma-1}$. Therefore, we can always find a value of b such that $|f_1| = f_2$ or $f_1 + f_2 = 0$. This guarantees that condition (iii) is verified. Concerning condition (i), it will be verified provided that f_1 is small enough, and this can always be guaranteed if – in the exercise described a moment ago – we keep $\hat{c}$ sufficiently close to $\psi^{1/(\alpha-\gamma)}$ (for which $f_1 = 0$). This completes the proof of Proposition 2.   □

Note that in Figures A1.1 and A1.2, we set $\psi_i = [b_i(b_i - 1)^{-1}]^\gamma$, $c_i = \psi_i^{1/(\alpha-\gamma)}$, $s_i = \gamma\alpha^{-1}[b_i(b_i - 1)^{-1}]^{\gamma-1}$, $t_i = \gamma\alpha^{-1}[(b_i - 1)b_i^{-1}]^{\gamma-1}$, where $i = 0, 1$. Note also that in Figure A1.3, we set, $b_i = a_i(a_i - 1)^{-1}$ and $a_i = (1 + r_i e^{-c})^{1/\gamma}$, where $i = 0, 1, 2$.

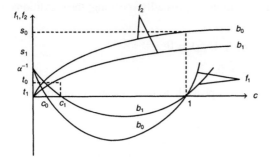

Figure A1.1. $f_1(c)$, $f_2(c)$ for 2 fixed values of b, $b_1 > b_0$; c_1 corresponds to $r = 0$ and $c = 1$ corresponds to $r_1 = e(\psi_i - 1)$.

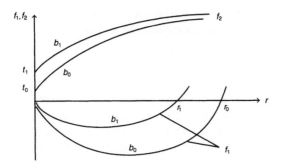

Figure A1.2. $f_1(r)$, $f_2(r)$ for 2 fixed values of b, $b_1 > b_0$.

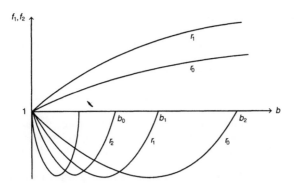

Figure A1.3. $f_1(b)$, $f_2(b)$ for 2 fixed values of r, $r_1 > r_0$; b_1 corresponds to $c = 1$.

Proof: [Proof of Proposition 1.3] Broadly speaking, the conditions for a flip bifurcation are

$$1 + b + f_1 + b(f_1 + f_2) = 0 \tag{A1.1}$$

$$1 - b(f_1 + f_2) > 0. \tag{A1.2}$$

We have seen above that it is possible to have a stable configuration of parameters with $(f_1 + f_2)$ as small as we please. As long as we keep it smaller than $1/b$, condition (A1.2) will hold. Condition (A1.1), however, can be violated by increasing b. This happens when the (small) equilibrium value of c results from a small value of b, so that increasing b leads to a relatively large decrease of f_1 (note that this effect requires that r should be neither too large nor too small, as will be seen). Condition (A1.1) also can be violated by decreasing α such that $f_1 + f_2$ is unchanged but f_1 is reduced. Finally, a flip bifurcation can occur when we increase r (and therefore c), given b. Again, if b at equilibrium is sufficiently small, an increase of r will produce a relatively large decrease of f_1.

Occurrence of the Neimark bifurcation requires that we have

$$1 + b + f_1 + b(f_1 + f_2) > 0 \tag{A1.3}$$

$$1 - b(f_1 + f_2) = 0. \tag{A1.4}$$

This can happen when the equilibrium E_2 obtains at a relatively large b, such that increasing b makes both f_1 and f_2 increase (or it makes f_2 more than it makes f_1 decrease). It can also occur at values of r sufficiently close to zero or to $\exp(\psi - 1)$. For both values, $f_1 = 0$ and condition (A1.3) obviously holds, whereas condition (A1.4) can be obtained by decreasing r (near $r = 0$, i.e., $c = 0$), or increasing it (near $c(\psi - 1)$, i.e., $c = 1$). The same result can be obtained by decreasing α.   □

REFERENCES

Benhabib, J., and Day, R. (1982). A characterization of erratic dynamics in the overlapping generations model, *Journal of Economic Dynamics and Control*, **4**, 37–55.
Benhabib, J., and Laroque, G. (1988). On competitive cycles in productive economy, *Journal of Economic Theory*, **45**, 145–70.
Grandmont J. M. (1985). On endogenous competitive business cycles, *Econometrica*, **53**, 995–1045.
Jullien, B. (1988). Competitive business cycles in an overlapping generations economy with productive investment, *Journal of Economic Theory*, **46**, 45–65.
Medio, A. (1992). *Chaotic Dynamics. Theory and Applications to Economics*, Cambridge University Press,
Reichlin, P. (1986). Equilibrium cycles in an overlapping generations economy with production, *Journal of Economic Theory*, **40**, 89–102.
Woodford, M. (1990). Equilibrium models of endogenous fluctuations: an introduction, *Nber Working Paper N. 3360*.

CHAPTER 2

Evolutionary chaos: Growth fluctuations in a Schumpeterian model of creative destruction

Gerald Silverberg and Doris Lehnert

A dynamic model of one of the authors of Schumpeterian competition and creative destruction, based on the Goodwin growth cycle, is generalized to allow for a continuing stochastic stream of new capital-embodied innovations. Mathematically, the model is equivalent to a large-dimensional Lotka–Volterra system with stochastically perturbed coefficients. Allowing for the introduction of new techniques according to various possible stochastic processes such as time-homogeneous or inhomogeneous Poisson, computer experiments reveal a robust pattern of distributed long waves and a $1/f^\alpha$-like spectrum in the productivity growth rate and other macroeconomic variables. Calculation of the Grassberger–Procaccia correlation dimension suggests that we may be dealing with an unusual form of low-dimensional deterministic chaos as an emergent property of a stochastically driven system. This is confirmed by a calculation of the embedding dimension using the notion of false nearest neighbors. We have termed this phenomenon evolutionary chaos. Evidence for a positive Lyapunov exponent as well as for nonlinearity based on the BDS test and a test for nonlinear predictability is also presented.

1   Introduction

Formal explanations of fluctuating behavior in complex systems appear to fall into a number of distinct classes. First, we find the periodically driven or forced case. Examples are seasonality in economic times series or the forced harmonic oscillator in physics. Next come linear dynamic systems driven by noise, which constitute the stock in trade of most mainstream econometric modeling. (In the absence of noise, linear dynamic systems can only display damped or explosive oscillations; sustained periodicity, such as in the multiplier–accelerator model, represents an exceedingly unlikely parameter constellation on a set of measure zero in the space of parameters.) These systems display fluctuating, but not strictly periodic, behavior; the underlying dynamics are presumed to be stable

45

(e.g., damped oscillations, or, as in recent work, unit root), whereas the persistence of fluctuations results from exogenous shocks of an unspecified character. They share with the first case the basic linear structure. In general, a spectral analysis will not reveal any pronounced concentration of cyclical activity at particular frequencies. Endogenous cycles without exogenous forcing terms can be generated by nonlinear dynamic systems in the form of limit-cycle or quasiperiodic motion, which will show up as sharp peaks in a spectral diagram.

This does not seem to be the case for most economic time series, however. A number of models and empirical methods have been proposed recently to investigate the possibility of deterministic chaos in economic systems. Here, fluctuations still would be generated endogenously but would not be strictly periodic. It is still a matter of controversy as to whether chaos can be detected empirically in economic time series and provides a better explanation than ARIMA-type time-series modeling. We propose a further alternative based on a nonlinear dynamic system driven in a novel way by innovation noise, which one might term an evolutionary oscillator. Its distinguishing characteristic is that it makes minimal assumptions about the frequency characteristics of stochastic variables and derives diffusion and wage/profit distributional and employment dynamics from only a few simple assumptions about Schumpeterian competition, yet produces distinctive and more plausible spectral patterns than the other classes of models proposed until now.[1] The spectrum also contains a region of $1/f^\alpha$ noise.[2] Not surprisingly, these times series are highly persistent (in the sense of a slowly decaying autocorrelation function). In addition to the linear time-series properties, the model displays characteristics of low-dimensional chaos, which can be distinguished statistically from a highly correlated stochastic process.

2   The model

Our approach is based on that of Silverberg (1984), which in turn is an extension of Goodwin (1967). First, a linear Phillips curve is postulated to govern the growth rate of real wages:

$$\dot{w} = -mw + nwv \tag{2.1}$$

where m and n are constants and v is the rate of employment aggregated over all technologies. Second, the economy is assumed to be composed of a number

---

[1] Two papers related in approach to ours are Mensch, Weidlich, and Haag (1987) and Mosekilde, Rasmussen, and Zebrowski (1987). Neither of these papers, however, provides any robust evidence for a long-wave spectral pattern.

[2] Thus our model could be considered a partial answer to Brock, Hsieh, and LeBaron's (1991, p. 188) fifth question: "What economic mechanisms are capable of converting independent outside noise impacting on individual economic units into economic aggregates that display characteristics of $1/f$ noise?"

of fixed-coefficient linear technologies. The rate of growth of the capital stock embodied in each technology is posited to be equal to that technology's own rate of (net) profit. Letting a_i, c_i, k_i, and r_i be the labor productivity, the capital-output ratio, the capital stock, and the rate of profit of any given technology i, respectively and γ be the rate of exponential physical deterioration of capital (economically motivated scrapping is an endogenous component of the model), we have

$$\frac{\dot{k}_i}{k_i} = r_i - \gamma = \frac{1}{c_i}\left(1 - \frac{w}{a_i}\right) - \gamma. \tag{2.2}$$

Soete and Turner (1984) propose an extension of this mechanism to allow the profits made with one technology to be invested in another technology with superior profitability. If the probability of making this jump on the technology ladder is proportional to the difference in profitability on the one hand and the relative size of the capital stock of the target technology on the other, then they show that equation (2.2) can be extended to

$$\frac{\dot{k}_i}{k_i} = r_i + s(r_i - \bar{r}) - \gamma = \frac{1}{c_i}\left(1 - \frac{w}{a_i}\right) + s(r_i - \bar{r}) - \gamma, \tag{2.3}$$

where s is a constant representing the strength of the cross-technology investment flows and

$$\bar{r} = \sum_{i=1}^{n} k_i r_i \left/ \sum_{i=1}^{n} k_i \right.$$

is the capital-stock-weighted average profit rate. Employment using this technology will grow at the same rate as the capital stock, so that the share of the labor force employing this technology, v_i, is given by

$$\frac{\dot{v}_i}{v_i} = \frac{\dot{k}_i}{k_i} - \alpha = \frac{1}{c_i}\left(1 - \frac{w}{a_i}\right) + s(r_i - \bar{r}) - \beta, \tag{2.4}$$

where α is the growth rate of the labor force and $\beta = \alpha + \gamma$.

Silverberg (1984) derives a criterion that determines whether a new technology initially introduced in a small quantity will displace an existing technology. This is based on evaluating the sign of the eigenvalue associated with the employment share of the new technology in the neighborhood of the old steady state. If it is positive, the old technology will be replaced by the new one; if it is negative, the new technology will not diffuse. This criterion reduces to comparing an expression specific to each technology based solely on technological and exogenous factors, independent of current relative prices and initial conditions:

$$T_i = a_i[1 - c_i(\alpha + \gamma)] = a_i(1 - c_i\beta). \tag{2.5}$$

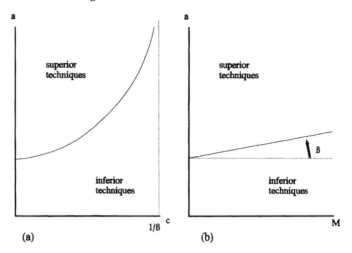

Figure 2.1. Contours of equal selective potential in the (**a**) a-c and (**b**) a-M planes. Technologies in the upper region are superior to those on or below the contour.

If T_i, which we term the technology's evolutionary potential, is higher than those of previous technologies, it will survive and gradually dominate the economy (see Figures 2.1a,b). The difference in evolutionary potential, $\Delta T = T_2 - T_1$, also determines the rate of replacement in the two-technology case:

$$v_2^{M_2}/v_1^{M_1} = \text{const} \cdot e^{\Delta T \cdot t}, \tag{2.6}$$

where $M_i = a_i c_i$ is the capital/worker ratio for each technology, as can be seen by simple algebraic manipulation of the two employment-share equations to eliminate w, and subsequent integration.

We now generalize the model to reflect the behavior of the capital stock and employment shares in the case of a continuing stream of capital-embodied innovations entering the economy over time. We envision each technology as being seeded with a fixed and very small employment share (say 0.01% of the labor force) at a specific moment in history. Formally, this is tantamount to "turning on" the corresponding employment-share equation à la equation (2.4) with the corresponding initial value for v_i at the time of innovation, thereby enlarging the dimension of the active state space of the system by one. Because the dimension of the state space is unbounded for such a process, we are forced in the numerical realization to restrict attention to only a finite number, n, of technologies most recently introduced. If the size of this subset is made sufficiently large with respect to the rate at which new technologies are being introduced, there is, in fact, no danger in this procedure, because old technologies automatically decline asymptotically to zero with time as they become relatively obsolete. Thus, in our implementation, when a new technology is introduced, the stack of technologies is pushed down by one, the oldest technology is eliminated, and the difference between the initial employment share of the new technology and the remaining employment share of the scrapped technology is proportionately removed from the rest of the economy to maintain a constant overall rate of employment. Then, the economy is allowed to evolve as an $n+1$ dimensional dynamic system starting with the n new (or shifted) technological parameters and initial employment shares and the previous real wage rate until the next innovation comes along.

In contrast to the macro dynamics of sectoral employment and wage formation, which are modeled deterministically, we wish to focus on the stochastic character of the innovation process. To this end, the model can be completed by filling the innovation "black box" with a fully specified stochastic process that can be either autonomous or subject to feedback from the economy. We have examined a number of stochastic models that are plausibly congruent with empirical studies of innovation and some hypotheses on modes of inducement in the economy. The first, which serves as a devil's advocate benchmark case, simply regards an innovation as a point event in time whose probability of occurrence is independent of other innovations and of time. This is precisely the definition of a time-homogenous Poisson process. For simplicity, we define an innovation as a fixed proportional increase in labor productivity over the last innovation, with the capital/output ratio unchanged, because this is consistent with the main implications of our choice of technique criterion, equation (2.5).[3] The resulting stochastic process can be characterized by two parameters: ω, the mean waiting time between innovations ($= 1/\rho$, the mean number of innovations per unit time), and Δ, the proportional jump in labor productivity between innovations. The approximate average growth rate of labor productivity τ will then be Δ/ω [more precisely $\ln(1+\Delta)/\omega$], which we can use to calibrate the model to historically reasonable values. As is well known, a time-homogeneous Poisson process is associated with the following distribution and probability density function:

$$\text{Prob}(n \text{ events during time interval } t) = \frac{(\rho t)^n}{n!} e^{-\rho t}, \qquad (2.7)$$

$$\text{Prob}(t < \text{interval between events} < t + dt) = \rho e^{-\rho t} \cdot dt. \qquad (2.8)$$

For the time-homogeneous case, the innovation process can be implemented exactly. The computer generates negative exponentially distributed variates for

---

[3] One could obviously regard the size and direction of an innovation jump in a-c space as themselves random variables, something we have opted not to do for the time being in order to leave the analysis as transparent as possible.

50   **Gerald Silverberg and Doris Lehnert**

a given mean waiting time by appropriately transforming a standard uniformly distributed random number generator. The system of differential equations is solved starting with some set of initial values for the length of the randomly generated time interval. Then, a stack updating is performed as outlined above and a new time interval is generated from our negative exponentially distributed variates, and the process iterates.

For the models described below involving a time-varying Poisson parameter, the process is discretely approximated as a Bernoulli process. The time axis is divided into small intervals, the Poisson parameter is scaled down proportionately, and a correspondingly weighted computer-generated "coin" is flipped to determine if an innovation is introduced during this interval. If no, the system is solved until the end of the interval and the coin tossing is repeated. If yes, a stack updating is also performed at the end of the interval. In all versions of the model, a fixed-step, fourth-order Runge–Kutta algorithm, which has proved more than adequate in accuracy for this well-behaved class of systems, is employed to solve the system of differential equations. It is important to select a step size small enough (on the order of 0.05–0.1 year) to maintain the correct qualitative features of the system.

The operation of the model can be visualized by plotting the share of each technology in the total capital stock as a bar graph (Figure 2.2). Denoting the share of technology i by f_i $(= k_i/k$, where k is the total capital stock) and rates of growth of a variable by a circumflex over it, we have

$$\hat{f}_i = \hat{k}_i - \hat{k}$$
$$= r_i + s(r_i - \bar{r}) - \gamma - (\bar{r} - \gamma) \tag{2.9}$$
$$= (1 + s)(r_i - \bar{r}).$$

In the absence of innovation, technologies with above-average profit rates will be growing in relative share; those with below-average profit rates will be declining. Equation (2.9) is an example of so-called replicator dynamics (cf. Hofbauer and Sigmund 1988). The average profit rate, $\bar{r}$, will increase monotonically in time (for constant wages) and is a Lyapunov function for the dynamics as the system converges to the most profitable technology. As innovations are introduced, however, the entire capital-stock distribution shifts to the right. Thus an "innovation wind" prevents the "diffusion wave" from washing up on the shore.

Artificial time series were generated under quasi-stationary circumstances by first allowing transients induced by the initial conditions (in particular, the shape of the initial capital-stock "vintage" structure) to die out by removing the first 200 years of each run. The variables of interest are the unemployment rate, the aggregate rate of gross profits, and the rate of growth of aggregate labor productivity. With respect to the last variable, only the deterministic component,

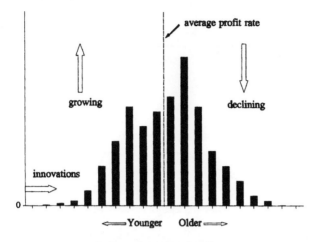

Figure 2.2. Schematic of the capital stock dynamics. Vertical bars represent the share of each technology in the total capital stock. As an innovation arrives at the left, the entire distribution shifts one step to the right.

that is the increase in labor productivity attributable to the shift in employment from existing-low to existing-high productivity sectors – the diffusion effect – was examined. The small, instantaneous jumps in productivity at the moment of introduction of a new technology, which can be made arbitrarily small by decreasing the initial employment share of an innovation, were neglected. This deterministic component can be expressed in the following form:

$$
\begin{aligned}
\hat{a} &= \frac{d}{dt} \ln \left(\frac{\text{output}}{\text{labor}} \right) = \frac{d}{dt} \ln \left(\frac{\sum_{i=1}^{n} \frac{k_i}{c_i}}{\sum_{i=1}^{n} \frac{k_i}{a_i c_i}} \right) \\
&= \frac{\sum_{i=1}^{n} \frac{k_i}{c_i}}{\sum_{i=1}^{n} \frac{k_i}{c_i}} - \frac{\sum_{i=1}^{n} \frac{k_i}{a_i c_i}}{\sum_{i=1}^{n} \frac{k_i}{a_i c_i}}
\end{aligned}
\tag{2.10}
$$

Because the c_i are identical, and by defining $\alpha_i = 1/a_i$, we can simplify equation (2.10) by substituting for $\dot{k}$ using equation (2.3):

$$
\hat{a} = \frac{w(1+s)}{c\alpha} \sigma_\alpha^2,
\tag{2.11}
$$

where $\bar{\alpha}$ and σ_α^2 are the mean and variance $\{\alpha_i\}$ over the distribution of technologies $\{f_i\}$. The proportionality between the rate of growth of average productivity and the variance of the technology distribution is fully parallel to the result derived by Soete and Turner (1984) for profit rates.

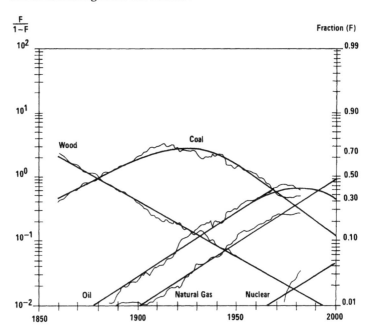

Figure 2.3a. An empirical case of multiple replacement taken from the primary energy sector in the United States (from Nakicenovic 1987).

3   Structural dynamics and linear time-series analysis

As new technologies come on-line, they diffuse into the economy because of their superior profitability. In the course of time, as their profitability declines to the average value prevailing in the economy, their share saturates, until they begin to diffuse out of the capital stock because of relative unprofitability. If this diffusion (either in or out) proceeds according to the well-known logistic equation, the share f of a technology will obey the following equation:

$$\ln[f/(1-f)] = \alpha \cdot (t - t_0). \tag{2.12}$$

Marchetti and Nakicenovic (1979) have extended this framework to the multiple replacement case, where new technologies saturate in terms of market share because of the advent of even newer technologies. An example from the primary energy sector is shown in Figure 2.3a.

To analyze the structural dynamics, we have plotted the transformed share of successive innovations (as measured by their share in the total capital stock) over time for a typical run with pure ploughback investment in Figure 2.3b.

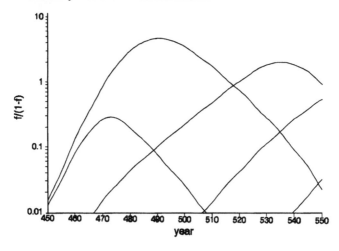

Figure 2.3b. Multiple replacement in our artificial economy ($\omega = 15, \tau = 2\%$).

Indeed, we do recover the characteristic features of the multiple replacement case uncovered in the empirical literature. Note that both the rate of diffusion (the slope of the quasi-linear segments) and the ultimate penetration levels vary between innovations, and are determined endogenously by the exact historical timing of preceding and subsequent innovations. Figure 2.3c shows the replacement pattern for a positive value of the Soete–Turner (ST) investment term s. As expected, diffusion proceeds more rapidly in this case, and technology life cycles become correspondingly shorter.

Figure 2.4 shows times series for a benchmark run of some of the macro-economic variables of primary interest. The unemployment and profit-rate variables may initially display short (Goodwin) cycles, which die out unless a period of constant productivity growth is encountered. Otherwise, they reflect the underlying long-period fluctuations in productivity growth. These are irregular but far from a random walk.

As opposed to the search for long waves in the historical statistics, where nonstationarity and the limited length and reliability of the data impose severe restrictions on the applicability of spectral methods, the model allows the unlimited generation of artificial data from a known stationary mechanism (assuming a constant innovation probability). In Figure 2.5a, the spectral density of the productivity growth rate that is presented is generated by running the model for 200 periods to allow transients to die off and performing a spectral analysis on the following 1,024 periods. What is remarkable is the sharp rise in spectral density in the 40- to 80-year region. Thus, in contrast to a naive expectation

54   **Gerald Silverberg and Doris Lehnert**

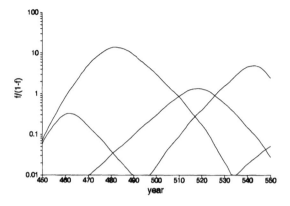

Figure 2.3c. Multiple replacement in the same run as in **2.3b** but with an ST investment parameter s of 0.5.

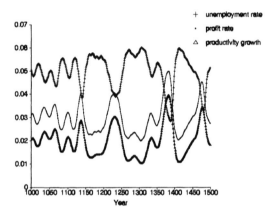

Figure 2.4. Artificial time series for unemployment, average profitability, and growth rate of productivity for a run with $\omega = 2$ years and $\tau = 2\%$.

of sharply defined 50- to 60-year Kondratieff cycles, our model also seems to provide strong evidence for long-period behavior, but in a spectrally distributed sense. In Figure 2.5b, we have plotted the related autocorrelation function for two key macrovariables, which both display the characteristic persistance of empirical macroeconomic time series, that is, the slow tapering off of autocorrelation with increasing lags. To see whether this result was not an artifact of the specific parameter values of this run, we ran the model through a range of relevant points in parameter space. Table 2.1 summarizes these experiments and shows the proportion of total spectral power concentrated between 40 and

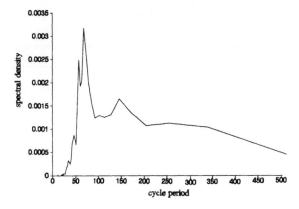

Figure 2.5a. Spectral density of aggregate productivity growth rate with $\omega = 2$ years, $\tau = 2\%/yr$. Spectral plots for the other macroeconomic variables are quite similar.

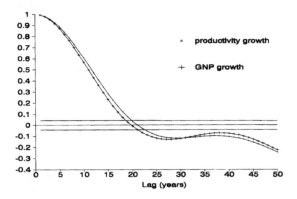

Figure 2.5b. Autocorrelation function of productivity and GNP growth rates. The horizontal lines give the 5% significance bounds.

80 years for a range of values of the three most significant parameters, for runs of length of 1024 periods. The capital/output ratio c has a direct effect on diffusion time (cf. Silverberg 1984) and thereby on the spectral pattern. The interaction of τ and ω also affects diffusion times, whereby the mean waiting time between innovations in the Poisson process, ω, does not itself directly determine the periodicity of the cycle. This is not the case if innovations are introduced nonstochastically with the precise period of ω; in this truly driven case, the macrovariables also will show a sharp spike in the spectrum at period ω, rather than in the long-range region.

Table 2.1. *Proportion of spectral variance in the range 40–80 years for runs of lengths 1,024 years and a range of relevant parameters.*

τ	ω	c			
		2	3	4	5
0.01	1	0.309	0.309	0.215	0.142
	2	0.385	0.219	0.143	0.116
	5	0.478	0.320	0.177	0.121
	10	0.378	0.259	0.139	0.098
0.02	1	0.422	0.426	0.369	0.307
	2	0.398	0.403	0.310	0.216
	5	0.423	0.467	0.406	0.291
	10	0.346	0.368	0.307	0.211
0.03	1	0.358	0.430	0.414	0.365
	2	0.309	0.397	0.375	0.302
	5	0.338	0.437	0.445	0.381
	10	0.295	0.357	0.343	0.276

Table 2.2. *Proportion of spectral variance in the range 40–80 years for runs of length 1,204 years and different values of β and τ*

β	τ		
	0.01	0.02	0.03
0.01	0.320	0.467	0.437
0.05	0.249	0.455	0.448
0.10	0.168	0.395	0.441
0.20	0.054	0.139	0.203

The parameters m and n, which control labor-market dynamics, only have an effect on the period of the Goodwin cycle, but none at all on the long-wave dynamics. The effect of varying β is shown in Table 2.2. Very large values of β tend to diminish the relative importance of the Kondratieff region in total variability.

By turning on the ST investment parameter, diffusion is progressively accelerated, which leads to a shortening of the cyclical pattern because of the emergence of an increasing number of time-series peaks. Table 2.3 shows the proportion of spectral variance between 40 and 80 years for different values of the ST investment parameter for our benchmark run. A plot of spectral density for an ST run is presented in Figure 2.6. It is apparent that the effect of turning on this investment mode is to shift the spectrum toward the shorter periods.

Table 2.3. *Proportion of spectral variance in the range 40–80 years for the benchmark run with different values of ST parameter.*

s				
0.0	0.2	0.5	2.0	5.0
0.568	0.562	0.534	0.343	0.183

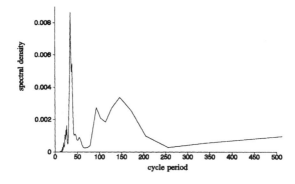

Figure 2.6. Spectral density of productivity growth rate of the same run as in Figure 2.4 but with an ST parameter value of 2.

In our model, causality runs from innovations to the macro dynamics. Our null hypothesis until now has been that the innovations are generated by a Poisson process, that is, by white noise. The model transforms this white noise into a particular long-wave spectral pattern, as we have seen above. To examine more closely the relationship between innovations and macro dynamics, Figure 2.7 plots innovation times against average productivity growth rate. It is readily apparent that clusters of innovations translate with a delay into a surge of productivity growth. By computing the cross correlation between moving averages of different orders of the time series of number of innovations per period, and the productivity growth rate, an optimal order and lag between the two time series can be determined. In the case of a run with $\omega = 2$ years and $\tau = 2\%$/year (which serves as our benchmark in the following), the cross correlation reaches a value as high as 83% for a 28-year moving average and a lag of 24 years (i.e., innovations leading productivity, as to be expected, see Figure 2.8). The plot of the productivity growth and innovation moving-average time series in Figure 2.9 confirms this relationship. The introduction of the ST investment term, not unexpectedly, shortens both the order of the moving average and the lag (Table 2.4).

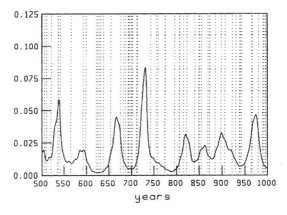

Figure 2.7. Time series of aggregate productivity growth rate and innovation dates (vertical dotted lines) for a run with $\omega = 8$ years.

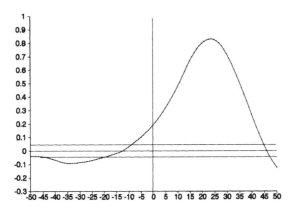

Figure 2.8. Cross correlation of the productivity growth rate and a 28-year moving average of the annual number of innovations.

Table 2.4. *Lag and moving-average order for maximal cross correlation between innovation and productivity growth rate time series with and without ST investment term.*

	$s = 0$			$s = 2$		
ω	MA	lag	r	MA	lag	r
2	28	24	0.83	16	14	0.79
5	26	27	0.66	18	13	0.65

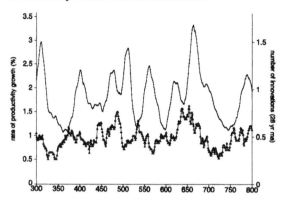

Figure 2.9. Time series of productivity growth rate (upper curve, left scale) and a 28-year moving average of innovations (lower curve, right scale) for the benchmark run. The lagged correlation is apparent.

This observation sheds some light on the so-called productivity paradox. If we attempt to predict the productivity growth rate of the present with a moving average of the innovation activity of the recent past, Figure 2.8 indicates that the two are essentially uncorrelated (lagged value at -14 years). The moving average of past innovation activity is only a good predictor of productivity growth for a point in time 10 years into the future in this case. This is not entirely unexpected, because our model makes clear that diffusion introduces significant time delays.

Our high-dimensional, nonlinear system thus appears to a certain extent to be imitating a moving-average process in converting the white-noise innovation input into the macrovariable cyclical output. It is well known that a moving-average process will extract a cyclical structure from white noise (the Slutsky–Yule effect). However, an examination of the spectrum of such a moving-average process reveals that it is still far from the characteristic long-wave pattern that we have discovered for the macrovariables (Figure 2.10). For this reason, we extended the analysis of drawing upon some of the relatively recent methods of the theory of nonlinear dynamic systems.

4   Nonlinear time-series analysis

It is by now well known that even very simple nonlinear dynamic systems can show an incredible richness of behavior, in particular, the resulting time series may mimic the properties of a stochastic process even though they are generated deterministically. The standard methods of linear time-series analysis are not, in general, sufficient to distinguish the two types of mechanisms (see, e.g., Baumol and Benhabib 1989; Lorenz 1989; Brock and Malliaris 1989; Brock

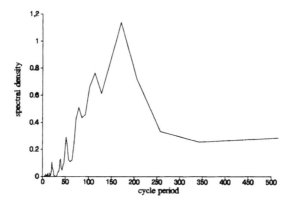

Figure 2.10. The spectral density of a 28-year moving average of the innovation rate. Notice that it differs significantly from the productivity spectrum despite the high cross correlation.

and Dechert 1991). In recent years, however, a number of new, specifically nonlinear methods have been developed that permit deterministic systems (so-called low-dimensional chaos) to be distinguished from truly stochastic ones based solely on an analysis of univariate time series.

One widely used method to investigate the dynamics of univariate time series is phase-space embedding. If $\{x_i\}$ is the original time series, then we can create a d-dimensional time series $\{(x_i, x_{i+k}, x_{i+2k}, \ldots, x_{i+(d-1)k})\}$, where k is a time delay. If d_A is the dimension of the attractor of the underlying dynamics, then an embedding of dimension $[2d_A]$, where brackets indicate the next largest integer, is sufficient to recover all topological properties and invariants of the attractor (Mañé 1981; Takens 1981). It is often the case, however, that a smaller embedding dimension will also do the trick. Kennel, Brown, and Abarbanel (1992) developed a technique for verifying the existence of an attractor and determining the minimum embedding dimension, using the concept of false nearest neighbors. False nearest neighbors are nearest neighbors in the Euclidean metric in a phase-space reconstruction of dimension n that cease to be close together according to some criterion in the next highest embedding $n + 1$. The minimum embedding dimension is determined to be that at which the proportion of false nearest neighbors is practically zero (to eliminate artifactual results resulting from sparse data, nearest neighbors are also considered false if their distance is comparable to a standard deviation of the data). The idea behind the technique appeals to the original justification for phase-space embedding: to lift the data into a space in which trajectories disentangle themselves from the crossings resulting from projection into too low-dimensional a space. We applied this method to a benchmark run of 8,192

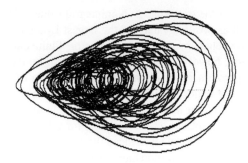

Figure 2.11a. View of strange attractor created by embedding productivity growth data in three dimension with a time delay of three years.

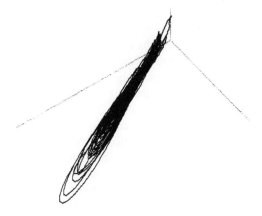

Figure 2.11b. Edgewise view of the same attractor.

data points and determined a minimum embedding dimension of 3. In Figures 2.11a and b we present two views of the reconstructed attractor, which does appear to be a nearly flat, almost two-dimensional object. By turning on the ST parameter, the minimum embedding dimension rises to 4 by $s = 0.5$ and to 5 by $s = 2$.

The calculation of the Grassberger–Procaccia correlation dimension [see Grassberger (1986a) for an overview] has been one of the main tools employed in nonlinear time-series analysis. By embedding a time series in successively higher dimensional spaces and calculating the correlation integral for a range of correlation lengths, it is possible to determine if convergence occurs and thus if a finite correlation dimension exists. In general a stochastic process will be infinite dimensional (i.e., no convergence will be observed), whereas a deterministic process will be characterized by a finite dimension (bounded from above by the dimension of the state space). Nonintegral values of the correlation dimension (as well as positive values of the largest Lyapunov exponent) are indicative of chaotic behavior on a strange attractor. Finite data sets introduce a severe restriction, however, because the upper limit on the calculated dimension increases approximately with the log of the number of data points. This restriction has been a major stumbling block in applying this method to economic time series. Using our model, however, we are in the position to be able to generate sufficient quantities of artificial data for valid analysis.

In Figures 2.12 and 2.13, we have reproduced the calculation of the correlation dimensions for the 28-year innovation moving average and the productivity growth rate of our benchmark run using 6,000 data points.[4] As we have pointed out above, these two series are highly correlated. Nevertheless, the correlation dimension plots permit them to be clearly differentiated. The moving-average series shows only weak convergence over a narrow scaling range at a value above 4. The productivity growth-rate data, in contrast, show convergence over a fairly wide range of scaling lengths to an estimate of the correlation dimension of approximately 2.9. The lack of convergence at very small scaling ranges is indicative of noise. Application of the so-called shuffle diagnostics (Scheinkman and LeBaron 1989), where the original time series is randomly scrambled, resulted in a total lack of convergence. This reinforces the impression that the finite correlation dimension is not spurious. In Figure 2.14, we also present the correlation dimension calculation for the same case, but with an ST investment parameter of 1. As with the calculation of the embedding dimension, the correlation dimension seems to increase with the ST parameter.

We first attempted to calculate the largest Lyapunov exponent using the method proposed by Wolf et al. (1985). The results were rather unstable with respect to parameter choices, however, and we refrain from presenting them here. Instead, we have computed the complete spectra with a programme developed by Kruel and Eiswirth (1991), based on the approach of Sano and Sawada (1985) (see also Kruel, Eiswirth, and Schneider 1993). Table 2.5 summarizes the results for a benchmark run of 8,192 years for a range of values of the two crucial parameters: ε, the maximum range from which test candidates are drawn (measured with respect to the extent of the attractor), and t_e, the evolution time over which two trajectories are traced. (A further parameter prevents points from being compared that are closer in time than the

---

[4] The box in the upper left corner of figures 2.12 and 2.13 shows the log of the correlation integral as a function of the log of the scaling length for different embedding dimensions. The slope of the regression line within the scaling range is an estimate of the correlation dimension. The accuracy of this estimate can be judged by examining the right-hand box, where the slope between consecutive points is plotted. The scaling range is selected by determining where these slopes converge with increasing embedding dimension. The estimated correlation dimension, with error bars, is displayed as a function of the embedding dimension in the lower left corner.

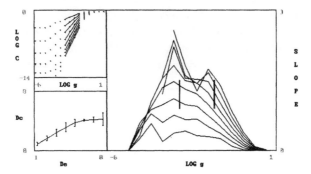

Figure 2.12. Correlation dimension for 28-year moving average of Poisson-distributed innovation rate ($\omega = 1$).

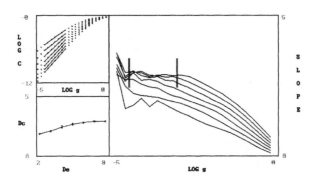

Figure 2.13. Correlation dimension for productivity growth rate ($\omega = 2$, $\tau = 2\%$) calculated with 6,000 data points. $D_c \approx 2.9$.

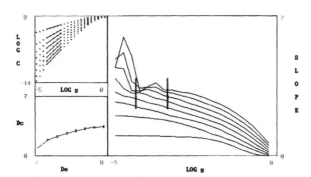

Figure 2.14. Correlation dimension for benchmark run and Soete–Turner investment function with $s=1$. $D_c \approx 3.35$.

Table 2.5. *Spectrum of Lyapunov exponents for the benchmark run (8,192 data points) computed for different values of the evolution time t_e and the shell radius ε.*

t_e	ε		
	0.02	0.05	0.10
5	0.0360	0.0172	0.0058
	−0.0044	−0.0048	−0.0117
	−0.0986	−0.0757	−0.0741
10	0.0405	0.0106	0.0026
	−0.0022	−0.0122	−0.0153
	−0.1047	−0.0995	−0.1089
20	0.0393	0.0121	−0.0013
	0.0120	−0.0055	−0.0163
	−0.0445	−0.0427	−0.0443

characteristic autocorrelation time of the series. For our benchmark run, this is 22 years). We can see that the spectra are relatively stable with respect to t_e, but vary considerably even with respect to sign as a function ε. We consider the values for $\varepsilon = 0.02$ or 0.05 to be the most reasonable, but must admit that the evidence for a positive Lyapunov exponent is not satisfactory in every respect. This is also underscored by the fact that the second Lyapunov exponent never as close to zero as one might expect (the method provides more reliable information about the largest Lyapunov exponent than about the rest of the Lyapunov spectrum, it should be noted).

We also computed the Brock–Dechert–Scheinkman (BDS) statistic for our benchmark time series using Dechert's computer program (for a thorough discussion of this statistic, see Brock et al. 1991). This statistic, based on the correlation integral, is actually a test of independence. By applying an optimal linear filter to the raw data, the BDS statistic on the residuals provides a test for nonlinearity. Following this procedure, we fitted an AR(14) process to 1,000 data points of our benchmark run and an AR(7) process to an ST run with $s = 1$ and then determined the BDS statistic on the sample residuals.[5] Tables 2.6 and 2.7 summarize the calculations. In both cases, linearity was rejected far below the 1% significance level.

We must qualify the above observations by noting a non sequitur of much nonlinear time-series analysis. Whereas we know that a low-dimensional attractor will be associated with a finite correlation dimension for a phase-space

[5] The order of the linear filter was determined by examining the autocorrelations and the partial autocorrelations.

Table 2.6. *Calculation of the BDS statistic on 1,000 residuals from fitting an AR (14) process to benchmark data[a]*

ε	D_c	C_1	C_m	SD	BDS
0.065600	2	160998	58471	0.03884	10.909
0.065600	3	160998	22394	0.02857	12.747
0.065600	4	160998	8845	0.01577	14.057
0.065600	5	160998	3587	0.00763	15.558
0.065600	6	160998	1574	0.00342	19.039
0.065600	7	160998	746	0.00145	24.936
0.065600	8	160998	371	0.00060	33.583
0.131200	2	292674	183075	0.07773	9.7311
0.131200	3	292674	116792	0.10306	10.298
0.131200	4	292674	75641	0.10243	10.628
0.131200	5	292674	49941	0.08913	11.233
0.131200	6	292674	33931	0.07177	12.372
0.131200	7	292674	23747	0.05492	14.012
0.131200	8	292674	17037	0.04053	16.091
0.196800	2	383759	304199	0.07064	8.932
0.196800	3	383759	243495	0.12212	9.298
0.196800	4	383759	195775	0.15812	9.165
0.196800	5	383759	159119	0.17916	9.414
0.196800	6	383759	130775	0.18781	9.875
0.196800	7	383759	108642	0.18706	10.473
0.196800	8	383759	91396	0.17967	11.256

[a] The BDS statistic is $N(0,1)$ on the null hypothesis of the data being independent and identically distributed (SD/Spread = 0.131, ε = 0.5, 1.0, and 1.5 × SD).

reconstruction at a sufficiently high embedding dimension, the converse does not necessarily follow: A finite value of a calculated correlation dimension need not imply that we are dealing with deterministic dynamics on a low-dimensional attractor. One reason, of course, is finite sample effects, because the correlation dimension will always yield a number (albeit perhaps for a vanishing scaling region), but the data requirements for a significant result increase exponentially with dimension. Another is that highly correlated (or colored-noise) stochastic systems such as $1/f^\alpha$ noise also may be associated with finite (and low) values of the correlation dimension (see, e.g., Osborne and Provenzale 1989; Theiler 1991). This was even (arguably) the case with our 28-year moving-average series of Poisson-distributed innovations (Figure 2.12), and had already been remarked upon by Grassberger (1986b).

Figure 2.15 presents a log–log plot of the spectral density against frequency for a 6,000-point dataset from the benchmark run (the plot is quite similar for ST runs). At very low frequencies, the spectrum is simply white noise. Starting at

Table 2.7. *BDS statistic for benchmark ST data*[a]

ε	D_c	C_1	C_m	SD	BDS
0.027260	2	206796	98768	0.06501	12.995
0.027260	3	206796	50332	0.06139	15.543
0.027260	4	206796	27406	0.04352	18.732
0.027260	5	206796	15658	0.02703	22.695
0.027260	6	206796	9154	0.01554	27.350
0.027260	7	206796	5502	0.00850	33.631
0.027260	8	206796	3330	0.00448	41.458
0.054520	2	348709	262595	0.09038	13.779
0.054520	3	348709	205181	0.14245	16.008
0.054520	4	348709	164309	0.16825	17.529
0.054520	5	348709	134114	0.17395	19.021
0.054520	6	348709	110550	0.16640	20.433
0.054520	7	348709	92252	0.15126	22.117
0.054520	8	348709	77529	0.13261	23.998
0.081780	2	426524	377106	0.06066	14.242
0.081780	3	426524	339506	0.11631	16.241
0.081780	4	426524	308853	0.16702	17.090
0.081780	5	426524	283124	0.20984	17.656
0.081780	6	426524	260236	0.24390	17.923
0.081780	7	426524	239957	0.26933	18.167
0.081780	8	426524	221831	0.28680	18.429

[a] Residuals of AR(7) process fitted to 1,000 data points of an $s = 2$ run; SD/Spread $= 0.0545$, $\varepsilon = 0.5$, 1.0, and 1.5 × SD).

around 0.02 (corresponding to cycles of 50-year length), the spectrum becomes a declining straight line before gradually reverting to white noise at a low level (corresponding to the innovation driving term?). This power-law region of the spectrum is characterized by an α of around 3.6. Thus, the big spectral picture shifts our model uncomfortably close to the class of colored-noise stochastic systems that may lead to spurious indications of low-dimensional chaos.

Kennel and Isabelle (1992) recently proposed a computational method to distinguish colored noise from chaos. It is based on the idea that a true deterministic system should have a significantly higher degree of nonlinear predictability than stochastic data sets with the same spectral signature. Kennel and Isabelle use a local constant predictor, which proved as efficient as other methods such as radial basis functions. To predict the future scalar value k steps ahead of the last component of a point x in a phase-space reconstruction, find the closest point y in the phase space and use its future iterate k steps ahead of its last component as the prediction. As with the calculation of the Lyapunov spectrum above, they exclude points y within the characteristic autocorrelation time to eliminate

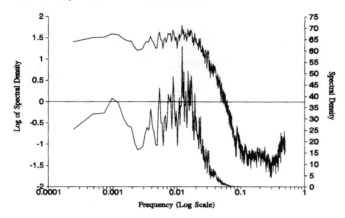

Figure 2.15. Power spectrum of rate of productivity growth plotted against log of frequency: (left scale) upper curve is the log of the spectrum; lower curve is the spectrum itself (right scale).

short-term, in-sample correlation effects. An ensemble of reference time series is generated by randomly perturbing the Fourier transform of the original data series and then transforming back into the time domain. Prediction errors are computed using the same method for these series and then compared with the prediction errors of the original series using a nonparametric test based on the Mann–Whitney rank-sum statistic. The resulting z-statistic will be $N(0,1)$ on the null hypothesis that the original series derives from the same distribution as the reference series. This comparison can be performed for a range of embedding dimensions and time delays. Kennel and Isabelle argue that the test also provides a means of choosing the most appropriate values for these parameters in the computation of such phase-space-based characteristics as the correlation dimension and the Lyapunov spectrum.

Figure 2.16 presents the values of this statistic for different times delays and embedding dimensions of our benchmark run using 8,192 points, one period prediction, and 20 randomly generated reference series. The evidence seems quite convincing that at least for short time delays there is indeed significantly higher nonlinear predictability in our data than in similar colored-noise series starting with an embedding dimension of 2. It is somewhat surprising that an embedding dimension of 2 seems to outperform higher dimensions, because a minimum embedding dimension of 3 was indicated by our previous work. For comparison, in Figure 2.17, we present the statistic computed on a 28-year moving average of Poisson data. Thus, we may conclude that although our model displays aspects of a colored-noise process, the indications of low-dimensional chaos that we have found do not seem to be merely spurious.

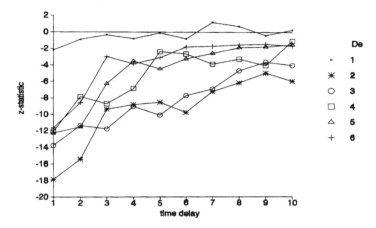

Figure 2.16. The z-statistic of nonlinear predictability for the benchmark run (8,192 data points) and different embedding dimensions and time delays for the phase-space reconstruction.

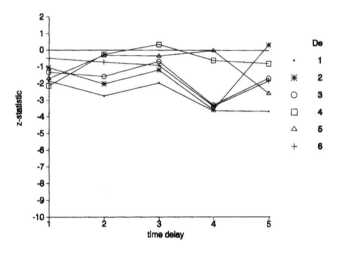

Figure 2.17. The z-statistic of nonlinear predictability for a 28-year moving average of Poisson-distributed innovations ($\omega = 2$).

Nevertheless, these emergent properties of our model require explanation, because it is neither a classic dynamic system (with interactive noise) nor a standard stochastic one. Rather, it can be characterized as a high-dimensional system of nonlinear ordinary differential equations whose coefficients are perturbed in a systematic way at random times. Nevertheless, its behavior seems to be reducible to a small number of degrees of freedom, but it is neither strictly periodic nor representable by linear time-series procedures. For this reason, we denote it as evolutionary chaos.

The power-law behavior of the spectrum over only a limited range before reverting to white noise is also characteristic of a phenomenon recently termed self-organized criticality (Bak, Tang, and Wiesenfeld 1988; Bak and Chen 1991; Bak et al. 1993). A sandpile with sand constantly falling onto the center and falling off the edges of a finite table provides the best intuitive illustration of this phenomenon. The pile will eventually organize itself into a heap with a characteristic slope, and additions of sand will trigger avalanches of all sizes (in fact, distributed according to a power law). In some respects, the capital stock of our model economy bears a certain resemblance to a sandpile (recall Figure 2.2). The finite lifetimes of technologies tracked in the model correspond to the finite size of the table. The nonlinear Lotka–Volterra dynamics of the technologies corresponds to the rearrangement of sand down the pile, and the innovation process corresponds to the addition of new sand to the pile at random times. The fluctuations in the rate of productivity growth correspond to fluctuations in the variance of the capital-stock distribution and thus the shape of the pile. The analogy is less precise than suggestive, but the log–log spectrum does seem to imply that we are dealing with a qualitatively similar kind of phenomenon.

5   Extensions of the model

Until now, we have assumed that the probability of making an innovation per unit time was constant and independent of economic variables. Although this is an intriguing null hypothesis for discussing long-period creative destruction, whether it can be maintained is an empirical question. It is intuitively plausible that the innovation Poisson parameter will, in fact, be influenced by economic variables, for example, investments in R&D in previous periods, and the size of the population of scientists and technologists. We examined a number of historical time series compiled from records of major innovations, such as that of Haustein and Neuwirth (Silverberg and Lehnert 1993). In Figure 2.18 we plot the number of innovations per year according to the Haustein–Neuwirth data. Although the series does appear rather stochastic, the existence of a trend cannot be rejected out of hand. Tests for an exponential trend in the mean (on the assumption that the data are generated by a Poisson process) confirm that the mean has been growing at a rate of about 0.86% per annum (see Silverberg and Lehnert 1993, Table V, for details on this and other aspects of the statistical analysis). Similar results emerge for the other innovation time series. A histogram of the Haustein–Neuwirth data reveals them to be approximately Poisson distributed (both before and after detrending) but over-dispersed (Figure 2.19).

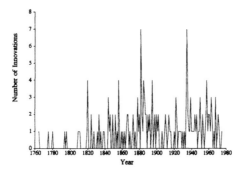

Figure 2.18. Haustein–Neuwirth innovation time series 1764–1975.

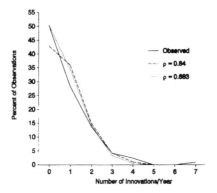

Figure 2.19. Histogram of Haustein–Neuwirth innovation time series with two fitted Poisson distributions ($\rho = 0.84$ is maximum likelihood estimate, $\rho = 0.683$ obtained by equating value for zero innovations).

To see what effect such assumptions about the innovation process may have on the robustness of long-wave spectral patterns, we modified the model to allow for feedbacks from economic activity to innovation and nonstationary of the innovation process.[6]

The simplest assumption about feedback is to make the innovation Poisson parameter a linear function of lagged profitability:

$$p = \max[p_{\min}, a\langle r\rangle + p_0], \tag{2.13}$$

---

[6] Ideally, one would like to extend the model to a full-fledged model of evolutionary endogenous growth, that is, to provide an economic accounting for the realized rate of innovation in terms of competitive self-organization or expected rates of return on R&D investment. We have refrained from this step here and restrict ourselves to an analysis of the robustness of the spectral results to different specifications of the variations in the innovation arrival rate.

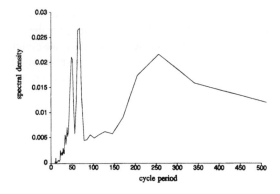

Figure 2.20. Spectrum of productivity growth rate when profits are allowed to feedback with a lag on the probability of innovation ($T = 10$, $p_{min} = 0$, $p_0 = 0.1$, $a = 1$)

where p is the innovation Poisson parameter, $\langle r \rangle$ is lagged profitability, and p_0 and p_{min} are constants. For simplicity, we use an exponential lag on profitability:

$$\frac{d}{dt}\langle r \rangle = \frac{1}{T}(r - \langle r \rangle), \qquad (2.14)$$

where T is the exponential lag and r is the current average profit rate. Spectral analysis of this feedback case for certain parameter values indicates that the long-wave structure may emerge even more distinctly (Figure 2.20).

To investigate the case of an exogenous trend in the Poisson parameter, we also have allowed the innovation parameter to grow logistically.

$$p = p_0 + \frac{p_1}{1 + e^{-a(t-t_0)}}, \qquad (2.15)$$

where p_0 and p_1 are the lower and upper bounds of the innovation Poisson parameter, a is the growth rate, and t_0 is the date of the inflection point of the logistic growth process. Thus, the Poisson parameter initially will grow exponentially but eventually will saturate at an upper bound. The resulting growth process will no longer be stationary, however, but will accelerate with time. The long-wave pattern still persists in the spectrum, but with a strong preponderance of very-long-period spectral power because of the nonstationarity.

6   Discussion and conclusions

The model we have proposed of creative destruction is related in some respects to the more neoclassical work of Aghion and Howitt (1992) and Cheng and Dinopoulos (1992). Innovations are produced stochastically according to a

Poisson process, but in these endogenous growth models, the advent of a new technology makes previous technologies obsolete, and they are immediately removed from production. In contrast to this work, however, we emphasize that diffusion is necessary before innovations manifest themselves in changes in aggregate productivity, and that different technologies coexist for long periods of time. Moreover, we do not impose any intertemporal equilibrium conditions; our interest is explicitly focused on the dynamics of the technological replacement process. In this respect, our model is closely related to the more evolutionary tradition of Iwai (1984a,b) and Henkin and Polterovich (1991), who attempt to derive analytical conclusions.

In neither the neoclassical nor the evolutionary camp, however, has much attention been directed to the time-series properties that necessarily follow from a particular class of models. (An exception perhaps is the Real Business Cycle school, but we do not consider their assumptions about major short-term technology shocks to be at all plausible.) Analytically, it is not at all obvious how to proceed, and for this reason we have contented ourselves with analyzing the model numerically. Nevertheless, we believe that this approach does yield some robust dividends. First, in contrast to a received but perhaps naive Schumpeterian view, it does not seem to be necessary for innovations to arrive in clusters (i.e., more tightly bunched than Poisson) or to vary systematically in time to motivate long waves of economic growth. Second, the characteristic persistence (slow tapering-off of the autocorrelation function) of economic time series is a robust emergent property of the model. Equivalently, the model generates $1/f^\alpha$ noise-like spectral patterns. Third, the model has many of the characteristics of low-dimensional chaos: a finite correlation dimension (in the range 2.5 to 3.5); a positive Lyapunov exponent; rejection of a linear stochastic model based on the BDS test; and statistically significant nonlinear predictability against time series with similar spectral patterns. The behavior of the model still demands a coherent explanation. We believe that the answer may lie in an understanding of the related class of phenomena known as self-organized criticality.

REFERENCES

Aghion, P., and Howitt, P. (1992). A model of growth through creative destruction, *Econometrica*, **60**, 323–51.
Bak, P., and Chen, K. (1991). Self-organized criticality, *Sci. Am. Jan.*, **269**, 26–33.
Bak, P., Chen, J., Scheinkman, J., and Woodford, M. (1993). Aggregate fluctuations from independent sectorial shocks: self-organized criticality in a model of production and inventory dynamics, *Rich. Econ.*, **47**, 3–30.
Bak, P., Tang, C., and Wiesenfeld, K. (1988). Self-organized criticality, *Phys. Rev. A*, **38**, 364–74.
Baumol, W., and Benhabib, J. (1989). Chaos: Significance, mechanism, and economic applications, *J. Econ. Perspect.*, **3**, 77–105.

Brock, W. A., and Dechert, W. D. (1991). Non-linear dynamical systems: Instability and chaos in economics. In *Handbook of Mathematical Economics*, Vol. IV, eds. W. Hildenbrand and H. Sonnenschein, North-Holland, Amsterdam.

Brock, W., and Malliaris, A. (1989). *Differential Equations, Stability and Chaos in Dynamic Economics*, North Holland, Amsterdam.

Brock, W. A., Hsieh, D. A., and LeBaron, B. (1991). *Nonlinear Dynamics, Chaos, and Instability: Statistical Theory and Economic Evidence*, MIT Press, Cambridge, MA.

Cheng, L., and Dinopoulos, E. (1992). Schumpeterian growth and international business cycles, *Am. Econ. Rev. Papers Proc.* **82**, 409–14.

Goodwin, R., (1967). A growth cycle. In *Socialism, Capitalism and Economic Growth*, ed. C. H. Feinstein, Macmillan, London.

Grassberger, P. (1986a). Estimating the fractual dimensions and entropies of strange attractors. In *Chaos*, ed. A. V. Holder, Manchestor University Press, Manchester. (1986b). Do climatic attractors exist?, *Nature*, **323**, 609–12.

Henkin, G. M., and Polterovich, V. M. (1991). Schumpeterian dynamics as a non-linear wave theory, *J. Math. Econ.*, **20**, 551–90.

Hofbauer, J., and Sigmund, K. (1988). *The Theory of Evolution and Dynamical Systems*, Cambridge University Press, Cambridge, England, UK.

Iwai, K. (1984a). Schumpeterian dynamics. I: An evolutionary model of innovation and imitation, *J. Econ. Behav. Org.*, **5**, 159–90.

(1984b). Schumpeterian dynamics. II: Technological progress, firm growth and "economic selection," *J. Econ. Behav. Org.*, **5**, 321–51.

Kennel, M. B., and Isabelle, S. (1992). A method to distinguish possible chaos from colored noise and determine embedding parameters, *Phys. Rev. A*, **46**(6), 3111–8.

Kennel, M. B., Brown, R., and Abarbanel, H. D. (1992). Determining embedding dimension for phase space reconstruction using a geometrical construction, *Phys. Rev. A*, **45**(6), 3403–11.

Kruel, T.-M., and Eiswirth, M. (1991). LCE_EXP. A program for the calculation of the complete spectrum of Lyapunov exponents from a time series of experimental data, University of Würzburg (available on Internet via anonymous ftp from ftp. phys-chemie.uni-wuerzburg.de).

Kruel, T.-M., Eiswirth, M., and Schneider, F. (1993). Computation of Lyapunov spectra: Effect of interactive noise and application to a chemical oscillator, *Phys. D*, **63**, 117–37.

Lorenz, H.-W., (1989). *Nonlinear Dynamical Economics and Chaotic Motion*, Springer, Berlin.

Mañé, R. (1981). On the dimension of the compact invariant sets of certain non-linear maps. In *Dynamical Systems and Turbulence Warwick 1980*, eds. D. A. Rand and L.-S. Young, Springer, Berlin.

Marchetti, C., and Nakicenovic, N. (1979). *The dynamics of energy systems and the logistic substitution model*, Research report RR-79-13, IIASA, Laxenburg, Austria.

Mensch, G. O., Weidlich, W., and Haag, G. (1987). Outline of a formal theory of long-term economic cycles. In *The Long-Wave Debate*, ed. T. Vasko, Springer, Berlin.

Mosekilde, E., Rasmussen, S., and Zebrowski, M. (1987). Technoeconomic Succession and the Economic Long Wave. In *The Long-Wave Debate*, ed. T. Vasko, Springer, Berlin.

Nakicenovic, N. (1987). Technological substitution and long waves. In *The Long-Wave Debate*, ed. T. Vasko, Springer, Berlin.

Osborne, A., and Provenzale, A. (1989). Finite correlation dimension for stochastic systems with power-law spectra. *Phys. D*, **35**, 357–81.

Sano, M., and Sawada, Y. (1985). Measurement of the Lyapunov spectrum from a chaotic time series. *Phys. Rev. Lett.*, **55**(10), 1082–5.

Scheinkman, J., and LeBaron, B. (1989). Nonlinear dynamics and stock returns, *J. Business*, **62**, 311–37.

Silverberg, G. (1984). Embodied technical progress in a dynamic economic model: The self-organization paradigm. In *Nonlinear Models of Fluctuating Growth*, eds. R. Goodwin, M. Krüger, and A. Vercelli, Springer, Berlin.

Silverberg, G., and Lehnert, D. (1993). Long waves and evolutionary chaos in a simple Schumpeterian model of embodied technical change, *Struc. Change Econ. Dynam.*, **4**, 9–37.

Soete, L., and Turner, R. (1984). Technology diffusion and the rate of technical change, *Econ. J.* **94**, 612–23.

Takens, F. (1981). Detecting strange attractors in turbulence. In *Dynamical Systems and Turbulence. Warwick 1980*, eds. D. A. Rand and L.-S. Young, Springer, Berlin.

Theiler, J. (1991). Some comments on the correlation dimension of $1/f^\alpha$ noise, *Phys. Lett. A*, **155**, 480–92.

Wolf, A., Swift, J., Swinney, J., and Vastano, J. (1985). Determining Lyapunov exponents from a time series, *Phys. D*, **16**, 285–317.

PART II

Nonlinearity in Financial Markets

CHAPTER 3

Detection of nonlinearity in foreign-exchange data

Paolo Guarda and Mark Salmon

The analysis in this paper is based on the common observation that many nonlinear dynamic processes may in fact be approximately linear over wide ranges of the economically relevant state space and hence over long periods of time. Only when state variables move into particular regions of the phase space may nonlinear reactions become apparent and, perhaps only then, statistically detectable. Standard unconditional methods of testing linearity do not seem to have recognized the potential importance of this observation, that a given sample may not be particularly informative regarding nonlinearity because it may be only occasionally important and not uniformly represented throughout a given observation period. This, we believe, could be one reason why evidence for nonlinearity in the conditional mean has been difficult to find in economic time series. We argue that an explicitly conditional approach to testing linearity in which the metric used in inference incorporates any potential ancillary information reflecting the statistical curvature of the underlying data-generation process may provide a more suitable framework for the detection of nonlinearity in economic time series.

We present theoretical arguments for adopting a conditional approach to testing linearity and discuss the difficulties in following this suggestion through in applied work. Then in order to explicitly investigate the periodic importance of nonlinearity, we apply a set of linearity tests recursively to both monthly and weekly observations on the U.S. dollar/UK pound sterling spot exchange rate over the period 1973–1990. Our main interest lies in the detection of nonlinearity in the first moment of the data, but we are also concerned that misspecification of the first moment may lead to error specifications that imply autoregressive conditional heteroskedasticity (ARCH) type processes and so also consider tests for conditional heteroskedasticity. The different tests we employ provide different indications of nonlinearity over different levels of temporal aggregation and under different transformations of the data, but the overwhelming conclusion is clearly in favor of the intermittent but not the

77

continuous importance of nonlinear effects in the first moment of the data. The weekly series display considerably more evidence of nonlinearity than the monthly data, and GARCH(1, 1) residuals show the least evidence of non-linearity both in the first moment and naturally in the second moment, with random-walk residuals clearly indicating further structure. Those periods in which the recursive tests indicate nonlinearity are briefly compared with an historical-event analysis in an attempt to identify potential behavioral causes for the deviations from linearity. Some of these episodes appear to be associated with public reversals of government policy and intervention in the market for foreign exchange, but others seem to have no obvious economic cause. We also find little association between periods of first-moment nonlinearity and periods of high volatility. Further, exploring such evidence for periodic non-linear effects in the first moment of financial data might aid the development of improved models of behavior in financial markets.

1   Introduction

Given that much of the physical world is characterized by nonlinearity, it would be surprising if economic behavior were any different. The real question is not whether nonlinearities ultimately describe both the economic and the physical worlds, but whether linear models provide adequate approximations that are able to capture observed behavior and whether standard statistical methods are appropriate to detect nonlinearity and provide valid inference when it is important.

We adopt a somewhat different position with regard to the detection of non-linearity in economic time series than has been taken in much of the previous literature. We are motivated by the observation that many models with globally complex nonlinear behavior can display approximate linearity over much of their economically meaningful phase space and only periodically exhibit nonlinearity, perhaps when the state variables pass through particular ranges. Econometricians need to consider how to detect evidence for nonlinearity of this form where the signal may be only intermittent and not uniformly present in the available sample. Standard unconditional inference techniques may not be suitable when the nonlinear signal is weak in this sense. Economists need to build structural models that match the empirical evidence and to assess whether volatile markets, where behavior is poorly explained by linear models such as those for foreign exchange, spend a significant portion of their time within nonlinear ranges or whether there are natural economic regulators that prevent the market from entering nonlinear or chaotic phases.

Few nonlinear structural models of exchange rates have been specified and, although standard linear specifications generally do not perform well, unam-biguous evidence in favor of nonlinearity in the first moment of exchange-rate data has been illusive with, it would seem, as much research accepting non-linearity as rejecting it [see Guarda and Salmon (1993)]. On the other hand, the one class of models, based on autoregressive conditional heteroskedastic (ARCH) processes, that has gathered considerable empirical support and exhibits periodic volatility or nonlinearity in the second moment does not appear to completely capture all of the systematic behavior found in financial time series and exchange rates. Given that misspecified first-moment behavior may lead to ARCH-type processes in the second moment, it would seem necessary to rigorously examine the first-moment specification before adopting an ARCH specification for the second moment. Moreover, even if economic behavior did imply periodic nonlinearity through the second moment, it might be expected that such behavior would also periodically affect the first and perhaps higher moments of the data. A broader class of nonlinear dynamic models might be needed to account for observed behavior in both the first and the second moments of financial data.

In what follows, we seek to contribute to this process by questioning the statistical methodology that is traditionally adopted for testing linearity in economic time series when nonlinearity may only be periodically important in the data and by providing some, apparently fairly clear, evidence for periodic non-linearity in the first moment of foreign-exchange data. Although we accept that arbitrage considerations might generally rule out continuous first-moment predictability, it may not at isolated periods. Moreover, the expected equilibrium return process may deviate periodically from constancy, leading to periodic non-random-walk behavior in efficient rates [see Levich (1979)].

We start in Section 2 by briefly discussing the statistical issues raised in the detection of nonlinearity and emphasize the difference between the use of conditional and unconditional inference in this context. Many, apparently linear, econometric models are statistically curved in the sense of Efron (1975), and this forces an important distinction between conditional and unconditional inference techniques to be drawn. Although we are able to discuss and demonstrate the importance of the difference between unconditional and conditional metrics in a simple statistically curved example, the determination of appropriate, approximate, or exact, ancillary statistics on which to condition when testing linearity will generally depend on the specific statistical model under consideration and represents an important unresolved research area. This discussion is therefore indicative of how we feel testing for linearity might be developed and may suggest one reason why clear statistical evidence for non-linearity in the first moment of economic time series has often been difficult to find.

Recognizing the arguments for conditional inference, we follow a conditional philosophy in the empirical analysis by applying a recursive approach to testing linearity in foreign-exchange data. Section 3 describes the eight tests that are applied to four different series based on the pound sterling U.S. dollar spot exchange rate: the raw data, the natural logarithms of the raw data, the log differences and the standardized residuals from a generalized autoregressive conditional heteroskedasticity–GARCH (1, 1)–model fitted to the log differences. The analysis in Section 4 is based on the use of the full sample and is carried out at both monthly and weekly frequencies. In common with other research, we find ambiguous results from this full-sample analysis, but in Section 5 the same tests are applied recursively, providing what we interpret as clear evidence in favor of nonlinearity in the first moment at particular periods within the sample, if not over the sample when taken as a whole. We also find, somewhat to our surprise, little association between periods of high volatility and those indicating first-moment nonlinearity. Section 6 concludes by suggesting that exchange-rate models should allow for periodic nonlinear reactions in both the first and the second moments and that future testing of linearity may benefit from adopting an explicitly conditional statistical framework.

2   A Conditional Approach to the Detection of Nonlinearity

Granger and Terasvirta (1993) recently provided a detailed discussion of a number of tests for linearity, which fall into two main classes: those for which a specific nonlinear alternative is specified, and general tests for which no particular alternative is identified. Where specific restrictions for linearity can be identified, it is natural that standard likelihood-based method be employed, through the use of either the likelihood ratio, Wald, or Lagrange multiplier (LM) tests. Wald tests seem to be particularly inappropriate for testing linearity, given their general lack of invariance to the algebraic form that a nonlinear restriction function may take (see, e.g., Gregory and Veall 1985; Critchley, Marriott, and Salmon 1996). However, a critical statistical issue when testing linearity is not simply a question of the lack of invariance of a particular statistic but the impact that the statistical curvature of the underlying statistical model has on inference regarding linearity. This issue in its simplest form concerns the choice of the norming metric in a test statistic.[1]

As Granger and Terasvirta (1993) show, a number of linearity tests correspond to LM tests which is natural, given that the LM approach only exploits restricted-parameter estimates. The same test may then be sensitive to a range of nonlinear alternatives because an LM statistic does not exploit information about the precise form of the alternative. Davidson and MacKinnon (1983) and Bera and McKenzie (1986) explored through Monte Carlo analysis, the

---

[1]   Much of the argument and material in this section has been drawn from Salmon (1993). Barndorff-Nielsen and Cox (1994) also provide for a more detailed discussion of conditional inference.

behavior of a number of different forms that an LM statistic may take, given alternative choices that can be made for the norming metric in the test statistic. Different finite-sample and robustness properties follow for these statistics, but in each case the norming metric was chosen so that is converged to the unconditional Fisher information matrix. The question of constructing conditional score statistics where the norming metric corresponds to the conditional variance of the score, given some suitably defined ancillary statistic, has not however been addressed and is essentially the issue we wish to raise in the context of testing for linearity.

Severini (1990) considered the conditional properties of unconditional likelihood-based tests. He showed that the asymptotic conditional size of these tests in a one-parameter case corresponds with the nominal size, provided the observed Fisher information matrix is used. If the expected Fisher information matrix is used instead, then the conditional size of the tests varies with the observed value of the (local) ancillary statistic, which in turn depends on the statistical curvature of the model under investigation. Hence, when statistical curvature is large, there is a clear argument in favor of using conditional inference but, more generally, the indication from Severini's results is that the use of the observed information-matrix forms of the likelihood-based tests will often insulate the results of inference from the effects of curvature. The wide divergence between the conditional and unconditional levels of these tests in curved statistical models was also apparent in the simulations carried out by Efron and Hinkley (1978).

Efron (1975) defined statistical curvature at θ of a one-parameter family of denisty functions as

$$\gamma_\theta = \left(\frac{|M_\theta|}{i_\theta^3} \right)^{\frac{1}{2}},$$

where i_θ represents the expected Fisher information per observation, and M_θ is the covariance matrix of the observed score and Hessian of the log likelihood function, $(\dot{l}_\theta \ddot{l}_\theta)$. As such, it describes the standard notion of the geometric curvature of a line (representing the parametric statistical family of distributions of interest) in some space of all suitably defined distributions as the rate of change of direction with respect to arc length – in other words, how fast the score statistic changes as θ moves through its range. Efron's main concern was to develop a measure of how far a given statistical family was from the exponential family, because one-parameter exponential families are known to have good statistical properties. In particular, in this case, the Maximum Likelihood Estimator (MLE) is known to be sufficient, and locally most powerful tests are also uniformly most powerful. Essentially, these properties follow because the exponential family can be viewed, in Efron's measure of curvature, as being flat or described by a straight line in the space of all distributions. Statistical curvature is then zero everywhere, and linear methods of statistical analysis – in other words, those based on linear approximations to the log likelihood function – work well. Efron's argument was then that a large value of statistical curvature would imply that these properties would break down and, in particular, that locally most powerful tests would have poor operating characteristics and that the variance of the MLE would exceed the Cramer–Rao lower bound in proportion to γ_θ^2. Under repeated sampling, Efron's measure of curvature will generally go to zero with sample size at a rate of $n^{1/2}$, and so, asymptotically, the effects of curvature will decay, but in finite samples, curvature depends on the particular model and the sample size. We also note that a distinction should be drawn between *parameter-effects* curvature and *intrinsic curvature* (see, e.g., Seber and Wild 1989). Parameter-effects curvature can be removed or reduced by reparameterizing the statistical model, whereas intrinsic curvature cannot, and it is intrinsic curvature that drives the wedge between conditional and unconditional inference techniques.

Most nonlinear dynamic models will be statistically curved, and indeed, so will many linear dynamic models. For instance, an autoregressive, AR(1), model has Efron curvature given approximately by $2/n$ independently of the autoregressive parameter, and an MA(1) model with parameter θ has curvature given, again approximately, by $2(3 - \theta^2)/(1 - \theta^2)n$. So, if we crudely take Efron's value of one-eighth as indicating when curvature will become important, then this implies that a sample size of at least 16 is needed with an AR(1) model to be able to ignore curvature effects, but a sample size of more than 185 is needed for a MA(1) model with $\theta = 0.9$. Multivariate models may also generate curved statistical families; for instance, a "linear" AR(p) model represents a $[(p + 1)(p + 2)/2, (p + 1)]$ curved exponential family and an ARMA(p, q) model is a $(n, p + q + 1)$ curved exponential family [see Ravishankar, Melnick, and Tsai (1990) for a more detailed discussion].

The importance of these results for testing linearity lies in the fact that because most dynamic models, whether linear or nonlinear, will be statistically curved, critically different results may arise from the use of conditional and unconditional metrics when testing for linearity. Standard forms of LM tests for linearity that employ unconditional metrics, through the use of the unconditional Fisher information matrix, may seriously misrepresent evidence for nonlinearity in the data, which may be detected using conditional metrics when the conditional variance of the score is calculated on the basis of suitably defined anciallary statistics.

The basic argument for adopting a conditional framework for inference follows from the conditionality principle in statistics (see, e.g., Cox and Hinkley 1974), and which may be stated as follows:

The Conditionality Principle

Suppose $S = (\hat{\theta}, A)$ is minimally sufficient for θ, and A is ancillary. Then, inferences about θ are appropriately drawn in terms of the sampling behavior of $\hat{\theta}$ under the assumption that A is constrained to the value, a, observed in the sample.

The Conditionality Principle dates back to Fisher (1925, 1934, 1935) and his fundamental work in establishing the concepts of sufficiency and ancillarity and their role in inference. The essential difference between the conditional and the unconditional approaches to inference lies in establishing a frame of reference that is relevant to the context of application. The following two quotes may be useful in conveying the role of ancillary information in inference:

Ancillary statistics are only useful when different samples of the same size can supply different amounts of information and serve to distinguish those which supply more from those that supply less . . .. (Fisher, 1935, p.)

The idea of ancillary statistics simply tells us how to cut down the sample space to those points relevant to the interpretation of the observations we have . . . (Cox, 1958, p.)

The mathematical analysis that we employ when determining the properties of tests and estimators rests on an *a priori* assumption that there will be some equivalence between the particular sample available and the assumed population. With frequentist inference, we embed the statistical problem *ex ante* in a sampling framework by assuming that the random variables are, for instance, independent and identically distributed and follow some prescribed distribution. A set of assumptions which, although standard, is not innocuous since frequentist probability calculations such as the construction of a confidence interval have the interpretation of covering the true value, say 95 percent of the time within a set of replications defined by these assumptions. A conditional frame of reference restricts the set of replications to that determined by the given value of the ancillary statistic, which essentially provides information about the experimental design of the observed sample or the adequacy of the assumed model, given the available sample. The implicit methodological assumption that is in question, is then, whether the pre-data mathematical calculations under the assumed statistical model are relevant to post-data inference, given the particular realization of the data.

This question of setting the appropriate frame of reference for econometric inference concerns the selection of appropriate tools for inference, in other words, which metric to use—conditional or unconditional—and if conditional, on what ancillary statistic should conditioning be taken. In particular, in the context of testing linearity, if statistical curvature is important and nonlinear reactions not uniformly represented in the sample, then the use of an unconditional metric may not provide relevant inference. Given the inability in economics to generate data from a well-designed experiment, economic data are potentially weak in that situations may exist where the available sample simply does not provide an adequate representation of the feasible range of behavior implied by the true data-generation process. The possibility exists for a true model to fail to be supported by a given data set in that some aspect of behavior implied by the economic model is simply not observed in the available data. A situation which could lead to the false statistical rejection of the true model. The relationship between the design of the available sample and the assumed statistical model should be explicitly recognized in the tools used for inference by conditioning on ancillary statistics that capture the appropriate frame of reference. Note that this issue concerns not only the potentially limited information content of the data but the mathematical forms of test statistics that are employed to assess this information. The emphasis on the unconditional approach to likelihood-based inference within econometrics has led to a situation in which we have developed few techniques to explore this issue where perhaps we should not reject the model but instead reject the data!

A major difficulty in following these arguments through for adopting a conditional framework for inference lies in isolating suitable (exact and unique) ancillary statistics on which to condition. One common definition of an ancillary statistic is as follows.

Ancillary Statistic

If the minimal sufficient statistic, S, has larger dimension than the unknown parameter θ, then A is called an ancillary statistic if we are able to write $S = (T, A)$, where A has a marginal distribution that does not depend on θ. T is often referred to as conditionally sufficient since it may be used as a sufficient statistic conditional on A.

Given that the MLE will in general be a function of the conditionally sufficient statistic, it can be seen from this definition that ancillary statistics capture that part of the total information lost when the sample is reduced to the MLE when it is not itself sufficient. This information is lost when unconditional inference is used, but may be recovered by conditioning on an ancillary statistic, which then serves to set the relevant frame of reference within which to conduct inference on the unknown parameter and measures the adequacy of the model's statistical assumptions, given the available sample. One intuitive explanation for the role of ancillary statistics is that they may contain information on the characteristics and shape of the likelihood function beyond simply the position of the MLE, and hence, to a first-order approximation, the Hessian or the observed information matrix will often provide a relevant ancillary and, in fact, a conditional precision measure for maximum likelihood inference. For many models, however, where the likelihood surface is irregular and locally nonquadratic around the MLE, the use of the observed information matrix cannot be guaranteed to provide an exact ancillary statistic and may only form an approximate ancillary.[2]

Because it is impossible to develop these arguments in detail here, we make our comparison between conditional and unconditional inference when testing linearity on the difference between the use of the observed information matrix, I, and the expected information matrix, $\mathcal{I}$, although, as we have stressed, a rigorous analysis would require the development of conditional metrics, $\mathcal{I}(\hat{\theta}|A = a)$, that recognize the higher-order effects of statistical curvature on inference in any particular case. These two measures of precision can obviously be quite different. One important observation of Efron and Hinkley (1978) is that, for large n, the difference between I and $\mathcal{I}$ is, under certain conditions, given by

$$\sqrt{n}\frac{I - \mathcal{I}}{\mathcal{I}} \sim N(0, \gamma_\theta^2)$$

where γ_θ^2, the statistical curvature of the model, varies with the parameter θ of the statistical model. This result clearly indicates the intimate connection between curvature, information loss, and the need for conditional inference. One natural approximate criterion for assessing the importance of conditional arguments can then be taken as the standardized ratio

$$A_n = \frac{\sqrt{n}}{\gamma_\theta}\left(\frac{I}{\mathcal{I}} - 1\right),$$

which serves as an approximate ancillary statistic and which will be asymptotically distributed as $N(0, 1)$. Given the approximate ancillarity of the observed information matrix, this statistic provides an indication of when the potential range of behavior under the assumed model's assumption is poorly represented in the available sample and, hence, when a significant difference between conditional and unconditional inference may arise. An obvious suggestion is then that it could be reported in applied econometric research to indicate at last the potential importance of conditioning.

The discussion above briefly emphasizes general aspects of the distinction between conditional and unconditional inference but, as we have stressed, the feasibility of applying conditional arguments to the testing of linearity rests on the construction of relevant ancillary statistics. One obvious, but invariably only-approximate, suggestion might be to use observed information-matrix forms of LM tests, although we suspect that further research into this question will lead to better approximate ancillaries and more appropriate conditional

---

[2] Cox (1980) considered how the notion of ancillarity can be extended when exact ancillaries do not exist.

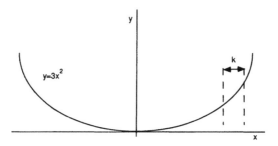

Figure 3.1. Nonlinear regression surface.

metrics when testing linearity.[3] However, even without suitable exact ancillary statistics, we can demonstrate how approximate ancillary statistics can pick up particular sample information that affects inference regarding nonlinearity by calculating the conditional and unconditional precision measures under different sampling schemes in the following simple Monte Carlo experiment.

We generate different samples drawn from a nonlinear, statistically curved, bivariate regression model that have different information regarding the nonlinearity in the true underlying expectation surface. Note that this data-generation process corresponds somewhat crudely, with the case made in the introduction for the periodic, but not uniform, presence of nonlinearity in the first moment of economic data.

We consider a bivariate regression model of the form

$$y_t = cx_t^2 + \varepsilon_t,$$

where $\{x_t, \varepsilon_t\}$ are independent standard normal variables. This stochastic linear regression model is statistically curved and, hence, from the arguments above, we can expect a distinction to arise between the use of conditional and unconditional inference that depends on the degree of statistical curvature. Let us also assume that the sampling structure determining the observations is constrained, as shown in Figure 3.1, in that observations on the regressor are drawn only from a fixed interval of width k around some fixed point, say $x = 3$, so that the mean of the standard normal variable x_t, becomes 3.

The maximum statistical curvature in this example occurs at the origin, and the sample observations are then drawn from a restricted, relatively linear part of the total potential reaction space where the statistical curvature is approximately

---

[3] Note that the Monte Carlo evidence of Davidson and MacKinnon (1983) and Bera and McKenzie (1986) regarding the relative slowness by which "observed" forms of the LM statistics approach the asymptotic χ^2 distribution is not strictly relevant to the discussion as to which statistic–conditional or unconditional – should be used for inference. The question of the finite sample distribution of the conditional LM statistic is a separate issue.

half the value of that at the origin. The index, k, serves essentially as an ancillary statistic that indicates the sampling stratification. We are interested in how inference varies as this ancillary takes different values and more "nonlinear" information is incorporated in the sample. A small Monte Carlo study, with 200 replications of 50 observations each, was carried out on this model, from which, we compute conditional and unconditional variances of the least-squares estimate of c, using the inverse of the observed and expected information, respectively, given our exact prior knowledge of the distribution of the regressor (noncentral χ^2), as well as the observed sampling variation of the parameter estimate drawn from the Monte Carlo experiments as the interval determined by the value of k increases in size from 0.05 to 5 in 100 steps.

Figure 3.2 shows these three measures of precision as k varies. The observed variance determined by the standard least-squares formula tracks the sampling variation relatively well, and only after the sampling interval has stretched sufficiently and k reaches a value of about 40 does the unconditional variance, calculated using the expected information matrix and the assumed distribution for the regressor, start to provide a reasonable approximation to the actual sampling variance of the estimate determined in the Monte Carlo. Note, in particular, how the unconditional estimate is insensitive to the sampling stratification, in that it does not reflect the way in which the information content of the sample changes with k. Both the sampling variance and the observed variance are higher than the expected variance, initially almost twice as large, until more evidence for nonlinearity becomes apparent in the sample and k increases. Note also that the expected information is calculated on the basis of the true nonlinear stochastic model that we, in fact, know in this case is generating the data. However, when testing linearity using LM tests based on restricted linear models, the null on which the expectation is formed will be the linear model. Hence, the question arises as to whether the unconditional metric is relevant and whether a conditional metric might provide more appropriate inference. We are also able to compute the A_n statistic given above to determnine if there is a statistical difference between the observed and expected information measures. Figure 3.3 plots this statistic while k again varies from 0.05 to 5. On a standard one-sided 95 percent significance test, we can see that the difference is significant up to about the value of $k = 25$.

What this simple exercise has shown is the fairly obvious point that different metrics may imply substantially different measures of precision when evaluated with the same data but, more important, that inference given the particular information content of an available sample when testing for linearity could be quite different when conditional and unconditional precision measures are employed.

The general argument for using conditional inference when testing linearity has been made, but the question of how to construct suitable exact or

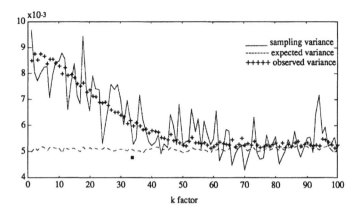

Figure 3.2. Conditional and unconditional precision measures.

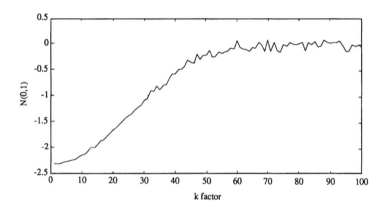

Figure 3.3. Ancillarity test for the significance of conditional inference as k varies.

approximate ancillary statistics for this purpose remains to be developed. We now consider explicitly testing for linearity, keeping in mind the arguments for conditional inference made above. In particular, we consider the use of recursive tests where the estimated metric used at each sample point changes as the sample size is increased and, therefore, inference is conditional on different sample information at each point, but the mathematical form of the metric does not change. We clearly are not formally using conditional metrics in the recursive LM tests below, but we hope the recursive approach at least provides a better inferential framework for detecting nonlinearity when it may not be uniformly represented in the sample.

3   Testing for linearity

Testing for linearity has generated a range of alternative statistics, perhaps starting with the work of Ramsey (1969); a recent survey and discussion can be found in Granger and Terasvirta (1993). We explicitly build on the work of Lee, White, and Granger (1993), concentrating on testing for linearity in the mean and extending their work by applying recursive forms of the tests described below.[4] They define a process $\{y_t\}$ to be *linear in mean* with respect to the information set X_t of dimension k (which may, but need not, contain lagged values of y_t) if there exists a $k \times 1$ vector of coefficients θ^* such that

$$P[E(y_t|X_t) = X_t'\theta^*] = 1 \text{ for some } \theta^* \in \mathcal{R}^k.$$

The alternative hypothesis of interest in this case is that the process $\{y_t\}$ is nonlinear in mean with respect to X_t so that

$$P[E(y_t|X_t) = X_t'\theta^*] < 1 \text{ for all } \theta^* \in \mathcal{R}^k.$$

We also adopt the same strategy of testing for *neglected nonlinearity*, so that the tests will be applied where appropriate, to the residuals of an AR(p) model, which we presume has extracted as much linear structure as possible from the data. The number of lags p is chosen using the Akaike Information Criterion (AIC).

3.1   *Keenan test*

The Keenan (1985) test is based on a truncated Volterra-series expansion. It restricts the information set, X_t, to the past p observations of y_t so that it regresses y_t on $(y_{t-1}, y_{t-2}, \ldots, y_{t-p})'$, although it can be generalized to include other explanatory variables. It consists of the following steps:

(1) Regress y_t on X_t linearly, $\quad y_t = X_t'\theta + e_t$, producing a vector of coefficient estimates, $\quad \hat{\theta}$, from which one can generate fitted values, $\quad \hat{y}_t = X_t'\hat{\theta}$ and estimated residuals $\quad \hat{e}_t = y_t - \hat{y}_t$.

(2) Regress the squares of the fitted values $\hat{y}_t^2$ on X_t and save the estimated residuals $\hat{\varepsilon}_t$. $\quad \hat{y}_t^2 = X_t'\lambda + \varepsilon_t$,

(3) Regress the residuals $\hat{e}_t$ on the residuals $\hat{\varepsilon}_t$ and save the estimated residuals $\hat{v}_t$. $\quad \hat{e}_t = \hat{\varepsilon}_t'\delta + v_t$,

---

[4] For completeness we repeat the description of these tests, which is often taken almost word for word from Lee, White, and Granger (1993).

(4)   Test the null hypothesis $H_0 : \delta = 0$ using the Keenan test statistic,

$$\frac{\hat{e}'\hat{\varepsilon}(\hat{\varepsilon}'\hat{\varepsilon})^{-1}\hat{\varepsilon}'\hat{e}}{\hat{v}'\hat{v}/(n - 2p - 2)},$$

where $\hat{e} = (\hat{e}_1, \ldots, \hat{e}_n)'$, $\hat{\varepsilon} = (\hat{\varepsilon}_1, \ldots, \hat{\varepsilon}_n)'$, and $\hat{v} = (\hat{v}_1, \ldots \hat{v}_n)'$.

The Keenan statistic has an $F(1, n - 2p - 2)$ distribution under the null hypothesis of no nonlinearity, where p is the number of explanatory parameters used (usually the number of lags in the autoregression). The Keenan test checks whether the squared fitted value ($\hat{y}_t^2 = \hat{\theta}' X_t X_t' \hat{\theta}$) has any additional explanatory power over the linear model. It has an LM interpretation similar to that of the Regression Error Specification Tests (RESET) below.

3.2   Ramsey RESET Test

The Ramsey (1969) RESET test can be seen as a generalization of the Keenan test because it examines the explanatory significance of higher powers of the fitted values $\hat{y}_t$ for y_t:

(1)   Regress y_t linearly on X_t as $y_t = X_t'\theta + e_t$,
      and save the estimated residuals $\hat{e}_t$ and fitted values $\hat{y}_t$.
(2)   Regress y_t on k powers of the fitted values $\hat{y}_t$ where k can be set at any level:

$$y_t = X_t'\theta + c_2\hat{y}_t^2 + c_3\hat{y}_t^3 + \cdots + c_k\hat{y}_t^k + v_t$$

and save the estimated residuals $\hat{v}_t$.
(3)   Test the null hypothesis $H_0 : c_2 = c_3 = \cdots = c_k = 0$ using the RESET statistic:

$$\frac{(\hat{e}'\hat{e} - \hat{v}'\hat{v})/(k - 1)}{\hat{v}'\hat{v}/(n - k)}.$$

This form of the RESET test follows an $F(k - 1, n - k)$ distribution under H_0. Another form suggested by Thursby and Schmidt (1977) was found to have superior power against nonlinear alternatives and can be obtained by regressing the error term from the autoregression against powers of the lagged dependent variables:

(1)   Regress y_t linearly on X_t as $y_t = X_t'\theta + e_t$
      and save the estimated residuals $\hat{e}_t$.
(2)   Regress the estimated residuals $\hat{e}_t$ on h powers of the explanatory variables X_t:

$$\hat{e}_t = X_t'\theta + X_t'^{(2)}\gamma_2 + X_t'^{(3)}\gamma_3 + \ldots + X_t'^{(h)}\gamma_h + v_t$$

and save the estimated residuals v_t. Note that $X_t^{'(j)}$ denotes the vector containing the elements of X_t', each raised to the power j where $j = 2, \ldots, h$, and h is chosen at will. Whereas, in the basic RESET test, c_h is a scalar, here γ_j is a different vector of k coefficients for each power from 2 to h.

(3) Test the null hypothesis $H_0 : \gamma_2 = \gamma_3 = \cdots = \gamma_h = 0$ using the RESET2 test statistic:

$$\frac{(\hat{e}'\hat{e} - \hat{v}'\hat{v})/(h - 1)}{\hat{v}'\hat{v}/(n - m - p - h)}.$$

This modified RESET statistic follows an $F(h - 1, n - m - p - h)$ distribution under the null, where p is the order of the autoregression (dimension of X_t), h is the highest power to which X_t is raised, and m is the number of coefficients estimated in the auxiliary equation ($h \times p$). Both of these RESET tests have LM interpretations and, in common with the Keenan test, are sensitive to departures from linearity in the mean.

3.3   Tsay test

Like the Keenan test, the Tsay (1986) test starts by regressing y_t on its past values so that X_t consists of $(y_{t-1}, \ldots, y_{t-p})'$. However, the Tsay test truncates the Volterra-series expansion at a higher order, and hence it features a more complicated second stage that involves the cross products of past observations, $y_{t-j}y_{t-k}$:

(1) Regress y_t on X_t linearly, $y_t = X_t'\theta + e_t$, and save the estimated residuals $\hat{e}_t$.

(2) Compose the vector P_t where $P_t = \text{vech}(X_t'X_t)$.
Because $\text{vech}(\cdot)$ denotes the half-stacking vector operator P_t consists of a $p(p + 1)/2$ element vector containing the elements of the lower triangular part of $X_t'X_t$. Thus, for each observation of y_t, there corresponds a vector P_t whose elements are the unique cross products of the last p observations of y' in other words, $y_{t-i}y_{t-j}$ for $i, j = 1, \ldots, p$ where $j \geq i$.
    Regress this vector P_t on the explanatory variables X_t : $P_t = X_t'\lambda + \varepsilon_t$, and save the estimated residuals $\hat{\varepsilon}$

(3) Regress the estimated residuals $\hat{e}_t$ on $\hat{\varepsilon}_t$: $\hat{e}_t = \hat{\varepsilon}_t'\delta + v_t$, and save the estimated residuals $\hat{v}_t$.

(4) Test the null hypothesis $H_0 : \delta = 0$ using the Tsay test statistic:

$$\frac{\hat{e}'\hat{\varepsilon}(\hat{\varepsilon}'\hat{\varepsilon})^{-1}\hat{\varepsilon}'\hat{e}/m}{\hat{v}'\hat{v}/(n - p - m - 1)},$$

where, again, m is the number of coefficients estimated in the auxiliary equation (i.e., step 3), so that $m = p(p+1)/2$.

The Tsay statistic has an $F(m, n - p - m - 1)$ distribution under the null. It tests the forecasting ability gained by including product terms such as $y_{t-i} y_{t-j}$ or y_{t-j}^2. Again, it has an LM interpretation, as shown by Granger and Terasvirta (1993) and is sensitive to departures from linearity in the mean.

3.4   *McLeod–Li test*

This test is based on the principle that if the residuals follow a linear independent and identically distributed process, the cross product of their squares should have the same correlation structure as the square of their cross products: $\text{corr}(y_t^2, y_{t-\kappa}^2) = [\text{corr}(y_t, y_{t-\kappa})]^2$ for all κ: McLeod and Li (1983) apply a standard Box–Ljung portmanteau test for serial correlation to the squared residuals from a linear model to test for linearity:

(1) Regress y_t linearly on X_t as $y_t = X_t'\theta + e_t$,
      and save the estimated residuals $\hat{e}_t$.
(2) Calculate the autocorrelation function of the squares of the estimated residuals $\hat{e}_t^2$ up to some order m:

$$\hat{r}(i) = \frac{\sum_{t=i+1}^{m}(\hat{e}_t^2 - \hat{\sigma}^2)(\hat{e}_{t-i}^2 - \hat{\sigma}^2)}{\sum_{t=1}^{n}(\hat{e}_t^2 - \hat{\sigma}^2)^2},$$

where $\hat{\sigma}^2 = n^{-1}\sum_{t=1}^{n}\hat{e}_t^2$.
(3) Test the null hypothesis of linearity using the statistic

$$n(n+2)\sum_{j=1}^{m}[\hat{r}(j)]^2/(n-j)$$

Under the null hypothesis, the McLeod–Li statistic tends to a $\chi^2(m)$ distribution, where the parameter m is chosen at the time of application. This test can be seen as an LM test against ARCH (again see Granger and Terasvirta 1993) although originally proposed as a general test for nonlinearity.

3.5   *Brock–Dechert–Scheinkman (BDS) test*

The BDS test developed by Brock, Dechert, and Scheinkman (1987) can be applied to the residuals of a linear autoregression to check whether they are generated by an independent and identically distributed process. It was derived from consideration of deterministic chaotic processes and is based on the Grassberger–Procaccia correlation exponent. Consider a vector of m observations, $Y_{q,r}$, which consists of a subsample of $\{y_t\}$ over the interval $t = q$ to

$t = r$ where $q \geq 0$ and $r \leq n$. Then compare a pair of such m-dimensional vectors $Y_{q,r}$ and $Y_{u,v}$. They are said to be no more than ε apart if it is true that for each pair of their corresponding elements:

$$\|Y_{q,j} - Y_{u,j}\| \leq \varepsilon, j = 1, \ldots, m$$

The correlation integral is then defined as

$$C_m(\varepsilon) = \lim_{T \to \infty} T^{-2} \text{ \{number of pairs of vectors such that the above holds\}},$$

which is a measure of the number of pairs of m-vectors (subperiods of length m within the sample) that are within a distance ε from each other. The correlation exponent, V_n, given below is used to distinguish chaotic from stochastic processes:

$$V_n = \lim_{\varepsilon \to 0} \frac{\partial \log[C_m(\varepsilon)]}{\partial \log(\varepsilon)}.$$

If a process is really stochastic, V_n will increase linearly in n. Conversely, if it is chaotic, C_m, $(\varepsilon) = \varepsilon^V$ and V is independent of the sample size n. The BDS test statistic below is based on the correlation integral, C_m:

$$\text{BDS} = \sqrt{n}[C_m(\varepsilon) - C_1(\varepsilon)^m]/\sigma_n,$$

where σ_n is a complicated variance expression, and the statistic follows a normal distribution under the null hypothesis. Note that the critical distance ε and the dimension m of the BDS test are chosen at the time of application. Hsieh and LeBaron (1988) establish by simulation that the test has good power against nonlinear alternatives, both stochastic and deterministic, and if the null of independence is rejected, it may be because of chaos or a nonlinear stochastic alternative. In samples of size $n = 500$, asymptotic normality seems accurate for ε between 0.5 and 1.5 times the standard deviation of the data and for dimensions m up to about 6. There appears to be no LM interpretation for the BDS test.

3.6 *ARCH LM test*

We have also included the basic ARCH LM test to explicitly consider questions of both first- and second-moment nonlinearity in the data. In principle, we could have attempted to "robustify" the first-moment tests for linearity from ARCH effects by using heteroskedastic-consistent forms of the test statistics, but for reasons similar to those discussed by Lee et al. (1993), we did not do so. The question of conditional second-moment structure is critically dependent on no misspecification in the first-moment structure and, given the methodological issues involved, we preferred to use the uncorrected forms. ARCH models, introduced by Engle (1982), describe series in which periods of high volatility alternate with periods of low volatility so that a large change is more likely to follow a large change and a small change is more likely to follow a small change. In its simplest form, this can be written formally as

$$y_t = X_t'\theta + \varepsilon_t$$

$$\varepsilon_t \sim N(0, h_t)$$

$$h_t^2 = \alpha_0 + \alpha_1\varepsilon_{t-1}^2 + \cdots + \alpha_p\varepsilon_{t-p}^2$$

Engle proposed an LM test of the null hypothesis that $\alpha_1 = \alpha_2 = \cdots = \alpha_p = 0$. The procedure is as follows:

(1) Regress y_t linearly on X_t as $y_t = X_t'\theta + e_t$,
and save the estimated residuals $\hat{e}_t$.

(2) Regress the squares of the estimated residuals $\hat{e}_t^2$ on an intercept and p lagged values of $\hat{e}_t^2$ as

$$\hat{e}_t^2 = \alpha_0 + \alpha_1\hat{e}_{t-1}^2 + \alpha_2\hat{e}_{t-2}^2 + \cdots + \alpha_p\hat{e}_{t-p}^2 + \varepsilon_t,$$

and save the estimated residuals $\hat{\varepsilon}_t$.

(3) Calculate the R^2 from the second regression and test the null hypothesis using the nR^2 statistic.

The ARCH LM test follows a $\chi^2(p)$ distribution under the null hypothesis of no ARCH dependence. This test, and the McLeod–Li test explicitly examine evidence for nonlinearity in the second moment, whereas the other tests we consider focus on nonlinearity in the mean.

3.7   Neural-Network test

White's (1989) Neural-Network test for neglected nonlinearity as described by Lee et al. (1993) is based on the premise that the observed series, $f(X_t, \delta)$, can be decomposed into a linear part $X_t'\theta$ and a nonlinear part $\sum_{j=1}^{q} \beta_j \psi(X_t'\gamma_j)$ constructed from a neural network. Thus, $f(X_t, \delta) = X_t'\theta + \sum_{j=1}^{q} \beta_j \psi(X_t'\gamma_j)$ and, under the null hypothesis of linearity, the β_j in the augmented neural network will be zero for all j. The neural-network test then checks the hypothesis $\beta_j = 0, j = 1, \ldots, q$ for a particular choice of q and $\gamma = (\gamma_0, \gamma_1, \ldots, \gamma_q)$. The test has power whenever $\sum_{j=1}^{q} \beta_j \psi(X_t'\gamma_j)$ is capable of extracting structure from the residuals of the linear regression $\hat{e}_t = y_t - X_t\hat{\theta}$.

The Neural-Network test exploits the fact that, under the null hypothesis of linearity, $E[e_t|X_t] = 0$ with probability one. Therefore, e_t is also uncorrelated with any measurable function of X_t, which we can denote $h(X_t)$, including the activations of the intermediate units $X_t' \gamma_j$. So, an alternative form of the null hypothesis is

$$E[h(X_t)e_t] = 0.$$

In implementing the Neural-Network test, we generate test functions of X_t, choosing for $h(X_t)$ the activations of hidden units $\psi(X_t' \gamma_j)$ for $j = 1, \ldots, q$, where γ_j are random vectors generated independently of y_t and X_t. Denoting the vector of activations thus generated as $\mathbf{\Psi}_t = [\psi(X_t' \gamma_1), \ldots, \psi(X_t' \gamma_q)]'$, the null hypothesis can be reformulated as

$$E(\mathbf{\Psi}_t e_t) = 0,$$

so that evidence of correlation between $\mathbf{\Psi}_t$ and e_t indicates that augmenting the linear network by including additional hidden units with nonlinear activations $\psi(X_t' \gamma_j)$ would improve forecasting performance. The Neural-Network test is implemented as follows:

(1) Regress y_t linearly on X_t as $y_t = X_t' \theta + e_t$, and save the estimated residuals $\hat{e}_t$.

(2) Choosing Γ independently of $\{X_t\}$ and $\{y_t\}$, form the vectors $\mathbf{\Psi}_j$ and regress $\hat{e}_t$ on X_t and $\mathbf{\Psi}_t$ as $\quad \hat{e}_t = X_t' \delta + \mathbf{\Psi}_t' \lambda + \varepsilon_t$, and save the estimated residuals $\hat{\varepsilon}_t$

(3) Test the null hypothesis using an nR^2 statistic.

Under the null hypothesis of linearity in the mean, the neural-network test asymptotically follows a $\chi^2(q)$ distribution and has a Lagrange Multiplier interpretation.

4   Full-sample analysis

We now apply the nonlinearity tests described above to the US dollar/UK pound sterling spot exchange rate. We adopt an AR(4) as linear filter, so that the null hypothesis is that the series under question is linear in the mean with respect to its last four lags. For the Keenan test and the RESET test, this means that the matrix X_t of explanatory variables consists of a constant and four lags, but, for the RESET2 test and the Tsay test, this would cause multicollinearity. Therefore, we exclude the constant when X_t is raised to a power for the RESET2[5] and also when the vector of unique cross products, P_t is constructed for the Tsay test. The tests are estimated with the following parameters: For the Keenan test, $p = 5$; for the RESET, $k = 4$; for the RESET2, $h = 4$, $p = 4$, and so, $m = 16$; and for the Tsay test, $p = 4$, and so, $m = 10$. For the McLeod–Li

---

[5] Note that this corresponds to the Thursby and Schmidt (1977) RESET, and not the RESET2 test as specified by Lee et al. (1993).

test, $m = 50$; for the BDS, ε is equal to the standard deviation of the input series and $m = 6$; and for the neural-network test, a network with two hidden units was estimated to provide the vector of activations Ψ_t.

Our monthly data cover the period January 1973 to June 1992, whereas the weekly data are over the shorter period of January 1, 1973, to May 7, 1990. We consider four separate transformation of the series:

(1)   Raw data: pound sterling against U.S. dollars;
(2)   Natural logarithms of the data;
(3)   Log differences (random-walk residuals);
(4)   GARCH(1,1) standardized residuals.

The raw data are seasonally unadjusted and neither differenced nor detrended, and the log differences are the equivalent of the residuals from a random walk (in logs) with a unit coefficient imposed on the lag and a zero-intercept term. The fourth series represents the standardized residuals of a GARCH(1,1) model fitted to the log differences.[6] These residuals are standardized by centering on their mean and dividing each one by the corresponding conditional variance as estimated by GARCH using the method described in Calzolari and Fiorentini (1992).

Table 3.1 reports the basic statistics for the series. Note immediately the difference between the monthly and the weekly data; weekly data consistently deviate further from normality than the monthly counterpart (the table reports the basic skewness and kurtosis coefficients). Note that transforming the raw data by taking logs improves kurtosis for both monthly and weekly series, increasing it toward its normal value 3.0; the Bowman–Shenton normality test (see, Kiefer and Salmon 1983) is correspondingly reduced. When the logs are differenced in the third column, kurtosis practically doubles, increasing the normality statistic, dramatically in the case of the weekly data. However, after the GARCH model is fitted to the log differences, kurtosis is reduced for the monthly series, reducing its normality statistic, whereas for the weekly series, kurtosis is dramatically increased and the normality test takes the value of 2,157 with a critical value of 5.99; this is probably due to two significant outliers. This table suggests that the normality assumption can be questioned for all of these series except the logs and GARCH residuals at the monthly frequency, that weekly data probably deviate further from normality than monthly data, and that the GARCH model is clearly better suited to the monthly series than to the weekly series.

Table 3.2 presents the autocorrelation function (ACF) of the monthly series. The strong autocorrelation frequently associated with a unit root in exchange rates is visible in the first two columns and, while taking logs has a very small impact, first differencing the logs eliminates most of the autocorrelation. Fitting

---

[6]   A more complex specification than the GARCH(1, 1) was not found to be necessary.

Table 3.1. *Descriptive statistics*

	Raw	Logs	Log diffs	GARCH
Monthly £ / $ spot exchange rate				
Observations	236	236	235	232
Maximum	2.5760	0.9462	0.1034	0.0111
Minimum	1.0961	0.0917	−0.1128	−0.0126
Skewness	0.2777	−0.1232	0.0067	0.0351
Kurtosis	2.3890	2.6140	4.1510	3.5320
Normality	6.704	2.062	12.974	2.74
Weekly £ / $ spot exchange rate				
Observations	906	906	905	902
Maximum	2.5800	0.9476	0.0658	0.0578
Minimum	1.0630	0.0612	−0.0412	−0.0790
Skewness	0.2219	−0.1262	0.2366	−0.5339
Kurtosis	2.1053	2.3313	5.3982	10.501
Normality	37.63	18.54	222.6	2.157

the GARCH model to the log differences transforms the pattern of autocorrelation and, if anything, appears to increase its significance. The lower panel of Table 3.2 presents the ACF for the squared values of each series. Again in this case, the ACF of the first two series takes the form of a gentle decline, the other two series producing ACFs that show little or no significance. Again, this indicates that taking log differences is successful in removing most of the second-moment linear dependence. However, the GARCH residuals provide some indication of residual nonlinear dependence.

Table 3.3 presents the ACF for the weekly data and their squared values. The results are much as for the monthly data except that the evidence of autocorrelation is considerably more pronounced except for the GARCH residuals.

Table 3.4 reports the full-sample results of the linearity tests run on the four basic monthly series. Note that each of the series provides some indication of nonlinearity except the GARCH standardized residuals. The Keenan, RESET, Tsay, McLeod–Li, and Neural-Net tests detect no evidence of nonlinearity in any of the series. However, the RESET2 test detects nonlinearity for both the logs and the random-walk residuals (i.e., log-differences). The BDS test rejects the null hypothesis of independence for the raw data, the logs, and the log differences, but not for the GARCH residuals. Predictably, the ARCH LM test is significant for the first three series and not for the GARCH(1, 1) residuals; however, note that it is sharply reduced by the log-differencing transformation. So, the conclusions from the full-sample tests on the monthly data appear to coincide with accepted wisdom that a GARCH model seems to capture most of the structure from the original series, although there is some weak evidence of residual autocorrelation in both the

Table 3.2. *Autocorrelation functions, monthly data*

	Raw	Logs	Log diffs	GARCH
£ / $ Spot exchange rate				
$\rho(1)$	0.9769	0.9802	0.3708	0.3322
$\rho(2)$	0.9522	0.9563	0.0493	0.0682
$\rho(3)$	0.9282	0.9832	0.0295	0.0082
$\rho(4)$	0.9030	0.9079	−0.0260	−0.0321
$\rho(5)$	0.8789	0.8848	−0.0340	−0.0252
$\rho(6)$	0.8571	0.8618	0.0438	0.0785
$\rho(12)$	0.6960	0.7145	0.0709	−0.0871
Squared series				
$\rho(1)$	0.9736	0.9752	0.0545	−0.0507
$\rho(2)$	0.9463	0.9490	−0.0292	−0.0855
$\rho(3)$	0.9203	0.9238	0.1926	0.0031
$\rho(4)$	0.8931	0.8977	−0.0128	−0.0863
$\rho(5)$	0.8671	0.8728	−0.0213	−0.0506
$\rho(6)$	0.8441	0.8505	0.0260	−0.0543
$\rho(12)$	0.6742	0.6832	−0.0130	−0.0116

Table 3.3. *Autocorrelation functions, weekly data*

	Raw	Logs	Log diffs	GARCH
£ / $ Spot exchange rate				
$\rho(1)$	0.9968	0.9969	0.2370	0.2647
$\rho(2)$	0.9938	0.9938	0.0168	0.1117
$\rho(3)$	0.9903	0.9905	0.0293	0.0939
$\rho(4)$	0.9866	0.9870	0.0935	0.1033
$\rho(5)$	0.9823	0.9831	0.0258	0.0301
$\rho(6)$	0.9780	0.9790	−0.0160	0.0009
$\rho(12)$	0.9506	0.9536	0.0113	0.0314
Squared series				
$\rho(1)$	0.9967	0.9968	0.1682	−0.0099
$\rho(2)$	0.9934	0.9937	0.0846	−0.0093
$\rho(3)$	0.9895	0.9900	0.1293	−0.0276
$\rho(4)$	0.9853	0.9860	0.1770	0.0050
$\rho(5)$	0.9805	0.9815	0.0442	−0.0362
$\rho(6)$	0.9756	0.9769	0.0370	−0.0234
$\rho(12)$	0.9448	0.9479	0.1075	0.0399

levels and the squared GARCH residuals from Table 3.2. Otherwise, the indicated misspecification relates to a lack of independence and ARCH structure in the other three series.

Table 3.5 reports the same tests for the series at a weekly frequency. Although the Keenan test again finds no evidence of nonlinearity, the RESET test

Table 3.4. *Linearity tests, monthly data £ / $ spot exchange rate*

Test	Raw	Logs	Log diffs	GARCH	Dist.
Keenan	0.1878	0.1518	1.2348	0.2994	$F(1,200)$
RESET	0.5512	0.1100	1.0307	1.1362	$F(3,200)$
RESET2	2.2736	4.6403**	4.9440*	2.0527	$F(3,200)$
Tsay	0.3841	0.8317	1.6549	0.7439	$F(10,200)$
McLeod–Li	29.178	28.681	30.664	47.210	$\chi^2(50)$
BDS(6)	69.381**	306.89**	−6.113**	−0.757	$N(0, 1)$
ARCH LM	219.69**	223.41**	17.492**	5.6808	$\chi^2(4)$
Neural net	1.1573	0.1543	0.1074	0.4635	$\chi^2(2)$

*Significance at the 5% level.
** Significance at the 1% level.

is now significant (at the 1 percent level) for the random-walk and GARCH residuals. The RESET2 test is significant at the 1 percent level for all four series (at monthly frequency, it was significant only for the logs and log differences). The Tsay test now indicates nonlinearity in the random-walk residuals at the 5 percent level. The McLeod–Li test has become significant at the 1 percent level for the first three series, but still indicates no nonlinearity for the GARCH residuals. At this frequency, the BDS test also rejects the independent and identically distributed hypothesis for the GARCH residuals as well as for the other three series. The ARCH LM test gives the same results as for the monthly series by rejecting homoskedasticity for all of the series except the GARCH residuals. The Neural-Network test is now significant at the 5 percent level, but only for the raw-data series. Overall, the number of significant rejections of linearity has more than doubled, compared with the monthly data.

This full-sample analysis may lead us to conclude that a GARCH(1, 1) model effectively eliminates any nonlinearities at the monthly level. At the weekly frequency, there is much wider evidence of nonlinearity in both the first and the second moments and the GARCH(1, 1) standardized residuals register significant nonlinearity (at the 1% level) for three different tests–RESET, RESET2, and BDS. Clearly, there is more structure here that needs to be explained, and for this we turn to the recursive analysis.

5   Recursive analysis

The tests are now applied recursively from the beginning of the sample, adding one observation at a time and reestimating the AR(4) linear filter andthe test

Table 3.5. *Linearity tests, weekly data £ / $ spot exchange rate.*

Test	Raw	Logs	Log diffs	GARCH	Dist.
Keenan	0.4916	0.9838	0.2368	0.9717	$F(1,1000)$
RESET	0.2365	0.2310	8.1210**	5.2759**	$F(3,1000)$
RESET2	6.2349**	10.076**	15.940**	7.3196	$F(3,1000)$
Tsay	1.5008	1.7439	2.152*	0.8031	$F(10,1000)$
McLeod–Li	106.59**	347.76**	332.45**	13.792	$\chi^2(50)$
BDS(6)	187.54**	1081.5**	9891.0**	404.08**	$N(0,1)$
ARCH LM	891.10**	895.15**	56.170**	0.8562	$\chi^2(4)$
Neural-net	4.7495*	2.3152	0.2514	0.6815	$\chi^2(2)$

* Significance at the 5% level.
** Significance at the 1% level.

statistics over the observations up to that point. To test the parameter stability of the linear filter, which itself provides a crude check of the adequacy of the linear approximation, the Hansen (1992) test is also run recursively. Figures 3.4–3.7 present the results graphically for the series taken at the weekly frequency, although the same general pattern of periodic nonlinearity can be seen in the monthly data. In each of the figures, the statistics are divided by their critical value (which is generated separately for each observation as the sample size grows); this means that, when the graphs reach the level of 1.0, the statistic has reached the indicated critical level.

For the weekly raw data, Figure 3.4 shows that the recursive Hansen test detects parameter instability in the linear AR(4) in 1982. The Tsay test indicates an isolated period around Nov. 8, 1976, which just hovers above 5 percent critical level before dropping off and then becoming significant again between 1987 and 1988, although it is not significant for the sample taken as a whole. The McLeod–Li test reveals a sudden rise to the 1 percent critical level about Oct. 19, 1981, and continues to be significant for the rest of the sample. The Neural-Network test is significant at two points within the sample around Mar. 8, 1976, and again from Nov. 19, 1984, to Feb. 4, 1985, although it is not significant over the sample as a whole. For the weekly logs, in Figure 3.5, the Hansen test detects parameter instability in the AR(4), starting around Aug. 17, 1981. Recursive analysis reveals a period of significance in the RESET test from about May 30 to Sept. 26, 1977, at the 5 percent level, which is again hidden in the full-sample analysis. The Tsay test is significant at the 5 percent level in full-sample analysis, but the recursive analysis reveals several different periods when it is significant at the 1 percent level: Mar. 22, to July 26, 1976; Sept. 6, 1976, to Oct. 10, 1977; Jan 10, to Aug. 1, 1977; and Nov. 7, 1977, to May 1, 1978. The McLeod–Li test passes the 1 percent threshold

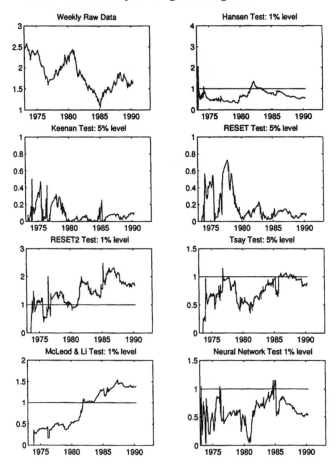

Figure 3.4. Weekly raw data

around Oct. 5, 1981, and begins a dramatic rise around Mar. 18, 1985. For the weekly log differences (Figure 3.6), the Hansen test is increasingly significant starting from mid 1982, indicating parameter instability in the AR(4) filter. The Keenan test is significant at the 5 percent level at just one isolated point in the sample at Mar. 18, 1985. The RESET identifies a sustained period of nonlinearity early in the sample from July 17, 1978, to Nov. 22, 1982, and then a period of effective linearity before a second rise breaking the 1 percent level again at Apr. 15, 1985. The Tsay test identifies two similar periods at the 1 percent level, but the first begins earlier toward Aug. 16, 1976, and ends at Nov. 20, 1978. The McLeod–Li test becomes significant at the 1 percent

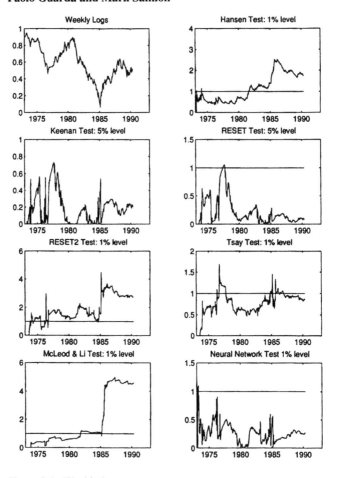

Figure 3.5. Weekly logs

level at Nov. 12, 1984, but again takes a sudden leap at July 22, 1985. For the weekly GARCH standardized residuals (Figure 3.7), the Hansen test detects no parameter instability in the AR(4) filter. The Keenan test has an isolated period from Feb. 9, 1976, to Oct. 3, 1977, during which it is significant at the 1 percent level. The start and end of this "bubble" correspond with the two negative and then positive outliers in the GARCH residual series. Their effect is also visible in several of the other tests. Intriguingly, the McLeod–Li test moves down on Feb. 2, 1976, where the other tests statistics increase. Both RESETs indicate first-moment nonlinearity for much of the sample starting in 1976 and 1977.

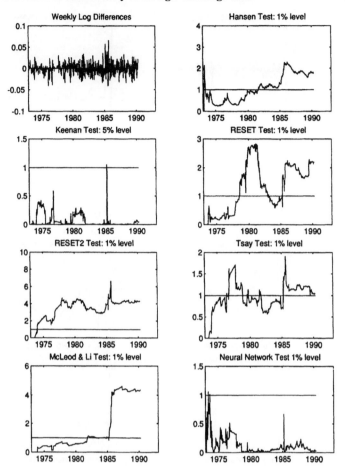

Figure 3.6. Weekly log differences

We present one final set of results in Figure 3.8, which attempts to correlate the observed evidence for first-moment nonlinearity detected in the recursive tests presented above with evidence of volatility in the conditional variances from the estimated GARCH(1, 1) process. In the individual graphs shown in Figure 3.8, the horizontal axis shows the estimated conditional variances, and the vertical axes show the indicated recursive first-moment test statistics for the log-difference series. The lack of association is clearly apparent, with significant first-moment nonlinearity being associated with periods of both high and low volatility. Although it may be easy to rationalize high volatility with evidence for first-moment nonlinearity, what was unexpected was the

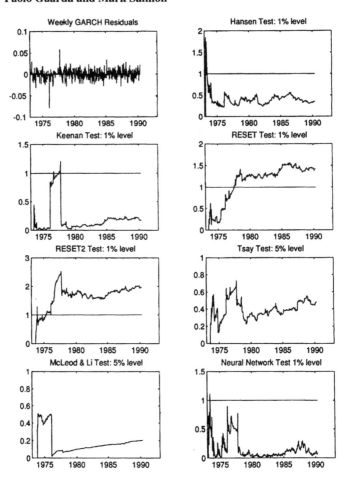

Figure 3.7. Weekly GARCH residuals

concentration, particularly with the RESET tests, of significant first-moment nonlinearity with low volatility. Clearly, our initial presumption that both first- and second-moment nonlinearity would occur at the same periods is not apparently supported by the data.

Given the different implicit alternative hypotheses that these tests have power against, it is difficult to draw precise conclusions from this recursive analysis. However, it does seem clear that there are indeed periods within the sample at which first-moment linearity breaks down and that these periods do not correspond necessarily with periods of high volatility. The conclusion we then draw is that modeling such data with GARCH / ARCH-type models may be

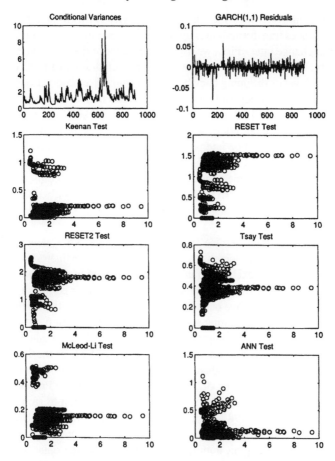

Figure 3.8. Conditional variances and first moment recursive tests

masking a more complicated nonlinear structure in the first moment of the data. Hence, it may be more appropriate to consider refined nonlinear conditional mean specifications than to adopt more complex second-moment specifications to model financial data of this sort.

6   Identifying periods of nonlinearity

Given the preceding evidence we now attempt to match those points in the sample that proved critical for the recursive nonlinear tests to macroeconomic events affecting the U.S. dollar/U.K. pound sterling exchange rate. The focus is limited to the log differences of the exchange rate at weekly frequency. This is the interval over which most nonlinear activity seems to take place, and the log-differences transformation is by far the most studied in the empirical literature on exchange rates. First, we used the graphics of the recursive nonlinearity tests to pick out the periods when each test moved dramatically, rising through its critical level or dropping back below it. From these observations, we traced the corresponding week and checked past issues of *The Economist* magazine for relevant news at that date. In particular, we looked for news identifying changes in government policy as to intervention in the foreign-exchange market, or news that could be interpreted as suggesting a shift in the fundamental determinants of the exchange rate. Of course, if the market is subject to fads or speculative bubbles, the appearance or disappearance of nonlinear dynamics may be unrelated to the arrival of any hard news but may only reflect a spreading misperception in the market or spreading awareness that average market expectations are incorrect.

The results of this exercise are reported in Table 3.6. Naturally, such an investigation is open to the charge that *ex post* any investigator can find some event to explain why exchange-rate behavior changed in any given week. That is to say that, *ex ante*, the news cited as an explanation for nonlinear behavior in a given week may not have been identifiable as such at the time. However, it is striking that just by examining a univariate series in isolation, these statistical tests for nonlinearity were capable of identifying such important events as the end of the fixed-exchange-rate regime in October 1977, or the 1978 decision by U.S. President Carter to abandon the noninterventionist policy and actively defend the dollar in October 1978, and the similar U-turn by President Reagan, who switched to a interventionist policy with the decision to stop the dollar's rise at the September 1985 summit of G7 leaders at the Plaza Hotel in New York. These three events suggest that models of discontinuous intervention could successfully exploit nonlinearities identified in the data. On the other hand, there are periods picked up by the nonlinearity tests for which there is no directly relevant news reported in the press. This suggests that some nonlinearities in exchange-rate data are independent of economic fundamentals and might be better explained by market psychology models such as those based on fads, chartists, and noise traders (see e.g., Frankel and Froot 1986; Scharfstein and Stein 1990; Delong et al. 1991; Banerjee 1992; Kirman 1993). In this case, bubbles burst not because of the arrival of some new information, but simply because enough agents in the market have learned that average market expectations are mistaken.

7   Conclusions

We may draw four conclusions from the empirical part of this study. First, the comparison of weekly and monthly data even in the full-sample analysis

Table 3.6. *Dates of significant indication of nonlinearity*

Date	Statistics	News
Jan. 28, 1974	Sharp rise in KEENAN (but not significant)	United States liberalizes international capital flows on Jan. 29, 1974. The reserve requirement on US deposits makes the dollar cheaper in London than in New York.
June 16, 1975	Sharp drop in KEENAN	Greenspan as chairman of Council of Economic Advisers announces the end of the sharpest US recession since World War II.
June 21, 1976	Sharp rise in KEENAN (but not significant)	Bank of England fails in attempt to block 4-month dive in Sterling due to liquidity from new Euromarket. US envoys to G5 meeting in Paris criticize the poor state of the UK economy.
Oct. 11, 1976	Sharp drop in KEENAN	Callaghan Government faced with domestic crisis seeks an International Monetary Fund (IMF) loan to stem slump in Sterling.
Oct. 18, 1976	TSAY turns significant	UK announcement shows soaring money supply. Deutch mark (DM) revalued upward in Snake.
Oct. 31,1977	TSAY drops sharply but remains significant	Sterling FLOATS as Bank of England abandons intervention. Expected relaxation of exchange controls does not appear in Healy's minibudget.
Oct. 30, 1978	TSAY drops to below significant level	Following poor reaction to economic program, Carter takes strong action to defend dollar: Fed doubles swaps with other Central Banks. United States borrows Special drawing rights (SDRS) from IMF for first time.
Sept. 10, 1979	Sharp rise in KEENAN (but not significant)	Basle meeting of Central Bank governors chooses not to realign EMS. Thatcher U-turn on selling North Sea oil, postponing privatization of British Petroleum
Aug. 10, 1981	Sharp drop in KEENAN	Reagan signs record tax break and sacks air-traffic controllers. Dollar and yen soar. Bank of England suspends MLR, abolishes reserve asset requirement, and cuts banks' cash ratio.

Table 3.6. *(cont.) Dates of significant indication of nonlinearity*

Date	Statistics	News
Mar. 18, 1985	Peak in KEENAN (5%) and in McLEOD–LI(1%)	Ohio Savings and Loan failure prompts bursting of dollar bubble. Volcker announces Fed is ready to lend. Moderate tax cuts in Lawson budget please Forex market. Pound soars.
Apr. 1, 1985	Sharp drop in RESET	United States announces faster money growth than expected. Volcker indicates dollar may fall.
Apr. 8, 1985	Sharp drop in KEENAN	Revised US GNP figures prove poor. Huge U.S. trade deficit ($11.4 billon) announced.
Apr. 15, 1985	RESET2 and TSAY rise	Dollar recovers despite Securities & Exchange Commission closing of a New Jersey trader.
Apr. 29, 1985	Sharp drop in RESET2	France obstacles GATT at Bonn G7 summit. British Gas privatization announced.
Aug. 5, 1985	Sharp rise in RESET2	United States announces record $13.4 billion trade deficit as Congress passes disappointingly big budget.
Sept. 16, 1985	Sharp drop in RESET2	EMS entry speculated as UK launches $2.5 billion floating rate note issue to rebuild reserves.
Sept. 23, 1985	Peak in TSAY	Plaza meeting. Reagan. performs U-turn abandoning nonintervention-ist stance to organize concerted effort to drive the dollar down. For the first time, United States becomes net debtor.
Feb. 24, 1986	Sharp drop in TSAY	Federal Reserve and US Treasury disagree publicly on dollar. Oil prices fall.

indicates that nonlinearity is much more pronounced at the higher frequency. This is to be expected as swings of opinion and speculative forces may dominate the market in the short run and fundamentals may dominate in the longer run. This is consistent with the contradictory picture of investor behavior portrayed in MacDonald and Taylor (1992) according to whom the market may hold irrational short-term expectations simultaneously with rational long-term expectations. The second conclusion is that when sample data are taken as a whole, there is only relatively weak evidence of nonlinearity in the mean. However, the recursive analysis reinforces the picture of separate episodes of significant nonlinear dependence. The third point that we can make is that nonlinearity seems to be found even in the residuals of the random-walk model and the GARCH residuals. Even after filtering these residuals with an AR(4), recursive nonlinearity tests exceed their critical levels at several points within the sample. This implies that the superior out-of-sample forecasting performance of the random-walk relative to structural exchange-rate models is likely to be uninformative as it is based on the comparison of two misspecified models. It also suggests that any well-specified model of exchange-rate determination must account for this observed periodic nonlinear dependence, which the GARCH specification fails to pick up. We also have found, admittedly to our initial surprise, little association between those periods indicating first-moment nonlinearity and periods of high volatility, suggesting that if GARCH processes are being used to approximate first-moment misspecification, then perhaps it may be more appropriate to consider respecifying the conditional first moment before formalizing our ignorance by fitting a GARCH model to the second moment.

We also emphasize that if economically meaningful behavior is restricted to approximately linear parts of the phase space, then nonlinearity in the first moment may be difficult to detect in economic data using standard methods, although questions of scale, both in terms of units of time and in the relative range of the state variables' variation, are critical in deciding whether linear approximations are likely to be adequate. Conditional inference may then provide a more relevant statistical framework for the detection of nonlinearity than the unconditional approach currently adopted.

REFERENCES

Banerjee, A. (1992). A simple model of herd behavior, *Q. J. Econ.* **107**(3), 797–817.

Barndorff-Nielsen, O. E., and Cox, D. R. (1994). *Inference and Asymptotics, Monographs on Statistics and Applied Probability* No. 52, Chapman and Hall, London.

Bera, A. K., and McKenzie, C. (1986). Alternative forms and properties of the score test, *J. App. Stat*, **13**(1) 13–25.

Brock, W., Dechert, W., and Scheinkman, J. (1987). A test for independence based on the correlation dimension, Discussion Paper No. 8702. Department of Economics, University of Wisconsin, Madison, WI.

Calzolari, G., and Fiorentini, G. (1992). Alternative methods for GARCH estimation, Working Paper No. 44, Dipartmento Statistico, Universita degli Studi di Firenze.

Cox, D. R. (1958). Some problems connected with statistical inference, *Ann. Math. Stat.*, **29**, 357–72.

(1980). Local ancillarity, *Biometrika*, **67**, 273–8.

Cox, D. R., and Hinkley, D. V. (1974). *Theoretical Statistics*, Chapman and Hall, London.

Critchley, F., Marriott, P., and Salmon, M. (1996). On the differential geometry of the Wald test with nonlinear restrictions, *Econometrica*, Sept.

Davidson, R., and MacKinnon, J. (1983). Small sample properties of alternative forms of the LM test, *Econ. Lett.* **12**, 269–75.

DeLong, B., Shleifer, A., Summers, L., and Waldmann, R. (1991). The survival of noise traders in financial markets, *J. Business*, **65**, 1–19.

Efron, B. (1975). Defining the curvature of a statistical problem (with applications to second-order efficiency) with discussion, *Ann. Stat.* **3**, 1189–1242.

Efron, B., and Hinkley, D. V. (1978). Assessing the accuracy of the maximum likelihood estimator: observed versus expected information, *Biometrika* **65**, 457–82.

Engle, R. (1982). Autoregressive conditionl heteroscedasticity with estimates of the variance of United Kingdom inflation, *Econometrica*, **50**(4), 987–1000.

Fisher, R. A. (1925). Theory of statistical estimation, *Proc. Cambridge Philos. Soc.*, **22**, 700–720.

(1934). Two new properties of mathematical likelihood, *Proc, Roy Soc. Ser A*, **144**, 285–307.

(1935). The logic of inductive inference, *J. Roy. Stat. Sco.* **98**, 35–54.

Frankel, J., and Froot, K. (1986). A tale of fundamentalists and chartists, NBER Working Paper No. 1854.

Granger, C. W. J., and Terasvirta, T. (1993). *Modeling nonlinear economic relations*, Advanced Texts in Econometrics, Oxford Univeristy Press, Oxford, England.

Gregory, A., and Veall, M. R. (1985). Formulating Wald tests of nonlinear restrictions, *Econometrica*, **50**, 549–63.

Guarda, P., and Slamon, M. (1993). Nonlinearity and exchange rate dynamics, *Cuardenos Economicos*, Special Issue on Exchange Rates and Foreign Exchange Markets, **53**(1), 173–219.

Hansen, B. (1992). Testing for parameter instability in linear models, *J. Policy Model*, **14**(4), 517–33.

Hsieh, D., and LeBaron, B. (1988). Finite sample properties of the BDS statistic, Working Paper, University of Chicago, Chicago. IL and University of Wasconsin at Madison, Madison. WI.

Keenan, D. M. (1985). A Turkey nonadditivity-type test for time series nonlinearity, *Biometrika*, **72**(1), 39–44.

Kiefer, N., and Salmon, M. (1983). Testing normality in econometric models, *Econ. Lett.*, **11**, 123–27.

Kirman, A. (1993). Ants, rationality and recruitment, *Q. J. Econ.*, **11**, 137–56.

Lee, T.-H., White, H., and Granger, C. W. J. (1993). Testing for neglected nonlinearity in time series models: a comparison of neural network methods and alternative tests, *J. Econ.*, **56**, 269–90.

Levich, (1979). On the efficiency of foreign exchange markets. In *International Economic Policy: Theory and Evidence*, eds. R. Dornbusch, and J. Frenkel, Johns Hopkins University Press.

McDonald, R. and Taylor, M. (1992). Exchange rate economics: a survey, *Int. Monetary Fund Staff Pap.*, **39**, 1–57.

McLeod, A. I., and Li, W. K. (1983). Diagnostic checking ARMA time series models using squared-residual autocorrelation, *J. Time Ser. Anal.*, **4**(4), 269–73.

Ramsey, J. (1969). Tersts for specification errors in classical linear least squares regression analysis, *J. Roy. Stat. Soc. Ser. B*, 350–71.

Ravishankar, N., Melnick, E. L., and Tsai, C.-H. (1990). Differential geometry of ARMA models, *J. Time Ser. Anal.*, **11**(3), 259–74. Salmon, M. (1993). Conditional inference, ancillarity and robustness in econometrics, mimeo, European University Institute,

Scharfstein, D., and Stein, J. (1990). Herd behavior and investment, *Am. Econ. Rev.*, **80**(3), 465–79.

Seber, G. A. F., and Wild, C. J. (1989). *Nonlinear Regression*, Wiley, New York.

Severini, T. A. (1990). Conditional properties of likelihood based significance tests, *Biometrika*, **77**(2), 343–52.

Thursby, J., and Schmidt, P. (1977). Some properties of tests for specification error in a linear regression, *J. Am. Stat. Assoc.*, **72**(359), 635–641.

Tsay, R. (1986). Nonlinearity tests for time series, *Biometrika*, **73**(2), 461–6.

White, H. (1989). An additional hidden unit test for neglected nonlinearity in multilayer feed forword networks, Proceedings of the International Joint Conference on Neural Networks, Washington DC (San Diego, SOS Printing), Vol 2: 451–5.

CHAPTER 4

Chaos and nonlinear dynamics in futures markets

Apostolos Serletis and Paul Dormaar

We test for deterministic chaos in 13 spot-month futures prices—Australian dollar, British pound, Canadian dollar, crude oil, copper, deutsche mark, gold, heating oil, unleaded gas, Japanese yen, platinum, Swiss franc, and silver. We use weekly data and two of the most reputable (nonparametric) inference methods: the Brock–Dechert–Scheinkman test for whiteness and the Nychka–Ellner–Gallant–McCaffrey test for positivity of the dominant Lyapunov exponent. We claim successful detection of chaos only in the Australian dollar, the Japanese yen, and possibly copper.

1   Introduction

The analysis and modeling of futures prices behavior has attracted a great deal of attention in the literature during the past three decades, ever since Samuelson (1965) advanced the hypothesis that futures prices follow a martingale. Although most of the empirical tests of the martingale model are based on linear models, interest in deterministic chaotic dynamics (i.e., the dynamics of systems that are both deterministic and stochastic) has recently experienced a tremendous rate of development, and the literature is still growing.

Besides its obvious intellectual appeal, chaos is interesting because of its ability to generate chaotic output that mimics the output of stochastic systems, thereby offering an alternative explanation for the behavior of asset prices. So, there is need to test for the presence of chaos. If, for example, chaos can be shown to exist, the implication would be that profitable, nonlinearity-based trading rules exist (at least in the short run and provided that the actual generating mechanism is known), raising questions about the efficient-markets hypothesis. Prediction, however, over long periods is all but impossible, because of the sensitive dependence on the initial-conditions property of chaos.

This paper tests for deterministic chaos in 13 futures markets, using weekly data. In doing so, we use two of the most reputable (nonparametric) inference

113

methods: the BDS (Brock, Dechert, and Scheinkman 1987) test for whiteness (independent and identically distributed observations) and the Lyapunov exponent estimator of Nychka et al. (1992). Both of these tests are explicitly derived for use with noisy data, with the latter being currently the only credible candidate as a test for chaos (Barnett et al. 1995).

The paper is organized as follows: Section 2 provides a review of the literature with respect to the martingale hypothesis and chaos. Section 3 provides a description of the key features of the two tests for chaos, focusing explicitly on each test's ability to detect chaos. Section 4 analyzes the univariate time-series properties of the 13 futures prices, and Section 5 presents the results of the BDS test and the Nychka et al. (1992) Lyapunov exponent test. Section 6 concludes the paper with a discussion of the implications of the results.

2   Theoretical foundations

2.1   *Martingale hypothesis*

The analysis and modeling of commodity futures price behavior has attracted a great deal of attention in the literature, ever since Samuelson (1965) advanced the hypothesis that (under the assumption that spot prices follow a stationary first-order autoregressive process, and futures prices are unbiased estimates for the settlement spot price) future prices follow a martingale process. Symbolically, a stochastic process x_t follows a martingale if

$$E_t(x_{t+1}|\Omega_t) = x_t,$$

where Ω_t is the time, t, information set that includes x_{t-j}, $j \geq 0$. The above equation says that if x_t follows a martingale, the best forecast of x_{t+1} that could be constructed on the basis of current information, Ω_t, would equal x_t. Alternatively, the martingale model implies that $(x_{t+1} - x_t)$ is a fair game:

$$E_t[(x_{t+1} - x_t)|\Omega_t] = 0$$

Clearly, x_t is a martingale if and only if $(x_{t+1} - x_t)$ is a fair game. It is for this reason that fair games are sometimes called martingale differences.

Note that the martingale difference model is less restrictive than the random-walk model – the forerunner of the theory of efficient capital markets. In particular, the martingale difference requires only independence of the conditional expectation of price changes from the available information, whereas the (more restrictive) random-walk model requires this and also independence involving the higher conditional moments of the probability distribution of price changes. By not requiring probabilistic independence between successive price changes, the martingale difference model is entirely consistent with the fact that price changes, although uncorrelated, tend not to be independent over time but to have clusters of volatility and tranquility (i.e., serial dependence in the higher conditional moments) – a phenomenon originally noted for stock-market prices by Mandelbrot (1963) and Fama (1965).

2.2   *Chaos*

Although most of the empirical tests of the martingale model are based on linear models, interest in deterministic chaotic processes has recently experienced a tremendous rate of development. Such processes have first- and second-moment properties that are the same as for white-noise processes – this is why they are also called white chaos. Deterministic white chaos represents a radical change of perspective in the explanation of fluctuations observed in economic time series. In this view, the fluctuations and irregularities observed in economic time series receive an endogenous explanation and are traced back to the strong nonlinear deterministic structure that can pervade the economic system.

Although a universally accepted and comprehensive characterization of chaos is still lacking, we follow the usage of Eckmann and Ruelle (1985) and take chaos to be synonymous with sensitive dependence on initial conditions. To be more specific, sensitivity to initial conditions implies that nearby identical chaotic systems in slightly different states will rapidly evolve toward very different states. This means that if asset prices have actually been generated by deterministic chaotic systems, then asset price changes will (at least in principle) be predictable over short periods, although prediction over long periods is all but impossible because of the sensitive dependence on initial conditions.

We test for deterministic chaos using two of the most reputable (nonparametric) inference methods – the BDS (Brock et al. 1987) test and the Lyapunov exponent estimator of Nychka, Ellner, Gallant, and McCaffrey (1992). The BDS test is currently the best available test for whiteness and can be used to test for residual nonlinear dependence, after any linear structure has been removed through prewhitening. The Nychka–Ellner–Gallant–McCaffrey (NEGM) test (Nychka et al. 1992) is currently the most credible nonparametric test for positivity of the maximum Lyapunov exponent. Both tests are explicitly derived for use with noisy data, with the latter being currently the only credible candidate for a test for chaos (Barnett et al. 1995).

Intuitively, Lyapunov exponents measure average exponential divergence or convergence between trajectories that differ only in having an infinitesimally small difference in their initial conditions, thereby providing a precise quantitative definition of sensitive dependence on initial conditions. If they are all negative, the system is stable, but if at least one of them is positive, then the system is unstable and forward orbits starting from close initial conditions will diverge on average at an exponential rate given by the same Lyapunov exponent. In fact, all chaotic systems have a positive Lyapunov exponent and so are always unstable. In what follows, we describe the BDS test for whiteness and the NEGM test for positivity of the maximum Lyapunov exponent, focusing explicit attention on each test's ability to detect chaos.

3   Testing methodology

We test for whiteness and chaos using the BDS test Brock et al. (1987) and the NEGM Lyapunov exponent estimator (Nychka et al. 1992). We describe these tests in Sections 3.1 and 3.2.

3.1   *BDS test*

The BDS test is based on the Grassberger and Procaccia (1983) correlation integral as the test statistic. In particular, under the null hypothesis of whiteness (independent and identically distributed observations), the BDS statistic is

$$W(T, m, \varepsilon) = \frac{\sqrt{T}[C(T, m, \varepsilon) - C(T, 1, \varepsilon)^m]}{\sigma(T, m, \varepsilon)},$$

where $C(T, m, \varepsilon)$ is the correlation function (integral), $T = N - m + 1$; N is the length of the series; m is the embedding dimension; ε is a sufficiently small number; and $\sigma(T, m, \varepsilon)$ is an estimate of the asymptotic standard error of $[C(T, m, \varepsilon) - C(T, 1, \varepsilon)^m]$. The BDS statistic converges in distribution to a standardized normal random variable (see, Brock et al. 1987).

Because the asymptotic distribution of the BDS test statistic is known under the null hypothesis of whiteness, the BDS test provides a direct (formal) statistical test for whiteness against dependence, which includes both nonwhite linear and nonwhite nonlinear dependence. Hence, the BDS test does not currently provide a direct test for nonlinearity or for chaos, because the sampling distribution of the test statistic is not known (either in finite samples or asymptotically) under the null hypothesis of nonlinearity, linearity, or chaos. It is, however, possible to use the BDS test to produce indirect evidence about nonlinear dependence (whether chaotic, that is, nonlinear deterministic, or stochastic), which is necessary but not sufficient for chaos [see Barnett and Hinich (1992), and Barnett et al. (1995) for a discussion of these issues].

3.2   *Nychka et al. (1992) Lyapunov exponent estimator*

The distinctive feature of chaotic systems is sensitive dependence on initial conditions (see, e.g., Eckmann and Ruelle 1985), that is, exponential divergence of trajectories with similar initial conditions. The most important tool for diagnosing the presence of sensitive dependence on initial conditions (and thereby chaoticity) in a dynamic system is provided by the dominant Lyapunov exponent, λ. This exponent measures the average exponential divergence or convergence between trajectories that have infinitesimally small differences in their initial conditions and remains well defined for noisy systems (see Kifer 1986). A bounded system with a positive Lyapunov exponent is an operational definition of chaotic behavior.

Consider the time series $\{x_t\}$. We can create the trajectory

$$X_t = F(X_{t-1}), F : R^m \to R^m \qquad (4.1)$$

where $X_t = (x_t, x_{t-1}, \ldots, x_{t-m+1})^T$ and $F(X_{t-1}) = [f(x_{t-1}, \ldots, x_{t-m}), x_{t-1}, \ldots, x_{t-m+1}]^T$. Gencay and Dechert (1992) show that the dynamic system (4.1) is topologically equivalent to the true (but unknown) system

$$Y_t = G(Y_{t-1}), G : R^n \to R^n$$

where $m \geq 2n + 1$ and x is seen through an observation function

$$x_t = h(Y_t), h : R^n \to R$$

Equation (4.1) can be written more generally as

$$
\begin{pmatrix} x_t \\ x_{t-L} \\ \vdots \\ x_{t-mL+L} \end{pmatrix}
=
\begin{pmatrix} f(x_{t-L}, \ldots, x_{t-mL}) \\ x_{t-L} \\ \vdots \\ x_{t-mL+L} \end{pmatrix}
+
\begin{pmatrix} e_t \\ 0 \\ \vdots \\ 0 \end{pmatrix},
\qquad (4.2)
$$

which reduces to $x_t = f(x_{t-L}, \ldots, x_{t-mL}) + e_t$ where m is the length of the embedding, L is the number of lags between observations, and $\{e_t\}$ is a sequence of zero mean (and unknown constant variance) independent random perturbations.

The definition of the dominant Lyapunov exponent, λ, can be formulated more precisely as follows: Let $X_0, X_0' \in R^m$ denote two "nearby" initial state vectors. After M iterations of model (4.2) with the same random shock, we have (using a truncated Taylor approximation)

$$\|X_M - X_M'\| = \|F^M(X_0) - F^M(X_0')\| \cong \|(DF^M)_{X_0}(X_0 - X_0')\|,$$

where F^M is the Mth iterate of F and $(DF^M)_{X_0}$ is the Jacobian matrix of F evaluated at X_0. By application of the chain rule for differentiation, it is possible to show that

$$\|X_M - X_M'\| = \|P_M(X_0 - X_0')\|,$$

where $P_M = J_M J_{M-1} \ldots J_1$ and $J_t = (DF)_{X_t}$. Letting $v_1(M)$ denote the largest eigenvalue of $P_M^T P_M$, the formal definition of the dominant Lyapunov exponent, λ, is

$$\lambda = \lim_{M \to \infty} \frac{1}{2M} \log |v_1(M)|.$$

In this setting, λ gives the long-term rate of divergence or convergence between trajectories. A positive λ measures exponential divergence of two nearby trajectories [and is often used as a definition of chaos (see, e.g., Deneckere and Pelikan 1986)], whereas a negative λ measures exponential convergence of two nearby trajectories. Regression methods generate estimates of λ through the intermediate step of estimating the individual Jacobian matrices.

In what follows we use the Nychka et al. (1992) Jacobian-based method and the LENNS program (see Ellner, Nychka, and Gallant 1992) to estimate the dominant Lyapunov exponent. In particular, we use a neural-network (or equivalently neural net) model to estimate f by nonlinear least squares, and use the estimated $\hat{f}$ and the data $\{x_t\}$ to produce an estimate of the dominant Lyapunov exponent. In doing so, we follow the protocol described by Nychka et al. (1992).

The predominant model in statistical research on neural nets is the single-(hidden) layer feedforward network with a single output. In the present context, it can be written as

$$\hat{f}(X_t, \theta) = \alpha + \sum_{j=1}^{k} \beta_j \psi \left(\omega_j + \gamma_j^T X_t \right),$$

where $X \epsilon R^m$ is the input, ψ is a known (hidden) univariate nonlinear activation function, $\theta = (\alpha, \beta, \omega, \gamma)$ is the parameter vector, $\gamma_j = (\gamma_{1j}, \gamma_{2j}, \ldots, \gamma_{mj})^T$, $\beta \epsilon R^k$ represents hidden unit weights, $\omega \epsilon R^k$, $\gamma \epsilon R^{k \times m}$ represent input weights to the hidden units, and k is the number of units in the hidden layer of the neural net. Note that there are $[k(m+2)+1]$ free parameters in this model.

Given a data set of inputs and their associated outputs, the network parameter vector, θ, is fitted by nonlinear least squares to formulate accurate map estimates. Because appropriate values of L, m, and k are unknown, the value of the triple (L, m, k) is chosen so that the Bayesian information criterion (BIC) is minimized. Gallant and White (1992) have shown that we can then use $\hat{J}_t$, the estimate of the Jacobian matrix J_t obtained from the approximate map $\hat{f}$, as a nonparametric estimator of J_t. The estimate of the dominant Lyapunov exponent then is

$$\hat{\lambda} = \frac{1}{2T} \log |\hat{v}_1(T)|,$$

where $\hat{v}_1(T)$ is the largest eigenvalue of $\hat{P}_T^T \hat{P}_T$ and where $\hat{P}_T = \hat{J}_T \hat{J}_{T-1} \ldots \hat{J}_1$.

4   Data trends, delinearization, and transformation

The data include weekly observations from Tick Data, Inc., on spot-month futures prices for the Australian dollar, British pound, Canadian dollar, crude oil, copper, deutsche mark, gold, heating oil, unleaded gas, Japanese yen, platinum, Swiss franc, and silver. Table 4.1 reports some summary statistics including (in the first two columns) details regarding the sample period and number of observations for each series.

Before conducting nonlinear dynamic analysis, the data must be rendered stationary, delinearized (by replacing the stationary data with residuals from an autoregression of the data), and transformed (if necessary) as described by Hsieh (1991). Table 4.1 reports some summary statistics along with tests for stochastic trends in the autoregressive (AR) representation of each individual time series. The unit root tests were conducted by estimating (by ordinary least squares) the following augmented Dickey–Fuller (ADF) regression (Dickey and Fuller 1981).

$$\Delta z_t = a_0 + a_1 t + a_2 z_{t-1} + \sum_{i=1}^{l} c_i \Delta z_{t-i} + \varepsilon_t, \qquad (4.3)$$

where z_t is the series under consideration (in logs), and l is selected to be large enough to ensure that ε_t is white noise. The null hypothesis of a single unit root is rejected if a_2 is negative and significantly different from zero.

The last two columns of Table 4.1 contain ADF tests of the null hypothesis that a single unit root exists in the logarithm of each series (z_t) as well as in the first (logged) difference of the series (Δz_t). Clearly, the null hypothesis of a unit root in log levels cannot be rejected, whereas the null hypothesis of a second unit root is rejected. Hence, we conclude that these series are characterized as $I(1)$, that is, having a stochastic trend. This evidence is consistent with the prevalent view that most time series are characterized by a stochastic rather than deterministic nonstationarity (see, e.g., Nelson and Plosser 1982).

Because a stochastic trend has been confirmed for each of the series, the data are rendered stationary by taking first differences of logarithms. Also, because we are interested in nonlinear dependence, we remove any linear dependence in the stationary data by fitting the best possible linear model. In particular, we prefilter the growth rates by the following autoregression:

$$\Delta z_t = b_0 + \sum_{j=1}^{q} b_j \Delta z_{t-j} + \varepsilon_t, \qquad \varepsilon_t | I_{t-1} \sim N(0, w_0), \qquad (4.4)$$

using for each series the number of lags, q, for which the Ljung–Box $Q(23)$ statistic is not significant at the 5% level (Ljung and Box 1978). This identifies q as 4 for crude oil, 10 for gold, 2 for the Japanese yen, 8 for silver, and 1 for each of the other series (see Table 4.2). The Akaike information criterion (AIC, Akaike 1978) and the BIC (Schwarz 1978) were also used. The lags identified by the AIC (Schwarz) are: Australian dollar 1 (1), British pound 1 (1), Canadian dollar 5 (1), crude oil 1 (1), copper 1 (1), deutsche mark 1 (1), gold 2 (2), heating oil 12 (1), unleaded gas 1 (1), Japanese yen 2 (2), platinum 3 (1), Swiss franc 3 (1), and silver 8 (1).

Table 4.1 Summary statistics for weekly logged differences and unit root tests [in log levels (z_t) and logged differences (Δz_t)]

Series	Sample period	Number observations	Mean	Standard deviation	Skewness	Kurtosis	ADF unit root tests	
							z_t	Δz_t
Australian dollar	Jan. 13, 1987 –June 2, 1993	330	0.014	1.329	-1.307 (0.134)	4.625(0.268)	-2.42	-6.77*
British pound	Feb. 13, 1975 –June 2, 1993	955	-0.043	1.660	-0.364 (0.079)	3.558 (0.158)	-1.92	-5.96*
Canadian dollar	Jan. 17, 1977 –June 2, 1993	854	-0.026	0.628	-0.438 (0.084)	3.424 (0.167)	-1.87	-6.92*
Crude oil	Mar. 30, 1983–June 2, 1993	530	-0.072	4.767	-0.806 (0.106)	8.834 (0.212)	-2.54	-5.46*
Copper	Aug. 22, 1972–Dec. 27, 1989	905	0.079	4.078	-0.107 (0.081)	2.640 (0.162)	-2.50	-5.24*
Deutsche mark	Feb. 13, 1975 –June 2, 1993	955	0.038	1.633	0.092 (0.079)	1.713 (0.158)	-1.65	-5.03*
Gold	Jan. 2, 1975 –June 2, 1993	961	0.079	3.046	0.221 (0.079)	13.855 (0.158)	-1.71	-4.74*
Heating oil	Mar. 6, 1979 –June 2, 1993	734	-0.009	4.616	-0.469 (0.090)	3.726 (0.180)	-2.85	-6.53*
Unleaded gas	Dec. 3, 1984 –June 2, 1993	439	-0.045	5.199	-0.070 (0.117)	3.076 (0.233)	-2.73	-5.13*
Japanese yen	Nov. 3, 1976 –June 2, 1993	865	0.117	1.573	0.453 (0.083)	2.362 (0.166)	-2.15	-4.79*
Platinum	Aug. 22, 1972–June 2, 1993	1,072	0.085	4.345	-0.237 (0.075)	4.409 (0.149)	-1.79	-5.31*
Swiss frank	Feb. 13, 1975 –June 2, 1993	955	0.056	1.896	0.322 (0.079)	1.234 (0.158)	-2.20	-5.25*
Silver	July 29, 1971 –June 2, 1993	1,140	0.079	4.894	-0.659 (0.072)	10.457 (0.145)	-2.15	-5.89*

Notes: Numbers in parentheses are standard errors. Unit root tests are conducted using the ADF regression, $\Delta z_t = a_0 + a_1 t + a_2 z_{t-1} + \sum_{i=1}^{l} c_i \Delta z_{t-i} + e_t$. The 90% critical value for the ADF test statistics is -3.12. An asterisk indicates significance at the 10% level.

Table 4.2. *Diagnostics of AR models under the Lung–Box (1978) $Q(23)$ test statistic*

$$\Delta z_t = b_0 + \sum_{j=1}^{q} b_j \Delta z_{t-j} + \varepsilon_t, \; \varepsilon_t | I_{t-1} \sim N(0, w_0)$$

		AR error-term diagnostics			
Series	AR lag, q	Q-Statistic	ARCH	Kurtosis	Skewness
Australian dollar	1	14.715	0.071	4.729 (0.268)	−1.320 (0.134)
British pound	1	22.053	12.369*	3.609 (0.158)	−0.362 (0.079)
Canadian dollar	1	24.317	3.404	3.447 (0.167)	−0.447 (0.084)
Crude oil	4	33.517	12.004*	8.551 (0.213)	−0.749 (0.107)
Copper	1	30.343	8.316*	2.628 (0.162)	−0.107 (0.081)
Deutsche mark	1	19.403	31.924*	1.685 (0.158)	0.100 (0.079)
Gold	10	31.053	158.025*	12.834 (0.158)	0.157 (0.079)
Heating oil	1	30.609	58.959*	3.408 (0.180)	−0.398 (0.090)
Unleaded gas	1	34.084	13.231*	3.115 (0.233)	−0.061 (0.117)
Japanese yen	2	29.200	3.335	2.517 (0.166)	0.457 (0.083)
Platinum	1	24.256	56.168*	4.370 (0.149)	−0.241 (0.075)
Swiss frank	1	17.811	22.210*	1.203 (0.158)	0.331 (0.079)
Silver	8	33.963	34.953*	8.352 (0.145)	−0.594 (0.073)

Notes: Numbers in parentheses are standard errors. The Q-statistic is distributed as a $\chi^2(23)$ on the null of no autocorrelation. ARCH is Engle's (1982) autoregressive conditional heteroskedasticity (ARCH) test distributed as a $\chi^2(1)$ on the null of no ARCH. An asterisk next to a Q-statistic or an ARCH statistic indicates significance at the 5% level; the 5% critical value for the Q-statistic is 35.173 and for the ARCH statistic is 3.842.

Although the autocorrelation diagnostics in Table 4.2 indicate that the chosen AR models adequately remove linear dependence in the stationary data, the autoregressive conditional heteroskedasticity (ARCH) test suggests the presence of a time-varying variance. Since variance-nonlinearity could be generated by either a (stochastic) ARCH process or a deterministic process, we use Bollerslev's (1986) generalized autoregressive conditional heteroskedasticity (GARCH) model to remove any stochastic nonlinear dependence. This model is a generalization of the pure ARCH model, originally from Engle (1982). GARCH models are useful in detecting nonlinear patterns in variance but not destroying any signs of deterministic structural shifts in a model (see, e.g., Lamoreux and Lastrapes 1990). Using the same AR structure as before, we estimate the following GARCH (1,1) model:

$$\Delta z_t = b_0 + \sum_{j=1}^{q} b_j \Delta z_{t-j} + \varepsilon_t, \quad \varepsilon_t | I_{t-1} \sim N(0, h_t)$$

$$h_t = w_0 + \alpha_1 \varepsilon_{t-1}^2 + \beta h_{t-1} \tag{4.5}$$

where $N(0, h_t)$ represents the normal distribution with mean zero and variance h_t.

The diagnostic tests are given in Table 4.3. First, estimated coefficients of the ARCH term, α_1, and the GARCH term, β_1, are positive and significant at the 5% level. Also, the Q-test finds no linear dependence and the ARCH test finds no ARCH effects, suggesting that the lag structure of the conditional variance is correctly identified. On the basis of these results, Lyapunov exponent estimates are next calculated for the standardized residuals, $\varepsilon_t / \hat{h}_t^{1/2}$, where ε_t is the residual of the mean equation and $\hat{h}_t$ is its estimated (time-varying) variance. We also use the BDS to test the null hypothesis of independent random variables (against the alternative of nonindependent random variables, thereby treating the BDS as an omnibus two-sided test) for the raw (log-differenced) data, the AR residuals, as well as the GARCH (1,1) standardized residuals.

5   Empirical results

5.1   *Results with the BDS test*

We now apply the BDS test of whiteness to the raw data, the AR residuals, and the GARCH (1,1) standardized residuals. The results are presented in Table 4.4 for dimensions 2 through 5 and ε equaling 0.5, 1, 1.5, and 2 standard deviations of the data. In the case of the raw data and the AR residuals, we use the asymptotic distribution of the BDS, whereas in the case of the GARCH standardized residuals, we use Hsieh's (1991, Table XIII) simulated critical values of the BDS. In this regard, Brock (1986) proved that the asymptotic distribution of the BDS test statistic is not altered by using residuals instead of raw data in linear models, and his theorem also can be extended to residuals of some nonlinear models, but not to ARCH-type models.

Except for the Australian dollar, in every case the BDS test on the raw data rejects the null hypothesis of independent and identically distributed observations, a finding that is consistent with deterministic chaos. Moreover, the BDS test statistics for the AR residuals do not differ substantially from those using the raw data, suggesting that the BDS test is not merely picking up linear dependence, but is in fact detecting strong nonlinear dependence in the data. The GARCH (1,1) model, however, removes considerable stochastic nonlinear dependence from the raw data. In particular, the BDS statistics for the standardized GARCH (1,1) residuals indicate some dependence for only the British pound, the Canadian dollar, crude oil, copper, and the Japanese yen, which is consistent with deterministic chaos.

5.2   *Results with the Nychka et al. test*

With the NEGM Lyapunov exponent test, the BIC point estimates of the dominant Lyapunov exponent for each parameter (L, m, k) are displayed in

Table 4.3 GARCH (1,1) Parameter estimates and error-term diagnostics

$$\Delta z_t = b_0 + \sum_{j=1}^{q} b_j \Delta z_{t-j} + \varepsilon_t, \; \varepsilon_t | I_{t-1} \sim N(0, h_t), \; h_t = w_0 + \alpha_1 \varepsilon_{t-1}^2 + \beta_1 h_{t-1}$$

Series	AR lag, q	GARCH (1,1) parameter estimates			GARCH (1,1) error-term diagnostics			
		w_0	α_1	β_1	Q-Statistic	ARCH	Kurtosis	Skewness
Australian dollar	1	0.061 (0.7)	0.011 (0.9)	0.956 (17.4)	14.158	0.170	4.893 (0.268)	−1.355 (0.134)
British pound	1	0.150 (2.9)	0.123 (4.6)	0.831 (23.7)	18.468	1.246	2.566 (0.158)	−0.320 (0.079)
Canadian dollar	1	0.093 (3.3)	0.161 (3.8)	0.615 (6.6)	24.021	0.197	3.925 (0.167)	−0.754 (0.084)
Crude oil	4	0.231 (1.6)	0.226 (4.3)	0.802 (20.6)	27.489	0.269	3.392 (0.213)	−0.584 (0.107)
Copper	1	0.499 (3.2)	0.093 (4.3)	0.877 (33.7)	20.678	2.734	1.110 (0.123)	0.107 (0.081)
Deutsche mark	1	0.164 (3.4)	0.153 (5.2)	0.793 (21.8)	22.672	0.116	0.981 (0.158)	0.167 (0.079)
Gold	10	0.238 (3.3)	0.198 (6.4)	0.790 (28.2)	33.096	0.093	1.693 (0.158)	−0.166 (0.079)
Heating oil	1	1.189 (4.0)	0.312 (6.3)	0.666 (16.4)	21.332	0.623	2.369 (0.181)	−0.305 (0.091)
Unleaded gas	1	2.580 (3.0)	0.213 (4.0)	0.700 (11.2)	30.283	0.164	1.427 (0.233)	−0.212 (0.117)
Japanese yen	2	0.048 (3.5)	0.025 (2.9)	0.957 (86.9)	27.474	0.310	3.492 (0.166)	0.631 (0.083)
Platinum	1	0.423 (3.0)	0.095 (5.4)	0.881 (44.6)	25.816	0.477	1.456 (0.149)	0.161 (0.045)
Swiss franc	1	0.025 (1.8)	0.070 (5.0)	0.927 (67.0)	24.549	0.598	1.083 (0.158)	0.391 (0.079)
Silver	8	0.379 (3.4)	0.121 (6.2)	0.865 (45.5)	27.012	0.032	1.618 (0.145)	0.188 (0.023)

Notes: Numbers in parentheses next to the GARCH(1,1) parameter estimates are t-ratios. Numbers in parentheses next to the kurtosis and skewness numbers are standard errors. The Q-statistic is distributed as a $\chi^2(23)$ on the null of no autocorrelation. The ARCH statistic is distributed as a $\chi^2(1)$ on the null of no ARCH. An asterisk next to a Q-statistic or an ARCH statistic indicates significance at the 5% level; the 5% critical value for the Q-statistic is 35.173 and for the ARCH statistic is 3.842.

Table 4.4 BDS Statistics (at dimensions 2–10 and ε = 0.5, 1, 1.5, and 2 standard deviations of the data) for weekly future returns

ε/σ	0.5			1			1.5			2		
m	Raw data	AR residuals	Standardized GARCH residuals	Raw data	AR residuals	Standardized GARCH residuals	Raw data	AR residuals	Standardized GARCH residuals	Raw data	AR residuals	Standardized GARCH residuals
						Australian dollar						
2	0.943	0.216	-0.179	0.965	0.318	-0.194	1.324	0.444	-0.582	1.564	0.808	-0.910
3	0.526	0.332	-0.174	0.432	0.042	-0.452	0.838	0.183	-0.626	1.215	0.678	-0.422
4	1.097	0.709	0.809	0.404	0.704	-0.344	0.708	0.041	-0.726	1.099	0.542	-0.384
5	1.421	1.054	0.323	0.388	0.158	-0.202	0.529	- 0.011	-0.706	0.891	0.393	-0.410
						British pound						
2	4.027*	4.124*	0.132	3.688*	3.625*	-0.574	3.807*	3.762*	-0.536	4.379*	4.301*	0.009
3	6.617*	6.613*	0.888	5.333*	5.284*	-0.534	5.040*	4.972*	-0.966	5.442*	5.371*	-0.565
4	9.951*	9.824*	2.222*	6.680*	6.607*	-0.308	6.070*	5.989*	-0.832	6.088*	6.022*	-0.681
5	14.182*	13.879*	3.739*	8.071*	7.971*	0.131	6.977*	6.894*	-0.472	6.706*	6.641*	-0.447
						Canadian dollar						
2	5.121*	5.260*	1.248	5.320*	5.261*	1.393	5.163*	4.929*	0.879	4.410*	4.040*	0.170
3	6.730*	6.669*	1.449	6.402*	6.319*	1.274	5.847*	5.583*	0.596	4.663*	4.315*	-0.135
4	9.639*	9.628*	2.596*	7.718*	7.650*	1.678	6.418*	6.173*	0.784	4.959*	4.659*	0.134
5	11.888*	11.353*	3.046*	8.778*	8.756*	1.911	6.644*	6.476*	0.711	4.864*	4.702*	-0.042

Crude oil												
2	8.050*	7.565*	-0.001	9.928*	9.503*	-0.567	10.248*	10.099*	-1.081	8.271*	7.679*	-1.050
3	10.691*	10.265*	0.465	11.398*	11.066*	-0.568	11.603*	11.139*	-1.169	9.622*	8.680*	-1.420*
4	12.658*	12.450*	0.295	12.098*	11.900*	-0.860	12.204*	11.799*	-1.449*	10.464*	9.482*	-1.596*
5	15.874*	16.005*	0.787	13.511*	13.370*	-0.648	13.207*	12.859*	-1.263*	11.492*	10.635*	-1.464*
Copper												
2	3.663*	3.675*	-1.663*	3.917*	3.962*	-2.070*	4.224*	4.215*	-2.037*	4.076*	4.119*	-1.636*
3	5.717*	5.820*	-1.515*	6.195*	6.267*	-2.146*	6.514*	6.534*	-2.156*	6.147*	6.188*	-1.766*
4	7.509*	7.560*	-1.035	7.943*	7.979*	-1.857*	8.205*	8.217*	-1.974*	7.579*	7.592*	-1.699*
5	9.360*	9.356*	-1.071	9.041*	9.070*	-1.845*	9.188*	9.200*	-2.001*	8.627*	8.637*	-1.753*
Deutsche mark												
2	6.142*	6.293*	1.145	5.639*	5.802*	0.687	6.053*	6.214*	0.504	6.032*	6.175*	0.242
3	8.331*	8.499*	1.190	7.226*	7.465*	0.515	7.627*	7.871*	0.399	7.783*	7.984*	0.032
4	12.188*	12.309*	2.390	9.368*	9.530*	1.263	8.861*	9.031*	0.952	8.669*	8.783*	0.423
5	15.227*	15.385*	3.055*	10.866*	11.033*	1.432	9.801*	9.940*	1.146	9.338*	9.408*	0.701
Gold												
2	7.193*	8.290*	-0.198	8.192*	8.894*	-0.236	8.514*	8.327*	-0.234	7.012*	6.244*	-0.147
3	9.224*	10.383*	-0.299	9.429*	10.251*	-0.281	9.717*	9.491*	-0.486	8.669*	7.619*	-0.325
4	12.262*	13.403*	0.652	11.519*	12.177*	0.439	11.144*	10.837*	0.176	10.177*	9.049*	0.027
5	15.670*	16.590*	0.991	13.193*	13.858*	0.718	11.930*	11.673*	0.378	10.672*	9.594*	0.077
Heating oil												
2	9.163*	9.301*	0.816	9.409*	9.554*	0.156	9.818*	10.098*	-0.253	9.427*	9.803*	-0.523
3	11.547*	11.431*	1.224	11.315*	11.417*	0.425	11.597*	11.892*	-0.017	10.932*	11.162*	0.003
4	13.685*	13.478*	1.205	12.578*	12.694*	0.355	12.675*	12.988*	0.006	11.766*	11.968*	0.244
5	16.679*	16.185*	0.552	14.040*	14.089*	-0.009	13.534*	13.859*	-0.168	12.355*	12.548*	0.262

Table 4.4 (Contd.)

	ε/σ											
	0.5			1			1.5			2		
m	Raw data	AR residuals	Standardized GARCH residuals	Raw data	AR residuals	Standardized GARCH residuals	Raw data	AR residuals	Standardized GARCH residuals	Raw data	AR residuals	Standardized GARCH residuals
						Unleaded gas						
2	4.494*	4.086*	-0.411	5.376*	5.023*	-0.441	5.383*	4.978*	-0.473	4.537*	4.323*	-0.640
3	5.574*	5.195*	0.187	6.560*	6.257*	-0.272	6.757*	6.347*	-0.359	5.702*	5.457*	-0.676
4	5.889*	5.627*	0.094	6.979*	6.630*	-0.662	7.104*	6.653*	-0.691	5.970*	5.740*	-1.072
5	6.865*	6.673*	0.186	7.679*	7.302*	-0.794	7.543*	7.094*	-0.823	6.280*	6.007*	-1.241*
						Japanese yen						
2	3.836*	3.914*	2.234*	3.525*	3.254*	1.577	2.556*	2.615*	0.849	1.984*	2.158*	0.687
3	6.279*	6.471*	3.336*	5.327*	4.733*	2.141*	4.072*	3.852*	1.332	3.582*	3.179*	1.000
4	6.999*	7.147*	3.433*	6.287*	5.735*	2.474*	4.888*	4.634*	1.685	4.350*	3.748*	1.217
5	8.848*	8.268*	3.942*	7.241*	6.678*	2.879*	5.568*	5.295*	2.141	4.885*	4.238*	1.606
						Platinum						
2	7.034*	7.570*	1.312	8.253*	8.681*	1.244	9.087*	9.496*	1.115	9.222*	9.486*	0.648
3	8.726*	9.137*	1.755	9.568*	9.877*	1.475	10.249*	10.508*	1.421	10.467*	10.584*	0.989
4	10.443*	10.860*	2.139	10.426*	10.707*	1.655	11.106*	11.295*	1.423	11.456*	11.517*	1.180
5	11.614*	12.107*	1.506	11.105*	11.373*	1.389	11.383*	11.541*	1.148	11.579*	11.622*	0.996
						Swiss frank						
2	3.815*	4.057*	0.178	4.424*	4.571*	0.781	4.607*	4.769*	1.085	4.943*	5.048*	1.630
3	5.553*	5.742*	0.397	6.101*	6.385*	1.014	6.121*	6.453*	1.136	6.128*	6.418*	1.350
4	7.661*	7.883*	0.870	7.975*	8.194*	1.566	7.793*	8.029*	1.720	7.536*	7.700*	1.766
5	10.353*	10.623*	1.260	9.606*	9.773*	1.831	8.686*	8.901*	1.902	8.227*	8.237*	1.844

Silver

2	10.766*	10.867*	1.384	11.109*	11.039*	1.445	11.629*	11.188*	1.252	11.960*	11.196*	0.667
3	13.514*	13.578*	1.101	13.513*	13.354*	1.083	13.454*	13.176*	0.876	13.595*	13.068*	0.582
4	16.429*	16.791*	1.332	15.684*	15.535*	1.354	14.865*	14.697*	1.205	14.392*	14.162*	0.913
5	19.478*	20.411*	1.246	17.788*	17.595*	1.026	15.926*	15.748*	0.941	14.825*	14.470*	0.909

Note: An asterisk indicates significance at the 5% (two-tailed) level. In the case of the raw data and AR residuals, we use the asymptotic distribution of the BDS. In the case of the GARCH standardized residuals, we use Hsieh's (1991, Table XIII) simulated critical values of the BDS:

		ε/σ			
m	0.5	1	1.5	2	$N(0,1)$
		2.5% Critical values			
2		−1.61	−1.52	−1.47	−1.49	−1.96
3		−1.65	−1.29	−1.29	−1.29	−1.96
4		−1.63	−1.17	−1.13	−1.12	−1.96
5		−1.94	−1.11	−1.00	−0.99	−1.96
		97.5% Critical values			
2		2.11	1.96	1.85	1.88	1.96
3		2.34	2.14	2.01	2.00	1.96
4		2.49	2.25	2.17	2.14	1.96
5		2.90	2.40	2.28	2.22	1.96

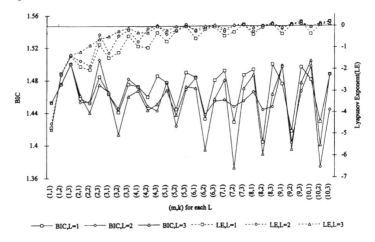

Figure 4.1. Estimated largest Lyapunov exponent for each triple (L, m, k) for the Australian dollar.

Table 4.5 along with the respective optimized value of the BIC criterion. Because this test is limited to short data sets [roughly 500 or so data points, see, e.g., Ellner et al. (1992)], for those series with more than 500 observations, we apply the test to the first 500 observations as well as the last 500 observations, implicitly assuming that any nonlinear deterministic structure will show up in the form of a positive Lyapunov exponent point estimate for at least one of the samples.

The Lyapunov exponent point estimates in Table 4.5 are all negative except for the Australian dollar (all observations), copper (for the first 500 observations), and the Japanese yen (for the first 500 observations as well as the last 500 observations), indicating the presence of a chaotic nonlinear generating process. Figures 4.1–4.3 indicate (for some representative futures contracts) the sensitivity of the dominant Lyapunov exponent estimate to variations in the parameters, by plotting the estimated dominant Lyapunov exponent for each of (L, m, k), where $L = 1, 2, 3$; $m = 1, \ldots, 10$; and $k = 1, 2, 3$; similar figures for the remaining futures contracts are available from the authors upon request.

6   Summary and concluding comments

We have tested for white chaos on 13 spot-month futures prices using two of the most reputable (nonparametric) inference methods. We find only limited robustness between the two inference methods, which is consistent with the evidence reported by Barnett et al. (1995). The BDS test rejects the null of whiteness for all of the original data and all of the AR residuals except for

Table 4.5 *BIC selection of the parameter triple (L, m, k), the value of the minimized BIC, and the dominant Lyapunov exponent point estimate for GARCH (1,1) standardized residuals*

Series	Total No. of Observations	(L,m,k) Triple that minimizes the BIC			Value of the minimized BIC			Dominant Lyapunov exponent point-estimate		
		First 500 Observations	Last 500 Observations	All Observations	First 500 Observations	Last 500 Observations	All Observations	First 500 Observations	Last 500 Observations	All Observations
Australian dollar	330			(3,7,2)			1.3717			0.043
British pound	955	(1,4,2)	(3,7,2)		1.4280	1.4210		−0.484	−0.003	
Canadian dollar	854	(2,5,2)	(1,10,2)		1.4118	1.3975		−0.114	−0.014	
Crude oil	530			(1,62)			1.4166			−0.319
Copper	905	(2,10,2)	(1,1,1)		1.4355	1.4412		0.057	−3.939	
Deutschemark	955	(1,1,1)	(3,2,1)		1.4397	1.4372		−5.519	−0.941	
Gold	961	(3,7,2)	(3,2,1)		1.4377	1.4376		−0.019	−1.301	
Heating oil	734	(3,7,2)	(2,6,2)		1.4366	1.4312		−0.025	−0.124	
Unleaded gas	439			(1,1,1)			1.4432			−4.952
Japanese yen	865	(3,9,2)	(3,8,2)		1.4099	1.4095		0.019	0.023	
Platinum	1,072	(1,1,1)	(2,3,1)		1.4382	1.4407		−3.485	−0.680	
Swiss frank	955	(3,5,1)	(2,2,1)		1.4323	1.4375		−0.220	−1.096	
Silver	1,140	(2,1,1)	(3,4,1)		1.4258	1.4276		−10.767	−0.416	

Note: Numbers in parentheses represent the BIC selection of the parameter triple (L, m, k), where L is the time-delay parameter, m is the number of lags in the autoregression, and k is the number of units in the hidden layer of the neural net.

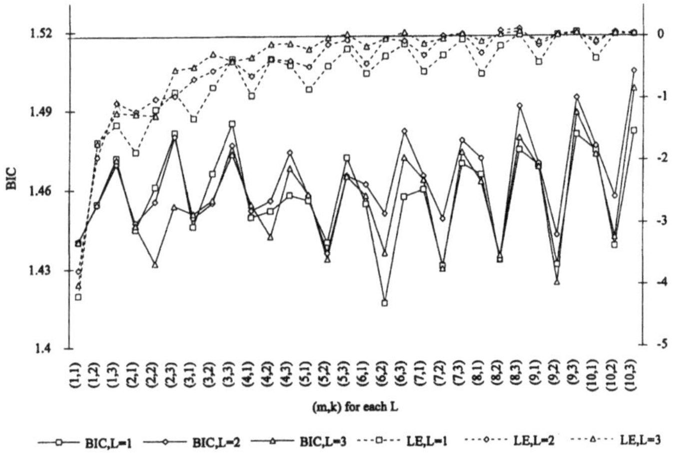

Figure 4.2. Estimated largest Lyapunov exponent for each triple (L, m, k) for crude oil.

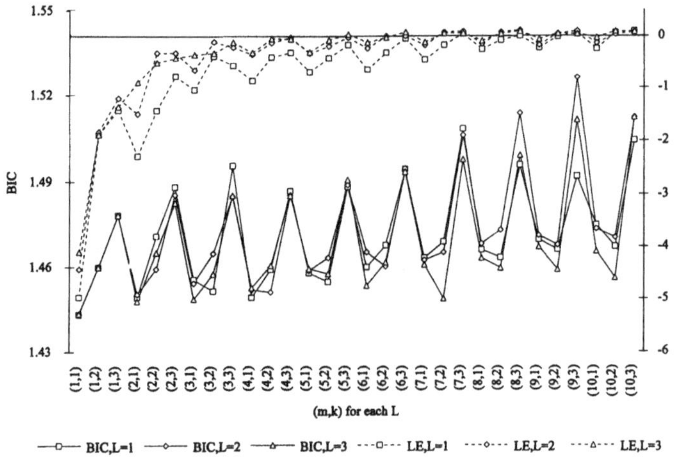

Figure 4.3. Estimated largest Lyapunov exponent for each triple (L, m, k) for unleaded gas.

the Australian dollar. With the GARCH (1,1) standardized residuals, however, the BDS statistic indicates some dependence for only the British pound, the Canadian dollar, crude oil, copper, and the Japanese yen. With the NEGM Lyapunov exponent test, however, we find evidence that only the Australian dollar, the Japanese yen, and perhaps copper and chaotic.

These findings have interesting implications. Most important, because chaos generates output that mimics the output of stochastic systems, it offers an alternative explanation of the behavior of futures prices. In particular, the existence of chaos implies that profitable, nonlinearity-based trading rules exist (at least in the short run and provided that the actual generating mechanism is known exactly), raising questions about the martingale-type behavior of futures prices. Prediction, however, over long periods is all but impossible, because of the sensitive dependence on the initial-conditions property of chaos.

Finally, in exploring the NEGM method, we have found it a very attractive test of positivity of the largest Lyapunov exponent. It is explicitly derived for use with noisy data and is a regression (or Jacobian) method, unlike the Wolf et al. (1985) direct method, which was the first method for calculating the largest Lyapunov exponent. In this regard, Brock and Sayers (1988) have found that the Wolf et al. (1985) procedure requires long data series and is sensitive to dynamic noise, and so, inflated estimates of λ are obtained. The NEGM test's only current limitation is its limitation to short data sets, which is exactly what motivated the use of weekly (rather that daily) observations in the current study.

REFERENCES

Barnett, W. A., Gallant, A. R., Hinich, M. J., Jungeilges, J., Kaplan, D., and Jensen, M. J. (1995). Robustness of nonlinearity and chaos test to measurement error, inference method, and sample size, *J. Econ. Behav. Organ.*, **27**, 301–320.

Barnett, W. A., and Hinich, M. J. (1992). Empirical chaotic dynamics in economics, *Ann. Oper. Res.*, **37**, 1–15.

Baumol, W., and Benhabib, J. (1989). Chaos: Significance, mechanism, and economic applications, *J. Econ. Perspect.*, **3**, 77–105.

Bollerslev, T. (1986). Generalized autoregressive conditional heteroskedasticity, *J. Econ. Theory*, **31**, 307–27.

Brock, W. (1986). Distinguishing random and deterministic systems: Abridged version, *J. Econ. Theory*, **40**, 168–95.

Brock, W. A., Dechert, W. D., and Scheinkman, J. (1987). A test for independence based on the correlation dimension, University of Wisconsin at Madison and University of Chicago.

Brock, W., and Sayers, C. (1988). Is the business cycle characterized by deterministic chaos? *J. Monetary Econ.*, **22**, 71–90.

Deneckere, R., and Pelikan, S. (1986). Competitive chaos, *J. Econ. Theory*, **40**, 13–25.

Dickey, D. A., and Fuller, W. A. (1981). Likelihood ratio statistics for autoregressive time series with a unit root, *Econometrica*, **49** (July), 1057–72.

Eckmann, J. P., and Ruelle, D. (1985). Ergodic theory of strange attractors, *Rev. Mod. Phys.*, **57**, 617–56.

Ellner, S., Nychka, D. W., and Gallant, A. R. (1992). LENNS, a program to estimate the dominant Lyapunov exponent of noisy nonlinear systems from time series data, Institute of Statistics Mimeo Series No. 2235 (BMA Series No. 39), Statistics Department, North Carolina State University, Raleigh, NC.

Engle, R. F. (1982). Autoregressive conditional heteroskedasticity with estimates of the variance of U.K. inflation, *Econometrica*, **50**, 987–1008.

Fama, E. F. (1965). The behavior of stock market prices. *J. Business*, **38**, 34–105.

Frank, M. Z., and Stengos, T. (1988). Chaotic dynamics in economic time-series, *J. Econ. Surv.*, **2**, 103–33.

Fuller, W. A. (1976). *Introduction to Statistical Time Series*, Wiley, New York.

Gallant, A. R., and White, H. (1992). On learning the derivatives of an unknown mapping with multilayer feedforward networks, *Neural Networks*, **5**, 129–38.

Gencay, R., and Dechert, W. D. (1992). An algorithm for the n Lyapunov exponents of an n-dimensional unknown dynamical system, *Phys. D*, **59**, 142–57.

Grassberger, P., and Procaccia, T. (1983). Measuring the strangeness of strange attractors, *Phys. D*, **9**, 189–208.

Hsieh, D. A., (1991). Chaos and nonlinear dynamics: Application to financial markets, *J. Finance*, **46**, 1839–1877.

Kifer, Y. (1986). *Ergodic theory of random transformations*, Birkhauser, Basel.

Lamoureux, C., and Lastrapes, W. (1990). Persistence in variance, structural change, and the GARCH model, *J. Business Econ. Stat.*, **8**, 225–34.

Ljung, G. M., and Box, G. E. P. (1978). On a measure of lack of fit in time series models, *Biometrica*, **65**, 297–303.

Mandelbrot, B. (1963). The variation of certain speculative prices, *J. Business*, **36**, 394–419.

Medio, A., and Gallo, G. (1992). *Chaotic Dynamics: Theory and Applications to Economics*, Cambridge University Press, Cambridge, England.

Nelson, C. R., and Plosser, C. I. (1982). Trends and random walks in macroeconomic time series: Some evidence and implications, *J. Monetary Econ.*, **10**, 139–162.

Nychka, D. W., Ellner, S., Gallant, A. R., and McCaffrey, D. (1992). Finding chaos in noisy systems, *J. Roy. Stat. Soc. B* **54**, 399–426.

Said, S. E., and Dickey, D. A. (1984). Testing for unit roots in autoregressive-moving average models of unknown order, *Biometrica*, **71**, 599–607.

Samuelson, P. (1965). Proof that properly anticipated prices fluctuate randomly, *Ind. Manage. Rev.*, 41–49.

Schwarz, G. (1978). Estimating the dimension of a model, *Ann. Stat.* **6**, 461–4.

Wolf, A., Swift, B., Swinney, J., and Vastano, J. (1985). Determining Lyapunov exponents from a time series, *Phys. D*, **16**, 285–317.

CHAPTER 5

Continuous-time chaos in stock market dynamics

Kehong Wen

Strong empirical evidence of continuous-time chaos is obtained from the log-linear detrended Standard and Poor 500 series of 1952–83. The result is reinforced by the finding of a remarkably similar series of a chaotic attractor from our behavioral model of the stock market. The empirical series is analyzed by using standard nonlinear-dynamics algorithms, with special care given to the data limitation, noise level, and time-unit consistency. The chaotic properties are evident in the log-linear detrended series and are obscured in the log-first-differenced series. We extensively analyze the detrending problem and find that the former detrending approach is the simplest, and most appropriate. Our continuous-time model for the price and return is an application of our earlier work on expectations and delay differential equations.

1   Introduction

Nonlinear dynamics and chaos have helped to revive the research interest in finding endogenous mechanisms to explain irregular fluctuations of economic variables, especially in the area of business cycles. There are a growing number of theoretical models that show that chaos is generic in virtually any model of a dynamic economic process (Day 1993). Many features of irregular regularity can be shown as results of deterministic dynamics without the influence of external noise. Many chaos models also can be constructed in a way consistent with optimization behaviors (Benhabib 1992). It is also easy to demonstrate that a deterministic-chaos model can generate the kind of data that look almost indifferent from the real data (Wen 1993a; and Section 5). With the aid of computers, solving nonlinear dynamics is now a common practice. The mathematical structure of nonlinear systems continues to be challenging and fascinating.

The progress is yet far from complete. One of the main reasons is that empirical evidence for economic chaos has not shown up very strong. The only claimed case of economic chaos that has been vigorously debated is the finding of monetary chaos by Barnett and Chen (1988). The other studies of nonlinearity or chaos, notably those by using the Brock–Dechart–Scheinkman (BDS) test (Brock, Dechart, and Scheinkman 1987), have been even more controversial (Granger 1991; Chen 1993; Barnett, Gallant, and Hinich 1993).

Despite the controversy, chaos has become a challenge to the dominating stochastic economics and econometrics. This is because deterministic chaos demonstrates its potential of replacing the role of noise, hence the issue of chaos versus noise, and the search for powerful tests that can discriminate chaos from noise. As rightly argued by Granger (1991); noise is not likely to go away in any economy; and if chaos exists, it is unlikely to be free from the contamination of noises such as measurement error. In the world of coexisting nonlinearity and noise, the right questions seem to be how we can disentangle their relative effects (Theiler et al. 1992), and how we should approach the complex systems with a broader perspective that recognizes the roles of both nonlinearity and/or chaos and noise (Wen 1993b).

We hope to clarify some confusion about these issues by considering the continuous-time chaos. There are basically two ways by which chaos is generated: by a discrete map or by a set of differential equations. Discrete maps are much easier to handle mathematically than the differential equations and thus are often the models that researchers have in mind when addressing the issue of chaos versus noise. This is especially true among econometricians because they are so used to discrete models. However, we know that almost all dynamics of physical systems are modeled by differential equations, and when using maps, physicists have in mind that they should be properly formed through the concept of Poincaré section [see discussion by Chen (1993) and Medio (1992)]. We show in this paper that this often-overlooked distinction between continuous-time chaos and discrete chaos has far-reaching effects.

First, a discrete chaos is much more easily contaminated by noise than a continuous chaos is. This is probably the reason why detecting chaos on a smooth time series can be more successful, whereas algorithms designed to test nonlinearity or chaos on prewhitened time series often generate mixed results. We therefore suggest in this paper that detecting continuous-time chaos may potentially be more fruitful than testing discrete chaos in economic research.

Second, a continuous-time model is theoretically more relevant than a discrete model. This argument goes back at least to Koopmans (1950), who argued that when the time series has long-term correlations, continuous-time model should be advised. Gandolfo (1981), has an excellent summary on the issue and the related problems of econometric estimation. He also explicitly pointed out that the best mathematical structure for economic dynamics is the difference–differential equation. We show, through a thorough demonstration on a time-series analysis, how effectively this theoretical argument can help the chaos-versus-noise debate. Our model using difference–differential equations for stock-market dynamics demonstrates the usefulness of this type of dynamic structure.

Third, by considering the possibility of continuous-time dynamics, one is forced to examine the time-unit consistency problem. By *time-unit consistency*, we mean that the dynamic model believed to explain the data with one time unit also should be consistent with data of the same variable but with different time units or sampling rates. It is true that different dynamics exist for different time scales; our argument is that when empirical data show time-unit-invariant properties, the corresponding models have no reason to alter their structures when only the time unit is different. When indeed the dynamics are changed because of different time scales involved, we have to be specific about the nature of the time scales involved [for discussion in physics, see Prigogine (1962)]. The common econometric practice is to perform a parametric estimation of a discrete model for a time series with a unique time unit. By raising the question of time-unit consistency, one has to examine the self-consistency of the underlying dynamics in different time scales. This examination helps lead to a more transparent result of economic chaos in this study.

Fourth, continuous-time dynamics allow for the coherent treatment of the stock variables and the flow variables. This is one of the difficult problems in macroeconomics (Tsiang 1988). A lesson we learned from elementary physics is that variables such as position and velocity are independent and always come in pairs in phase space when a physical system is described. We also know in economic dynamics that the level and increment are equally important, but their roles in modeling are often in disparity. Some models are concerned with only levels, whereas others are concerned only with increments. An important example for the former is the static supply–demand analysis, and for the latter, the random-walk model for the stock-market returns. We demonstrate in the case of empirical analysis and theoretical modeling of stock-market dynamics that it is possible and fruitful to consider both the stock and the flow variables in one picture or model.

In Section 2, we introduce the data and discuss the problems associated with detrending. We devote a lengthy discussion to the detrending problem because this is the starting point of many controversies involving the deterministic and stochastic interpretations. We propose a simple method to observe the deviation from stationary linear stochastic processes. This method also provides information for choosing a proper detrending scheme and gives a rough estimation of the noise level. In Section 3, the time-unit consistency problem is studied by applying nonlinear-dynamics analysis on the time series with different time units. The results show that the empirical series is a continuous-time chaos with noise, rather than something generated from a linear stochastic process. Section 4 proposes a theoretical model and provides some related results. Section 5 concludes.

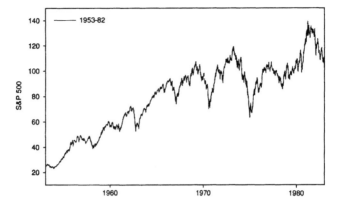

Figure 5.1. S & P 500 weekly time series with a growth trend. The price index is recorded every fifth trading day. Our selected data range starts from the 1,250th point to the 2,750th point, approximately covering a period from January 1953 to December 1982. Source: The original data set with 3,121 points beginning from January 2, 1928, is provided by Edgar E. Peters, who also provides the daily data.

2   Data and detrending

The Standard & Poor 500 is a commonly used composite index that reflects the aggregate movements of the stock market. The series that we study, as shown in Figure 5.1 is the every fifth-day closing index with 1,500 points. It covers the 30-year period starting from January 1953 to December 1982. The daily index with 7,500 points covering the same period also is used throughout the analysis. We choose the stock composite data as our demonstrating case because the data are much more detailed than most macroeconomic indices such as the gross national product (GNP).

As one can see, there are approximately seven to eight irregular cycles going along with a growth trend. The series contains all of the basic elements of business cycles: irregularity, persistency, fluctuations, trends, and so on. An analysis on the data is to obtain whatever information they have to reveal the underlying process – be it stochastic, deterministic, static, or dynamic. We therefore want to preserve as much as possible the original information before analysis.

A common feature of macroeconomic time series is that the irregular fluctuations are usually associated with trends. The trends may be growing or decreasing irregularly. There may be short-term and long-term trends, and sometimes the short-term trends also can be interpreted as fluctuations. Even more puzzling is the question of whether or not the trends are interacting with fluctuations; therefore, the trend and the fluctuation are, after all, interdepen-

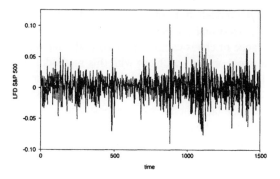

Figure 5.2. Time series of the first-differenced logarithms of the original S & P data in Figure 5.1. ($N = 1,499$).

dent. Nevertheless, one has to detrend or decompose the data in one way or another to allow for further analysis. But how one does it is not a simple matter, which often leads to quite different interpretations and results. Despite the importance of this problem, there have been rather few systematic studies. The best discussion we have found in economics literature is the one by Friedman (1969), who obviously favors the differencing approach. Our analysis raises a serious question about his conclusion.

There are two distinct simple approaches to remove the trends. One approach is to consider exclusively the increment.

$$r_t = \log P(t+1) - \log P(t), \tag{5.1}$$

where $P(t)$ indicates the original index. Here, r_t is a flow variable, but the time unit is fixed. It is often referred to as the compounded return. We use the subscript t to indicate that the variable is discrete. Usually, people take the logarithm before doing differencing to make the resulting series more stationary (Fama 1970). The early work on the random-walk hypothesis of the stock market is based on the analysis on this type of series by looking into the autocorrelation properties.

Figure 5.2 shows the resulting time series after applying the first-differencing to the logarithms of the S & P 500 series in Figure 5.1. It looks like white noise, but it is not. Its distribution is well-known leptokurtic, and the variance is changing over time showing heteroskedasticity (Ding, Granger, and Engle 1993). Most of the recent econometric models following Engle's autoregressive conditional heteroskedasticity (ARCH) model (Engle 1982) are proposed to characterize the properties of the change of conditional variance.

The work using the BDS test follows the same tradition to test the nonlinearity of the resulting series, by examining the residuals of linear models or the residuals of ARCH-type models fit to the r_t series (Scheinkman and LeBaron 1989; LeBaron 1991). No strong evidence of chaos turns up, however; but even if it does, the importance of chaos can be seriously undermined, as argued by Ganger (1991). The most obvious problem with this methodology, as argued by Theiler et al. (1992) and by Chen (1993), is that nonlinear structure can be "bleached" away through the operation of removing linear structures. The less obvious problem is the fact that the test is, at best, a test for discrete chaos, but the time unit arbitrarily chosen from the differencing has no connection with the underlying dynamics. Thus, even if a chaotic dependence is identified from the discrete data, we have no reason to believe that the orbit on a Poincaré section has this unique, constant time unit.

The other approach of detrending is to decompose the time series into a long-term trend and a fluctuating component around the trend. The commonly used log-linear detrending method is the following:

$$p(t) = \log P(t) - (r_0 t + b_0), \tag{5.2}$$

where $r_0 t + b_0$ is the linear trend and the parameters r_0 and b_0 can be obtained through regression.

The difficulty of this approach appears quite serious because one is forced to choose the specific historical period to pick up the trend, which requires historical judgment. This approach has an implicit assumption that there exists only weak interaction between the trend and cycles, even though the trend is certainly an integrated part of the dynamics governing the economic growth. However, this approach does not necessarily assume that the trend is fixed, and it allows for the consideration that the data are generated from a continuous process. In addition, we show in the rest of this section that in terms of removing the trend, first-differencing is as artificial as, if not more artificial than the linear detrending.

Figure 5.3 shows the log-linear detrended S & P 500 stock series. There are about seven to eight medium cycles within a probable long wave. The average period of medium cycles ranges about 3–4 years. These cycles are aperiodic, and noisy fluctuations coexist. Figure 5.4 shows the autocorrelation functions for the same data using different detrending methods. One can see that the log-linear-detrended (LLD) series keeps the patterns that we observe from the original series. Its autocorrelation function has a long-term decaying and oscillating property. The autocorrelation function for the log-first-differenced (LFD) series, however, shows little sign of serial correlation.

From equations (5.1) and (5.2), we have

$$r_t = p(t+1) - p(t) - r_0. \tag{5.3}$$

Equation (5.3) shows that the resulting LFD series r_t is equivalent to the first-differenced $p(t)$ minus a constant. One can deduce r_t series from $p(t)$, but one cannot obtain $p(t)$ from r_t unless the initial condition and the time

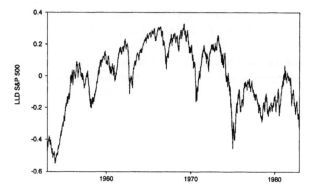

Figure 5.3. Log-linear detrended S & P 500 time series ($N = 1,500$).

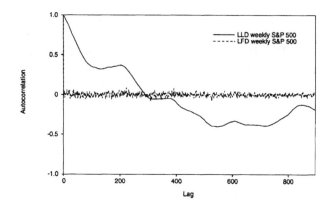

Figure 5.4. Autocorrelation functions for the log-linear detrended S & P data and the log-first-differenced S & P time series.

unit are specified. Therefore, the first-differencing operation is secondary to the LLD operation. In terms of artificially choosing the long-term trend, the first-differencing has the same degree of accuracy as linear detrending, because the resulting series is often modeled by assuming a drift or a positive constant mean to allow for the trend. This constant drift term in a stochastic model is as deterministic as the growth rate in a deterministic model. Although the return series can provide useful statistical properties, its models statistically fitted to the data cannot guarantee to capture the properties of the price series such as the LLD series.

It can be observed from the LLD series that the price has evolving multi-humped distributions and coexisting complex spectra, which are in good agreement with the experience of American business cycles in the period covered by the series (Wen, Chen, and Zhang 1992; Zhang, Wen, and Chen 1992). The results support the view that the stock market is operating in non-equilibrium situations.

To show that the stock return is also nonstationary, both in mean and in variance, and that the price and return have an integrated nonlinear relationship, we propose a simple method for further observation. By properly choosing a moving time-window, we obtain the short-term averages and numerical variances of the LFD and the log second-differenced (LSD) series. We also obtain the short-term numerical variances of the LLD series in the corresponding time-windows. The calculations are done on the daily S & P 500 series with 7,500 points.

Figure 5.5 shows these results. We see not only that the variances of all of these series are changing over time as the phenomenon pointed out by Mandelbrot (1963) and modeled by Engle (1982), but also that the average of the return is changing over time in a magnitude of order 10^{-3}. The magnitude is over five times the overall average of the return, that is, the drift term or long-term growth rate, which is 1.93×10^{-4}. It is also 10 times larger than the average variance of the return (but about one-tenth of the average standard deviation), and in the same order of magnitude as the range of change of the standard deviation (estimated to be 6×10^{-3}).

Ding et al. (1993) recently analyzed the daily S & P 500 return series. They recognize that the return series is nonstationary and has long memory. They propose a new class of model more general than the ARCH model to account for the long-term correlations. They do not recognize, however, the mean-changing feature of the return series. The changing mean may be a more important factor that gives rise to the long memory that they attribute to the changing variances. However, the second-differencing indeed gives a near unchanging sample mean but with changing sample variance. Their model may be better suited for this series.

Why is the average of the compounded returns changing? If one accepts the fact that the original series show upturns and downturns of business cycles, it is straightforward to see that during the upturn/downturn periods, the returns must be on average greater/smaller than the long-term increment index (the drift term). Therefore, by ignoring the changing mean of returns, one is bound to misaccount for the business cycles.

We also can conclude that the first-differencing cannot avoid the problem of dealing with trends and cycles as Friedman (1969) believed, because we still have to explain in a stochastic setting how the mean is changing. On the contrary, the task may become more difficult, because the mean-changing feature can be obscured by the volatility that we observe from the variances. This finding is consistent with the finding of mean reversion in stock returns, (Poterba and Summers 1988).

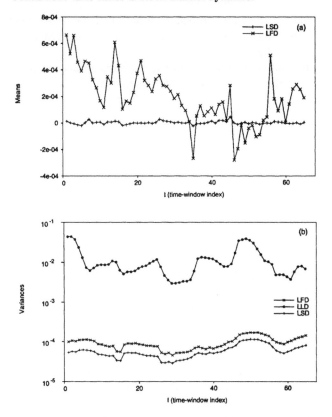

Figure 5.5. Numerical mean and variance of daily S & P 500 series obtained by a sliding time-window. The window size is 500 points, and the window is shifted every 100 points. (a) The averages of the LFD and the LSD S & P 500. (b) The variances of the log-linear-detrended (LLD), the LFD and the LSD S & P 500.

From the variances of the LSD series in Figure 5.5(b), we also may have a rough estimate of the noise level, being less than 10^{-4} or 1% of the averaged variance of the LLD series.

The data that we have obtained permit an observation for nonlinearity.

Suppose that we form a null hypothesis that the price $p(t)$ is generated from a stationary linear stochastic process. The process in discrete time can be an ARMA process, or in continuous time can be some type of Brownian diffusion process. In both cases, the resulting variance of the price $p(t)$ is linearly proportional to the variance of the driving noise (Wang and Uhlenbeck 1945; Box and Jenkins 1970). Because the $p(t)$ series has zero mean, we can show that the linear proportional relationship also must hold between the variance of the $p(t)$ series and the variance of first-differenced $p(t)$ or the second-differenced $p(t)$ series.

We test this null hypothesis by plotting one variance against the other in log scale. If the relationship is linear, the dots should fall on a straight line parallel to the 45-deg line. The results are shown in Figure 5.6. From Figure 5.6(a), one sees that the variances between the first- and the second-differenced data have a nearly linear relationship. But the variances between the LLD and the LSD series have a nonlinear relationship. The null hypothesis clearly can be rejected for the $p(t)$ variable (linear regression statistic: slope $b = 1.25$, $R^2 = 0.61$), but one cannot say so for the r_t variable ($b = 0.97$, $R^2 = 0.96$). This result suggests that nonlinearity or chaos is more evident in the $p(t)$ series than in the r_t series.

In summary, this section shows that differencing as a whitening process does not necessarily make the time series stationary, even with the sacrifice of imposing limitations such as the unique time unit. It actually may obscure the right statistical inference by amplifying the noise and shortening the correlation length. For the purpose of discerning nonlinear dynamic structure or chaos, we argue that it is potentially misleading to work solely on the variable r_t. We reason that stronger evidence of chaos can be found from variables such as $p(t)$ which is less contaminated by noise and can be viewed as a continuous time series. Although we argue that $p(t)$ is more original and informative than r_t, it is useful to make reference to the properties of r_t when analyzing primarily $p(t)$. Our simple method proposed above shows that the r_t series is most likely to be nonstationary not only in variance but also in mean. This is consistent with the finding that $p(t)$ most probably is generated by a nonlinear and nonstationary process. The noise level that we have estimated is only intuitive and is confirmed by our analysis on the correlation dimension in Section 3.

We argued favorably for the log-linear detrending over the log-first-differencing as a simple detrending technique. In Section 3, a standard nonlinear dynamics test is conducted on the $p(t)$ series with special care taken in data limitation, noise level, and especially time-unit consistency. A more sophisticated and potentially more promising technique for trend-cycle decomposition has been developed by Chen (Chapter 13, this volume). We will consider using it in the future.

3   Time-unit consistency in testing economic chaos

There are now many introductions to the various algorithms for testing chaos, such as computing the correlation dimension and the Lyapunov exponent (e.g., Chen 1988, 1993). In sections 3.1–3.4, we discuss the results directly without detailing these algorithms, so as to focus on the main argument of this paper.

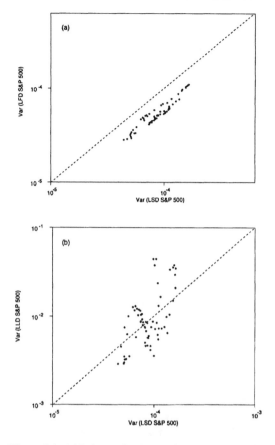

Figure 5.6. (a) In log scale, the moving variances of the LFD S & P 500 versus the moving variances of the LSD S & P 500. The dashed line indicates the 45-deg line. (b) In log scale, the variances of the LLD versus the LSD S & P 500.

3.1   *Autocorrelation*

The autocorrelation function is a very important concept in analyzing time series. A time series generated by a stationary process can be usefully described by its mean, variance, and autocorrelation function (Box and Jenkins 1970). Correlation is also the best way to explicitly make the sharp contrast between equilibrium states and non-equilibrium states in physics (Prigogine and Stengers in press), because the correlations that characterize far-from-equilibrium situations may extend over macroscopic distances, whereas the correlations that characterize the equilibrium states are within microscopic

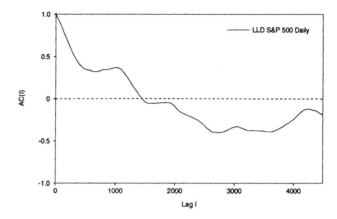

Figure 5.7. Autocorrelation function for the LLD S & P daily data ($N = 7,500$).

range. Further, oscillating decaying correlation is one of the characteristics of many chaotic attractors, especially the continuous-time chaos. Therefore, it is not appropriate to test for chaotic dependence by filtering out correlations.

We have already seen the autocorrelation function for the weekly S & P 500 series in Figure 5.4. The function is obviously oscillating decaying. We show elsewhere (Zhang et al. 1992) that the autocorrelation function can be decomposed into several oscillating decaying modes called correlation resonances. They indicate for each independent mode the frequency in which the correlation oscillates and how fast the correlation decays. The oscillating rate and the decay rate form the complex spectrum. The result shows that the stock-market dynamics follow a non-Markovian process and it support the chaos interpretation.

It is useful to examine the decorrelation time T_d, which is determined by the first vanishing autocorrelation. For the LLD weekly series, the T_d is about 290 weeks. For an AR(n) model to capture this long-term correlation, the order n must be way over ten! This is the main reason why Koopmans (1950) suggested using a continuous-time model in a case like this. But a better way to argue is by looking at the autocorrelation of the same series with a different time unit.

Figure 5.7 shows the autocorrelation function for the daily LLD S & P 500 series. Note that the correlation structure is the same as that of the weekly LLD series. In other words, if we decompose the function into its characteristic oscillating and decaying modes, the complex spectra will be the same as those of the weekly data after rescaling. This means that the correlation property is the same for the weekly dynamics and the daily dynamics.

Note also that this new function has a T_d of about 1,450 days. In practice, we have no hope to determine the right linear discrete dynamics with such long lags.

Now, the question that we asked in the introduction (Section 1) about the time-unit consistency problem can be asked about the autocorrelation as follows. Can any estimated discrete model have the same form of autocorrelation when its time unit is changed from weekly to daily without changing the parameters or its structure? Suppose that a discrete model – be it linear or nonlinear, deterministic or stochastic – fits exactly the autocorrelation of weekly data. As a dynamic process, this model tells how every successive point is generated, and the data are decorrelated at about 290 successions. If we now turn this process into a shorter time unit, say daily, the 290 successions would give a decorrelation time of 290 days instead of the 290 weeks, which is the T_d that we have for the daily series. This model necessarily will be either time-unit specific or time-unit inconsistent. If a dynamic model works for one time unit only, it does not qualify as a dynamic model for the variable that we can observe and want to forecast in many time units. If instead it is time-unit inconsistent, it does not stand up to empirical facts, because we observe empirically a time-unit-invariant property.

This argument excludes the possibility of any discrete process, including discrete chaos, for the purpose of finding the underlying dynamics that can account for both the weekly and daily serial correlations.

3.2   *Phase portrait*

Phase portrait allows a picturesque examination of the movement in phase space. It is also a proper way to select a Poincaré section. We constructed the phase portraits for both the LLD and the LFD series following Takens' (1981) time-delay method.

The phase portrait for the LFD S & P 500 series, as expected, is almost a Gaussian noise. This is usual for first-differenced economic data. In contrast, the phase portrait for the LLD S & P 500 series shows structured dots (the two phase portraits have been deleted because of space limitations). When following the plotting of the dots on the computer screen, one observes the movement of a changing spiral.

To pick up more clearly the deterministic pattern of the LLD data, we can employ the moving-average technique before detrending. It can be confirmed easily that a reasonable moving average will not significantly change the autocorrelation structure of a time series. For example, when a 10-point moving average is applied to the original S & P 500 data, the autocorrelation function of the corresponding LLD series is almost no different, and the cyclical pattern in its resulting series looks almost exactly the same as the original, except that it is smoother. Figure 5.8 shows the phase portrait of the smoothed S & P 500 series. This picture reveals the changing spiral structure. However, the moving-averaged series is used here only for looking at the phase portrait.

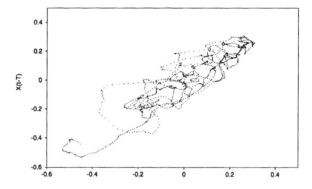

Figure 5.8. Two-dimensional phase portrait for the LLD, 10-point moving-averaged S & P 500 series ($T = 20$ weeks, $N = 1,471 = 1500$-9-20).

The phase portraits also show that we have no simple way to construct a Poincaré map to describe the trajectory.

The same construction is also done on the daily series, resulting in the similar and thicker phase-space pattern with more dots in between any two successive dots previously observed. This is also a way to exclude the possibility of discrete models, despite the fact that Ramsey, Sayers, and Rothman (1990) show that a spiraling pattern exists in an AR(6) model.

However, the autocorrelation and phase portrait do not show whether the $p(t)$ series is chaos with noise or it is a noise-contaminated periodic pattern with a very long period. The latter alternative, though, is very unlikely, because business experience of the stock market suggests that the market never repeats its pattern over a long period of time. This is also a point made by Slutzky (1937) for general economic time series.

We still need to obtain more direct evidence of chaos.

3.3   *Correlation dimension*

One of the most important characteristics of deterministic chaos is its fractal dimension (Mandelbrot 1977), which provides a lower bound to the degrees of freedom for the system (Grassberger and Procaccia 1983). Low dimensionality of the strange attractor comes from the dissipation effect. Normally, a complex system would involve many degrees of freedom. But because of the dissipation, only a few degrees of freedom are needed to describe a chaotic attractor. This is why finding a low dimension is useful both in identifying and modeling chaos.

By using the Grassberger–Procaccia (GP) algorithm, we obtain the numerical results on the correlation dimension D of the LLD weekly S & P 500 series as shown in Figure 5.9. We can clearly identify a saturated plateau region, which

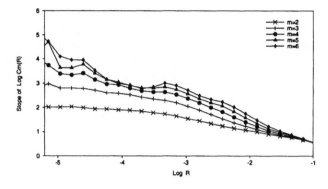

Figure 5.9. Correlation dimension for LLD S & P 500 series (delay $T = 10$, m is the embedding dimension).

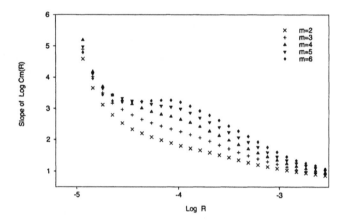

Figure 5.10. Correlation dimension for LLD S & P 500 (daily) series.

gives an estimation of correlation dimension between 2.5 and 3.5 and close to 3.0. Because this dimension is low, the number of our data points–1,500–is sufficient (see Ramsey et al. 1990).

We run the GP program for the LLD daily S & P 500 series with 7,500 points covering the same time period. The result is very encouraging. The plateau region in Figure 5.10 gives an estimate of the dimension between 3.0 and 3.5. The curves are much smoother than those in Figure 5.9. We therefore have obtained another time-unit-consistent measure of our $p(t)$ series.

The fact that both plots show a plateau around $R = 10^{-4}$ confirms our earlier estimation that the noise level is less that 1 percent of the variance of the LLD series.

The daily data that we use cover more than five cycles, and each cycle has more than 150 points. The noise level is not high enough to mask the pattern that we observe in the phase portrait. The estimate of D around 3.0 is from both the weekly data and the daily data. We therefore believe that a low-correlation dimension exists and does not change when the sampling rate is increased but within the time scale of concern. This suggests that the series is very likely to be chaos with small noise.

In our numerical experiments, noise filtering techniques, such as moving average and interpolation, may artificially create low dimensionality, especially when one obtains a correlation dimension lower than 2. This is because these techniques usually rearrange the points in phase space along some smooth lines, which can effectively lower the dimensions. We have been cautious about this, and use the moving-average technique only for showing the phase portrait of Figure 5.8.

The results also suggest that if one tries the linear stochastic model such as AR(n), the order n must be kept low. But with such low order, the corresponding model definitely will not be able to produce the long autocorrelations that we showed earlier. The facts of low dimensionality and long correlation are other effective arguments against the possibility of a linear stochastic process.

Because the $p(t)$ series cannot be discrete chaos and our phase portraits show no signs of having a Poincaré map that has a time unit of one week or one day, the first-differenced series r_t also cannot be a discrete chaos.

3.4   *Largest Lyapunov exponent*

Chaotic motion is sensitive to initial conditions. Its measure is the Lyapunov exponents, which are the exponential rates of divergence of nearby orbits in phase space. Theoretically, the largest Lyapunov exponent, λ, is negative for stable systems with fixed points, zero for periodic or quasiperiodic motion, and positive for chaos.

The λ can be calculated numerically by the Wolf algorithm (Wolf et al. 1985) where the limiting procedure to obtain the divergence rate is approximated by an averaging process over the evolution time EVOLV. This algorithm is applicable when the noise level is low and the data length is long enough to cover more than a few cycles. Although the algorithm can produce spurious results for the return variable because of the high relative level of noise, we believe that it can be reliable for the price $p(t)$ series, because this series contains a noise level of less than 1 percent relative to its average variance.

After experimenting with the Wolf program with the LLD weekly S & P 500 series by choosing different parameters, we found a stable range of parameters. We then chose one set of parameters within this range. We chose the embedding dimension DIM $= 4$, because the correlation dimension that we have estimated

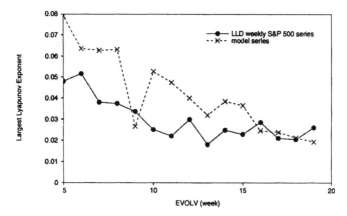

Figure 5.11. Average largest Lyapunov exponents for the LLD weekly S & P
500 and the series generated from our model ($N = 1,500$, DIM $= 4$, TAU $=$
20, DT $= 1$, SCALMX $= 0.1$, SCALMN $= 0.0001$).

is around 3. We choose SCALMN $= 0.0001$, because the estimated higher
bound of the noise level is 10^{-4}. Figure 5.11 shows the average largest Lyapunov
exponents versus EVOLV produced by the Wolf algorithm. We estimate that
the exponent is about 0.025 week^{-1} by taking the average of the points that
fall in the range of EVOLV between 10 and 20 weeks, where the numerical
exponents become stabilized and where the evolution lengths are appropriate.

The dashed curve in Figure 5.11 shows the same calculation for a chaotic
series produced from our model (Section 4, Figure 5.13). The series contains
no external noise, The Lyapunov exponent approaches the same magnitude as
the empirical number as EVOLV is increased.

Usually, researchers stop at confirming that the series has a positive Lyapunov exponent. But the numerical positive exponent may still be a result of
noise, despite the fact that the Wolf algorithm has a parameter SCALMN to
partly exclude the noise effect. This is precisely the reason that some researchers
avoid using this algorithm in testing economic chaos.

The examination of time-unit consistency allows a further test on the predictive power of the number that we have obtained. We ask: If the exponent
indicates the chaotic divergence, what can we expect from the exponent of
the daily series? For discrete chaos, there is no clear relationship between the
Lyapunov exponents of the series with different time units because of the ill-
defined nature of the corresponding maps. For continuous-time chaos, however,
we know theoretically that the two exponents should be the same. Therefore,
we can expect that, for continuous-time chaos, the exponent estimated from the
weekly data will have predictive power for the daily data, that is, the largest

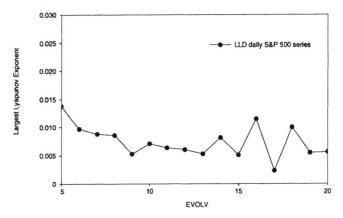

Figure 5.12. Average largest Lyapunov exponents for the LLD daily S & P 500 series (N = 7,500, DIM = 4, TAU = 50, DT = 1, SCALMX = 0.1, SCALMN = 0.0001).

Lyapunov exponent for the daily series would be roughly one-fifth of 0.025 day^{-1} or 0.005 day^{-1}.

Figure 5.12 shows our numerical calculation on the LLD daily S & P 500 series. The average value of the largest Lyapunov exponent is around 0.005 day^{-1}. The number is estimated from the average number in the EVOLV range between 10 and 20 days. This result is wonderfully satisfactory. Note that we have chosen the same embedding dimension, DIM, and the same level of noise, SCALMN, as in the weekly case. Our choice of delay-TAU and the observation range of EVOLV in both cases follows the suggestion given by Wolf et al. (1985). The data also have sufficient number of points and low level of noise for reliable use of their program.

Figures 5.11 and 5.12 not only show that local divergence is indeed positively exponential, but also show the time-unit consistency that we expect from a continuous-time chaos.

We have performed the standard nonlinear dynamics analysis on both the daily and the weekly LLD S & P 500 series. The analysis were not carried out on the differenced series because of our argument presented in Section 2. Special care has been taken for the data limitation, noise level, and most important, the time-unit consistency. The basic nonlinear-dynamics structures for both series are the same, even quantitatively. They are *time-unit invariant* within the time scales of concern. This property is important for excluding the possibility of ARMA-type models and virtually any other more general but discrete stochastic models. It also rejects the possibility of discrete chaos. A consistent picture, that is, the continuous-time chaos, emerges as the best interpretation.

But a question still remains. We do not know whether this continuous-time chaos is generated from a deterministic chaos contaminated by disturbing noises, or if it is a noise-induced chaos. If it is the latter, the chaos will disappear without noise. But, either way, continuous-time chaos provides the right framework for modeling the stock-market dynamics.

In Section 4, we build a nonlinear-dynamics model using delay differential equations to explain the empirical results. We demonstrate that a deterministic chaos generated from the model accounts for all of the basic properties observed. We believe that this is the right way to start. The effects of external noises on the model's behavior is touched upon but not fully discussed.

4   The model

The analyses and results in Sections 2 and 3 provide a clear guide for constructing a dynamic model. The model that can capture the empirical properties must include the following important elements:

(1) It must have nonlinear dynamics and produce chaos;
(2) it must be formulated in continuous time;
(3) it should display empirically comparable complex dynamics for the $p(t)$ variable.

Relating to point (3) and our discussion about the problem of modeling stock variable and flow variable, we need a model that takes into consideration both the price and the change of price. In particular, we treat these variables as interacting independent variables. For this purpose, we define variable $r(t)$, the instantaneous stock-market return to replace the compounding return r_t as

$$r(t) = \frac{d\log P(t)}{dt}$$
$$= \dot{P}(t)/P(t). \tag{5.4}$$

Recall our definition of $p(t)$ in equation (5.2); we have the following equation for $p(t)$ and $r(t)$:

$$\dot{p}(t) = r(t) - r_0. \tag{5.5}$$

To formulate the equation for the change of $r(t)$, we consider three types of stylized market participants. Following the interpretation given by Huang and Day (1993), they are: (1) the α-investor, who uses fundamental information, sometimes referred to as "information trader," "sophisticated investor," or "fundamentalist"; (2) the β-investor, who uses extrapolative rules, sometimes known as "sheep," "noise trader," or "chartist"; and (3) the market-maker or "specialist," who mediates transactions and whose legal function is to "maintain an orderly market." We propose the following equation to capture their effects on the dynamics of stock return $r(t)$:

$$\dot{r}(t) = -\alpha[r(t - \tau) - r_0] + \beta[r(t - \tau) - r_0]e^{-[r(t-\tau)-r_0]^2/\sigma^2}$$

$$- \gamma p(t - \tau'). \tag{5.6}$$

We perceive that the effects of the behaviors of the participants on the dynamics are competing feedbacks. More specifically, the α-investor gives a negative feedback on the market return, whereas the β-investor gives a positive feedback, with reference to the long-run rate r_0. These two types of participants are competing against each other directly and share the same response time. The effect of the specialist, although also a negative feedback, is quite different from the above two. The main distinction is that the specialist should stabilize the potential deviation of price from its smooth long-term trend. Therefore, its feedback on the return $r(t)$ is formed by the deviation $p(t)$ with a different response time. For simplicity, all of the negative feedbacks take linear forms. Only the positive-feedback term is nonlinear. The particular exponential function of the positive feedback has a theoretical judgment by virtue of the fact that it captures the rule-induced expectations (Wen 1993a). This function, together with the second term, produces multiregime expectations (Wen and Chen 1992). The delayed-response structure is able to give rise to extremely complex and interesting behaviors (Wen 1993a). More detailed theoretical reasonings for model (5.6) based on expectations-driven excess-demand flows are presented elsewhere (Wen 1994). Suffice it to show in this paper that the model can capture the observed empirical properties.

Equations (5.5) and (5.6) give our complete model of stock-market price and return in continuous time. By substituting a new variable, "excess return" $r'(t)$ for $r(t) - r_0$, and dropping the prime, we have

$$\dot{r}(t) = -\alpha\tau(t - \tau) + \beta r(t - \tau)e^{-\frac{r^2(t-\tau)}{\sigma^2}} - \gamma p(t - \tau')$$

$$\dot{p}(t) = r(t). \tag{5.7}$$

The model structure is the same as that of our earlier freeway-driving model (Wen 1993a) proposed to describe the monetary growth. It is a Liénard equation with two delays. A detailed mathematical and numerical treatment can be obtained from Wen, Chen, and Turner (1994).

We want to emphasize that this model follows the modeling methodology of Chen (1993) and is different from the Huang–Day model in the following ways:

First, we consider delayed feedbacks and soft-bouncing mechanisms (Wen 1993a), whereas they formulate the model with rigid bounds and without time delays. Second, we consider the multiregime expectations and formulate the model in continuous time, whereas their model has been a discrete chaos model. Third, a more important difference is the variables. They consider the price level $P(t)$, whereas we choose the price deviation $P(t)$ and the instantaneous return $r(t)$ as defined above. Therefore our model is aimed at explaining most of the features that we have seen from the data, whereas theirs concentrates on the chaotic switching. Fourth, we build the model also to obtain realistic time series that are comparable with the real data, whereas their model uses discrete time that does not provide realistic series and time scales.[1]

The model can be adapted readily to any model that tries to capture the irregular growth patterns in business cycles. As one can see, the r_0 parameter is the trend parameter. It can be treated as a bifurcation parameter for investigating the effects that the long-term growth rate will have on the cycles. The parameter also can be treated as a variable that may be influenced by the technological change, by the specification of the neoclassic capital accumulation process, or by the cycle variables $p(t)$ and $r(t)$.

The two-variable model has the richest dynamic behaviors that one can ever expect from a nonlinear dynamics model (Wen 1993a).

Figure 5.13 shows a time series $p(t)$ from a chaotic attractor of model (5.7). It looks remarkably like the series in Figure 5.3. The time series has seven to eight irregular cycles with their durations, relative amplitudes, and turning points mimicking almost perfectly those of the empirical data. In terms of realism, we cannot ask for more.

The corresponding phase portrait constructed by Takens' (1981) method displays similarities with Figure 5.8. It also shows that there is no clear way to construct a Poincaré map for this complicated chaos. the corresponding first-differenced series looks much more random and displays similarities with the series in Figure 5.2.

The autocorrelation of the chaotic $p(t)$ series is also oscillating decaying and that of the first-differenced series decays much faster. The autocorrelation function of $p(t)$ is also very similar to that of the LLD S & P 500 series (not shown).

Figure 5.14 shows the correlation dimension produced by the GP algorithm for the chaotic $p(t)$ series. It gives an estimation of D between 2.5 and 3.0 and close to 3.0. This is almost identical to the empirical result.

Because our model is a continuous-time model, by changing the sampling rate the overall picture for dimensionality and correlation will not change unless we have an oversampling or undersampling problem. Furthermore, the time scales for the business cycles can readily be estimated from a specification of the time unit in the model that corresponds to a realistic value.

---

[1] For a discussion of realism of time series and time scales, see Zarnowitz (1992), Sims (1986), and Woodford (1989) pp. 197–198.

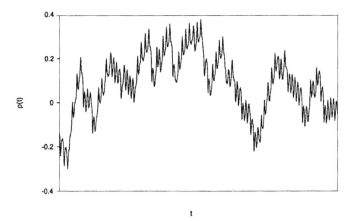

Figure 5.13. A portion of the time series $p(t)$ from a chaotic attractor of model (5.7). ($\alpha = 6\beta = 100$, $\sigma^{-2} = 200$, $\gamma = 1$, $\tau = 0.183$, $\tau' = 0.048$, time step $= 0.001$, sampling rate $= 85$, $N = 1{,}500$; about 2,500 transient sample points were thrown out before taking the data).

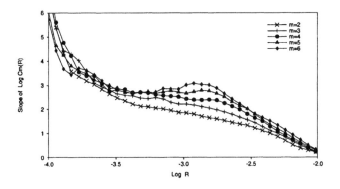

Figure 5.14. Correlation dimension for the chaotic $p(t)$ series (delay $T = 10$).

The numerical Lyapunov exponent for the simulated time series is calculated and shown earlier in Figure 5.11. It approaches the empirical value nicely.

We also have studied the effects to the dimension test from first-differencing and adding noise. As estimated, the noise level for the S & P 500 series is less than 10^{-4} (Sections 2 and 3). When adding such measurement error into the series in Figure 5.13, the dimension plot still gives a clear plateau at around 3.0. The continuous-time chaos does not seem to be masked by the measurement error. When running the GP algorithm on the first-differenced $p(t)$ series, however, the structure totally disappears. The result shows that the methodology of the BDS test on chaotic residuals resulting from differencing or fitting linear stochastic models is not justified (Wen 1996).

The simulation power of the deterministic chaos model for the original S & P 500 series greatly reinforces the conclusion that the empirical data are a continuous-time chaos.

We do not claim, however, that stochastic forces do not play a role in the price dynamics. On the contrary, it is our understanding that a model such as (5.7) should be viewed as a nonlinear propagator. When external shocks such as multiplicative noises are considered, the model becomes an extension of the Slutzky–Frisch impulse-propagation mechanism into the nonlinear regime. Interesting phenomena such as noise-induced chaos and noise-induced transition can be expected. Some preliminary results have been obtained from this model (Wen 1993b).

The stochastic version of model (5.7) may well provide a natural generalization to the ubiquitous price dynamics of modern finance, that is, the geometric Brownian motion model (Merton 1990). We hope in the near future to look into its implication for finance theory by studying the continuous-time stochastic nonlinear dynamics.

5   Conclusion

We believe we have obtained strong evidence that continuous-time chaos exists in the stock-market price dynamics. The mixed results obtained by others by studying the differenced series or return variable are due to the fact that the nonlinear structures are obscured by the operation of differencing or discrete filtering.

Checking the time-unit consistency has proved an effective means to show self-consistent interpretation for nonlinearity or chaos, even in a noisy situation. We have demonstrated that it is potentially more fruitful and more conclusive to identify the continuous-time chaos than the discrete chaos. The discovery of more convincing cases of empirical chaos will help advance the use of nonlinear dynamics in economics and finance.

Continuous-time modeling provides a coherent treatment of stock variable and flow variable, and of time scales. This is certainly important to economic dynamics. We have constructed such a deterministic model that accounts for most of the empirical features that we have obtained. The result reinforces our conclusion about continuous-time chaos.

To demonstrate the out-of-sample forecasting power of our model is on our research agenda. The following points can be offered at this stage. Our results show a Lyapunov divergence rate of 0.025 week^{-1}, which gives an upper bound of the prediction time span of about 40 weeks. The series that we have shown in Figure 5.13 is not in any way a result of overfitting.

However, chaos research should by no means be restricted to the deterministic approach. Both stochasticity and deterministic nonlinearity should play critical roles in the study of evolutionary complexity of business cycles. Rather, studying the deterministic version of the nonlinear dynamics is a strategy, because the properties of the deterministic counterpart provide valuable information for investigating the dynamic nonlinear response to external or internal shocks. We hope to treat this interesting new topic in the future.

Before ending, we feel compelled to give a thought on finance theory. We believe that the finding of chaotic dynamics in the stock market provides an alternative to the understanding of the aggregate movements. Currently, there are two standard reference points for the stock-market movements. One is the efficient-market hypothesis (Fama 1970), and the other is the "fads" (Shiller 1984), "noise trader" (De Long et al. 1990), or "bubbles" view. The former views that the price changes efficiently reflect the unexpected flow of news about fundamentals and the price changes approximately follow a random walk. The latter view leaves room for psychological factors or market sentiments, and market inefficiency. This latter view seems to be consistent with the fact that stock-market prices can change abruptly even when no substantial news appears, as in the case of 1987 Black Monday. The recent literature based on asymmetric information and market heterogeneity points to a reconciliation of these two extreme views, by looking into the complexity of the trading process [e.g., Romer (1993), and the references therein]. The view of chaos and complex dynamics provides some deeper insights, that dynamic uncertainty inherently prohibits complete assessment of fundamentals either by the market or by the market participants.[2] Economists or traders strive to be rational, but we can never be completely rational about the market. We have shown in this paper that the price is not a result of simple random processes, the market is not in equilibrium, and complex dynamics are required to describe the stock market. There is a limit to the unambiguity of the information revealed by the stock prices, in terms of the deterministic components such as trend and cycles, and in terms of the statistical distributions. The information ambiguity cannot be overcome through buying out the information asymmetry, but can be reduced through discerning the nonlinear dynamics.

Acknowledgment

I am indebted to Dr. Ping Chen for his comments in numerous discussions we have had over the past years. I thank especially Professor Ilya Prigogine for his continuing support and encouragement. Invaluable comments and suggestions also have been provided by Professors William Barnett, Richard Day, and Michael Woodford. I also thank Professor Victor Zarnowitz, the seminar

---

[2] For more general view on bounded rationality based on dynamic instability, see Prigogine (1993).

participants from the Economics Department of the Washington University in St. Louis, and the seminar participants from the Solvay Institute in Brussels. This study is supported by the I. Prigogine Center at the University of Texas at Austin. Any errors are mine.

REFERENCES

Barnett, W. A., and Chen, P. (1988). The aggregation–theoretic monetary aggregates are chaotic and have strange attractors: An econometric application of mathematical chaos. In eds. W. A. Barnett, E. R. Berndt, and H. White, *Dynamic Econometric Modelling*, Cambridge University Press, Cambridge, England 199–245.

Barnett, W. A., Gallant, A. R., and Hinich, M. (1993). Detection of nonlinearity and chaos: Application to money stock, Working Paper No. 178, Department of Economics, Washington University, St. Louis, MO.

J. Benhabib, ed. (1992). *Cycle and Chaos in Economic Equilibrium*, Princeton University Press, Princeton, NJ.

Box, G. E. P., and Jenkins, G. M. (1970). *Time Series Analysis: Forecasting and Control*, Holden–Day, San Francisco, CA.

Brock, W. A., Dechart, W. D., and Scheinkman, J. (1987). A test for independence based on the correlation dimension, SSRI Working Paper No. 8702, University of Wisconsin at Madison.

Chen, P. (1988). Empirical and theoretical evidence of monetary chaos, *Sys. Dynam. Rev.*, **4**, 81–108.

(1993). Searching for economic chaos: A challenge to econometric practice and nonlinear tests. In eds. R. Day and P. Chen, Oxford University Press, New York.

Day, R. H. (1993). Nonlinear dynamics and evolutionary economics. In eds. R. H. Day and P. Chen Oxford University Press, New York.

Day, R. H., and Chen, P. eds. (1993). *Nonlinear Dynamics and Evolutionary Economics*, Oxford University Press, New York.

De Long, J. B., Shleifer, A., Summers, L. H., and Waidmann, R. J. (1990). Noise trader risk in financial markets, *J. Political Eco.*, **98**, 703–38.

Ding, Z. X., Granger, C. W. J., and Engle, R. F. (1993). A long memory property of stock market returns and a new model, *J. Empirical Finance*, **1**(1), 83–106.

Engle, R. F. (1982). Autoregressive conditional heteroskedasticity with estimates of the variance of U.K. inflation, *Econometrica*, **50**, 987–1008.

Fama, E. F. (1970). Efficient capital markets: A review of theory and empirical work, *J. Finance*, **25**, 384–433.

Friedman, M. (1969). *The Optimum Quantity of Money and Other Essays*, Aldine, Chicago, IL, chap. 11.

Gandolfo, G. (1981). *Quantitative Analysis and Econometric Estimation of Continuous Time Dynamic Models*, North-Holland, New York.

Granger, C. W. J. (1991). Development in the nonlinear analysis of economic series, *Scand. J. Econ.*, **93**(2), 263–76.

Grassberger, P. and Procaccia, L. (1983). Measuring the strangeness of strange attractors, *Phys. Rev. Lett.*, **50**, 346–9.

Huang, W. H., and Day, R. H. (1993). Chaotically switching bear and bull markets: The derivation of stock price distributions from behavioral rules. In eds. R. H. Day and P. Chen.

Koopmans, T. C. (1950). Models involving a continuous time series. In ed. T. C. Koopmans, *Statistical Inference in Dynamic Economic Models*, Wiley, New York.

LeBaron, B. (1991). The changing structure of stock returns. In eds. W. A. Brock, D. A. Hsieh, and B. LeBaron., *Nonlinear Dynamics, Chaos, and Instability: Statistical Theory and Economic Evidence*, MIT Press, Cambridge, MA.

Mandelbrot, B. (1963). The variation of certain speculative prices, *J. Business*, **36**, 394–419.

Mandelbrot, B. B. (1977). *Fractals, Forms, Chances and Dimension*, Freeman, San Francisco, CA.

Medio, A. (1992). *Chaotic Dynamics: Theory and Applications to Economics*, Cambridge University Press.

Merton, R. C. (1990). *Continuous-Time Finance*, Basil Blackwell Publishers, Cambridge, MA.

Poterba, J. M., and Summers, L. H. (1988). "Mean reversion in stock prices: Evidence and implications," *J. Financial Econ.*, **22**, 27–59.

Prigogine, I. (1962). *Nonequilibrium Statistical Mechanics*, Wiley, New York.
(1993). Bounded rationality: From dynamical systems to socio-economic models. In eds. R. Day and P. Chen, Oxford University Press, New York.

Prigogine, I., and Stengers, I. (in press) *Time, Chaos and the Quantum: Towards the Resolution of the Time Paradox*, Harmony House.

Ramsey, J. B., Sayers, C. L., and Rothman, P. (1990). The statistical properties of dimension calculations using small data sets: Some economic Applications, *Int. Econ. Rev.*, **31**(4), 991–1020.

Romer, D. (1993). Rational asset-price movements without news, *Am. Econ. Rev.*, **83**(5), 1112–30.

Scheinkman, J. A., and LeBaron, B. (1989). Nonlinear dynamics and stock returns, *J. Business*, **62**(3), 311–38.

Shiller, R. J. (1984). Stock prices and social dynamics, *Brookings Pap. Econ. Act.*, **2**, 457–98.

Sims, C. (1986). Commentaries on the Grandmont paper "On endogenous competitive business cycles," In ed. H. F. Sonnenschein. *Models of Economic Dynamics*, Lecture Notes in Economics and Mathematical Systems, Vol. 264, Springer–Verlag, Berlin, pp. 37–39.

Slutzky, E. (1937). The summation of random causes as the source of cyclic processes, *Econometrica*, 105–46.

Takens, F. (1981). Detecting strange attractors. In eds. D. A. Rand and L. S. Young, *Dynamical Systems and Turbulence*, Lecture Notes in Mathematics, No. 898, Springer–Verlag, Berlin, pp. 366–81.

Theiler, J., Galdrikian, B., Longtin, A., Eubank, S., and Farmer, J. D. (1992). Using surrogate data to detect nonlinearity in time series. In eds. M. Casdagli and S. Eubank, *Nonlinear Modeling and Forecasting*, Addison–Wesley, Reading, MA.

Tsiang, S.-C. (1988). The flow formulation of a monetary for an open economy and the determination of the exchange rate. In eds. M. Kohn and S.-C. Tsiang, *Finance Constraints, Expectations, and Macroeconomics*, Oxford University Press, New York.

Wang, M. C., and Uhlenbeck, G. E. (1945). On the theory of Brownian motion II, *Rev. Mod, Phys.*, **17**(2–3), 323–42.

Wen, K. H. (1993). Complex dynamics in nonequilibrium economics and chemistry, Ph.D. dissertation, University of Texas at Austin.
(1993b). Evolving properties and complex dynamics in stock market prices – A perspective for unifying deterministic and stochastic approaches in business cycles, Working Paper, Ilya Prigogine Center for Studies in Statistical Mechanics and Complex Systems, University of Texas at Austin.

(1996). Continuous-time chaos and expectations-driven dynamics – an excess demand flow model of the stock market, in revision.

Wen, K. H., and Chen, P. (1992). Multi-regime expectations and complexity of soft-bouncing oscillator – a delayed response model of business cycles, IC^2 Institute Working Paper No. 92-10-03, University of Texas at Austin.

Wen, K. H., Chen, P., and Zhang, Z. L. (1992). Evolving multi-humped distributions and switching business modes – empirical observations of nonequilibrium behavior, IC^2 Institute Working Paper No. 92-09-05, University of Texas at Austin.

Wen, K. H., Chen, P., and Turner, J. S. (1994). Bifurcations in a Liénard equation with two delays. In eds. G. S. Ladde and M. Sambandham, *Proceeding of Dynamic Systems and Applications*, Vol. 1, Dynamic, Atlanta, GA.

Wolf, A., Swift, J., Swinney, H., and Vastano, J. (1985). Determining Lyapunov exponents from a time series, *Phys. D.*, **16**, 285–317.

Woodford, M. (1989). Imperfect financial intermediation and complex dynamics. In eds. W. A. Barnett, J. Geweke, and K. Shell, *Economic Complexity: Chaos, Sunspots, Bubbles, and Nonlinearity*, Cambridge University Press, Cambridge, England.

Zarnowitz, V. (1992). *Business Cycles, Theory, History, Indicators, and Forecasting*, University of Chicago Press, Chicago, IL.

Zhang, Z. L., Wen, K. H., and Chen, P. (1992). Complex spectral analysis of economic dynamics and correlation resonances in market behavior, IC^2 Institute Working Paper No. 92-09-02, University of Texas at Austin.

PART III

Tests for nonlinearity and chaos

An experimental design to compare tests of nonlinearity and chaos

William A. Barnett, A. Ronald Gallant, Melvin J. Hinich,
Jochen A. Jungeilges, Daniel T. Kaplan, and Mark J. Jensen

In recent years, there has been growing interest in testing for nonlinearity and chaos in economic data, but much disagreement and controversy has arisen about the available results. For example, Barnett and Chen published a case in which successful detection of chaos has been claimed with economic data. That published claim has generated considerable controversy, as have all such published findings of chaos. Similar controversies have arisen regarding publication of the weaker claim of nonlinearity. In short, there seems to be little agreement about the existence of nonlinearity or chaos in economic data, with some economists continuing to insist that linearity remains a good assumption for all economic time series, despite the fact that economic theory provides little support for the assumption of linearity.

In an attempt to explore the reasons for these empirical difficulties, five tests for nonlinearity or chaos were applied to various monetary aggregate data series. Inferences varied across tests for the same data, and within tests for varying sample sizes and various methods of aggregation of the data. In short, robustness of inferences in this area of research seemed to be low. It has been argued that it is this robustness problem that accounts for the controversies surrounding empirical claims of nonlinearity and chaos in economics.

A likely explanation for the results with those five tests is that they have different power functions, and hence some may have more power against some alternatives than others. If that is the case, then none uniformly dominates the others, but each may have its own uses. However, the power functions cannot be explored with real economic data, because the true generating mechanism is not known. We therefore designed an experiment, in the form of a competition,

This research was partially supported by the National Science Foundation (NSF) in the United States (Barnett, Gallant), the U.S. Office of Naval Research (Hinich), the Medical Research Council in Canada (Kaplan), and the German Science Foundation in Germany (Jungeilges). Mark Jensen was employed as a research assistant under Barnett's NSF grant. We benefited from the comments of William Brock.

to determine how each test would perform, when the data was generated by Monte Carlo methods from known structures, and with each test conducted by an expert in the use of that test, but without his having knowledge of the model that generated the data. In this paper, we provide the details of the experimental design used in controlling the competition.

1   Introduction

1.1   *Competition design*

We describe the details of the design of an ongoing single-blind controlled competition, in which we compare the power of five highly regarded tests for nonlinearity or chaos against various alternatives. The data used in this competition were simulated using five different generating models and two different sample sizes. Hence, there were 10 samples involved in the complete competition. One model, and hence two of the data sets, was purely deterministic (and chaotic). The other four models, and hence eight of the data sets, were stochastic processes in which the randomness was produced by Monte Carlo methods. One of the stochastic processes was linear, and the other three were nonlinear, but not chaotic. Although the same five generating models were used to produce both sample sizes, the participants in the experiment were not aware of that fact. Hence, the participants had no reason to believe that fewer than 10 generating models were used to produce the simulated data. When completed, the competition will result in a paper providing the results of the competition. To retain the integrity of the process, none of the results can be revealed until the competition is complete.[2] This conference paper was produced while the competition was still under way, and hence none of the results available at that time can be revealed. When the results of the competition are published, that publication will include only an outline of the experimental design, because the details of the design are available from this paper.

The data were generated at Washington University in St. Louis and sent by electronic mail to the participants in the experiment, who were provided with no information regarding the nature of the simulated data. Each participant used one test to analyze each of the data series. Throughout the competition, William Barnett and Mark Jensen at Washington University generated the data and were the only participants having any knowledge of the nature of the data. They did not reveal the generating models to the other participants until the competition was complete and all results from all participants had been received.

Only one of the tests used in this competition – the BDS test was run at Washington University, and that test is available in a widely used computer program. We acquired the computer program from William Brock and report

---

[2] The results will be revealed in Barnett, Gallant, Hinich, Jungeilges, Kaplan, and Jensen (1996).

the results acquired with his program. The simulated data are available to anyone who might wish to replicate the reported results with the BDS test. The other five tests are more complicated to run and possibly could have been prejudiced in some ways if the generating model were known to the person running the test. Hence, each of those tests was run by a competition participant who was supplied with no prior information about the generating models. In addition, each of those participants has established expertise in the test that he ran and a possible vested interest in producing the best possible results. In three of those cases, the participant was among the originators of the test, and in the remaining case, the participant has produced and used a computer program that is especially well suited to executing the test that he ran.

All five of the tests used in this competition are purported to be useful with noisy data of moderate sample size. The two sample sizes used in this competition were intended to include a sample of small size relative to the capabilities of the tests and a sample of large size. The computational cost of running some of these tests is very high with the large sample. With one of the tests, months of execution time on a workstation are needed to complete the test with each of the five large sample data sets. These computation costs limited to five the number of generating models that reasonably could be used to produce the simulated data in the competition, at least in the large sample case.

1.2   *Motivation for competition*

In recent years, there has been growing interest in testing for nonlinearity and chaos in economic data, but much disagreement and controversy has arisen about the available results. For example, Barnett and Chen (1986, 1988a,b) claimed a successful detection of chaos. That conclusion was further confirmed with the same data by DeCoster and Mitchell (1991, 1994). However, the finding was subsequently disputed by Ramsey, Sayers, and Rothman (1988) and Ramsey and Rothman (1994), who also raise questions regarding virtually all of the other published tests of chaos. Various replies have been published, including those of Barnett and Hinich (1992, 1993) and that of DeCoster and Mitchell (1994). Further results relevant to those controversies recently were provided by Serletis (1994). In short, there is little agreement about the existence of chaos or even of nonlinearity in economic data, and some economists continue to insist that linearity remains a good assumption for all economic time series, despite the fact that economic theory provides very little support for the assumption of linearity. This paper explores the reasons for these empirical difficulties.

In earlier papers of less scope, Barnett and Hinich (1992, 1993) argue that the controversies stem primarily from two sources; the high noise level that exists in most aggregated economic data and the relatively low sample sizes that are available with economic data. The algorithms currently available to detect chaos, such as the Lyapunov exponent test and the Grassberger–Procaccia dimension computation, were originated primarily for use with experimental data in physics. Because physicists often can generate very large samples of high-quality data, they find these algorithms to be directly applicable to their research. Unfortunately, economists are not so favorably situated.

In a sense, the controversies regarding the existence of nonlinearity or chaos in economic data seem surprising. The statistical tests used in this paper, as well as the conventional deterministic tests used by Barnett and Chen, do not test specifically for the existence of nonlinearity or chaos produced from within the structure of the economy. In fact, the tests have no way of determining the source of the nonlinearity or chaos, because the tests have no way of knowing the boundaries of the economic system. Hence, any of these tests could find chaos in an economic system, even if the economic system is entirely linear and stable, but is subject to chaotic shocks from an unstable surrounding weather system. If, in such a case, shocks from the surrounding environment are important in explaining economic fluctuations, nonlinearity or even low-dimensional chaos could be found in economic data, despite the fact that the origins of the chaos are in the nonlinear dynamics of weather formation.

To be able to isolate the source of nonlinear dynamics to be within the structure of the economy, we would need a parametric structural model of the economy, and we would then need to test the hypothesis that the parameters lie within the subset of the parameter space that supports chaos, or some other nonlinear bifurcation regime for which we may wish to test. However, mathematicians currently do not have the ability to solve for the boundary of that set in the chaotic case, when the number of parameters exceeds three. Hence with plausible structural economic models, we do not have the ability to locate the boundaries of the set that define the null hypothesis of chaos within the economic structure, and hence we do not have the ability to test for chaos within such a structure. The situation in the nonchaotic nonlinear cases is not much better, except in the case of very simple forms of nonlinearity, such as single-frequency cycles.

Because the available tests are not structural and hence are unable to identify the source of detected chaos, the alternative hypothesis of the available tests is that no natural deterministic explanation exists for the observed economic fluctuations anywhere in the universe. In other words, the alternative hypothesis is that the economic fluctuations are produced by supernatural shocks or by inherent randomness in the sense of quantum physics. Considering the implausibility of the alternative hypothesis, one would think that findings of chaos in such a nonparametric test would produce little controversy, whereas any claims to the contrary would be subjected to careful examination. Yet, the opposite seems to be the case. The resistance to the results of tests for nonchaotic nonlinearity are even more surprising.

It would appear that the controversies must be produced by the nature of the tests themselves, rather than by the nature of the hypothesis. In particular, there may be very little robustness of such tests. The fact that the likelihood function has been found to be extremely irregular under chaos (see, e.g., Geweke 1989, El-Gamal 1991) might suggest that results may be difficult to find that are consistent across variations in sample size, test method, and aggregation. That possibility was the subject of Barnett, Gallant, Hinich, Jungeilges, Kaplan, and Jensen (1994), who used five of the most widely used tests for nonlinearity or chaos with various monetary aggregate data series of various sample sizes and acquired results that differed substantially across tests and over sample sizes, as well as over the statistical index-number formulas used to aggregate over the same component data.

It is possible that none of these tests completely dominates the other, because some tests may have higher power against certain alternatives than other tests, without any of the tests necessarily having higher power against all alternatives. If this is the case, each of the tests may have its own comparative advantages, and there may even be a gain from using more than one of the tests in a sequence designed to narrow down the alternatives. This competition was designed to explore the relative powers of the five tests used by Barnett, Gallant, Hinich, Jungeilges, Kaplan, and Jensen (1994), against various alternatives.

2   Data generation

The sample sizes generated consisted of a small sample of size 380 and a large sample of size 2000. The observations were produced with each of the two sample sizes from each of the following five models:

Model I is the fully deterministic, chaotic Feigenbaum recursion of the form:

$$y_t = 3.57 y_{t-1}(1 - y_{t-1}),$$

where the initial condition was set at $y_0 = 0.7$.

Model II is a generalized autoregressive conditional heteroskedasticity (GARCH) process of the following form:

$$y_t = h_t^{1/2} u_t,$$

where h_t is defined by

$$h_t = 1 + 0.1 y_{t-1}^2 + 0.8 h_{t-1},$$

with $h_0 = 1$ and $y_0 = 0$.

Model III is a nonlinear moving-average (NLMA) process of the following form:

$$y_t = u_t + 0.8u_{t-1}u_{t-2}.$$

Model IV is an autoregressive conditional heteroskedasticity (ARCH) process of the following form:

$$y_t = (1 + 0.5y_{t-1}^2)^{1/2}u_t,$$

with the value of the initial observation set at $y_0 = 0$.

Model V is an autoregressive moving average (ARMA) model of the form:

$$y_t = 0.8y_{t-1} + 0.15y_{t-2} + u_t + 0.3u_{t-1},$$

with $y_0 = 1$ and $y_1 = 0.7$.

With the four stochastic models, the white-noise disturbances, u_t, are sampled independently from a standard normal distribution. Those, white-noise disturbances were generated using the fast acceptance-region algorithm of Kinderman and Ramage (1976), with the initial seed value set by the clock of the computer at the time the program was run. Of the five generating models, only Model V is linear, only Model I is chaotic, and only Model I is noise free.

3   Test methods and capabilities

We use five inference methods to test for nonlinearity or chaos with the simulated data: the Hinich bispectrum test, the BDS test, Lyapunov exponent estimator of Nychka, Ellner, Gallant, and McCaffrey (1992), White's test, and Kaplan's test.

The tests used by Barnett and Chen (1988a) are commonly used in the experimental physics literature. With noise-free data: the connection between those tests and chaos is well understood [see, e.g., Brock and Dechert (1988) for proofs of the relevant theorems]. But the appropriate way to use those tests with noisy data is not entirely clear, because the sampling distributions of the test statistics are not known. This ambiguity may be one source of the controversies that have arisen in economics regarding tests for chaos.

In this competition, we use tests derived for use with noisy data. The Hinich bispectral test is a test in the frequency domain of flatness of the bispectrum. The sampling properties of the test statistic are known, and the approach is based on conventional time-series inference methodology. The test was run by Hinich in Austin, Texas, without knowledge of the models that generated the data. The BDS test is a test for whiteness, which can be used to test for residual nonlinear structure, after linear structure has been removed through prewhitening. The test was run by Mark Jensen at Washington University. Although he was aware of the generating models, he used the BDS test program that has been supplied widely on floppy disk by William Brock. The Nychka–Ellner–Gallant–McCaffrey (NEGM) test is a nonparametric test for positivity of the maximum Lyapunov exponent.[3] The NEGM test was run by Gallant in North Carolina without knowledge of the models that generated the data. White's test is a test for nonlinearity and was run by Jochen Jungeilges without knowledge of the models that generated the data. He used his own program, which implements White's test. Kaplan's test can be used to test either for nonlinearity or for more focused special cases of nonlinearity, such as chaos. Kaplan's test was run by Kaplan in Quebec without knowledge of the models that generated the data.

4   Available conventional tests

By using conventional stochastic-process methods for testing for nonlinear dynamics, we are limited largely to tests for general nonlinearity, which is necessary but not sufficient for chaos. There are three well-known tests currently in use for testing for nonlinearity: the BDS test (Brock et al. 1986), White's neural-network test, and the Hinich bispectrum test.

The BDS test provides an important advance in testing for stochastic dependence, and hence the BDS test is a significant new contribution to the field of statistics. But the BDS test does not provide a direct test either for nonlinearity or for chaos, because the sampling distribution of the test statistic is not known, either in finite samples or asymptotically, under the null hypothesis of nonlinearity, linearity, chaos, or the lack of chaos. The asymptotic distribution is known under the null of independence. Hence, the hypotheses of nonlinearity and chaos are nested within the alternative hypothesis, which includes both nonwhite linear and nonwhite nonlinear processes.

In conventional statistical methodology, one tests a hypothesis by equating it with the null – not by using the power function of the test to try to discriminate among subsets of the alternative hypothesis. Under the latter nonstandard approach, virtually every known hypothesis would be a test for nonlinearity or chaos, because nearly every statistical test contains nonlinearity and chaos as subsets somewhere within either the null or the alternative hypothesis. Nevertheless, it is possible to use the BDS test to test any estimated parametric stochastic process against the remaining alternatives, if the parametric process null has been removed from the data by prefiltering. For example, if all linear

---

[3] Gencay and Dechert (1992) have proposed a test that is similar in some respects to the NEGM test. As a result of that similarity, we did not believe that a comparison between those two tests was a likely place to look for a robustness problem. In addition, we believe that a comparison between such related tests would require a much larger number of comparisons than we had available with the data used in the current study. From this class of tests, we therefore decided to run only the NEGM test.

possibilities have been removed by fitting the best possible linear model, the BDS test can be used to test the residuals for remaining nonlinear dependence.

Similarly, if all nonchaotic possibilities could be removed by fitting the best possible nonchaotic model, the BDS test could be used to test the residuals for remaining chaotic dependence. But filtering out all possible nonchaotic possibilities with certainty seems to be beyond the state of the art. Hence, it is not clear how the BDS test can be used to produce a convincing inference regarding chaos, where we here define noisy chaos to be a stochastic process having chaotic signal. For a more formal definition, see Nychka, Ellner, Gallant, and McCaffrey (1992).

Filtering out all linear possibilities with certainty is difficult at best, but, nevertheless, prefiltering by autoregressive integrated moving average (ARIMA) fit is often viewed as a reputable means of prewhitening, and hence we use the BDS test to test for remaining nonlinear dependence in the residuals of an ARIMA process fitted by the Box–Jenkins approach. There have been a number of other recent attempts to apply the BDS test to nonlinearity testing of filtered data. For one such interesting example, see Scheinkman and LeBaron (1989). We describe the BDS test in Section 6. Despite our reservations regarding the usefulness of the BDS test in testing for chaos, we believe that the BDS test produces a viable test of linearity against the omnibus alternative of nonlinearity, when the data are prefiltered by ARIMA fit. We use the BDS test for that purpose.

The Hinich bispectrum approach provides a direct test for nonlinearity as well as a direct test for Gaussianity, because Hinich's approach produces a test statistic having known asymptotic sampling distribution under the null of linearity, as well as another test statistic having known asymptotic sampling distribution under the null of Gaussianity. However, the alternative hypothesis is not as broad as that for the BDS test. With the bispectrum test, the alternative hypothesis is all nonlinear processes having nonflat bispectrum. However, there are some nonlinear processes displaying nonflat polyspectra only at the trispectrum or higher order. Hence, the bispectrum test has zero power against some forms of nonlinearity. In such cases, the nonlinearity can be detected by subsequently running the trispectrum test of Dalle Molle and Hinich (1989, 1991) or of Walden and Williams (1993). The BDS test, on the other hand, has high power against a vast class of nonlinear alternatives.

In Section 5, we describe the Hinich bispectrum approach, which is related to the approach of Subba Rao and Gabr (1980). Note that Hinich (1994) has a related newer test, which is an analogue to the bispectrum test in the time domain. Although that newer test may have power against a broader alternative than the frequency-domain bispectrum test, Hinich's newer test is not yet as widely known as his popular bispectrum test. As a result, we have not included Hinich's newer test in this competition.

White's test uses neural-net methods to test for nonlinearity. A connection exists between the White test, which we use as a candidate for a test of nonlinearity, and the NEGM test for chaos, because the NEGM test prefilters with a neural net before testing for chaos with the fitted neural net. Because chaos is a stronger hypothesis than nonlinearity, the connection between the two tests could be useful in sequential testing. In particular, if nonlinearity is rejected with the White test, then there is diminished reason to proceed further with the NEGM test for chaos, because chaos is a strictly nested special case of nonlinearity.

Although the BDS, White, and Hinich tests are among the best-known tests available for testing nonlinearity in noisy data, we believe that there is only one well-established candidate for a test for chaotic signal in small samples of noisy data. That is the NEGM test.[4] We describe the NEGM test in Section 7.

A new test that examines the evidence for the continuity of dynamic maps has been proposed by Kaplan (1993). At present, Kaplan's test has not been subjected to the extensive Monte Carlo comparisons that are available for the NEGM test. The Kaplan test compares a test statistic computed directly from the data with the test statistic produced from surrogate data. Here, the surrogate data have been produced from linear processes having the same histogram and an almost identical autocorrelation function as the actual data. The null hypothesis is linearity of the dynamics found in the data. However, depending on the manner in which the surrogate data are produced, the method appears relevant to the investigation of more sharply focused forms of complex dynamics. We describe the test briefly in Section 9. For more details, see Kaplan (1993).

5 Hinich bispectral approach

5.1 *Definitions and background*

If $\{x(t)\}$ is a zero-mean third-order stationary time series, then the mean $\mu_x = E[x(t)] = 0$, the covariance $c_{xx}(m) = E[x(t+m)x(t)]$, and the general third-order moments $c_{xxx}(s, r) = E[x(t+r)x(t+s)x(t)]$ are independent of t. If $c_{xx}(m) = 0$ for all nonzero m, the series is white noise. Priestly (1981) and Hinich and Patterson (1985) stress that although a series may be white noise, $x(n)$ and $x(m)$ may be stochastically dependent unless $\{x(t)\}$ is multivariate Gaussian. Only under multivariate Gaussianity are lack of correlation (whiteness) and stochastic independence the same. If the distribution of $\{x(n_l), \dots, x(n_N)\}$ is multivariate normal for all $n_1, \dots, n_N$, then the series

---

[4] The method of Gencay and Dechert (1992), mentioned above, is among the other promising possibilities, but that test as well as the others have not been subjected to the degree of experimentation that currently is available for the NEGM test with noisy data.

is defined as Gaussian, where N is the sample size.[5] Hinich and Patterson (1985, p. 70) fault Box and Jenkins (1970, p. 8 vs p. 46) and Jenkins and Watts (1968, p. 149 vs p. 157) for blurring the definitions of whiteness and independence.

We define a pure-white-noise series as one in which $x(n_1), \ldots, x(n_N)$ are independent random variables for all values of $n_1, \ldots, n_N$. All pure-white-noise series are white. All white-noise series are not pure white noise unless, in addition, they are Gaussian.

In addition to stationarity, whiteness, and pure whiteness, linearity is another often assumed property of a time series. Many researchers implicitly assume that the errors of their models are Gaussian, and test for pure white noise by using the covariance function $c_{xx}(m)$, but ignore the information regarding possible nonlinear relationships that are found in the third-order moments $c_{xxx}(s, r)$.

The above discussion suggests the need to test for both nonlinearity and Gaussianity, in addition to testing in the usual ways for whiteness.

5.2   *Test method*

Hinich (1985) argues that the bispectrum in the frequency domain is easier to interpret than the multiplicity of third-order moments $\{c_{xxx}(r, s): s \leq r, r = 0, 1, 2, \ldots\}$ in the time domain. For frequencies f_1 and f_2 in the principal domain,

$$\Omega = \{(f_1, f_2) : 0 < f_1 < 0.5, f_2 < f_1, 2f_1 + f_2 < 1\},$$

the bispectrum, $B_{xxx}(f_1, f_2)$, is defined by

$$B_{xxx}(f_1, f_2) = \sum_{r=-\infty}^{\infty} \sum_{s=-\infty}^{\infty} c_{xxx}(r, s) \exp[-i2\pi(f_1 r + f_2 s)]. \quad (6.1)$$

The bispectrum is the double Fourier transformation of the third-order moments function.[6]

---

[5] In accordance with time-series conventions, we equate Gaussianity of the time series with multivariate Gaussianity.

[6] The bispectrum is the third-order polyspectrum, whereas the ordinary power spectrum is the second-order polyspectrum. Strictly speaking, the polyspectrum of order k is the Fourier transform of the cumulant function (not the moment function) of order k. Cumulants are defined as the coefficients of the terms in the power-series expansion of the *logarithm* of the characteristic function of a distribution, whereas the moments are the coefficients of the terms in the power-series expansion of the *level* of the characteristic function of the distribution. Unlike the moments, the cumulants have the merit of being semi-invariants. However for a stationary time series with zero mean, the second- and third-order cumulant functions are identical to the second- and third-order moment functions. Only at the fourth and higher orders do the cumulant functions differ from the moment functions. But, because we use only the second and third orders under the assumption of stationarity and zero mean, we need draw no distinction between moments and cumulants.

The statistical tests based on the sample bispectrum that we briefly discuss in this section were applied with success to the study of acoustic signals and noise by Brockett, Hinich, and Wilson (1987) and to stock prices and exchange rates by Hinich and Patterson (1985, 1989) and Brockett, Hinich, and Patterson (1988).

The skewness function $\Gamma(f_1, f_2)$ is defined in terms of the bispectrum as follows:

$$\Gamma^2(f_1, f_2) = |B_{xxx}(f_1, f_2)|^2/S_{xx}(f_1)S_{xx}(f_2)S_{xx}(f_1 + f_2), \qquad (6.2)$$

where $S_{xx}(f)$ is the (ordinary power) spectrum of $x(t)$ at frequency f. Because the bispectrum is complex valued, the absolute value (vertical) lines in equation (6.2) designate modulus. Brillinger (1965) proves that the skewness function $\Gamma(f_1, f_2)$ is constant over all frequencies $(f_1, f_2)\epsilon\Omega$, if $\{x(t)\}$ is linear, whereas $\Gamma(f_1, f_2)$ is zero over all frequencies, if $\{x(t)\}$ is Gaussian. Linearity and Gaussianity can be tested using a sample estimator of the skewness function $\Gamma(f_1, f_2)$. We now outline the procedure that we use to obtain the bispectrum.

5.3   Computation of the test statistics

Let $f_k = k/N$ for each integer k. For the sample $\{x(0), x(1), \ldots, x(N - 1)\}$, define $F_{xxx}(f_j, f_k)$ to be an estimate of the bispectrum of $\{x(t)\}$ at the frequency pair (f_j, f_k) such that:

$$F_{xxx}(f_j, f_k) = X(f_j)X(f_k)X^*(f_j + f_k)/N, \qquad (6.3)$$

where

$$X(f_j) = \sum_{t=0}^{N-1} x(t)\exp(-i2\pi f_j t).$$

The asterisk in equation (6.3) designates complex conjugate.

The function $F_{xxx}(f_j, f_k)$ must be smoothed as follows to form a consistent estimator: Let $\langle B_{xxx}(f_m, f_n)\rangle$ denote a smoothed estimate of $B_{xxx}(f_m, f_n)$, which is obtained by averaging over values of $F_{xxx}(f_j, f_k)$ at adjacent frequency pairs such that

$$\langle B_{xxx}(f_m, f_n)\rangle = M^{-2} \sum_{j=(m-1)M}^{mM-1} \sum_{k=(n-1)M}^{nM-1} F_{xxx}(f_j, f_k). \qquad (6.4)$$

This estimator $\langle B_{xxx}(f_m, f_n)\rangle$, is the average of the $F_{xxx}(f_j, f_k)$ over a square on M^2 points. It is a consistent and asymptotically complex normal estimator of the bispectrum, $B_{xxx}(f_1, f_2)$, if the sequence (f_m, f_n) converges to (f_1, f_2) (see Hinich 1982).

As discussed earlier, the estimated skewness function, $\Gamma(f_m, f_n)$, will not be significantly different from a constant at any frequency pair in Ω under the null hypothesis of linearity. If the null hypothesis is Gaussianity as well as linearity, then that constant is zero. The skewness function can be used to motivate construction of the normalized test statistic, $2|\delta(f_m, f_n)|^2$, where

$$\delta(f_m, f_n) = \langle B_{xxx}(f_m, f_n) \rangle / [(N/M^2) \langle S_{xx}(f_m) \rangle \langle S_{xx}(f_n) \rangle$$
$$\times \langle S_{xx}(f_m + f_n) \rangle]^{1/2}. \tag{6.5}$$

In this formula, $\langle S_{xx}(\cdot) \rangle$ is defined as a consistent and asymptotically normal estimator of the power spectrum $S_{xx}(\cdot)$, and $f_m = (2m - 1)M/2N$ for each integer m. Hinich has shown that $2[\delta(f_m, f_n)]^2$ is approximately distributed as an independent noncentral chi-squared variate with two degrees of freedom at frequency pair (f_m, f_n).

The larger that M is, the less the finite sample variance is and the larger the sample bias is. Because of this trade-off, there is no unique M that is appropriate to use for performing nonlinearity and Gaussianity tests based upon the estimated statistics given by equation (6.5). When M is large, the bandwidth is large, the variance is reduced, and the resolution of the tests is small, because there are too few terms for the linearity test. If M is small, there is a large number of terms to sort for the linearity tests, the variance may be too large, and the chi-square approximation used for the linearity test may not be good. Hinich (1982) suggested that M should be selected to be approximately the square root of the number of observations, N.

Let P denote the number of frequency pairs in the principal domain, Ω, and let

$$D = \{(m, n) : (f_m, f_n) \epsilon \Omega\},$$

so that P is the cardinal number of the set D. Hinich (1982) showed that the P values of $2|\delta(f_m, f_n)|^2$ for $(m, n) \epsilon D$ are approximately distributed as independent, noncentral chi-square variates with noncentrality parameter $\lambda(f_m, f_n)$, where

$$\lambda(f_m, f_n) = (2M^2/N)|B_{xxx}(f_m, f_n)|^2/S_{xx}(f_m)S_{xx}(f_n)S_{xx}(f_m + f_n)$$
$$= (2M^2/N)\Gamma^2(f_m, f_n). \tag{6.6}$$

Define the test statistic

$$\text{CHISUM} = 2 \sum_{(m,n)\epsilon D} \sum |\delta(f_m, f_n)|^2. \tag{6.7}$$

The distribution of CHISUM is approximately a noncentral chi-square with $2P$ degrees of freedom with a noncentrality parameter that is the sum of the $\lambda(f_m, f_n)$ over all $(m, n) \epsilon D$.

Under the null hypothesis that $\{x(t)\}$ is Gaussian and thus the skewness function $\Gamma(f_m, f_n)$ is identically zero over all $(m, n) \in D$, CHISUM is approximately a central chi-square $2P$ variate. Equation (6.7) gives us an asymptotic chi-square test of the Gaussianity hypothesis. If the time series is linear but not necessarily Gaussian, then the skewness function is constant, which implies from equation (6.6) that the noncentrality parameters are constant. The Hinich linearity test uses the empirical distribution function of $\{2|\delta(f_m, f_n)|\}$ in the principal domain to test the null hypothesis that the $\lambda(f_m, f_n)$ are all the same. A robust single test statistic for this dispersion is the 80th quantile of these statistics.

For details of the test, see Hinich (1982), Hinich and Patterson (1985, 1989), and Ashley, Patterson, and Hinich (1986). In particular, the final transformed test statistics are distributed as standard normal random variates under the respective null hypotheses. When the null is Gaussianity, the resulting test statistic is denoted by H. When the null is linearity, the test statistic is denoted by Z. In both cases, the distribution of the standard normal is used to produce a one-sided test, in which the null is rejected if the test statistic is large.

Ashley, Patterson, and Hinich (1986, p. 174) presented an equivalence theorem that proves that the Hinich bispectral linearity test statistic is invariant to linear filtering of the data. An important implication of the theorem is that if $x(t)$ is found to be nonlinear, then the residuals of a linear model of the form $y(t) = f[x(t)]$ will also be nonlinear, because the nonlinearity in $x(t)$ will pass through any linear filter, f. The above paper further reported tables on the power of the Hinich linearity test for detecting violations of the linearity and Gaussianity hypotheses for a number of sample sizes and M values. The table indicates substantial power for both tests, even when N is as small as 256, if the value of M used is between 12 and 17. For this sample size, the power of the test falls off, as M increases above 17.

6   The BDS test

6.1   *General features of the test*

The details of the BDS test (Brock et al. 1986) are well known in this literature. The test uses the correlation function (also called the correlation integral) as the test statistic. This choice is in contrast to the Grassberger–Procaccia test, which uses the correlation dimension. The correlation function is needed in deriving the correlation dimension, but the two are not the same. The correlation dimension's value has a direct connection with the Hausdorf dimension of the attractor. Hence, the correlation dimension, in principle, has a direct connection with chaos. In particular, low fractional Hausdorf dimension is the result sought by those looking for useful chaos. The determinism in high-dimensional chaos cannot be modeled without large numbers of variables, and in the limit, infinite-dimensional chaos is white noise.

Although correlation dimension is therefore potentially very useful in testing for chaos, the sampling properties of the correlation dimension are unknown. If the only source of stochasticity is noise in the data, and if that noise is slight, then it is possible to filter the noise out of the data and use the correlation-dimension test deterministically. However, if the economic structure that generated the data contains a stochastic disturbance within its equations, the correlation dimension is stochastic and its derived distribution is important in producing a reliable inference.

The BDS test uses the correlation function as the test statistic. The asymptotic distribution of the correlation function is known under the null hypothesis of whiteness (independent and identically distributed observations). As a result, the BDS test can be used to produce a formal statistical test of whiteness against general dependence. However, the sampling distribution of the BDS test statistic is not known under the nulls of chaos, nonlinearity, or linearity. We are left with the uncomfortable choice between the correlation dimension, which produces a direct test for chaos, but only when no stochastic shocks exist within the model, or the correlation function, which does have known sampling properties when there are stochastic shocks within the model, but only under a different null hypothesis (i.e., pure whiteness).

Nevertheless, the BDS test can be used to produce indirect evidence about nonlinearity. In particular, an ARIMA process can be fitted to the data in an attempt to remove linear structure. The BDS test then can be used to determine whether there is evidence of remaining dependence in the data. If all linear dependence has already been removed, then any remaining dependence must be nonlinear. In principle, there are some difficulties with this approach. The Box–Jenkins estimate of the ARIMA process may not succeed in removing all forms of linear dependence. In addition, the sampling distribution of the BDS test statistic is affected in largely unknown ways by the nonzero variances of the coefficient estimators in the ARIMA process.

Despite such necessary qualifications about pretesting, we use the BDS test as one of our tests, because it has high power against an unusually large class of nonlinear alternatives. In fact, the BDS test's conclusion tends to be especially convincing when the test accepts the null. With high power against such a vast class of alternatives, acceptance of the null tends to be very strong evidence for the null. In that sense, the BDS test could be viewed as an extremely conservative test of the null.

In particular, we use the Box–Jenkins approach to fit an ARIMA (i, j, k) model to the data, where i is the order of the AR(i) autoregressive part, k is the order of the $MA(k)$ moving-average part, and j is the number of times that the data are differenced before fitting the moving average. In every case, the

Box–Jenkins approach resulted in setting $j = 0$ (so that the fit was ARMA) or $j = 1$(so that there was prior first differencing).

Formally, the equation of an ARMA (i, k) process, x_t, is:

$$x_t = \sum_{n=1}^{i} a_n x_{t-n} + \sum_{n=1}^{k} b_n u_{t-n},$$

where u_t is a zero-mean, white-noise process. The AR(i) autoregressive part is $\sum_{n=1}^{i} a_n x_{t-n}$, and the MA(k) moving-average part is $\sum_{n=1}^{k} b_n u_{t-n}$. As mentioned above, a process that is ARIMA (i, j, k) becomes ARMA (i, k), if differenced j times.

The BDS test statistic is a transformation of the correlation function. That transformed test statistic asymptotically becomes a standard normal Z statistic, under the null of pure whiteness. The null of pure whiteness is rejected if the test statistic is large. By convention with a Z statistic, large means larger than 2 or perhaps 3. Strictly speaking, the definition of large should depend upon sample size.

The correlation function has two arguments (variables) and one free parameter. The arguments are the embedding dimension, m, and the metric bound, ε, which is the maximum difference between the pairs of observations counted in computing the correlation function. In the case of the Grassberger–Procaccia test, ε and M are not free, because the limits of those two variables are taken in defining the correlation dimension. In particular, in defining the correlation dimension, the limit is taken as ε goes to zero and as m goes to infinity. But the BDS test uses the correlation function rather than the correlation dimension, and the values of ε and M are finite and arbitrary in the definition of the correlation function.

In addition to the two free variables, there is a free parameter in the correlation function. That parameter is the time delay used in embedding the univariate observations into a multivariate phase space. In this case, a finite choice for that parameter must be made in either the Grassberger–Procaccia test or the BDS test. In the BDS test, the convention is to set the time delay equal to one, so that m successive observations are stacked, without skipping any intervening observations, in producing the embedded-phase-space vectors. There is, in fact, much controversy regarding the best choice of the time delay with the Grassberger–Procaccia test, and various competing selection methods have been proposed, including one based on information theory. In the case of the BDS test, the argument for the use of the unitary time delay rests on the prewhitening by ARIMA fit of the data used with the BDS test.

The need to choose the values of ε and m can be a complication in using the BDS test. We adopt the approach used by advocates of the test. In particular, we set ε equal to the standard deviation of the data.[7] At our chosen setting for ε, we produced the BDS test statistic for all settings of embedding dimension from 2 to 8, in the hope that the same inference would be produced at each of those embedding dimensions. Fortunately, in our cases, the inference was always robust to the setting of m within the 2 to 8 range.

Hsieh and LeBaron (1988) have found that type I error is large with the BDS test when the sample size is not adequately large, because the nonzero standard error of the ARIMA coefficient estimators biases the BDS test. By their criterion, our sample size is barely adequate. Hence, to avoid rejecting a true null hypothesis, we should refrain from rejecting the null unless the test statistic is very large. Instead of rejecting when the test statistic exceeds conventional critical values of 2 or 3, perhaps we should resist rejecting unless the test statistic exceeds 4. In addition, Brock, Hsieh, and LeBaron have found that the asymptotic properties of the BDS test deteriorate when the embedding dimension increases to more than 3 at sample sizes comparable to ours. Although we report results with embedding dimensions varying from 2 to 8, the results with embedding dimensions of 2 or 3 should be given the most serious consideration. But again, we generally acquired inferences that were robust to variation of embedding dimension from 2 to 8, so that the issue regarding deteriorating asymptotic properties with large embedding dimensions did not arise.

6.2   *Details of the test statistic*

The above discussion assumes knowledge of the correlation-function (integral) and correlation-dimension formulas. For convenient reference within this chapter, the formulas are supplied below.

Suppose that we have a time series of observations on a scalar random variable, m_t. We first embed them into a multivariate phase space as follows. Select an embedding dimension, n, and then stack the resulting n values of m_t into an n-dimensional vector, with successive elements of the vector being separated by τ periods. If the first observation in the n-history is m_t, then we can designate the resulting n-history at t by $m(n, \tau)t$, where we define

$$m(n, \tau)_t = [m_t, m_{t+\tau}, m_{t+2\tau}, \ldots, m_{t+(n-1)\tau}]$$

---

[7] Through Monte Carlo studies, Hsieh and LeBaron (1988) found that the power and size of the test are maximized when ε is selected to be between $\frac{1}{2}$ and $1\frac{1}{2}$ times our choice. Hence, our choice is in the center of that region. We further investigated variations of the setting throughout that range. Our inferences were not changed at either the upper or lower bound of the region. Lower settings for ε, including the square of the standard deviation, produced results evidencing domination of the test by noise in the data. In particular, the test statistic became a strong function of embedding dimension and varied between very positive and very negative values as m was increased at fixed ε.

at each t. For notational simplicity below, the τ is usually dropped in $m(n, \tau)_t$. The existence of the argument τ should be understood.

We first define the Grassberger–Procaccia method of measuring dimension. The dimension measure resulting from that method is called the correlation dimension, because the procedure uses the correlation function, $C_n(\varepsilon)$, defined by

$$C_n^*(\varepsilon) = {}^\#\{(i, j) : \|m(n)_i - m(n)_j\| < \varepsilon, 1 \le i \le N_n,$$

$$1 \le j \le N_n, i \ne j\}/(N_n^2 - N_n), \tag{6.8}$$

where $N_n = N - (n - 1)\tau$ is the number of n-histories that can be produced from a sample of size N with time lag τ, and ${}^\#A$ denotes the cardinality of (number of distinct points in) the set A. The correlation function measures the correlation of points along the time series. In practice, there is no need to divide by $N_n^2 - N_n$. The Grassberger–Procaccia correlation dimension in phase space is defined as

$$D(n) = \lim_{\varepsilon \to 0}[{}^n\log_2 C_n^*(\varepsilon)/\log_2 \varepsilon]. \tag{6.9}$$

If we then take the limit as the embedding dimension goes to infinity, and we apply the Takens Embedding Theorem, we get the correlation dimension of the attractor set in state space,

$$D = \lim_{n \to \infty} D(n). \tag{6.10}$$

As discussed above, the BDS test is based on the correlation function, $C_n^*(\varepsilon)$, which has n, τ, and ε as unspecified parameters. The Grassberger–Procaccia test is based upon D in which only ε remains free and unspecified. But the sampling distribution of D is unknown for stochastic data.

7   Lyapunov exponent test

7.1   *General features of the test*

When there are stochastic shocks within the structure of a system, measures of dimension are sensitive to the amount of noise in the system. An alternative method of testing for chaos is to compute the dominant Lyapunov exponent. Testing for a positive value for that exponent for a bounded system is equivalent to testing for the sensitivity to the initial-conditions property of chaos. Hence, testing for positivity of that exponent produces a direct test for chaos.

Algorithms for estimating that exponent fall into two classes: the Jacobian method (see, e.g., Ellner et al. 1991) and the direct method. In the past, such computations were applied deterministically. In physics experiments with very large sample sizes and no stochastic shocks internal to the system, noise in the data could be filtered out (see, e.g., Smith 1992) and the Lyapunov exponent computed by one of the two approaches. Recently, an estimator became available that is applicable with more modest sample sizes and with systems containing internal stochastic shocks. The approach is presented and explored with simulated data and biological data by Nychka (1992). The approach proceeds as follows.

Assume that the data $\{x_t\}$ are real valued and are generated by a nonlinear autoregressive model of the form

$$x_t = f(x_{t-L}, x_{t-2L}, \ldots, x_{t-dL}) + e_t \tag{6.11}$$

for $1 \leq t \leq N$, where L is the time-delay parameter and d is the length of the autoregression. Here, f is a smooth, unknown function, and $\{e_t\}$ is a sequence of independent random variables with zero mean and unknown constant variance. According to Taken's theorem (Eckmann and Ruelle 1985) for dynamic systems, the above nonlinear autoregression can represent any deterministic chaotic system on an attractor with finite dimension. Nychka et al. fit f nonparametrically using either a spline or a neural net. They then compute the Lyapunov exponent from the fitted function, f, using the Jacobian approach.

On the basis of the findings of Nychka et al., Gallant used the neural-net approach with the simulated data. As in their study, he used the feedforward single-hidden-layer networks with a single output. The neural-net approach to nonlinear regression has a selection parameter, q, that equals the number of units in the hidden layer of the neural net. Hence, in addition to the coefficients of the neural net, there are three parameters that must be selected in the NEGM approach: q, L, and d. The approach uses a Bayesian information criterion (BIC) to select q, L, and d. The details of that BIC approach can be found in Gallant and Tauchen (1991).

Recently, Nychka et al. switched from the use of the BIC criterion to the closely related generalized cross-validation (GCV) criterion. Gallant used the neural-net fit and the GCV criterion in this experiment, in the same manner now used by Nychka et al. In particular, the value of the triple (q, L, d) is determined to minimize GCV, whereas the coefficients of the neural net are selected to minimize least squares conditionally upon (q, L, d). For more details regarding the neural-net fit, see McCaffrey et al. (1992). For proof of the consistency of the nonparametric function estimator by neural net, see Gallant and White (1988, 1991).

In principle, it should be possible to produce a standard error for the Lyapunov exponent point estimate, perhaps by bootstrapping. But when noise is large, the properties of such a bootstrapped standard error are not known, and there has not yet been any published research on the computation of a standard error for the Nychka et al. Lyapunov exponent estimate. Hence, we report only the point estimates of the dominant Lyapunov exponents, as computed by Gallant in this competition.

7.2   Point estimation

Here we provide a more technical discussion of the NEGM approach to estimation of the maximum Lyapunov exponent, λ. We begin by producing a state-space representation of equation (6.11) as follows: Define the vectors

$$\mathbf{X}_t = \begin{pmatrix} \mathbf{x_t} \\ x_{t-L} \\ \cdot \\ x_{t-dL+L} \end{pmatrix}, \mathbf{F}(\mathbf{X}_{t-L}) = \begin{pmatrix} f(x_{t-L}, \ldots, x_{t-dL}) \\ x_{t-L} \\ \cdot \\ x_{t-dL+L} \end{pmatrix},$$

$$\text{and } \mathbf{E}_t = \begin{pmatrix} e_t \\ 0 \\ \cdot \\ 0 \end{pmatrix}.$$

The state-space representation is:

$$\mathbf{X}_t = \mathbf{F}(\mathbf{X}_{t-L}) + \mathbf{E}_t. \tag{6.12}$$

Data analyses based on Taken's theorem include the widely used method of "attractor reconstruction in time-delay coordinates" (Schuster 1988). Thus, the nonlinear autoregressive model in equation (6.11) is a generalization of attractor reconstruction to allow for random perturbations. Most methods of attractor reconstruction are data intensive, because they rely on the availability of a large number of nearly identical data segments that are separated in time to generate various numerical approximations to the local behavior of the system. The method of McCaffrey et al. (1992) is more efficient in its use of data, because it uses nonparametric statistical methods to approximate f directly.

Ruelle (1989) provides a definition of chaos that extends to noisy dynamic systems such as the nonlinear autoregressive model: a system is chaotic if it exhibits sensitive dependence to initial conditions for all initial conditions. A quantitative measure of the rate at which similar trajectories diverge is the dominant Lyapunov exponent, λ. A bounded system with positive λ is one operational definition of chaotic behavior. See Nychka et al. (1992) for a discussion of Lyapunov exponents that is specific to the nonlinear autoregressive model.

The NEGM method is a Jacobian-based method that estimates λ through the intermediate step of estimating the individual Jacobian matrices,

$$\mathbf{J}_t = \partial \mathbf{F}(\mathbf{X}_t)/\partial \mathbf{X}'.$$

After examining several nonparametric methods, McCaffrey et al. (1992) recommended using either thin-plate splines or neural nets to estimate J_t. Here, we use neural nets and follow the protocol described by Nychka et al. (1992). Briefly, the method is as follows:

The neural net with q units in the hidden layer is

$$f(\mathbf{X}_{t-L}, \theta) = \beta_0 + \sum_{j=1}^{q} \beta_j \psi \left(\gamma_{0j} + \sum_{i=1}^{d} \gamma_{ij} x_{t-Li} \right),$$

where

$$\psi(u) = \frac{u(1 + |u/2|)}{2 + |u| + u^2/2},$$

and where the parameter vector

$$\theta = (\beta_0, \beta_1, \ldots, \beta_q, \gamma_{01}, \gamma_{11}, \gamma_{21}, \ldots, \gamma_{d1}, \ldots, \gamma_{0q}, \gamma_{1q}, \gamma_{2q}, \ldots, \gamma_{dq})$$

is fitted to data by nonlinear least squares. That is, one computes the estimate $\hat{\theta}$ to minimize the sum of squares

$$S(\theta) = \sum_{t=1}^{N} [\mathbf{x}_t - f(\mathbf{X}_{t-1}, \theta)]^2,$$

and uses

$$\hat{\mathbf{F}}(\mathbf{X}_t) = \begin{pmatrix} f(x_t), \ldots, x_{t-dL+L}, \hat{\theta}) \\ x_{t-L} \\ \cdot \\ x_{t-dL+L} \end{pmatrix}$$

to approximate $\mathbf{F}(\mathbf{X}_t)$.

The surface of $S(\theta)$ is replete with local minima. In view of this fact, Nychka et al. (1992) suggest that one randomly select on the order of 1,000 starting values for θ and iterate each to a local minimum using the nonlinear optimizer of NPSOL (Gill, Murray, Saunders, and Wright 1986) with a lax termination criterion. The 20 best of these are then used as starting values with a stringent termination criterion. The value of $\hat{\theta}$ that corresponds to the smallest $S(\theta)$ of these 20 is selected as the estimate.

Because appropriate values of d, L, and q are unknown, they must be estimated. Nychka et al. (1992) recommend selecting that value of the triple (d, L, q) that minimizes the BIC criterion (Schwarz 1978) jointly in (d, L, q, θ), where

$$\text{BIC} = S(\hat{\theta}) + p \log(N)$$

and where $p = 1 + q(d + 1)$ is the number of elements in θ. As shown by Gallant and White (1992), we can use $\hat{\mathbf{J}}_t = \partial \hat{\mathbf{F}}(\mathbf{X}_t)/\partial \mathbf{X}'$ as a nonparametric estimator of J_t, when (d, L, q) are selected to minimize BIC, or in the more recent version to minimize the closely related GCV criterion. The estimate of the dominant Lyapunov exponent then is

$$\hat{\lambda} = \frac{1}{2N} \log |\nu_1(N)|$$

where $\nu_1(N)$ denotes the largest eigenvalue of the matrix $\hat{\mathbf{T}}'_N \hat{\mathbf{T}}_N$, and where

$$\hat{\mathbf{T}}_N = \hat{\mathbf{J}}_N \hat{\mathbf{J}}_{N-1} \cdots \hat{\mathbf{J}}_1.$$

7.3   Precision

Although the standard error of the estimate $\hat{\lambda}$ is not known, Nychka (1992) display plots that are informative about precision. One plot illustrates the sensitivity of the estimate of λ to variations in the initial conditions used in estimating the coefficients, θ, of the neural net and to variations in (L, d). We refer to that plot as the NEGM sensitivity plot. The other plot illustrates the effect on the estimate of λ of variations in (L, d) and also indicates the precision of the point estimate of (L, d). We find the NEGM sensitivity plot to be especially useful, and hence we supply only that plot, both for our large and small samples, in the cases in which evidence of chaos was found with the NEGM test. That plot is an indication of the sensitivity of $\hat{\lambda}$ to variations in θ about the least-squares estimate at various settings of (L, d).

The procedure for producing the NEGM sensitivity plot is the following: For each setting of (L, d) where $L = 1, 2, \ldots, 5$ and $d = 1, 2, \ldots, 6$, the value of q that minimizes GCV conditionally upon (L, d) is found. Let $\hat{q}(L, d)$ be that value. As described above, the estimation of θ proceeded by first narrowing down the estimates of that vector to 20 possibilities, through a nested optimization procedure. The one among the 20 that minimized least squares then was selected as the optimum estimate. In the NEGM sensitivity plot, box plots are displayed indicating the range of values of the estimated dominant Lyapunov exponent at each setting of (L, d), with q set at $\hat{q}(L, d)$. The range within the box was acquired at each such setting of $(L, d, \hat{q})$ by varying θ over the 20 possibilities for θ attained through the nested iteration. A bar within each box indicates the median of the estimates among the 20 possibilities. The scatter within any such box illustrates the numerical stability of recovering a similar estimate of λ, when only the starting values of θ are varied. Moving between boxes indicates the sensitivity of the estimate of λ to variations in (L, d).

8   White's test

The basic idea of White's test involves modeling the elements of the generating process as being generated by an augmented single hidden-layer feedforward neural network. Recent simulation studies have produced evidence demonstrating that the test has power against a variety of nonlinear processes. All results using White's test were obtained using an implementation of White's test, programmed and applied in this competition by Jochen Jungeilges.

The test procedure applied is essentially the neural-network test of Halbert White (1989a,b) Efforts to study the operational characteristics of this test for nonlinearity were undertaken by Lee et al. (1993) and Jungeilges (1993). These studies demonstrate that the test has appropriate size as well as power against various types of nonlinearity. The version of the test used in the current investigation is equivalent to the version called NEURAL 1 by Lee et al. Details of the algorithm used are given by Jungeilges (1993).

The rationale for White's test can be summarized as follows: Under the hypothesis of linearity in the mean, the theoretical residuals obtained by applying a linear filter to the process (i.e., affine part of the network) should not be correlated with any measurable function of the history of the process under scrutiny. When carrying out White's test, one basically correlates the residuals from an affine network with the output generated by the hidden-layer phantom units of a single hidden-layer feedforward network. White chooses an exponential cumulative distribution function as the measurable test function. The vector of connection strength associated with the signals arriving at each of the hidden-layer phantom units is chosen at random and independently of the process at hand. This amounts to choosing the direction in which the test looks for nonlinearity at random. This strategy appears to be a viable way out of the dilemma generated by the fact that the connection-strength parameters can be identified only under the alternative of nonlinearity in the means. See, e.g., White (1989a), Kuan, and White (1991).

White (1989b), points out that, under certain assumptions, the parameters of the network do not have to be estimated. White argues that a procedure involving regression and the extraction of principal components leads to an equivalent test procedure. Basically, the test statistic of the network test is shown to be asymptotically equivalent to a function of the multiple correlation between the residuals from the affine network and a low-dimensional representation of the hidden-layer output. See White (1989b), Jungeilges (1993), and Lee et al. (1993).

The dimension of the affine network, that is, the order of the autoregressive process, is chosen by a conventional selection criterion. For each series, Jungeilges chose the order that minimized the Schwarzian Bayesian information criterion (SBIC). This criterion provides asymptotically unbiased order estimates. Alternatives, for example, Akaike's information criterion, are known to overestimate the order. In the light of recent results presented by Theiler and Eubank (1993), it may be preferable to have parsimonious order-selection criteria when testing for nonlinearity. Also, Jungeilges (1993) demonstrated that choosing the dimension of the affine part of the network via the SBIC may improve the power of White's test against nonlinear chaotic data-generating processes relative to the power of the version of the test involving alternative selection criteria.

9   Kaplan's test

In the case of chaos, a time-series plot of the output of a chaotic system may be very difficult to distinguish visually from a stochastic process. Hence, it can be very difficult to detect the continuity of the system, even when the data are entirely deterministic. However, it is well known that plots of the solution paths in phase space (x_{t+1} plotted against x_t and lagged values of x_t) often reveal deterministic structure that was not evident in a plot of x_t versus t. A test based on continuity in phase space has been proposed by Daniel Kaplan at the Center for Nonlinear Dynamics, Department of Physiology, McGill University.

He has used the fact that deterministic solution paths, unlike stochastic processes, have the following property: points that are nearby are also nearby under their image in phase space. That is, if x_t and y_t are close to each other and their lagged values also are close to each other, then x_{t+1} and y_{t+1} also are close to each other. Using this fact, he has produced a test statistic, ε, that has a strictly positive lower bound for a stochastic process, but not for a deterministic solution path. With relatively small sample sizes, this statistic can be used to test the hypothesis that the data are deterministic versus the alternative that they come from a particular stochastic process. If ε is found to be smaller for the data than for the stochastic process by a statistically significant amount, then the stochastic process is rejected as an alternative to determinism. Producing results on statistical significance requires multiple Monte Cario trials with the process.

By computing the test statistic from an adequately large number of linear processes that plausibly might have produced the data, the approach can be used to test for noisy nonlinear dynamics against the alternative of linear stochasticity. The procedure involves producing linear-stochastic-process surrogates for the data and determining whether the surrogates or a noisy continuous nonlinear dynamic solution path better describe the data. A noisy continuous dynamic solution is concluded if the value of ε from the surrogates is never small enough relative to the value of ε computed from the data.

More formally stated, the procedure is the following: In a time series from a deterministically chaotic dynamic system, the value of $x_{t+\tau}$ for any fixed positive integer τ is a single-valued function of the state of the system at time t.

If we define the vector $\mathbf{x}_t = (x_t, x_{t-\tau}, x_{t-2\tau}, \ldots, x_{t-(m-1)\tau})$ embedded in m-dimensional phase space as a stand-in for the m-dimensional state vector in state space, then for a chaotic, system, there is a function giving $x_{t+\tau} = f(x_t)$ with the fixed-positive-integer time delay τ. Here, $x_{t+\tau}$ is called the image of the point x_t in phase space. The Kaplan test examines the evidence provided by a time series that this function f is continuous. For perfectly deterministic systems with a continuous f, nearby points in m-dimensional phase space will have nearby images. For a stochastic system, on the other hand, nearby points in phase space may have quite different images.

In terms of the delta-epsilon proofs of continuity familiar from calculus, distance in phase space plays the role of δ, and distance of the images plays the role of ε. For a given choice of embedding dimension m, one calculates $\delta_{ij} = |\mathbf{x}_i - \mathbf{x}_j|$ and $\varepsilon_{ij} = |\mathbf{x}_{1+\tau} - \mathbf{x}_{j+\tau}|$, for all pairs of subscripts (i, j). The average of the values of ε_{ij} over those (i, j) satisfying $\delta_{ij} < r$ is defined as $E(r)$. For a perfectly deterministic system with continuous f, one expects to have $E(r) \to 0$ as $r \to 0$.

For a system that is not perfectly deterministic, one way of interpreting the nonzero value of the limit of $E(r)$ as $r \to 0$ is as a goodness-of-fit measure from fitting a continuous model of some fixed order to an infinite amount of data (so that overfitting was not an issue). If this measure of fit is smaller for the data than for surrogate data generated from a model that satisfies a stated null hypothesis, then there is evidence that the null hypothesis should be rejected. When the measure is computed directly from the data, the interpretation is goodness of fit under the maintained hypothesis that the unknown model is continuous, although the model may not satisfy the more restrictive assumptions defining the null.

To test for linear dynamics, surrogate data can be generated using phase randomization with amplitude adjustment. See Theiler, Eubank, Longtin, Galdrikian, and Farmer (1992). In practice, though, one does not have enough data to take the limit as $r \to 0$. A practical test statistic E can be constructed in a number of ways. Hence, Kaplan has linearly extrapolated $E(r)$ to $r = 0$ from the computed positive values of r to acquire an approximation to $K = \lim_{r \to 0} E(r)$. This value of the Kaplan test statistic, K, for the simulated data then can be compared with that value of K generated from surrogate data, with statistical significance assessed using multiple Monte Carlo trials.

With the simulated data, Kaplan used his statistic on 20 surrogates generated to have the same histogram and a similar autocorrelation function. The time series were embedded in one-, two-, three-, and four-dimensional spaces.[8] If the value of the test statistic for the simulated data was less than the minimum

---

[8] Kaplan's convention for defining embedding dimension differs from that used by the NEGM and BDS tests. Add 1.0 to each embedding dimension to get the embedding dimension using the BDS and NEGM conventions. In Kaplan's convention, the embedding dimension is the dimension of the space in which δ_{ij} is calculated.

value acquired with the surrogates data at an embedding dimension, nonlinearity was deemed to be detected. Results on statistical significance are not reported, because adequate Monte Carlo replications for that purpose were not conducted. For details of the computation and test, see Kaplan (1993).

The time delay, τ, was determined in accordance with the method defined by Kaplan (1993). That time delay was 1.0 in each case except for the two ARMA cases (Model V with both sample sizes). In the ARMA cases, Kaplan's method resulted in setting the time delay to 20. Two methods exist for computing the minimum value of K consistent with the surrogates. The simplest method is to compute the minimum value K from the finite number of surrogates, and impute that to the population of surrogates consistent with the procedure.

A more appealing approach is to compute the mean and standard error of the values of K from the sample of 20 surrogates and then subtract a multiple (conventionally, two or three) of the standard error from the mean to get an estimate of the population minimum. By use of a multiple of two, the conclusions reached below from the Kaplan test are the same for either of the two methods. In the tabulated results, we provide both the minimum value of K from the 20 surrogates and the mean and variance of K from the surrogates. Under the assumption of normality of the distribution of K from the population of surrogates, conclusions could be reached about statistical significance. But we do not provide such an interpretation, because the normality assumption may be a poor approximation, and not enough surrogates were generated to produce a Monte Carlo inference about statistical inference.

10   Conclusions

This competition has been under way for three years. We expect the results to be very informative. When completed, the competition's results will be published. Although we were not free at the time of the conference to reveal the results, we can say that the competition at that time was proving to be very productive. Following the conference, the competition was completed, and the results will appear in Barnett, Gallant, Hinich, Jungeilges, Kaplan, and Jensen (1996). We believe that further competitions and experiments of this sort would be useful, because the number of relevant tests that merit this kind of investigation is large, as is the size of the set of alternative hypotheses against which each has unknown power, and as is the number of potentially relevant sample sizes, and relevant noise levels.

REFERENCES

Ashley, R. A., and Patterson, D. M. (1989). Linear versus nonlinear macroeconomies: A statistical test, *Int. Econ. Rev.*, **30**(3), 685–704.

Ashley, R. A., Patterson, D. M., and Hinich, M. (1986). A diagnostic test for nonlinear serial dependence in time series fitting errors. *J. Time Ser. Anal.*, **7**(3), 165–78.

Barnett, W. A., and Chen, P. (1986). Economic theory as a generator of measurable attractors, *Mondes Develop.*, **14**(453); reprinted in *Laws of Nature and Human Conduct: Specificities and Unifying Themes*, eds. I. Prigogine and M. Sanglier, Brussels, Belgium, pp. 209–24.

   (1988a). The aggregation–theoretic monetary aggregates are chaotic and have strange attractors: An econometric application of mathematical chaos. In *Dynamic Econometric Modelling*, Proceedings of the Third International Symposium in Economic Theory and Econometrics, eds. W. Barnett, E. Berndt, and H. White, Cambridge University Press, Cambridge, England, pp. 199–246.

   (1988b). Deterministic chaos and fractal attractors as tools for nonparametric dynamical econometric inference, *Math. Comput. Model.*, **10**, 275–96.

Barnett, W., and Hinich, M. J. (1992). Empirical chaotic dynamics in economics, *Ann. Oper. Res.*, **37**, 1–15.

   (1993). Has chaos been discovered with economic data. In *Evolutionary Dynamics and Nonlinear Economics*, eds. P. Chen and R. Day, Oxford University Press, Oxford, England, pp. 254–63.

Barnett, W. A., Gallant, A. R., Hinich, M. J., Jungeilges, J., Kaplan, D., and Jensen, M. J. (1994). Robustness of nonlinearity and chaos tests to measurement error, inference method, and sample size, *J. Econ. Behav. Organ.*, **27**, 301–320.

   (1996). A single-blind controlled competition among tests for nonlinearity and chaos, *J. Econometrics*, to be published.

Box, G. E. P., and Jenkins, G. M. (1970). *Time Series Analysis–Forecasting and Control*, Holden Day, San Francisco, CA.

Brillinger, D. R. (1965). An introduction to polyspectrum, *Ann. Math. Stat.*, **36**, 1351–74.

Brock, W. A., and Dechert, W. D. (1988). Theorems on distinguishing deterministic from random systems, In *Dynamic Econometric Modelling, Proceedings of the Third International Symposium in Economic Theory and Econometrics*, eds. W. Barnett, E. Berndt, and H. White, Cambridge University Press, Cambridge, England, pp. 247–68.

Brock, W. A., Dechert, W. D., and Scheinkman, J. (1986). A test for independence based on the correlation dimension, Working Paper, University of Wisconsin–Madison and University of Chicago.

Brock, W. A., Hsieh, D. A., and LeBaron, B. (1991). *Nonlinear Dynamics, Chaos, and Instability: Statistical Theory and Economic Evidence*, MIT Press, Cambridge, MA.

Brockett, P. L., Hinich, M., and Wilson, G. R. (1987). Nonlinear and non-Gaussian ocean noise, *J. Acoust. Soc. Am.*, **82**(4), 1386–94.

Brockett, P. L., Hinich, M., and Patterson, D. (1988). Bispectral-based test for the detection of Gaussianity and linearity in time series, *J. Am. Stat. Assoc.*, **83**(403), 657–64.

Dalle Molle, J. W., and Hinich, M. J. (1989). The trispectrum. In *Proceedings of the Workshop in Higher Order Spectral Analysis*, eds. J. M. Mendel and C. L. Nicias, pp. 68–71.

   (1991). Cumulant spectra-based tests for the detection of coherent signal in noise, In *Proceedings of the International Signal Processing Workshop on Higher Order Statistics*, eds. J. L. Lacoume, M. A. Lagunas, and C. L. Nikias, pp. 151–54.

DeCoster, G. P., and Mitchell, D. W. (1991). Nonlinear monetary dynamics, *J. Bus. Econ. Stat.*, **9**, 455–62.

   (1994). Reply, *J. Bus. Econ. Stat.*, **12**, 136–7.

Eckmann, J. P., and Ruelle, D. (1985). Ergodic theory of chaos and strange attractors, *Rev. Mod. Phys.*, **57**, 617–56.

El-Gamal, M. (1991). Non-parametric estimation of deterministically chaotic systems, *Economic Theory*, Vol. **1**, Springer–Verlag, Berlin, pp. 147–67.

Ellner, S., Gallant, A. R., McCaffrey, D., and Nychka, D. (1991). Convergence rates and data requirements for Jacobian-based estimates of Liapunov exponents from data, *Phys. Letts. A*, **153**, 357–63.

Gallant, A. R., and Tauchen, G. (1991). A nonparametric approach to nonlinear time series analysis: Estimation and simulation. In *New Dimensions in Time Series Analysis*, part II, eds. D. Brillinger, P. Caines, J. Geweke, E. Parzen, M. Rosenblatt, and M. S. Taqqu, Springer–Verlag, New York, pp. 71–92.

Gallant, A. R., and White, H. (1981). There exists a neural network that does not make avoidable mistakes. In *Proceedings of the Second IEEE International Conference on Neural Networks*, San Diego, CA, July 24–27, SOS Printing, San Diego, CA, Secs. 1.657–1.664.

(1992). On learning the derivatives of an unknown mapping with multilayer feedforward networks, *Neural Networks*, **5**, 129–38.

Gencay, R., and Dechert, W. D. (1992). An algorithm for the *n* Lyapunov exponents of an *n*-dimensional unknown dynamical system. *Phys. D*, **59**, 142–57.

Geweke, J. (1989). Inference and forecasting for chaotic nonlinear time series, Institute of Statistics and Decision Sciences DP. No. 89–06, Duke University, Durham, NC.

Gill, P. E., Murray, W., Saunders, M. A., and Wright, M. H. (1986). Users guide for NPSOL (version 4.0): a Fortran package for nonlinear programming, Technical Report SOL 86–2, Systems Optimization Laboratory, Stanford University, Stanford, CA.

Hinich, M. J. (1982). Testing for Gaussianity and linearity of a stationary time series, *J. Time Ser. Anal.*, **3**(3), 169–76.

(1994). Testing for dependence in the input to a linear time series model, Working Paper, Department of Government, University of Texas at Austin.

Hinich, M. J., and Patterson, D. (1985). Identification of the coefficients in a nonlinear time series of the quadratic type, *J. Econometrics*, **30**, 269–88; reprinted in *New Approaches to Modelling, Specification Selection, and Econometric Inference*, Proceedings of the First International Symposium in Economic Theory and Econometrics, eds. W. Barnett and R. Gallant, Cambridge University Press, Cambridge, MA, 1989.

(1989). Evidence of nonlinearity in the trade-by-trade stock market return generating process. In *Economic Complexity: Chaos, Sunspots, Bubbles, and Nonlinearity*, Proceedings of the Fourth International Symposium in Economic Theory and Econometrics, eds., W. Barnett, J. Geweke, and K. Shell, Cambridge University Press, Cambridge, England, pp. 383–409.

Hsieh, D., and LeBaron, B. (1988). Finite sample properties of the BDS statistic, Working paper, University of Chicago and University of Wisconsin, Madison.

Jenkins, G., and Watts, D. (1968). *Spectral Analysis and its Applications*, Holden-Day, San Francisco, CA.

Jungeilges, J. A. (1993). Operational characteristics of White's test for neglected nonlinearities, Working Paper, Department of Economics, Washington University in St. Louis, St. Louis, MO.

Kaplan, D. T. (1993). Exceptional events as evidence for determinism, Department of Physiology, McGill University, Quebec, Canada, *Phys. D*. in press.

Kinderman, A. J., and Ramage, J. G. (1976). Computer generation of normal random numbers, *J. Am. Stat. Assoc.*, **71**, 893–6.

Kuan, C., and White, H. (1991). Artificial neural networks: An econometric perspective, Department of Economics and Institute for Neural Computation, Working Paper, University of California at San Diego, San Diego, CA.

Lee, T. H., White, H., and Granger, C. (1993). Testing for neglected nonlinearities in time series models. *J. Econometrics*, **56**, 269–90.

McCaffrey, D. F., Ellner, S., Gallant, A. R., and Nychka, D. W. (1992). Estimating the Lyapunov exponent of a chaotic system with nonparametric regression, *J. Am. Stat. Assoc.*, **87**, 682–95.

Nychka, D., Stephen, E., Gallant, R., and McCaffrey, D. (1992). Finding chaos in noisy systems, *J. Roy. Stat. Soc. B*, **54**(2), 399–426.

Priestley, M. (1981). *Spectral Analysis and Time Series*, Vol. 2, Academic Press, New York.

Ramsey, J. B., and Rothman, P. (1994). Comment on "Nonlinear Monetary Dynamics" by DeCoster and Mitchell, *J. Bus. Econ. Stat.*, **12**, 135–36.

Ramsey, J. B., Sayers, C. L., and Rothman, P. (1990). The statistical properties of dimension calculations using small data sets: Some economic applications, *Int. Econ. Rev.*, **31**, 991–1020.

Ruelle, D. (1989). *Chaotic Evolution and Strange Attractors*, Cambridge University Press, Cambridge, England.

Scheinkman, J., and LeBaron, B. (1989). Nonlinear dynamics and GNP data. In *Economic Complexity: Chaos, Sunspots, Bubbles, and Nonlinearity*, Proceedings of the Fourth International Symposium in Economic Theory and Econometrics, eds. W. Barnett, J. Geweke, and K. Shell, Cambridge University Press, Cambridge, England, pp. 213–27.

Schuster, H. G. (1988). *Deterministic Chaos: An Introduction*, 2nd ed., VCH, Weinheim.

Schwarz, G. (1978). Estimating the dimension of a model, *Ann. Stat.*, **6**, 461–4.

Serletis, A. (1994). Random walks, breaking trend functions, and the chaotic structure of the velocity of money, Working paper, Department of Economics, University of Calgary, Calgary, Alberta, Canada.

Smith, R. L. (1992). Estimating dimension in noisy chaotic time series, *J. Roy. Stat. Soc. B*, **54**, 329–51.

Subba Rao, T., and Gabr, M. (1980). A test for linearity of stationary time series, *J. Time Ser. Anal.*, **1**, 145–58.

Theiler, J., and Eubank, S. (1993). Don't bleach chaotic data, Working Paper, Center for Nonlinear Studies and Theoretical Division, Los Alamos National Laboratory, Los Alamos, NM.

Theiler, J., Eubank, S., Longtin, A., Galdrikian, B., and Farmer, J. (1992). Testing for nonlinearity in time series: The method of surrogate data. *Phys. D*, **58**, 74–94.

Walden, A. T., and Williams, M. L. (1993). Deconvolution, bandwidth, and the trispectrum, *J. Am. Stat. Assoc.*, **88**, 1323–29.

White, H. (1989). Some asymptotic results for learning in single hidden-layer feedforward network models, *J. Am. Stat. Assoc.*, **84**, (408), 1003–13.

    (1989b), An additional hidden unit test for neglected nonlinearity in multilayer feedforward networks, *Proceedings of the International Joint Conference on Neural Networks*, Washington, DC, IEEE Press, New York, pp. 451–55.

CHAPTER 7

Testing time series for nonlinearities: The BDS approach

W. D. Dechert

1   Introduction

The Brock–Dechert–Scheinkman (BDS) method (Brock, Dechert, Scheinkman 1987; Brock et al. 1991) for testing time series for nonlinearities is presented. The basis for the method is the use of the correlation integral (Grassberger and Procaccia 1983b) as a test statistic on time-series data. The correlation integral was originally used as a measure of the fractal dimension of a set of data (Grassberger and Procaccia, 1983a,b). It has the advantage over other measures (such as the Hausdorff measure) that it is relatively easy to calculate. As a measure of chaos, it calculates the frequency of repeated patterns in the data. Because chaotic orbits are dense on their attractors, and because chaotic attractors have a dense subset of periodic points, the chaotic orbits will have many patterns that are nearly periodic. It is these patterns that the correlation integral measures.

In applying the correlation integral and related measures to stochastic time series, one is testing for the presence of patterns in the data. However, even independently generated data will occasionally have patterns in it. In the method of by Brock et al. (1987, 1991) the correlation integral is used to test for patterns that occur more (or less) frequently than would be expected in independent data. As a formal statistical test, the BDS test has as its null hypothesis, that the data were generated by an independent and identically distributed stochastic process. The method can be generalized to a strictly stationary process that is weakly dependent. At this stage, it is unclear what other processes fall under the null hypothesis (Dechert 1993).

The BDS test does not specify an alternative hypothesis, but rather is a partial test for independence and identical distribution. However, a number of Monte Carlo experiments (Brock, Hsieh, and LeBaron 1991; Liu, Granger, and Heller 1993) have been performed with the BDS test against a variety of alternative stochastic specifications. The BDS test has good power against many of the alternatives that are often used in analyzing economic time series.

191

The use of the test in economics [see Brock, Hsieh, and LeBaron (1991) for an extensive bibliography] has primarily followed the prescription of testing the residual errors of a fitted model (Brock 1986; Brock and Dechert 1989a). This method depends on the model being correctly specified and can be used as a general test for specification error. It is worth emphasizing that it depends on the researcher having a model for the data in the first place. When that is so, it is not so common that one also has a specific alternative against which to test. The use of a general-purpose test may be justified under these circumstances.

2   BDS statistic

The BDS test uses the correlation integral (Grassberger and Procaccia 1983b) as the basis for a statistic to test the hypothesis that a set of data are independent and identically distributed. However, the correlation integral was designed as a numerically efficient method of calculating a measure of the fractal dimension of the data, and hence was originally applied only to deterministically generated data. How then does it apply to stochastic data?

The correlation integral for a set of data $\{x_t, 1 \le t \le n\}$ is

$$C_n(\varepsilon) = \frac{1}{n^2} \sum_{s=1}^{n} \sum_{t=1}^{n} H(\varepsilon - |x_s - x_t|) \tag{7.1}$$

where H is the Heaviside function,

$$H(r) = \begin{cases} 1 & \text{if } r > 0 \\ 0 & \text{otherwise} \end{cases}$$

If the data are generated by a stationary stochastic process that is weakly dependent,[1] or by a deterministic process with an invariant measure, the correlation integral converges to

$$C(\varepsilon) = \iint H(\varepsilon - |x - y|) d\mu(x) d\mu(y), \tag{7.2}$$

where μ is understood to be the univariate distribution function in the stochastic case, or the invariant measure in the deterministic case. All of the results in this paper generalize to the vector case [see Baek and Brock (1992) for an analysis of a vector version of BDS] in the obvious way.

On the basis of the theory of state-space reconstruction (Takens 1981, 1983), m-histories of the data are constructed as

$$x_t^m = (x_t, x_{t-1}, \ldots, x_{t-m+1})$$

---

[1] See Denker and Keller (1983) for definitions and results for U-statistics.

and a correlation integral is calculated on the basis of these constructed vectors,

$$C_{m,n}(\varepsilon) = \frac{1}{n^2} \sum_{s=1}^{n} \sum_{t=1}^{n} H\left(\varepsilon - ||x_s^m - x_t^m||\right), \tag{7.3}$$

where $||u|| = \max_i |u_i|$ for $u \in R^m$. The value of m is called the embedding dimension. If the data are deterministically generated by an n-dimensional system,

$$z_{t+1} = f(z_t) \tag{7.4}$$

with observations

$$x_t = h(z_t), \tag{7.5}$$

then it is a theorem (Takens 1981) that for $m \geq 2n + 1$ the map

$$J^m(z) = [h(z), h \circ f(z), \dots, h \circ f^{m-1}(z)] \tag{7.6}$$

is an embedding.[2] The implication is that certain dynamic properties such as the fractal dimension, the correlation integral, and the Lyapunov exponents (among others) are the same whether calculated with the actual dynamics, $\{z_t\}$, or with the embedded data, $\{x_t^m\}$.

The correlation dimension (Grassberger and Procaccia 1983b) of $\{x_t\}$ at embedding dimension m is

$$\alpha_m = \lim_{\varepsilon \to 0} \lim_{n \to \infty} \frac{\ln C_{m,n}(\varepsilon)}{\ln \varepsilon}. \tag{7.7}$$

By Takens' (1981, 1983) theorem, α_m is constant for $m \geq 2n + 1$ when the data are deterministic, and $\alpha_m = m$ when the data are and independent and identically distributed. This, in part, accounts for the power of the BDS test in identifying independent and identically distributed sequences. The principal reason that the BDS test does so well against a variety of alternatives is that the nature of the correlation integral is to count the number of repetitions of patterns in the data. The BDS test is constructed to measure this against the expected frequency of patterns in the data under the hypothesis of independence and identical distribution.

Chaotic systems have infinitely many periodic points, each of whose neighborhood is visited infinitely often by the chaotic orbit, Hence, there are numerous repetitions of patterns in chaotic data. In the stochastic processes that are often used in economics [e.g., autoregression, (AR), (MA), autoregressive conditional heteroskedasticity (ARCH), generalized ARCH(GARCH)] there is sufficient intertemporal dependence so that patterns are repeated with higher

---

[2] See Bröckner and Jänich (1982) for the precise definitions and properties of embeddings.

probability than they would be if the data were independent and identically distributed. This accounts for the success of the BDS test.

When the data are weakly dependent, then

$$\lim_{n\to\infty} C_{m,n}(\varepsilon) = C(\varepsilon)^m,$$

and

$$\sqrt{n}\left[C_{m,n}(\varepsilon) - C(\varepsilon)^m\right] \tag{7.8}$$

is asymptotically normal (Brock et al. 1987). The expression for the variance of (7.8) requires

$$K_n(\varepsilon) = \frac{1}{n^3}\sum_{r=1}^{n}\sum_{s=1}^{n}\sum_{t=1}^{n} H(\varepsilon|x_r - x_s|)H(\varepsilon - |x_s - x_t|)$$

$$= \frac{1}{n}\sum_{s=1}^{n}\left[\frac{1}{n}\sum_{t=1}^{n} H(\varepsilon - |x_s - x_t|)\right]^2,$$

which has a limit of

$$K(\varepsilon) = \lim_{n\to\infty} K_n(\varepsilon) = \int\left[\int H(\varepsilon - |x - y|)d\mu(x)\right]^2 d\mu(y). \tag{7.9}$$

The asymptotic variance (7.8) under the hypothesis of independence and identical distribution is

$$\frac{V_m^2}{4} = K^m - C^{2m} + 2\sum_{i=1}^{m-1}\left(K^{m-i}C^{2i} - C^{2m}\right), \tag{7.10}$$

where the dependence on ε has been suppressed.

If $K = C^2$ then the value of the variance in (7.10) is zero. This is the degenerate case (Serfling 1980) and the statistic (Brock, Hsieh, and LeBaron 1991) is asymptotically χ-square. This case occurs (Dechert 1993) only if the data are uniformly distributed on a circle.[3]

The BDS statistic is based on equation (7.8) with an estimate for the second term:

$$\sqrt{n}\left[C_{m,n}(\varepsilon) - C_n(\varepsilon)^m\right]. \tag{7.11}$$

---

[3] Equivalently, the data could be uniformly distributed on the interval [0,1] with a wrap-around metric $d(x, y) = \min(|x - y|, 1 - |x - y|)$ to measure closeness. The kernel in Equation (7.1) would be $H[\varepsilon - d(x, y)]$ and similarly for the kernel in equation (7.3). A study of the degenerate case has been published (Theiler 1988).

Under the hypothesis that the data are weakly dependent, this statistic is also asymptotically normal (Brock et al. 1987, 1991) with zero mean. When the data are independent and identically distributed, the asymptotic variance is

$$\frac{\sigma_m(\varepsilon)^2}{4} = 2 \sum_{j=1}^{m-1} \left(K^{m-j} C^{2j} - C^{2m} \right)$$

$$+ K^m - C^{2m} - m^2 C^{2m-2}(K - C^2), \tag{7.12}$$

where the dependence of K and C on ε has been suppressed for notational ease. The BDS statistic is

$$S_{m,n}(\varepsilon) = \sqrt{n} \frac{C_{m,n}(\varepsilon) - C_n(\varepsilon)^m}{\sigma_{m,n}(\varepsilon)}, \tag{7.13}$$

where $\sigma_{m,n}$ is σ_m evaluated with the (consistent) estimators K_n and C_n of K and C, respectively.

Equation (7.11) has a negative bias because

$$E\left[C_{m,n}(\varepsilon) - C_n(\varepsilon)^m\right] = C(\varepsilon)^m - E\left[C_n(\varepsilon)^m\right] \tag{7.14}$$

$$\leq C(\varepsilon)^m - C(\varepsilon)^m = 0. \tag{7.15}$$

The bias can found from

$$C_{m,n}(\varepsilon) - C_n(\varepsilon)^m = \left[C_{m,n}(\varepsilon) - C(\varepsilon)^m\right] - \left[C_n(\varepsilon)^m - C(\varepsilon)^m\right] \tag{7.16}$$

where the first term in equation (7.16) is unbiased, and so, the (negative) bias of the BDS statistic is the expected value of the second term. It follows from the asymptotic normality of (7.8) that $E[C_n(\varepsilon)^m - C(\varepsilon)^m]$ is $O(n)$. When $m = 2$ the bias is

$$E\left[C_n(\varepsilon)^2 - C(\varepsilon)^2\right] = \frac{4(n-2)}{n(n-1)}(K - C^2) + \frac{4}{n(n-1)}(C - C^2) \tag{7.17}$$

From equation (7.12), $\sigma_2(\varepsilon) = 2(K - C^2)$, and so, for $m = 2$, the (negative of the) bias of the BDS statistic (7.13) is approximately

$$\frac{2(n-2)}{\sqrt{n}(n-1)} + \frac{2}{\sqrt{n}(n-1)} \frac{C - C^2}{K - C^2}, \tag{7.18}$$

which is asymptotic to $2\sqrt{n}$.

3   Other correlation-integral statistics

To date, there are two alternative statistics based on the correlation integral that are used in testing time series for nonlinear structure. In one (Dechert 1993), a generalized correlation integral is used as a refinement of the BDS statistic, whereas in the other (Scheinkman and LeBaron 1989), a ratio of correlation integrals is used as a conditional probability test. Savit and Green (1991) also used a ratio of correlation integrals as a conditional probability. These extensions are designed to determine the exact structure of the nonlinearity in the time-series data.

Dechert (1993) generalized the correlation integral by using different values of ε for each of the components:

$$\tilde{C}_{m,n}(\varepsilon_1, \ldots, \varepsilon_m) = \frac{1}{n^2} \sum_{i=1}^{n} \sum_{j=1}^{n} \prod_{k=0}^{m-1} H(\varepsilon_{k+1} - |x_{i+k} - x_{j+k}|). \tag{7.19}$$

This allows one to adjust the extent to which the patterns have to be exact on specific components of the pattern. It also leads to some interesting properties of the correlation integral. Dechert (1993) studied a special case of equation (7.19):

$$D_{m,n}(\varepsilon_1, \varepsilon_2) = \frac{1}{n^2} \sum_{i=1}^{n} \sum_{j=1}^{n} H(\varepsilon_1 - |x_i - x_j|) H(\varepsilon_2 - |x_{i+m} - x_{j+m}|) \tag{7.20}$$

which is the same as equation (7.19) with the intervening values of ε set to $+\infty$. Defining the limit as

$$D_m(\varepsilon_1, \varepsilon_2) = \lim_{n \to \infty} D_{m,n}(\varepsilon_1, \varepsilon_2), \tag{7.21}$$

it was shown that, for a stationary Garussian process, x_i and x_{i+m} are independent if and only if

$$D_m(\varepsilon_1, \varepsilon_2) = C(\varepsilon_1)C(\varepsilon_2) \tag{7.22}$$

holds for all $\varepsilon_1, \varepsilon_2$ (Dechert 1993). This is an alternative characterization of stochastic independence that comes from a measure that is designed to detect the presence of nonlinearity in deterministic systems. It was also shown that if a system that generates deterministic data satisfies a Lipschitz condition, then for suitably chosen values of ε_1 and ε_2 the limiting behavior of equation (7.21) is different than it is for stochastic data. In this way, a test for stochastic versus deterministic data can be fashioned using the generalized correlation integral.

The asymptotic variance (Dechert 1993) for the statistic (7.20) is

$$\sigma_m(\varepsilon_1, \varepsilon_2) = 4\left[K(\varepsilon_1) - C(\varepsilon_1)^2\right]\left[K(\varepsilon_2) - C(\varepsilon_2)^2\right] \tag{7.23}$$

and

$$\tilde{S}_{m,n}(\varepsilon_1, \varepsilon_2) = \sqrt{n}\frac{D_{m,n}(\varepsilon_1, \varepsilon_2) - C_n(\varepsilon_1)C_n(\varepsilon_2)}{\sigma_{m,n}(\varepsilon_1, \varepsilon_2)} \tag{7.24}$$

is asymptotically $N(0, 1)$.

Scheinkman and LeBaron (1989) make use of the fact that the limiting value of the correlation integral of a stationary stochastic process has a probabilistic interpretation,

$$C_m(\varepsilon) = P\{|X_s - X_t| < \varepsilon, \ldots, |X_{s+m-1} - X_{t+m-1}| < \varepsilon\} \quad (7.25)$$

to calculate the conditional probability

$$\frac{C_{m+1}(\varepsilon)}{C_m(\varepsilon)} = P\{|X_{s+m} - X_{t+m}|$$

$$< \varepsilon \,||\, X_s - X_t| < \varepsilon, \ldots, |X_{s+m-1} - X_{t+m-1}| < \varepsilon\}. \quad (7.26)$$

This definition also can be extended by using the generalized correlation integral (7.19). Under the null hypothesis of independence,

$$\frac{C_{m+1,n}(\varepsilon)}{C_{m,n}(\varepsilon)} - C_n(\varepsilon) \quad (7.27)$$

converges to zero, and by the techniques of Brock et al. (1987, 1991),

$$\sqrt{n}\left[\frac{C_{m+1,n}(\varepsilon)}{C_{m,n}(\varepsilon)} - C_n(\varepsilon)\right] \quad (7.28)$$

is asymptotically normal. The asymptotic variance can be calculated by the methods of Brock et al. (1987, 1991).

4   BDS tests

The BDS statistic was originally designed to test for model misspecification (Brock and Dechert 1989a,b, 1991) of the following type. Suppose that the data are stochastically generated by

$$y_t = f(Y_{t-1}, X_{t-1}) + u_t, \quad (7.29)$$

where the errors $\{u_t\}$ are independent and identically distributed and $Y_{t-1} = (y_{t-1}, y_{t-2}, \ldots)$ and X_{t-1} are other variables that are measurable at date $t-1$. If there is an $\sqrt{n}$-consistent estimator, f_n, then for f it was shown by Brock and Dechert (1989a) that the residual errors

$$u_{t,n} = f(Y_{t-1}, X_{t-1}) - f_n(Y_{t-1}, X_{t-1}) + u_t \quad (7.30)$$

converge to the true (independent and identically distributed) errors, and that the BDS statistic (7.13) is asymptotically $N(0, 1)$ when calculated with the residuals (i.e., there is no correction term for estimated nuisance parameters). In the case that f is linear in Y_{t-1} and not a function of any other variables, then a necessary and sufficient condition for

$$\lim_{n \to \infty} f_n = f$$

Table 7.1. *Values of BDS and $\tilde{S}_{m,n}$ for Hénon and independent and identically distributed data.*

m	ε	BDS	ε_1	ε_2	$\tilde{S}_{m,n}$	ε_1	ε_2	$\tilde{S}_{m,n}$
1	0.0641	−3.110	0.445	0.445	−2.966	0.150	0.400	−3.488
2	0.0641	17.63	0.445	0.445	53.19	0.150	0.400	11.71
3	0.0641	18.13	0.445	0.445	−2.070	0.150	0.400	−2.389
4	0.0641	29.29	0.445	0.445	27.99	0.150	0.400	72.19
5	0.0641	31.01	0.445	0.445	−2.858	0.150	0.400	−4.133
6	—	—	0.445	0.445	9.266	0.150	0.400	43.36

is that the limit residuals

$$v_t = \lim_{n \to \infty} u_{t,n}$$

be independent and identically distributed. A nonlinear version of this result also is presented by Brock and Dechert (1989a). The BDS test also has been successfully applied to other types of models as well, such as ARCH, GARCH, GARCH-m, AR, TAR, and VAR. See Brock, Hsieh, and LeBaron (1991) for these applications, as well as for a bibliography of BDS tests on economic time series.

5   Applications

In terms of using the BDS statistic versus a generalized correlation integral statistic, the latter can be more sensitive to hidden nonlinearities in the data. The drawback is that there are more free tuning parameters to choose. By way of comparison, two data sets each of 2,000 observations are constructed (see Table 7.1).

They are an interleaving of random data[4] with nonlinear data. Specifically, let $\{y_t\}$ be independent and identically distributed data (in this case, uniformly distributed on $[-1, 1]$), and let $\{x_t\}$ be a nonlinear time series. Define

$$\left. \begin{array}{l} z_{2t} = y_t \\ z_{2t+1} = x_t \end{array} \right\} \text{ for } t = 0, 1, \ldots, n.$$

In Table 7.1, there is a comparison of the performance of the BDS statistic with the generalized statistic (7.24) for $\{x_t\}$ generated by the first component of the Henon map:

$$x_{t+1} = 1.0 + y_t - 1.4x_t^2$$

$$y_{t+1} = 0.3x_t$$

[4] Pseudorandom data, of course. The random-number generator is a compound generator that uses 17 linear congruential generators as inputs. See Collings (1987).

Table 7.2. *Values of BDS and $\tilde{S}_{m,n}$ for ARCH and independent and identically distributed data.*

m	ε	BDS	ε_1	ε_2	$\tilde{S}_{m,n}$	ε_1	ε_2	$\tilde{S}_{m,n}$
1	0.0412	−1.510	0.500	0.500	−1.368	0.170	0.450	−1.267
2	0.0412	1.526	0.500	0.500	7.693	0.170	0.450	7.363
3	0.0412	1.872	0.500	0.500	0.3002	0.170	0.450	0.4942
4	0.0412	2.114	0.500	0.500	2.828	0.170	0.450	2.524
5	0.0412	1.965	0.500	0.500	0.4400	0.170	0.450	0.1651
6	—	—	0.500	0.500	0.3221	0.170	0.450	0.3054

Although the BDS does pick up the nonlinearity in the every other component, the generalized statistic reveals this structure much more clearly.

The second data set was constructed as above, but with $\{x_t\}$ as an ARCH process with conditional variance

$$\sigma_t^2 = \frac{1 + x_{t-1}^2}{2}.$$

The comparisons are in Table 7.2.

In this case, the BDS does not pick up the alternating-sequence nonlinearity, whereas the $\tilde{S}_{m,n}$ does at dimension $m = 2$. The BDS statistic does not have a lot of power against ARCH alternatives (Brock, Hsieh, and LeBaron 1991). This example shows that, nevertheless, a generalized correlation integral statistic can have more power by virtue of its increased flexibility.

It was also shown previously (Dechert 1993) that the generalized statistic could be used to distinguish between deterministic and stochastic sequences. This is another direction in which this test is more flexible than the BDS test, which cannot distinguish between the two types of sequences.

REFERENCES

Baek, E. G., and Brock, W. A. (1992). A nonparametric test for independence of a multivariate time series, *Stat. Sinica*, **2**, 137–56.

Brock, W. A. (1986). Distinguishing random and deterministic systems: Abridged version, *J. Econ. Theory*, **40**, 168–95.

Brock, W. A., and Dechert, W. D. (1989a). A general class of specification tests: The scalar case. In *Business and Economics Statistics Section of the Proceedings of the American Statistical Society*, pp. 70–79.

(1989b). Statistical inference theory for measures of complexity in chaos theory and nonlinear science. In *Measures of Complexity and Chaos*, eds. N. B. Abraham et al., Plenum Press, New York, pp. 79–97.

(1991). Non-linear dynamical systems: Instability and chaos in economics. In *Handbook of Mathematical Economics*, eds. W. Hildenbrand and H. Sonnenschein, Elsevier, pp. 2209–35.

Brock, W. A., Dechert, W. D. and Scheinkman, A. (1987). A test of independence based on the correlation dimension, Department of Economics, University of Wisconsin at Madison, University of Houston, and University of Chicago.

Brock, W. A., Dechert, W. D., Scheinkman, J. A., and LeBaron, B. (1991). A test for independence based on the correlation dimension, Department of Economics, University of Wisconsin at Madison, University of Houston, University of Chicago, and University of Wisconsin.

Brock, W. A., Hsieh, D. A., and LeBaron, B. (1991). *Nonlinear Dynamics, Chaos, and Instability: Statistical Theory and Economic Evidence*. MIT Press, Cambridge, MA.

Bröckner, Th., and Jänich, K. (1982). *Introduction to Differential Topology*, Cambridge University Press, Cambridge, England.

Collings, B. J. (1987). Compound random number generators, *J. Am. Stat. Assoc.*, **82**(398), 525–7.

Dechert, W. D. (1993). An application of chaos theory to stochastic and deterministic observations, Department of Economics, University of Houston.

Denker, M., and Keller, G. (1983). On U-statistics and von Mises statistics for weakly dependent processes, *Z. Wahrscheinlichkeitstheor. verwandte Gebiete*, **64**, 505–22.

Grassberger, P. and Procaccia, I. (1983a). Estimating the Kolmogorov entropy from a chaotic signal, *Phys. Rev.*, **28A**, 25–91.

(1983b). Measuring the strangeness of strange attractors, *Phys. D*, **9**, 189.

Liu, T., Granger, C. W. J., and Heller, W. P. (1993). Using the correlation exponent to decide whether an economic series is chaotic. In *Nonlinear Dynamics, Chaos and Econometrics*, eds. M. H. Pesaran and S. M. Potter, Wiley, New York, pp. 17–32.

Savit, R., and Green, M. (1991). Time series and dependent variables, *Phys. D*, **50**, 95–116.

Scheinkman, J. A. and LeBaron, B. (1989). Nonlinear dynamics and stock returns, *J. Bus.*, **62**, 311–37.

Serfling, R. J. (1980). *Approximation Theorems of Mathematical Statistics*, Wiley, New York.

Takens, F. (1981). Detecting strange attractors in turbulence, In *Dynamical Systems and Turbulence, Waruick 1980*, eds. D. Rand and L. Young, Springer–Verlag, Berlin, pp. 366–81.

(1983). Distinguishing deterministic and random systems. In *Nonlinear Dynamics and Turbulence*, eds. G. Borenblatt, G. Iooss, and D. Joseph, Pitman, Boston, MA, pp. 315–33.

Theiler, J. (1988). Statistical precision of dimension estimators, *Phys. Rev.*, **41A**(6), 3038–51.

CHAPTER 8

Searching for nonlinearity in mean and variance

Ted Jaditz and Chera L. Sayers

We use nonlinear time-series models to predict movements in the level and the volatility of a high-frequency economic time series. We extend earlier work by showing that linear-in-mean processes with autoregressive conditional heteroskedasticity (ARCH) or generalized ARCH (GARCH) class innovations are linear in squares, and hence, nonlinear diagnostics can be applied to higher moments as well as levels. We examine whether nearest-neighbor methods can exploit this dependence to improve out-of-sample forecasting of features of our data. In addition, we use the Mizrach method to determine whether the forecast improvements identified by the nonparametric methods are statistically significant. We find little evidence of strong nonlinearities in our data in either levels or squares.

1   Introduction

We discuss an approach to identifying important nonlinearities in economic data sets. Briefly, we advocate using out-of-sample predictive accuracy as a standard for evaluating model specification: One model is to be preferred to an alternative model if the former can generate out-of-sample forecasts that are significantly better than the forecasts generated by the latter.

We illustrate how this approach can be used to identify whether there are important nonlinearities in the level or in the variance of a time series. We compare forecasts generated from linear models to forecasts generated by a black-box procedure that is known to do well at approximating arbitrary nonlinear functions. Prior applications of the methodology have focused exclusively

We wish to thank but not otherwise implicate Rochelle Antoniewicz. The views expressed here do not necessarily reflect the policy or views of the Bureau of Labor Statistics (BLS) or the views of other BLS staff members. This paper was delivered at the 1993 Summer Meetings of the American Statistical Association and an edited version appears in the *Proceedings of the Business and Economics Statistics Section*, 1993.

on identifying nonlinearities in the level equation of a process. Here, we show how the methodology can be applied in some interesting ways to identify non-linearities in variance as well.

Nonlinear time-series methods in general are receiving increasing attention in the economics profession. One reason for this attention is that specification tests applied to the residuals of linear models often signal additional dependencies that are inconsistent with a linear data generator. Thus, nonlinear methods have been viewed as a means to achieve better in-sample fits. A second reason for the interest in nonlinear methods in what one might call the forecasting paradox: Standard linear statistical models of economic phenomena invariably fit very well in sample, but usually fail miserably at out-of-sample prediction. One is therefore tempted to explore means by which apparent dependencies in linear model residuals can be exploited to generate superior forecasts.

Numerous authors have looked for general evidence of nonlinearity by looking for dependencies in the residuals of models that represent an a priori best guess of the underlying data generator. The justification for this approach is the well-known Specification Test Theorem (Brock and Dechert 1988). Suppose, for example, that we observe a time series $\{y_t\}_{t=1,T}$ that is generated by the model.

$$y_t = \sum_{i=1,p} a_i y_{t-i} + u_t, \qquad (8.1)$$

where u_t is (IID), but instead, we filter with the model

$$y_t = \sum_{i=1,q} b_i y_{t-i} + v_t. \qquad (8.2)$$

We have

Theorem 8.1: *If* $||a|| < \infty$, $||b|| < \infty$, *and* $Var[t] < \infty$, $\{v_t\}$ *IID implies* $a_i = b_i \forall i$.   □

Statistics based on the correlation integral, such as the Brock–Dechert–Scheinkman (BDS) statistic, dimension numbers, and Kolmogorov entropy numbers, are known to be quite effective at identifying dependence in the residuals of linear null models. A general strategy is then to estimate a linear model, and test to see if the residuals are IID. If we (fail to) reject the null hypothesis that the residuals of an underlying model are IID, then we (fail to) reject the hypothesis that our null model is correctly specified. This general approach to testing for residual nonlinearity is followed by Brock and Sayers (1988), Frank and Stengos (1988) and DeCoster and Mitchel (1991), to name just a few early examples.

It is natural to try and extend this approach to test the specification of AR(GARCH)-class models. One might estimate an AR-GARCH model and test whether the standardized residuals are IID, as is done by Scheinkman and LeBaron (1989). A problem is that for models with higher moment dependence, nuisance-parameter theorems remain elusive for these statistics. For example, De Lima (1992) shows that the nuisance-parameter theorems developed for the case of linear residuals do not apply to the case of residuals from ARCH or GARCH-class models. Simulations by Brock, Hsieh and LeBaron (1991) suggest that the asymptotic distribution of the BDS test statistic depends on the values of the estimated parameters of the null model. Thus, test statistics calculated on the standardized residuals of ARCH-class models cannot be taken at face value.

Although this problem can be resolved (e.g., via the bootstrap), other problems remain. The typical test procedures are what one might refer to as factorization tests: The researcher is interested in testing for factorizations of joint distributions characteristic of independence. When such factorizations fail, the source of the failure is difficult to identify. The procedure seldom offers concrete suggestions for how the model might be changed to eliminate the dependence. This suggests that alternative approaches to identifying nonlinearity may be worth exploring.

Diebold and Nason (1990) argue that the relevant test for nonlinearities is what one might refer to as the prediction test. They point out several reasons why apparent in-sample nonlinearity may not necessarily imply out-of-sample forecast improvement. First, nonlinearities may be present only in even-numbered moments, and thus may be uninformative for level prediction. Thus, in spite of evidence of general dependence in the residuals, it may not be possible to improve level specification. Second, the apparent in-sample nonlinearities may be caused by rare regime breaks, structural shifts, or outliers, which are of limited use for out-of-sample prediction. Third, very slight nonlinearities may be present and detectable with large data sets, yet offer negligible ex ante forecast improvement. Hence, failure of in-sample diagnostics are not completely persuasive that there are important, exploitable dependencies in a time series.

Given these considerations, the most persuasive demonstration that there are exploitable nonlinear dependencies in a data set is to construct a forecast rule that does, in fact, exploit the dependence to generate superior forecasts. The methodology that we use here is quite similar to the methodology employed by Diebold Nason with some further refinements. We divide out sample into two parts: a fitting set and a prediction set. We estimate a nonlinear, nonparametric model on the fitting set; we then use parameter values estimated on the fitting set to form forecasts of the elements of the prediction set. We then compare the mean square error of these forecasts to the mean square error of forecasts generated by linear models, using a test statistic of Mizrach (1992a) which is a refinement of a procedure of Granger and Newbold (1986) and Meese and Rogoff (1988). Following Diebold and Nason (1990) we focus on near-neighbor forecast algorithms. One important reason for this focus is that this technique has been demonstrated to do very well at forecasting nonlinear deterministic systems. A recent review by Casdagli (1992) reports that near-neighbor techniques are able to forecast moderately high-dimensional deterministic nonlinear functions extremely well out of sample. This class of data generators is of particular interest in light of claims by Barnett and Chen (1988) and DeCoster and Mitchel (1991) that there is evidence of nonlinear determinism in various economic data sets. Thus, the results for near-neighbor forecasting can be interpreted as a diagnostic for significant nonlinear determinism in economic data.

A second reason for focusing on near-neighbor methods is their relation to the correlation-integral-based tests of dependence. For example, the Kolmogorov entropy test (Brock and Baek 1991) is essentially a test of whether x_{s+1} can predict x_{t+1}, given that the m-history $\{x_t, x_{t-1}, \ldots, x_{t-m+1}\}$ is close to the m-history $\{x_s, x_{s-1}, \ldots, x_{s-m+1}\}$. The near-neighbor algorithm is essentially a method of systematically sifting through a data set looking for just this type of structure. If the correlation-integral-based test are, in fact, identifying important structural features of the data, then the near-neighbor algorithm ought to forecast the data very well.

We extend the usual technique of looking for nonlinearities in level to looking for nonlinearities in squares of the process as well. Squares of the underlying data are interesting in their own right: Witness for proliferation of models of conditional heteroskedasticity over the last 10 years, including ARCH (Engle 1983), GARCH (Bollerslev 1986), and EGARCH (Nelson 1990). More recently, there is emerging an appreciation that nonlinearities in variance may be important. See, for example, Hamilton and Susmel (1992) who point out that the usual linear-variance-equation ARCH or GARCH models fail to capture certain important features of stock-price volatility. We show below that if the underlying process is linear in level, and if the variance equation is of the GARCH class, then the process will be linear in squares. Thus, testing for linearity in the squares of the process can be a useful diagnostic of nonlinearity in the variance equation.

We apply our methodology to a data set of observations on an interest-rate risk premium. We analyze the difference between the one-month treasury bill rate and the one-month rate on high-grade commercial paper. This data set has three interesting features. Firstly, it is highly variable over time; see Lauterbach (1989) and references therein. Second, it is economically important in that it has been identified by researchers such as Friedman and Kuttner (1989, 1992), Stock and Watson (1989) and Bermanke (1990), as a financial variable that contains significant information about the future course of the economy. Third, it is available on a relatively high frequency. Our data consist of 1,712 weekly observations over the time period January 8, 1960, to October 16, 1992.

The results of test for nonlinearity in the level equation of this data set were reported by Jaditz and Sayers (1993); we review the results from that study briefly before proceeding to new results for squares. To summarize our results, our methods are unable to exploit apparent nonlinear residual dependence to improve out-of-sample forecast accuracy in either the level or the squares of the data. It is therefore possible that there are no important nonlinearities in either the level equation or the variance equation. Further, the results indicate that the ARCH effects explain very little of the total variation of the squares of the process. This suggests that ARCH-class models may not be the sole cause of the failure of the nonlinearity diagnostics in the data. Alternatives, such as regime shifts, structural breaks, and multivariate relationships, must be considered more seriously.

2   Linearity in level, linearity in squares

To be able to talk about nonlinearity, we must first be specific about what we mean by a linear time series. Suppose that we have a stationary time series with bounded unconditional moments, $\{x_t\}_{t=1,\infty}$. Under what circumstances is it appropriate to model the sequence $\{x_t\}$ using only linear techniques?

By the Wold decomposition, this time series has a representation

$$x_t = u_t + v_t \tag{8.3}$$

where v_t is deterministic, and v_t and u_t are uncorrelated. Further, u_t has the representation

$$u_t = \sum_{i=1}^{\infty} a_i \varepsilon_{t-i} = A(L)\varepsilon_t \tag{8.4}$$

where $\{\varepsilon\}_t$ is an uncorrelated process (see Priestly 1981). Appeal to the Wold representation is often made to justify a focus on linear modeling techniques. For a process $\{x_t\}$ that has no deterministic component, it is possible to specify conditions under which linear models say virtually all that there is to say about a process.

One restrictive class of nonlinear process is defined by Priestly (1981):

Definition 1: $\{x_t\}$ is IID linearly if it has the representation

$$x_t = \sum_{i=1}^{\infty} a_i \varepsilon_{t-i} = A(L)\varepsilon_t \tag{8.5}$$

and the innovations $\{\varepsilon_t\}$ in equation 8.5 are IID with mean 0 and variance σ^2.

□

Note that applying the BDS test to the estimated residuals of a linear model is testing for IID linearity. On the other hand, a process can fail to be IID linear, and yet offer no meaningful improvement in level specification. If the process $\{x_t\}$ has no deterministic component, and if any error dependence cannot be used to help in forecasting the conditional mean of the process, then we say that the process $\{x_t\}$ is Martingale-difference-sequence (MDS) linear:

Definition 2: (Hall and Heyde 1980) $\{x_t\}$ is MDS linear if the innovations $\{\varepsilon_t\}$ in equation 8.5 are an MDS (Loosely speaking, e_t is an MDS if the expectation of e_t conditional on all information available at time $t-1$ is 0. See Brock and Potter (1991) for a further discussion.) □

Our approach might be interpreted as a constructive diagnostic for the claim that the series $\{x_t\}$ is MDS linear. To conduct the diagnostic, one generates a forecast of the time series using a linear null model. One then compares the (out-of-sample) forecast performance of the linear model to a black-box alternative. If the alternative method can generative forecast errors that are smaller (on average) than the forecast errors of the best available linear model, then the underlying data generator cannot be MDS linear.

Although nonparametric methods have been used to study variation in the level, they are less frequently applied to the study of volatility. Volatility clustering appears to be generic in economic data. There are several approaches to the modeling of conditional volatility. The most popular approach is the GARCH or ARCH line of modeling, from Engle (1983) and Bollerslev (1986). Here, the conditional variance of the process is assumed to follow an autoregressive (AR) or autoregressive moving average (ARMA) process. One might then ask just how much we can infer about the variance equation in the absence a specification for the level. Here we show that an MDS linear process driven by ARCH or GARCH errors is MDS linear in squares.

We write the level equation of the process as

$$x_t = A(L)x_t + \varepsilon_t, \ \varepsilon_t \text{ MDS} \tag{8.6}$$

We recast into the familiar form

$$[1 - A(L)]x_t = \varepsilon_t \tag{8.7}$$

or

$$x_t = [(1 - A(L)]^{-1}\varepsilon_t. \tag{8.8}$$

The GARCH variance specification is written

$$\varepsilon_t = e_t h_t, \tag{8.9a}$$

$$e_t \text{ white noise, } E[e_t] = 0, E[e_t^2] = 1. \tag{8.9b}$$

$$h_t^2 = \alpha + B(L)h_{t-1}^2 + C(L)\varepsilon_{t-1}^2. \tag{8.9c}$$

When we square x_t, we obtain

$$(x_t)^2 = [1 - A(L)]^{-1}\varepsilon_t^2. \tag{8.10}$$

(Note that in the model, ε_t^2 is correlated with ε_{t-i}^2 for small i, but $E[\varepsilon_t \varepsilon_{t-i}] = 0$ as a consequence of equation (8.9b).)

Given the GARCH specification for the variance equation, we can rewrite equation (8.10) as an AR process in squares of x_t. To illustrate: Rewrite equation (8.9c) to convert the GARCH specification into an ARCH specification:

$$[1 - B(L)]h_t^2 = \alpha + C(L)\varepsilon_{t-1}^2, \tag{8.11}$$

which yields

$$h_t^2 = \alpha' + [1 - B(L)]^{-1}C(L)\varepsilon_{t-1}^2. \tag{8.12}$$

Because $E[\varepsilon_t^2] = h_t^2$, we can write

$$\begin{aligned}
\varepsilon_r^2 &= h_t^2 + \zeta_t \\
&= \alpha' + [1 - B(L)]^{-1}C(L)\varepsilon_{t-1}^2 + \zeta_t,
\end{aligned} \tag{8.13}$$

where $E[\zeta_t] = 0$, $\zeta_t \in [-h_t^2, \infty)$. Here, we might point out that if the GARCH specification is correct, then $\{\zeta_t\}$ is an MDS sequence. So,

$$[1 - D(L)]\varepsilon_t^2 = \alpha' + \zeta_t \tag{8.14}$$

and

$$\varepsilon_t^2 = \alpha' + [1 - D(L)]^{-1}\zeta_t \tag{8.15}$$

We substitute this result into equation (8.10) to obtain

$$\begin{aligned}
x_t^2 &= [1 - A(L)]^{-1}\{\alpha' + [1 - D(L)]^{-1}\zeta_t\} \\
&= a + E(L)\zeta_t,
\end{aligned} \tag{8.16}$$

and finally,

$$E(L)^{-1}x_t^2 = a' + \zeta_t \tag{8.17}$$

The point is this: Even in the presence of GARCH effects, the process $\{x_t^2\}$ has a linear representation in terms of a white-noise error process ζ_t. If the data generator is not linear in both level and variance, then this series of substitutions does not work. Indeed, we can search for nonlinearities in the variance of the process using exactly the same hardware that we used to search for nonlinearities in the level. Black-box forecasts can help us to test whether there are nonlinearities in either the first or the second moment of the process.

3   Methodology

Nearest-neighbor methods are beginning to find use in economics and finance. Recent efforts include Diebold and Nason (1990), Meese and Rose (1990), LeBaron (1992), and Mizrach (1992b). To motivate the method, suppose that we observe a time series where the data generator is a smooth function of the form

$$x_t = f(x_{t-1}, x_{t-2}, \ldots, x_{t-d}) + \varepsilon_t, \ \varepsilon_t \ \text{uncorrelated} \tag{8.18}$$

If the data-generating function $f(\cdot)$ is fixed over time, and given enough observations, we may be able to deduce aspects of the local structure of the function. If the signal-to-noise ratio is high, then when $(x_{t-1}, x_{t-2}, \ldots, x_{t-d})$ is close to $(x_{s-1}, x_{s-2}, \ldots, x_{s-d})$, we expect that x_t will be close to x_s. Linear models estimated from points that are close to $(x_{t-1}, x_{t-2}, \ldots, x_{t-d})$ may have forecast errors that have a lower component of bias or (functional) specification error, compared to a global linear model. Thus, forecast errors may be lowered even though we reduce estimator efficiency by discarding some of our data.

Our implementation follows the scheme suggested by Casdagli (1992). We start with observations on a time series $\{x_t\}_{t=1,T}$ which we partition into a fitting set $\mathcal{F}$ and a prediction set $\mathcal{P}$. The aim is to use the information in $\mathcal{F}$ to predict observations in $\mathcal{P}$.

For a given lag length m, construct for each observation $\{x_t\}_{t=m+1,T}$ an m-history x_{t-1}^m,

$$x_{t-1}^m = (x_{t-1}, x_{t-2}, \ldots, x_{t-m}). \tag{8.19}$$

Thus we have a set of ordered pairs $\{(x_t, x_{t-1}^m)\}_{t=m+1,T}$. For each x_t in the prediction set, we calculate the distance between x_{t-1}^m and $x_{s-1}^m \forall s \in \mathcal{F}$. Following Casdagli (1992), we use the sup norm to calculate distances:

$$||x_{t-1}^m - x_{s-1}^m|| = \max_i |x_{t-i} - x_{s-i}|. \tag{8.20}$$

We then select the k nearest pairs (x_s, x_{s-1}^m) to estimate the parameters in the local regression

$$x_s = \alpha_{0,k} + x_{s-1}^m \alpha_k + \varepsilon_s. \tag{8.21}$$

The estimated parameters $\hat{\alpha}_{0,k}$ and $\hat{\alpha}_k$ are used to calculate the prediction

$$\hat{x}_t = \hat{\alpha}_{0,k} + x_{t-1}^m \hat{\alpha}. \tag{8.22}$$

The prediction is then used to calculate the prediction error $x_t - \hat{x}_t = e_{t,k}$.

Other implementations of nearest-neighbor estimation (notably Cleveland and Devlin, 1988) differ from the Casdagli approach in certain technical details, notably weighting and the distance measure. See Jaditz and Sayers (1993a) for a further discussion of these differences. To summarize, the scheme described here appears to be numerically stable and computationally less demanding when compared with alternative approaches.

Rather than adopt a model based on goodness of fit, we evaluate our model solely on the basis of prediction efficiency. One measure of forecast efficiency is the normalized root mean square error (RMSE) of the forecast,

$$R_k(m) = \frac{1}{P} \left(\sum_{t \in \mathcal{P}} e_{t,k}^2 \right)^{(0.5)} \Big/ \sigma_{\mathcal{P}}, \tag{8.23}$$

where $\sigma_{\mathcal{P}}$ is the sample standard deviation of the $x_t \in \mathcal{P}$. We use plots of $R_k(m)$ to help identify specifications that are particularly successful at forecasting the series. We then use a test statistic of Mizrach (1992a) to evaluate whether the improvement is statistically significant.

The statistic is a refinement of an approach of Granger and Newbold (1986) and Meese and Rogoff (1988). To review the test, let $\{\varepsilon_{1,t}\}$ be the forecast residuals from method 1, and let $\{\varepsilon_{2,t}\}$ be the forecast residuals from method 2. Granger and Newbold test whether $\mathrm{var}(\varepsilon_{1,t}) = \sigma_1^2$ is significantly less than $\mathrm{var}(\varepsilon_{2,t}) = \sigma_2^2$ by looking at the orthogonalized residuals $u_t = \varepsilon_{1,t} - \varepsilon_{2,t}$, $v_t = \varepsilon_{1,t} + \varepsilon_{2,t}$. The correlation between u_t and v_t is just $\sigma_1^2 - \sigma_2^2$. Thus, if the correlation between u_t and v_t is significantly greater (less) than zero, then σ_1^2 is significantly greater (less) than σ_2^2.

Mizrach's refinement is to generalize the test to biased, heterokedastic forecast residuals, using Newey and West (1987) hardware. Mizrach (1992a) shows that given that the two sequences are α mixing, the statistic

$$R = \sqrt{T} \left\{ \frac{\frac{1}{T} \sum_{i=1}^{T} u_i v_i}{\left[\sum_{i=-k}^{k} w(i) S_{uvuv}(i) \right]^{1/2}} \right\} \sim \mathcal{N}(0, 1) \tag{8.24}$$

asymptotically, where

$$w(i) = 1 - \frac{|i|}{k+1}$$

$$S_{uvuv}(t) = \frac{1}{T-j} \sum_{j=1}^{T} u_j v_j u_{j-i} v_{j-i} \quad j \geq 0$$

$$\frac{1}{T+j} \sum_{j=t+1}^{T} u_{j+t} v_{j+t} u_j v_j \quad j < 0$$

$$k = k(T), \text{ with } \lim_{n \to \infty} \frac{k(T)}{T^{1/2}} = 0.$$

$$= \mathrm{int}(T^{1/3}) + 1, \text{ for example.}$$

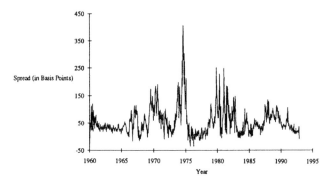

Figure 8.1. Six month tresaury bill/six month commercial paper interest rate spread.

Mizrach's (1992a) Monte Carlo analysis indicates that the statistic is properly sized in samples greater than $T \geq 100$.

One final caveat is in order. To apply this statistic to level forecasts, we need to estimate fourth-order moments from out data. To apply it to variance forecasts, we need to estimate eighth-order moments. There is some concern in the literature about whether we may assume that moments of this order exist generically in time series (see, e.g., Loretan and Phillips 1992). Thus, some caution should be used in the application of our tests.

4   Results

Our data are a time series of 1,711, weekly observations on the spread between 6-month treasury bills and 6-month commercial paper. The treasury bill rate used to compute the spread is the average issuing price for the weekly Monday Treasury auction of 6-month bills. The commercial paper rate is the average dealer issuing rate for 6-month prime commercial paper, as of the Monday of the Treasury auction. Thus, our data series represents an ex ante risk premium, rather than an ex post realized difference in returns.

Figure 8.1 displays the plot of the raw time series. To induce greater stationary in the data, we first difference. Figure 8.2 displays the first difference of the interest-rate premium. Summary statistics for this series are given in Table 8.1. The data are highly correlated both in level and in squares, and are highly persistent. Figure 8.3 plots the squared risk premium.

We apply an AR filter to see how well the linear model fits the data. Table 8.2 describes the filter. Note the extremely large number of lags required to induce white residuals. Further, nonlinear diagnostics indicate that the residuals still appear to exhibit significant nonlinear structure.

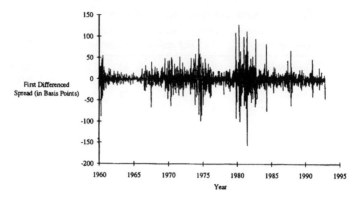

Figure 8.2. First difference of the interest-rate spread.

Table 8.1. *Summary statistics for the differenced data*

Summary statistics			
Mean	0.000		
Standard deviation	18.95		
Median	0.000		
Maximum	128		
Minimum	−156		
Diagnostic tests	Test statistic	Degrees of freedom	Probability
Ljung–Box Q test	195.89	41	0.000
McLeod-Li test	1101.1	41	0.000
χ^2 test (stationarity)	47.92	29	0.015

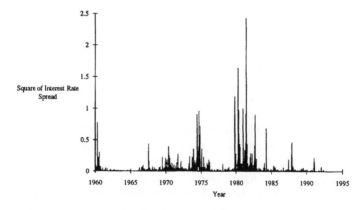

Figure 8.3. Squares of interest rate data.

Table 8.2. *Auto regression filter summary*

Diagnostic tests	Test statistic	Degrees of freedom	Probability
Ljung–N Box Q test	53.49	40	0.075
McLeod-Li test	1485.65	40	0.000
χ^2 test	35.34	28	0.160
BDS test $m = 5$, $\varepsilon = 0.9$	14.62		0.000

[a] AR(p) filtered residuals: $p = 54$

For both levels and squares, we calculate our near-neighbor forecasts for embedding dimensions 5, 10, 15, and 20. Three alternative-fitting set specifications were utilized. First, we have the fixed-window-fitting set: For all t,

$$\mathcal{F} = \{x_t : m + 1 < t \leq N_f\}$$
$$\mathcal{P} = \{x_t : N_f < t \leq T\}$$

for some $N_f < T$. Second, there is the expanding-window-fitting set: For a given t,

$$\mathcal{F}_t = \{x_s : m + 1 \leq s < t\}$$
$$\mathcal{P}_t = \{x_t\}.$$

Finally, we have the sliding-window-fitting set: For a given t and N_f, we have

$$\mathcal{F}_t = \{x_t : m + 1 + (t - N_f) < s \leq t\}$$
$$\mathcal{P} = \{x_t\}.$$

For every lag length and window scheme, we calculate the best AR forecast and the best near-neighbor forecast.

4.1   *Nonlinearity in Mean*

To review the earlier results from Jaditz and Sayers (1993). There appears to be significant linear structure in the mean of this process. Evidence for nonlinearity in level is quite weak.

The results are summarized in Table 8.3. The near-neighbor methodology can generate only modest improvements over AR specifications. For fixed- and sliding-window specifications, the near-neighbor approach can offer improvements of at most, 2 percent of the AR RMSE.

A representative $R_k(m)$ plot is given in Figure 8.4. As Casdagli (1992) points out, if there are important nonlinearities, the $R_k(m)$ plot will typically reach its minimum at a relatively small number of near neighbors, and then have a noticeable upward slope. Note that the plots in Figure 8.5 exhibit a smooth

Table 8.3. *Results for out-of-sample level prediction*

Prediction method	m	Best k	$R_k(m)$
Fixed-window near-neighbor	5	1,352	0.948
	10	1,319	0.948
	15	1,276	0.920
	20	1,247	0.918
Sliding-window near-neighbor	5	1,361	0.946
	10	1,336	0.926
	15	1,283	0.919
	20	1,259	0.919
Expanding-window nearest-neighbor	5	1,387	0.954
	10	1,343	0.942
	15	1,263	0.933
	20	1,141	0.933
AR model, fixed-fitting set	5		0.950
	10		0.933
	15		0.933
	20		0.934
AR model, sliding-fitting set	5		0.949
	10		0.933
	15		0.931
	20		0.935
Martingale prediction			1.646
unconditional mean			1.026

Notes: m = embedding dimension; Best k = number of near neighbors that minimizes $R_k(m)$; $R_k(m)$ = relative efficiency of forecast, equal to the normalized RMSE.

downward slope. This provides additional confirmation that local information does not appear to be important for forecast performance.

Table 8.4 gives the results of the comparison of the best AR and near-neighbor forecasts using Mizrach's test of forecast efficiency. Both the AR forecast and the near-neighbor forecast offer significant improvements over the unconditional mean forecast. However, the difference between the AR model and the near-neighbor forecast is not significant. Thus we do not have strong evidence of nonlinearity in levels in our data set.

4.2 *Nonlinearity in Squares*

Given the lack of evidence for nonlinear structure in mean, we square the data and try again. Results for near-neighbor prediction of the squared data are

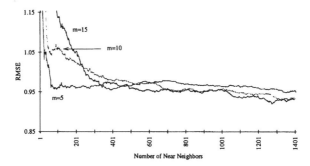

Figure 8.4. $R_k(m)$ plot for the level equation: Fixed-window, varying embeddings.

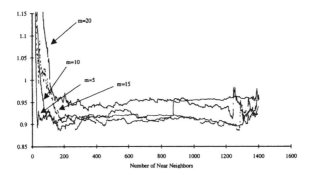

Figure 8.5. $R_k(m)$ plot for the variance equation: expanding-window, varying embeddings.

Table 8.4. *Mizrach's robust forecast comparison: Levels*

Data set 1	Data set 2	Test statistic
Unconditional mean forecast	Fixed-window, embedding dimension 20	2.29
Unconditional mean forecast	AR(15), fixed fitting set	2.07
AR(15), fixed fitting set	Fixed-window, embedding dimension 20	1.61

given in Table 8.5. Here, the near-neighbor forecasts are about 3 percent better than the best AR forecasts, which are about 6 percent better than the Martingale forecasts and 20 percent better than the unconditional mean forecasts.

Comparing the forecasts using the Mizrach test statistic (Table 8.6): both the AR (15) forecast and the near-neighbor forecast are significantly better than

Table 8.5. *Results for out-of-sample level prediction*

Prediction method	m	Best k	$R_k(m)$
Fixed-window near-neighbor	5	168	0.890
	10	1,200	0.895
	15	1,224	0.887
	20	1,250	0.898
Sliding-window near-neighbor	5	143	0.890
	10	1,170	0.890
	15	1,174	0.891
	20	1,266	0.905
Expanding-window nearest-neighbor	5	176	0.885
	10	1,259	0.895
	15	1,278	0.885
	20	1,306	0.906
AR model, fixed-fitting set	5		0.934
	10		0.929
	15		0.917
	20		0.919
AR model, sliding-fitting set	5		0.949
	10		0.933
	15		0.931
	20		0.935
Martingale prediction			0.984
unconditional mean			1.143

Notes: m = embedding dimension; Best k = number of near neighbors that minimizes $R_k(m)$; $R_k(m)$ = relative efficiency of forecast, equal to the normalized RMSE.

the unconditional mean forecast. Neither AR(15) nor near the neighbor method is significantly better than the Martingale forecast. Although the expanding-window specification has the lowest RMSE, it is not significantly better than the AR(15) forecast.

The $R_k(m)$ plot for the expanding-window case is given in Figure 8.5. Note that the plot is somewhat more erratic that the plot for the levels, and does appear to have some jumps that could be interpreted as evidence of local structure. It is also possible that these jumps are an artifact of the data: Recalling Figure 3, the squares data exhibit a significant number of spikes in the fitting set, and minor changes in the fit about one of those spikes can have a major effect on the overall RMSE. Further detailed examination of the forecast residuals suggests that fitting about one of the spikes accounts for most of the difference

Table 8.6. *Mizrach's robust forecast comparison: Squares*

Data set 1	Data set 2	Test statistic
Unconditional mean forecast	Expanding-window, $m = 5$	2.64
Martingale forecast	AR(15), fixed-fitting set	0.94
Martingale forecast	Expanding-window, $m = 5$	1.44
AR(15), fixed-fitting set	Expanding window, $m = 5$	0.70

among forecasts. Thus, although the $R_k(m)$ plot is intriguing, the balance of the evidence suggests that there is no important nonlinearity in squares.

5   Summary

This paper has illustrated how nonparametric black-box forecasting procedures, combined with a robust test for forecast improvement, can be used to assist in model selection. We apply the approach to a data set for which the usual diagnostics illustrate significant nonlinear dependence.

We find that there is little evidence in the data for forecastable nonlinearities in either the level or the variance equations for this time series. This suggests that ARCH or GARCH-class models are as good a way as any to model this data set. In particular, it is unlikely that the data are generated by a simple, stationary nonlinear deterministic function.

The failure of nonparametric methods to identify any significant nonlinear effects is highly surprising. Note that over the sample period, we observe several complete business cycles and at least one (if not two) major changes in the conduct of monetary policy. One could also list several important changes in institutions and technologies over the sample period. Any one of these effects might have been expected to leave a mark in our time series, leaving a shift in level or a change in the speed of adjustment that the nonparametric methods might be expected to exploit.

The issue is whether our findings represent a power problem with the procedure, or whether they illustrate a true feature of the underlying data generator. Someone with a strong belief that business-cycle effects are important, for example, might estimate a parametric regime shift model, similar to Neftci (1984) or Hamilton (1989), for example, and perhaps one would find significant coefficients on the relevant parameters. On the other hand, apparent significance may be a result of inappropriate modeling of the error structure. (If a modeling procedure neglects important dependence in the data, then the standard errors calculated under the assumptions of the model will, in general, be too small.) In an effort to help resolve this issue, we continue to study the power of the nonparametric forecasting procedure in detecting nonlinearities in simulated data, using popular nonlinear models as data generators.

REFERENCES

Barnett, W. A., and Chen, P. (1988). The aggregation-theoretic monetary aggregates are chaotic and have strange attractors: An econometric application of mathematical chaos. In *Dynamic Econometric Modeling, Proceedings of the Third International Symposium on Economic Theory and Econometrics*, eds. W. A. Barnett, E. R. Berndt, and H. White, Cambridge University Press, Cambridge, MA, pp. 199–245.

Bemanke, B. S. (1990). On the predictive power of interest rates and interest rate spreads, *New England Econo. Rev.* (Nov./Dec.). 51–68.

Bollerslev, T. (1986). Generalized autoregressive conditional heteroscedasticity, *J. Econ.* **31**, 307–27.

Brock, W. A., and Baek, E. G. (1991). Some theory of statistical inference for nonlinear science, *Rev. Econ. Studies*, **58**, 697–716.

Brock, W. A., and Dechert, W. D. (1988). A general class of specification tests: The scalar case, *Proceedings of the Business and Economic Statistics of the American Statistical Association*, Published by American Statistical Association, Alexandra, VA, 70–79.

Brock, W. A., Hsieh, D., and LeBaron, B. (1991). *A Test of Nonlinear Dynamics, Chaos, and Instability*, MIT Press, Cambridge, MA.

Brock, W. A., and Potter, S. M. (1991). Nonlinear time series and macroeconomics, mimeo, University of Wisconsin–Madison, Madiso, WI.

Brock, W. A., and Sayers, C. L. (1988). Is the business cycle characterized by deterministic chaos? *J. Monetary Econ.*, **22**, 71–80.

Casdagli, M. (1992). Chaos and deterministic versus stochastic non-linear modeling, *J. Roy. Stat. Soc. Ser. B*, **54**, 303–28.

Cleveland, W. S., and Devlin S. J. (1988). Locally weighted regression: An approach to regression analysis by local fitting, *J. Am. Stat. Associ.* **83**, 596–610.

DeCoster, G. P., and Mitchell, D. W. (1991). Nonlinear monetary dynamics, *J. Bus. Econ. Stat.* **9**, 455–461.

De Lima, P. (1992). Testing nonlinearities under moment condition failure, mimeo, Johns Hopkins University, Battimore, MD.

Diebold, F. X., and Nason, J. A. (1990). Nonparametric exchange rate prediction? *J. Int. Econ.* **28**, 315–22.

Engle, R. F. (1983). Autoregressive conditional heteroscedasticity with estimates of the variance of U.K. inflation, *Econometrica* **50**, 987–1008.

Frank, M., and Stengos, T. (1988). Chaotic dynamics in economic time series, *J. Econ. Surv.* **2**, 103–33.

Friedman, B. A., and Kuttner, K. N. (1989). Money, income and prices after the 1980's, NBER Working Paper 2852.

(1992). Why does the paper-bill spread predict real economic activity? In *New Research in Business Cycles, Indicators, and Forecasts*, eds. J. Stock and M. Watson, University of Chicago Press, Chicago, ID, and National Bureau of Economic Research, Cambridge, MA.

Granger, C. W. J., and Newbold, P. (1986). *Forecasting in Business and Economic Time Series*, Academic Press, San Diego, CA.

Hall, P., and Heyde, C. C. (1980). *Martingale Limit Theory and Its Application*, Academic Press, New York.

Hamilton, J. D. (1989). A new approach to the economic analysis of nonstationary time series and the business cycle, *Econometrica* **57**, 357–84.

Hamilton, J. D. and Susmel, R. (1992). Autoregressive heteroscedasticity and changes in regime, mimeo, Department of Economics, University of California San Diego, La Jolla, CA 92093.

Jaditz, T., and Sayers, C. L. (1993). Non-linearity in the interest rate risk premium, Bureau of Labor Statistics Working Paper 242.

Lauterbach, B. (1989). Consumption volatility, prediction volatility, spot-rate volatility, and the returns on treasury bills and bonds, *J. Finan. Econ.* **24**, 155–79.

LeBaron, B. (1992). Forecast improvements using a volatility index, *J. Appl. Econo.* **7**, S137–49.

Loretan, M., and Phillips, P. C. B. (1992). Testing the covariance stationarity of heavy tailed time series: An overview of the theory with applications to several financial data sets, Social Systems Research Institute Working Paper 9208, University of Wisconsin, Madison, WI.

Meese, R., and Rogoff, K. (1988). Was it real? The exchange rate differential relation over the modern floating rate period, *J. Finance* **43**, 933–48.

Meese, R. A., and Rose, A. K. (1990). Non-linear, nonparametric, nonessential exchange rate estimation, *Am. Econ. Rev.* **80**, 192–6.

Mizrach, B. (1992a). Forecast comparisons in L^2, Federal Reserve Bank of New York, Research Function, April.

   (1992b). Multivariate nearest neighbor forecasts of EMS exchange rates, *J. Appl. Econ.* **7**, S151– 63.

Neftci, S. (1984). Are economic time series asymmetric over the business cycle? *J. Polit. Econ.* **92**, 307–28.

Nelson, D. B. (1990). Conditional Heteroscedasticity in Asset Returns: A New Approach, *Econometrica* **59**, 347–70.

Newey, W., and West, K. (1987). A simple positive semi-definite heteroscedasticity and autocorrelation consistent covariance matrix, *Econometrica* **55**, 703–8.

Priestly, M. B. (1981). *Spectral Analysis and Time Series*, Academic Press, New York.

Scheinkman, J., and LeBaron, B. (1989). Nonlinear dynamics and stock returns, *J. Bus.* **62**, 311–37.

Stock, J. H., and Watson, M. K. (1989). New indexes of coincident and leading economic indicators. In *NBER Macroeconomics Annual*, eds. O. J. Blanchard and S. Fisher, MIT Press, Cambridge, MA., pp. 351–94.

CHAPTER 9

Operational characteristics of White's test for neglected nonlinearities

J. A. Jungeilges

White's neural-network test NNT for neglected nonlinearity is introduced, and the operational characteristics of a test procedure that is asymptotically equivalent to the NNT is studied. The main element of this effort consists in a simulation experiment that uses economic models as data generators. The design of the experiment allows for the generation of information about the size and the power of various versions of the test procedure. Special emphasis is put on the exploration of the effects of uncertainty about the dimension of the affine network on the performance of the test. The findings corroborate earlier results concerning the test's appropriate size. The test has moderate power against a nonlinear Hicksian macroeconomic system that is prone to non-economic noise and has high power against chaotic processes generated by two microeconomic models. Moreover, the solution to the order-selection problem definitely influences the power of the test.

1   Introduction

The current change of paradigm observable in major areas of science also has led to a surge of interest in nonlinear phenomena in economics. As a consequence, the intensity of research geared toward the design of neoteric statistical tests for nonlinearity of data-generating processes has increased. Moreover, various efforts have been launched to reevaluate existing testing procedures in the light of recent developments in nonlinear dynamics. There are conceptual as well as practical reasons for the interest in nonlinearities. The identification of economic processes for which the existing linear models are inadequate may lead to new modeling efforts dominated by a nonlinear structural modeling

The paper reflects research performed while the author held a position as visiting scholar at the Department of Economics, Washington University, One Brookings Drive, St. Louis, MO 63130. The author's work was supported by a grant from the German Science Foundation approach. The practical aspect is associated with prediction problems. If the process generating a given time series is indeed nonlinear, the conventional linear predictors may be outperformed by nonlinear predictors or they are even totally irrelevant if the process underlying the data exhibits sensitive dependence on initial conditions.

There already exists a variety of tests for nonlinearities. An explicit account of such procedures can be found, for example, in Schuhr (1991, pp. 120–140), Lee, White, and Granger (1993) and Tong (1990, pp. 221–281). In the present effort, we scrutinize the operational characteristics of a neoteric procedure proposed by White (1989a). This test is of special interest because it is based on the outstanding approximation ability of neural nets. It tests the hypothesis of linearity in the mean against the wide alternative of nonlinearity in the mean. In a previous simulation study, the neural-network test (NNT) has been found to have proper size and power against various forms of nonlinearities (Lee et al. 1993). This study tries to broaden the knowledge concerning the operational characteristic of White's test. The primary focus is on size and power in the presence of small sample sizes as well as on the relation between the performance of the test and the choice of the autoregressive model (i.e., the affine part of the network) used to remove linear correlation from the data. We arrive at our results on the basis of a simulation experiment. Although we adopt a traditional technique for the analysis of the properties of the test, we chose an alternative approach with respect to the processes representing the "true state of nature" in the simulation study.

Operating under the assumption that nonlinear dynamic models provide a parsimonious abstraction of economic reality, we argue that prior to the application of a test for nonlinearity to economic data the characteristics of the tests used should be evaluated using artificial data-generating processes based on an economic rationale. At the present state, it seems impossible to evaluate the power of a given test against all possible forms of nonlinearity. Acknowledging this fact, researchers working toward an understanding of tests for nonlinearity typically use artificial data generated by some process (dynamic map) whose properties have been studied extensively (e.g., bilinear processes, threshold autoregressive models, nonlinear MAs), to arrive at statements concerning the power properties of some given test. This strategy is adequate if one wants to generate results concerning the general usefulness of the test at hand. But, given the intended application in a specific area, characterized by specific forms of nonlinearities, this strategy might not be very helpful. The potential user of the test would have to evaluate whether or not the maps used as data generators provide a valid abstraction for the process being studied. While trying to solve this problem, an economist might very well run into a lot of conflicting evidence in the existing econometric literature. What makes the problem worse is that the major body of econometric evidence is based on the assumption that economic processes are indeed linear!

As an alternative strategy, we propose the use of artificial nonlinear data-generating processes motivated by economic theory. Using a set of processes based on economic axioms and arguments from various economic paradigms should lead to results of higher informational value to those who intend to apply tests for nonlinearity to economic data. In the present effort, we implement this strategy by choosing a macroeconomic data generator based on an early nonlinear business-cycle model by Hicks (1950), a nonlinear model of a financial market by Huang and Day (1993), and a microeconomic model of interdependent consumer behavior from Gaertner and Jungeilges (1988, 1993).

The strategy outlined above is not without precedence. Consider, for example, the strategy chosen by Granger (1966) to exemplify the spectral shape of economic data. A simple accelerator multiplier model is used to demonstrate that, for realistic parameter values, the typical shape of the power spectrum occurs. Another example is provided by the work of Ashley and Patterson (1988) who generate trajectories of a nonlinear Keynesian-type model to demonstrate that Hinich's bispectral test has power against a chaotic alternative. So far, the work related to operational characteristics of White's test relied on the conventional simulation approach. Additional reference related to the NNT include White (1889b) and Kuan and White (1991). Reports on applications of the test are found in Lee et al. (1993), who apply the test to various macroeconomic series, and in Hiemstra and Jones (1992), who use the test on stock-return data as well as on data reflecting trading volume at the New York Stock Exchange.

Note that our results are valid for our own implementation of White's test. With respect to the size of the test, we find that, given that the true linear generating process is a low-dimensional autoregressive process, the size of the test is appropriate and fairly stable throughout the domain of stable first-order autoregressive models. The distribution of the test statistic deviates significantly from the theoretical null distribution if the data-generating process has a negative unit root. Drastic deviations from the theoretical null are also possible in the presence of a positive unit root. The choice of the order of the linear filter used to eliminate linear correlation does not seem to have a significant influence on the size of the test, given that the true underlying model is stable. If instabilities are present, then using the Schwarzian Bayesian information criterion (SBIC) to select the order of the linear filter is advantageous.

The simulation experiments in which the hypothetical true state of nature is nonlinear provide evidence for the fact that the NNT is indeed able to detect even Hicksian nonlinearities coupled with a noisy environment, given that the time series are long enough. Faced with data taken from chaotic attractors, White's test detects the underlying nonlinearity with high probability even for small sample sizes. In all cases, it becomes evident that the distribution of the test statistic under the alternative is not independent of the way that the order of the linear filter is chosen. Our results indicate that a criterion known to prefer parsimonious models, i.e., the SBIC, tends to choose a dimension for the linear filter for which the probability of rejecting linearity in the mean is maximized.

Prior to outlining the rationale of White's NNT as well as the algorithm of the test procedure in Section 2, we give a short introduction into feedforward-type neural nets. A discussion of the design for the simulation experiment is found in Section 3. Section 3.1 contains a description of the economic data generators. We also make an effort to characterize the data basis used in the experiment. Finally, the results are explicated in Section 4. A set of concluding remarks (Section 5) carries the paper to completion.

2   White's NNT

The present treatment of White's NNT intends to familiarize the reader with the conceptual basis of White's test for neglected nonlinearities. Prior to the description of the computational procedure, we discuss a specific type of neural network, thereby providing the main structural element of the testing procedure. The outline of the so-called feedforward network with hidden layers is succeeded by a sketch of the probabilistic model, the main assumptions, as well as the course of the argument motivating the utilization of this type of network in a test for nonlinearities. We describe the computational procedure in the final subsection.

2.1   *Introduction to neural-network models*

The research geared at understanding the nature of the human brain has generated various models sharing the characteristics of a network structure. Theoretical work done by scientists studying cognitive processes has motivated the development of an interesting class of nonlinear statistical models that are able to learn. The learning process, which involves some kind of interaction with an environment, can be viewed as a statistical procedure of the recursive type. Because those models reflect to some degree our understanding of the brain's neural structure, it has become customary to refer to elements in this class of models as neural-network models, or NNMs. This neoteric type of statistical model has been used in various disciplines in the solution of problems that seemed to be resistent to satisfactory solutions prior to the introduction of NNMs. White (1989b) identifies pattern recognition, classification, nonlinear feature detection and nonlinear forecasting as areas of successful application. Also recently, McCaffrey et al. (1992) demonstrated the usefulness of NNMs for the estimation of Lyapunov exponents of chaotic systems. An extensive introduction to NNMs, especially aimed at the needs of econometricians, also can be found in Kuan and White (1991).

Although network learning is a relatively new concept, the methods implied by the concept rely on statistical methods that have been well established since the early fifties. It is stochastic approximation theory that is applied to a new class of nonlinear models. The usefulness of the NNMs for testing of nonlinearity is primarily due to the fact that the models are capable of approximating any arbitrary nonlinear function. NNMs have properties of flexible functional forms. Prior to the introduction of the test, it seems useful to offer a heuristic treatment of the type of NNM providing the main structural element for White's testing procedure.

One constituting element of neural networks are units potentially able to receive and to process information. In some models, one finds units that exhibit only subsets of such abilities. The connections between those units constitute the second important structural element of the class of network models under scrutiny. They represent channels suitable for the transmission of information between units. The quality of the connection is reflected by the concept of connection strength. If the information is distorted along the channel, then a low connection parameter reflects such circumstances. Imagine, for instance, that four units are only able to send information to other units. In network jargon, these units are referred to as neurons. The information issued by each unit l is denoted by $x_l, l = 0, 1, 2, \ldots, k$. Let x denote the column vector of messages sent by the neurons (or input units):

$$x = \begin{pmatrix} x_0 \\ x_1 \\ x_2 \\ \vdots \\ x_k \end{pmatrix}.$$

Those messages are perceived by units that can sense information, process it, and transmit the processed information to an output unit. In network lingua, the units are said to be arranged in a hidden layer. The jth unit, $j = 1, 2, \ldots, q$, in the layer receives the signal sent by neuron l as $\gamma_{jl} x_l$, where γ_{jl} denotes some real constant. Processing of information in hidden-layer unit j can be modeled as follows: In a first step the incoming information is summed up; the next step consists in the application of a nonlinear, measurable function $\psi : R \to R$ to the accumulated information. That is, unit j produces the output

$$\psi \left(\sum_{l=0}^{k} \gamma_{jl} x_l \right).$$

Let

$$\gamma_j = \begin{pmatrix} \gamma_{j0} \\ \gamma_{j1} \\ \gamma_{j2} \\ \ldots \\ \gamma_{jk} \end{pmatrix}$$

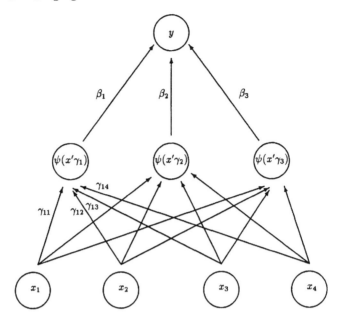

Figure 9.1. A single hidden-layer feedforward network.

denote the vector of connection strength associated with hidden-layer unit j; then the value of the activation function can be represented as $\psi(x'\gamma_j)$. After generating the new information $\psi(x'\gamma_j)$, the hidden-layer unit transmits this information to an output unit, a unit functioning exactly like a hidden-layer unit. It sums the filtered information, applies the identity map to it, and produces an output y. Figure 9.1 contains a sketch of the network just described. Because there exists only one hidden layer, and because information only flows in one direction, this network is referred to as a single-layer feedforward network (SLFFN).

Now, suppose that we augment this network by adding direct channels or connections from each neuron l to the output unit. Upon receipt of these filtered, though direct, signals from the neurons, this information is also summed up and then added to the sum of the filtered signals received from the hidden-layer units by the output unit. The single-hidden-layer feedforward network extended in such a fashion is referred to as an augmented single hidden-layer feedforward network (SHLFFN). A sketch of the structure is given in Figure 9.2.

In compact vector notation, we can represent the SHLFFN model as

$$y = x'\theta + [\psi(x'\gamma_1)\psi(x'\gamma_2)\dots\psi(x'\gamma_q)]\beta \qquad (9.1)$$

where $\theta_{(k+1,1)}$ and $\beta_{(q,1)}$ denote column vectors of connection strength. Next, suppose that we have obtained data, that is, realizations of some stochastic

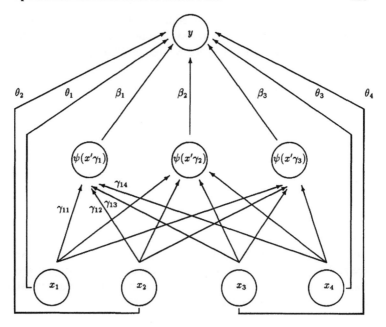

Figure 9.2. Augmented single hidden-layer feedforward network.

process $\{Y_t, X_t\}$ for the periods $t = 1, 2, 3 \ldots, n$. The matrix representation of equation (9.1), useful for the simultaneous representation of data and model, is provided by

$$
\begin{pmatrix} y_1 \\ y_2 \\ y_3 \\ \vdots \\ y_n \end{pmatrix} = \begin{pmatrix} 1 & x_{11} & \cdots & x_{1k} \\ 1 & x_{21} & \cdots & x_{2k} \\ 1 & x_{31} & \cdots & x_{3k} \\ \vdots & \vdots & \ddots & \vdots \\ 1 & x_{n1} & \cdots & x_{nk} \end{pmatrix} \theta
$$

$$
+ \begin{pmatrix} \phi(x_1'\gamma_1) & \phi(x_1'\gamma_2) & \cdots & \phi(x_1'\gamma_q) \\ \phi(x_2'\gamma_1) & \phi(x_2'\gamma_2) & \cdots & \phi(x_2'\gamma_q) \\ \phi(x_3'\gamma_1) & \phi(x_3'\gamma_2) & \cdots & \phi(x_3'\gamma_q) \\ \vdots & \vdots & \ddots & \vdots \\ \phi(x_n'\gamma_1) & \phi(x_n'\gamma_2) & \cdots & \phi(x_n'\gamma_q) \end{pmatrix} \beta, \tag{9.2}
$$

which may alternatively be expressed as

$$
Y_{(n,1)} = X_{(n,k+1)}\theta_{(k+1,1)} + \Psi_{(n,q)}\beta_{(q,1)}. \tag{9.3}
$$

In the case of $\beta = 0$, the model reduces to an affine-type network, a structure resembling a linear regression model. As outlined in Section 2.2, the residuals from this affine network play a crucial role in White's NNT for nonlinearity.

2.2   *Theoretical rationale for White's test*

Starting out from a probability model, we give a sketch of the main steps of the derivation of White's test for nonlinearity. The test statistic is derived and a relatively inexpensive way of computing the test is discussed. Throughout this treatment, special attention is given to the assumptions under which the test is derived. Violations of such assumptions might explain certain operational characteristics becoming evident in the simulation experiments.

Suppose there exists a probability space (Ω, Σ, P) where Ω denotes the n-dimensional Euclidean sample space, Σ represents a sigma algebra of Borel sets of R_∞^n, that is, Σ represents a Borel algebra generated by all measurable finite-dimensional product cylinders. Probabilities are assigned to sets in Σ by the probability function P. Next, let us define the key concept in the argument that follows. The definition of a martingale difference sequence (MDS) relies on the concept of an adapted stochastic sequence (ASS).

Definition 1: (ASS). Let b_t denote a sequence of random scalars, and Σ_t represent an increasing sequence of sigma algebras in Σ. If b_t is measurable with respect to Σ_t, then $\{b_t, \Sigma_t\}$ is called an adapted stochastic sequence (ASS).

Definition 2: (MDS). Let $\{b_t, \Sigma_t\}$ denote an ASS. Then $\{b_t, \Sigma_t\}$ is a martingale difference sequence (MDS) if and only if $E(b_t|\Sigma_{t-1}) = 0$.

Now suppose that we are interested in explaining or forecasting some observable variable at time t on the basis of previous realizations of the variable $(y_{t-1}, y_{t-2}, \ldots)$ as well as by considering the realizations of other variables at time t, $x_t = (z_{t1}, z_{t1}, \ldots, z_{tl})$. Under the assumption that observations on the lagged y variable and on the z variable exist, we let the sigma algebra Σ_{t-1} contain the information used to explain or forecast the y variable at time t:

$$\sum_{t-1} = \sigma \left[\cdots \begin{pmatrix} z_{t-1} \\ y_{t-2} \end{pmatrix}, \begin{pmatrix} z_t \\ y_{t-1} \end{pmatrix} \right]. \tag{9.4}$$

Proceeding in such a way, we can generate an increasing sequence of sets

$$\cdots \subset \sum_{t-3} \subset \sum_{t-2} \subset \sum_{t-1}. \tag{9.5}$$

In such a situation, there exists a regression function—linear or nonlinear—relating the value of y_t to z_t. The existence is guaranteed by the following theorem.

Theorem 9.1: *(Doob 1954, p. 603). Suppose the conditional expectation*

$$E\left[y_t | \cdots \begin{pmatrix} z_{t-1} \\ y_{t-2} \end{pmatrix}, \begin{pmatrix} z_t \\ y_{t-1} \end{pmatrix} \right] \tag{9.6}$$

is measurable with respect to $\sum_{t-1}$. Then there exists a function

$$f\left[\cdots \begin{pmatrix} z_{t-1} \\ y_{t-2} \end{pmatrix}, \begin{pmatrix} z_t \\ y_{t-1} \end{pmatrix} \right] \tag{9.7}$$

which is also measurable with respect to $\sum_{t-1}$ such that

$$E\left(y_t | \sum_{t-1} \right) = f\left[\cdots \begin{pmatrix} z_{t-1} \\ y_{t-2} \end{pmatrix}, \begin{pmatrix} z_t \\ y_{t-1} \end{pmatrix} \right]. \tag{9.8}$$

Aware of the existence of a regression function, econometricians usually specify the function $f(\cdot)$ based on evidence from economic theory. Typically, such specifications are linear.

For the motivation of White's test, it is crucial to demonstrate that pairs consisting of the residual at time t from a regression model given above and the information set available at time t form an MDS. To demonstrate this point, assume that $E(|y_t|) < \infty$, for all t, and observe that, by definition, y_t is measurable w.r.t. Σ_t. Therefore, $\{y_t, \Sigma_t\}$ is an ASS. Also, $E(y_t|\Sigma_{t-1})$ is measurable w.r.t. Σ_t, which implies that $\{y_t - E(y_t|\Sigma_{t-1}), \Sigma_t\} = \{\varepsilon_t|\Sigma_t\}$ is an ASS. In addition, the subsequent argument establishes that the expected value conditional on the information set Σ_{t-1} equals 0:

$$E\left(y_t | \sum_{t-1} \right) - E\left(y_t | \sum_{t-1} \right) = 0$$

$$E\left(y_t | \sum_{t-1} \right) - E\left[E\left(y_t | \sum_{t-1} \right) \Big| \sum_{t-1} \right] = 0$$

$$E\left[y_t - E\left(y_t | \sum_{t-1} \right) \Big| \sum_{t-1} \right] = 0$$

$$E\left(\varepsilon_t | \sum_{t-1} \right) = 0 \tag{9.9}$$

Because $\{\varepsilon_t, \Sigma_t\}$ is an ASS and $E(\varepsilon_t|\Sigma_{t-1}) = 0$, the sequence $\{\varepsilon_t, \Sigma_t\}$ is a martingale sequence.

The final step toward establishing the idea underlying White's test consists in assuming that there exists a function $h(\cdot)$ measurable w.r.t. the information set $\sum_{t-1}$. From $E(\varepsilon_t | \sum_{t-1}) = 0$, it follows that

$$h\left(\sum_{t-1}\right) E\left(\varepsilon_t \bigg| \sum_{t-1}\right) = 0. \tag{9.10}$$

By applying the substitution theorem, we obtain

$$h\left(\sum_{t-1}\right) E\left(\varepsilon_t \bigg| \sum_{t-1}\right) = E\left[\varepsilon_t h\left(\sum_{t-1}\right) \bigg| \sum_{t-1}\right] = 0. \tag{9.11}$$

Using the expectation operator on both sides of the equation implies that

$$E\left[\varepsilon_t h\left(\sum_{t-1}\right)\right] = 0. \tag{9.12}$$

Let us summarize the argument: Assuming the existence of a probability space (Ω, Σ, P), the existence of a regression function is guaranteed under general conditions. If one assumes that the process y_t is linear in the mean, then the residuals ε_t are not correlated with any measurable function of the information set available to explain or forecast the process in period t. We shall now assume that the function $f(\cdot)$ takes the following form:

$$f\left[\cdots \binom{z_{t-1}}{y_{t-2}}, \binom{z_t}{y_{t-1}}\right] = x_t \theta + \wp(x_t), \tag{9.13}$$

where $\wp(x_t)$ is a nonlinear function of the covariates z and the lagged values of y. Choosing such a specification is equivalent to stating that the process y_t is nonlinear in the mean. Under the assumptions made so far, we can restate equation (9.13) as

$$E\left[\{y_t - x_t\theta - \wp(x_t)\}h\left(\sum_{t-1}\right)\right] = 0, \tag{9.14}$$

which is equivalent to

$$E\left[\{y_t - x_t\theta\}h\left(\sum_{t-1}\right)\right] = E\left[\wp(x_t)h\left(\sum_{t-1}\right)\right]. \tag{9.15}$$

If we formulate the hypothesis "y_t is linear in the mean," then we assign the value 0 to $\wp(x_t)$ in equation (9.13), and equation (9.15) takes the form:

$$E\left[\{y_t - x_t\theta\}h\left(\sum_{t-1}\right)\right] = 0. \tag{9.16}$$

Consequently, under the hypothesis of linearity in the mean, there should be no correlation between the theoretical residuals from the linear part of the model and any measurable function of the history of the process y_t. On the other hand, if one finds that the expected value of $E[\{y_t - x_t\theta\}h(\sum_{t-1})]$ differs from zero, then this can only be so if the expectation $E[\wp(x_t)h(\sum_{t-1})]$ differs from 0, that is, if there exists structure over and above the linear part $X_t\theta$. Expression (9.15) also provides an insight into the reason why test procedures based on the idea outlined so far may indicate that there is no evidence against linearity in the mean although there is nonlinear structure. If the nature of the nonlinearity and the form of the test function $h(x_t)$ is such that the expectation $E[\wp(x_t)h(\sum_{t-1})]$ just compensates $E[\{y_t - x_t\theta\}h(\sum_{t-1})]$, then the associated test will have low power against the alternative hypothesis.

Carrying out White's test for neglected nonlinearity, one basically correlates the residuals from the affine network (i.e., the first summand in equation (9.1) with the output of the hidden-layer phantom units). White specifies the test function $h(x_t)$ as

$$h(x_t) = \phi(x_t'\gamma_j) = (1 + e^{-x_t'\gamma_j})^{-1}. \tag{9.17}$$

The vector of connection strength associated with the signals arriving at each of the q hidden-layer phantom units is chosen at random and independently of the process $\{y_t, x_t\}$. At first sight, the random choice of connection strength may seem awkward. But this strategy is indeed well motivated. One should note that under the null hypothesis, the elements of γ are not identified. In fact, identification holds only under the alternative of nonlinearity. As pointed out by White (1989b), a hypothesis with respect to the irrelevance of phantom hidden-layers is equivalent to the problem of testing when nuisance parameters are identified only under the null hypothesis. This problem has, for instance, been treated by Davies (1977, 1978), and in connection with test of functional form by Bierens (1990). Typically, solutions to this problem are computationally prohibitive or involve subjective judgments on behalf of the analyst. The solution to the problem chosen by White amounts to letting chance determine the type of nonlinearity against which the test has power. Considering the nature of available alternative solutions, White's procedure seems appropriate.

In principle, one could estimate the parameters of the network specified in 9.1 and then test the hypothesis $H_0 : \beta = 0$. Although the estimation technology is available, such effort can be avoided in the present situation. White proposes estimating the population mean $E[\phi(x_t'\gamma_j)\varepsilon_t]$ by the average over the rows of Ψ multiplied by the observable residuals $\hat{e} = Y - X\hat{\theta}$, where $\hat{\theta}$ denotes the least-squares estimate of θ in the affine part of the network. Of course, an estimate of θ under the alternative is not available. The resulting test statistic, as well as its null distribution, is given in the theorem below.

Theorem 9.2: *(White 1991). Let $\hat{e} = Y - X\hat{\theta}$ with $\hat{\theta} = (X'X)^{-1}X'Y$ and let $\mathbf{1}$ denote an $n \times 1$ vector of ones. Then, White's test statistic is given by*

$$\text{WNN}_{(1,q)} = \frac{1}{n}\mathbf{1}' \text{diag}\,(\hat{e})\Psi, \qquad (9.18)$$

and if the hypothesis of linearity in the mean holds, then as $n \to \infty$,

$$\sqrt{n}\text{WNN} \overset{d}{\sim} \text{MVN}[0_{(1,q)}, W_{(q,q)}]. \qquad (9.19)$$

Under the null hypothesis, $\sqrt{n}\text{WNN}$ converges in distribution to a multivariate normal distribution with mean vector $0_{(1,q)}$ and covariance matrix $W_{(q,q)}$. Given a consistent estimate of W, one can construct a Wald-type test statistic, $\tilde{W}_n$:

$$\tilde{W}_n = \frac{1}{n}[\mathbf{1}' \text{diag}\,(\hat{e})\Psi]\hat{W}_n^{-1}[\mathbf{1}' \text{diag}\,(\hat{e})\Psi]' \qquad (9.20)$$

which is asymptotically chi-square distributed, $\hat{W}_n \chi^2(q)$, under the null hypothesis. The decision rule for White's test consequently reads:

if $\tilde{W}_n > \chi^2_{(1-\alpha)}(q)$,

then reject H_0 of linearity in the mean,

else fail to reject H_0

Conceptually, the computation of $\tilde{W}_n$ is no problem. But White has shown (see, e.g., White 1992), that a numerically cheaper test procedure, under certain conditions, is asymptotically equivalent to the procedure outlined above. For the equivalence to hold, it is sufficient that any of the two assumptions listed below be fulfilled:

Assumption 9.1: *$\{y_t, x_t\}$ is an independent process and $E[\varepsilon_t^2 | x_t] = $ constant.*

Assumption 9.2: *Let $\{y_t, x_t\}$ be a dependent process for which*

$$E[\varepsilon_t^2 | x_t] = \text{ constant.}$$

$$E[y_t | x_t, (y_t, x_t)^{-1}] = E[y_t | x_t].$$

If these assumptions do not hold, then the test statistic of the alternative procedure given below converges to a mixture of chi-square distributions (White 1989). In the remaining sections of this paper, we describe some simulation experiments that reflect the properties of White's alternative testing procedure. The procedure relies on two well-known statistical concepts: on OLS estimation of linear models and principal component analysis. The APL program used to carry out the test for nonlinearity is based on the algorithm NNTEST.

Algorithm: NNTEST

Comments:	given: data $Y, X \in [0,1]$
	given: functions PCA(l, M), $u(a, b)$
	$\diamond$ the function PCA computes component scores based on the l largest principal components of the Matrix M.
	$\diamond$ the function $u(a, b)$ generates uniformly distributed pseudorandom numbers
Initialization:	$n \leftarrow$ number of observations
	$q \leftarrow$ number of phantom units
	$\phi \leftarrow$ test function
	$q^* \leftarrow$ number of principal components
Step 1	GENERATE RESIDUALS FROM AFFINE NETWORK
	$Y = X\theta + e$(model)
	$\hat{\theta} \leftarrow (X'X)^{-1}X'Y$
	$\hat{e} \leftarrow Y - X\hat{\theta}$
Step 2	GENERATION OF Φ
	For $j = 1$ to q do

$$\gamma_j = \begin{pmatrix} \gamma_{j0} \\ \gamma_{j1} \\ \gamma_{j2} \\ \cdots \\ \gamma_{jk} \end{pmatrix} \leftarrow u(-2, 2)$$

	$\Gamma \leftarrow (\gamma_1 \gamma_2 \gamma_3 \cdots \gamma_q)$
	$\Phi \leftarrow \phi \circ X\Gamma$ ($\circ \equiv$ apply to each element of)
Step 3	EXTRACTION OF PRINCIPAL COMPONENTS
	$\Psi^* \leftarrow$ PCA (q^*, Φ)
Step 4	REGRESS RESIDUALS ON $[\Psi^*, X]$
	$\hat{e} = [\Psi^*, X]\delta + z$ (model)
	$\hat{\delta} \leftarrow ([\Psi^*, X]'[\Psi^*, X])^{-1}[\Psi^*, X]'\hat{e}$
	$\tilde{e} \leftarrow [\Psi^*, X]\hat{\delta}$
	$R^2 \leftarrow \frac{(\hat{e}'\tilde{e})^2}{\hat{e}'\hat{e}(\tilde{e}'\tilde{e})}$
	$\tilde{W}_n \leftarrow nR^2$
Step 5	DECISION
	if $\tilde{W}_n > \chi^2_{(1-\alpha)}(q^*)$,
	then reject H_0 of linearity in the mean,
	else fails to reject H_0.

This algorithm gives the basic version of the test in which the dimension of the affine part of the network is assumed to be known. In the simulation experiments, we also utilize a version of this test in which, prior to step 1, an autoregression-order selection procedure determines the order of the affine network. The order is estimated by the three-order selection criteria: Akaike's final prediction error criterion (FPE), Akaike's information criterion, and SBIC. The simulation experiments designed to validate the code and to further our knowledge of forms of nonlinearities that can be successfully detected by White's procedure are the subjects of the subsequent sections.

3   Design of the simulation study

It is the primary goal of our present effort to generate additional knowledge about the operational characteristics of White's NNT for nonlinearity. Apart from considering the performance of the test if a linear mechanism is generating the data, we focus on the test's ability to detect economically motivated nonlinearities. To realize the latter goal, we generate artificial time series from economic models. That is, we use theoretical insights into the economic processes to build evidence for or against the usefulness of the NNT in an economic context. This approach is, of course, only valid if one is willed to make the assumption that existing economic theories are indeed able to explain and mimic salient features of the economic process. Although earlier evaluations of White's test (see, e.g., Lee et al. 1993), followed the typical strategy of using nonlinear models and maps that have been studied in statistics and nonlinear mathematics, our simulation experiments are designed such that they are informative for a specific group of researchers, namely economists or econometricians.

The four models reflecting the true state of nature are:

(1)   An autoregressive process of order 1 [AR(1)]
(2)   A stochastic Hicks-type model of the business cycle
(3)   Day and Huang's model of the stock market
(4)   A model of interdependent consumer behavior.

We generate time series of varying length ($T = 50, 100, 150, \ldots, 300$) from each model. For each choice of parameters in the models given above, 500 realizations of the associated process are generated, that is, there are 500 replications at each design point. For the assessment of the size of the test, the coefficient of the AR(1) model is varied over the interval $[-1,1]$, whereas we choose only one set of parameters for each of the nonlinear processes listed above. Because we consider three alternative order-selection criteria (i.e., three versions of the test), the investigation of the size of the test is based on a $6 \times 10 \times 3$ complete factorial, allowing for the evaluation of effects on the performance of White's test attributable to changes of sample size T, to changes of models across a subspace of the space of linear autoregressive processes of order one, as well as to changes in the strategy of filter selection. In the group of experiments focusing on the test's ability to detect economically motivated nonlinearities, the current design only allows for the assessment of sample-size effects and order-selection effects. Assuming that autoregressive processes are common knowledge, we do not discuss them. Because the same assumption most likely does not hold for the nonlinear models employed in the study, we discuss the background for and the merits of each model and give a characterization of the sample processes generated on the basis of each stochastic or deterministic model.

3.1   *Economic time-series generators*

At the present state of the study, we consider various nonlinear economic models from different spheres of economic theory. First of all, we discuss a stochastic business cycle model based on one of the early formal nonlinear explanations of the trade cycle due to Sir J. Hicks. The original model is modified by connecting it to some non-economic environment. The second model represents a recent contribution to the theory of financial markets. Deeply rooted in the nonlinear paradigm, it reflects certain views of the behavior of agents in financial markets which are attributed to Keynes. The third model is a simple model of interacting consumers. It is the main feature of this model that consumers' preferences change endogenously over time. The dynamics of the consumption of two goods by two types of agents can be described by a nonlinear map in two dimensions. While the latter two models are deterministic maps, the series generated by them can be interpreted as random processes since in each case we will model uncertainty with respect to the initial condition. As the discussion below will demonstrate, the dynamics of these models representing various areas of economics do, infact differ tremendously.

3.2   *A stochastic nonlinear multiplier–accelerator model*

The early business-cycle models by Samuelson (1939) and Metzler (1941) were succeeded by the nonlinear trade-cycle model of Hicks. Hicks (1950) presents a model that is nonlinear in the sense that the induced investment function is not valid over the entire cycle. In the remaining paragraphs of this section, we give a sketch of a simplified Hicks-type model with stochastic components. The specification of the stochastic difference equation used to generate the test data is discussed and the main characteristics of the generated time series are described.

   As point of departure, consider the following simple dynamic system typical for early macroeconomic dynamics, combining the Keynesian multiplier and the accelerator. Let Y_t, C_t, and I_t refer to national income (output), consumption, and investment in fixed capital in period t. Then, a system, that, under certain conditions, produces oscillations is given by

$$C_t = C_0 + mY_{t-1}$$

$$I_t = I_0 + v(Y_{t-1} - Y_{t-2})$$

$$Y_t = I_t + C_t \tag{9.21}$$

with $C_0 \geq 0$, $m \in (0, 1)$, $I_0 \in R$, and $v \geq 0$. These equations imply that desired and actual investment are identical. Firms can always install or get rid of capital as the economy moves through upswings and downswings. Also, factors of production can be mobilized *ad infinitum*. With respect to the dynamics, the steady state is stable for $v \leq 1$. Realistic estimates of the marginal increase in capital necessary to achieve a marginal increase in national income do indeed exceed 1. In terms of the model given above, this would imply unstable oscillatory dynamics. Motivated by such drawbacks of the linear multiplier–accelerator model, Hicks augmented the basic model by enforcing a lower bound on disinvestment in the downswing and an upper bound on the development of the national income in the boom phase. The lower bound, I_f, referred to as investment floor, enforces positive gross investment, given that depreciation is constant and exogenous. In terms of net investment, it is required that the sum of autonomous investment and induced investment has to be larger than or equal to the replacement of the depreciated portion of the capital stock. Consequently, at a certain instance in the downswing, the accelerator is defunct.

The upper bound, Y_c, on output reflects the limited availability of factors of production. During a boom, the economy may experience a state in which it realizes its maximal growth path under given resource restrictions. The two bounds guarantee that the model realizes economically meaningful trajectories even if the accelerator values exceed 1. The system of equations implied by the foregoing reads

$$C_t = C_0 + mY_{t-1}$$

$$I_t = \max [I_f, I_0 + v(Y_{t-1} - Y_{t-2})]$$

$$Y_t = \min (Y_c, I_t + C_t), \tag{9.22}$$

which leads to the following difference equation:

$$Y_t = \min \{Y_c, C_0 + mY_{t-1} + \max [I_f, I_0 + v(Y_{t-1} - Y_{t-2})]\} \tag{9.23}$$

In a detailed discussion of this deterministic model, Blatt (1983, pp. 189–98) demonstrates that this model is able to produce cycles. One also should mention the recent treatment of the model by Hommes (1991) in which it is proven that versions of the Hicks model generate various forms of chaos.

In our effort, we consider that the economic system (9.23) is embedded in a non-economic environment. A multitude of random processes and events occurring in that environment influences the economic system in the sense that the agents' fundamentals are affected. It is assumed that the signals from the non-economic sphere do not have an impact on those spheres of the household's decision mechanism responsible for generating consumption decisions depending on last period's income. Also, in firms, those levels of the hierarchy responsible for capital adjustment necessitated by recent development of demand for goods are thought to be largely unaffected by signals from the non-economic sphere. It seems more likely that interpretations of such signals on the board level might lead to deliberate policy decisions triggering variations in the firms' long-run (or autonomous) investment activity. Our assumptions concerning the impact of non-economic information on the microlevel implies that stochastic terms are added to the intercepts of the consumption and net investment equation in the laws of the economic macromotion.

Moreover, it is assumed that even in the short run, events in the non-economic sphere may have an impact on the conditions restricting the economy in the upswing. The investment floor is not modeled as a stochastic entity. That is, we restrict ourselves to a situation in which the dominant reason for depreciation is of a purely technical nature. Although one has to acknowledge the fact that there exist many economies in which, because of frequently occurring events, the causes of which are not directly related to the economic activity (e.g., natural catastrophies such as flood or hurricanes), the actual depreciation rate apparently fluctuates in a random fashion.

The assumptions made above allow us to study the performance of White's test for nonlinearity when faced with national income data generated by an idealized economy. The data-generating economy is prone to noise from the non-economic sphere. At least during certain phases of the trade cycle, such classic concepts as the multiplier or the accelerator drive the dynamics of national income.

For the present series of simulation experiments, the parameters of the model were specified as follows:

$$C_0 = 20 + u(-5, 5)$$
$$m = 0.8$$
$$I_f = -5$$
$$I_0 = 0 + u(-10, 1)$$
$$v = 1$$
$$Y_c = 110(1 + u[-0.1, 0.1]), \tag{9.24}$$

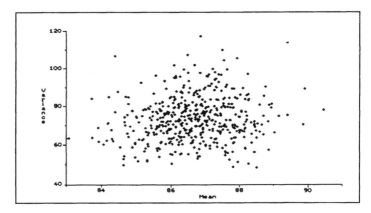

Figure 9.3. Estimated mean and variance for the stochastic Hicks process.

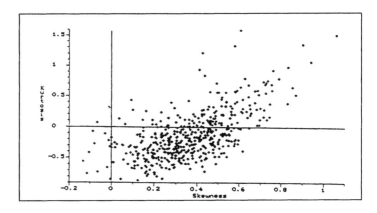

Figure 9.4. Estimated skewness and kurtosis for the stochastic Hicks process.

where $u(a, b)$ denotes the realization of a uniform random variable.

This specification reflects an economy in which the decision mechanism leading to the autonomous investment activities is volatile to noise from the non-economic sphere. In fact, the accelerator can even be disfunct in the time period right before the peak of the upswing. There is only little variation in the resource constraints and in long-term consumption decisions.

As indicated above, we generated 500 replications of the process for sample sizes varying from $T = 50$ to $T = 300$. To characterize the sample of processes, we plotted the estimated moments for the 500 series for the case $T = 250$. Estimated mean and variance as well as the estimated skewness and kurtosis are shown in Figures 9.3 and 9.4, respectively.

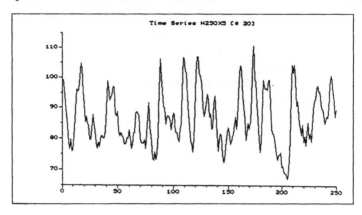

Figure 9.5. Typical stochastic Hicks process.

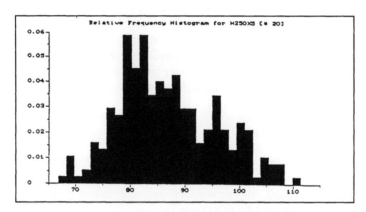

Figure 9.6. Marginal distribution of a typical stochastic Hicks process.

   The second plot reveals that most of the realizations have left-steep marginal distributions, which are bulkier than the normal distribution. A Hicks process with such typical characteristics is displayed below, along with a classic density estimate of its marginal distribution (cf. Figures 9.5 and 9.6).

3.3   *Deterministic excess-demand model of stock-market behavior*

Recently, Huang and Day (1993) proposed a model of stock-market behavior that implies a deterministic map as the law of motion for stock prices. The model is able to mimic salient features of asset price movements as, for instance, so called bearish and bullish markets. The authors also established that a piecewise linear version of their model is able to generate observable chaotic motion.

Considering the novelty of the approach, we provide a conscript of the main ideas underlying the model prior to discussing the map that represents the data generator in our experiments.

According to the Day and Huang approach, the three behavioral elements representing the main factors generating the characteristics of stock markets are: thoughtful evaluation, speculative consideration, and animal spirits. The roots of the latter factor are found in the work of Keynes. Subsets of the behavioral elements are associated with certain types of economic agents participating in the market. Although investors and specialists are characterized by the ability of thoughtful investigation and the presence of speculative considerations, the animal spirits are the features defining the market sheep.

Investors typically are able to contain estimates of the current value, v, of shares based on current information about firms. Also, they have the ability to generate estimates of the value that shares will have if anticipated long-term conditions materialize. In the sequel, u denotes this share value based on long-term expectations. Assuming a nonnegative, convex, differentiable chance function, $f(p)$, reflecting that the chance of missing a capital gain is low if the price p is close to the low end of the market, m, and reflecting that high chances of losing a capital gain are great if the market is near the high end, M, the authors arrive at an excess demand function of the Keynesian type:

$$a\alpha(p) = \begin{cases} a(u-p)f(p) & p \in [m, M] \\ 0 & \text{o.w.} \end{cases} \tag{9.25}$$

when $a \in R$ is interpreted as an adjustment coefficient. Assuming that the chance functions of investors with varying estimates of the long-run value of shares are identical, one can represent aggregate excess demand as a multiple of the excess demand for an average investor.

The term market sheep refers to small investors who believe that market prices convey relevant information about the future. Such individuals enter the market when prices are high, expecting further features. In the case of falling prices, they leave the market expecting a further decline in prices. In that sense, they follow the market like sheep. The excess-demand function of the market sheep is modeled as a monotonic, increasing function of the share price $\beta(p)$.

The third group of agents on the market consists of specialists. Reacting to aggregate excess demand, they make the market in the sense that they supply excess demand from their inventories of stocks and they accumulate inventories when there is excess supply. The key assumption concerning specialists' price-setting behavior is given below:

Assumption 9.3: *Let E(p) denote aggregate excess demand at price p and $\gamma(\cdot)$ is a continuous, monotonically increasing function with $\gamma(0) = 0$. Then,* *specialists' price-setting behavior is reflected in the following law of motion:*

$$p_{t+1} - p_t = c\gamma[E(p)]. \tag{9.26}$$

In the analysis of the model, Day and Huang show that a full market equilibrium represents a singularity. Typically, the equilibrium is temporary. Indeed, the equilibrium could only be sustained under the condition that the sheep would have a portfolio of infinite size. It is also demonstrated that switching between bearish and bullish markets occurs. In addition, there exist chaotic regimes as well as cycles of all orders. For the case of a piecewise linear version of equation (9.26), it can be shown that chaos is thick and strong, that is, it will be observable.

We choose the piecewise linear equation for the price dynamics as a generator of economic time series:

$$p_{t+1} = p_t + \theta(p_t) \tag{9.27}$$

where $\theta(\cdot)$ is defined as

$$\theta(p_t) = \begin{cases} -cbv + (1+cb)p_t & 0 \le p_t < m; \\ c(\pi n - bv) + [1 + c(b - \pi)]p_t & m \le p_t < n; \\ -cbv + (1+cb)p_t & n \le p_t < N; \\ c(\rho N - bv) + [1 + c(b - \rho)]p_t & N \le p_t < M; \\ -cbv + (1+cb)p_t & M \le p_t. \end{cases} \tag{9.28}$$

For our simulations, we choose a specification that is able to generate the data pattern resembling bearish and bullish markets:

$$m = 0, n = 0.05, N = 0.9, M = 1,$$

$$b = 0.15, c = 1, v = 0.5, \rho = 9.03, \pi = 9.15 \tag{9.29}$$

This piecewise linear map has two equilibrium points. For the given constellation of parameter values, both of them are unstable. Consequently, a trajectory tends to oscillate around one of the two equilibrium points for a while before it moves over to the other equilibrium point. Eventually, the trajectory will leave the vicinity of that fixed point again to return to the first one. The process will continue *ad infinitum*. Day and Huang study the probabilistic characteristics of this deterministic process. They conclude that if one assumes a uniform distribution for the initial value of the trajectory, then one can interpret the trajectories generated by the map (9.28) as realizations of a random variable with a given distribution function.

As in the case of the stochastic Hicks model, we characterize the realizations generated by this deterministic difference equation by the mean versus variance and skewness versus kurtosis plots associated with the case $T = 250$

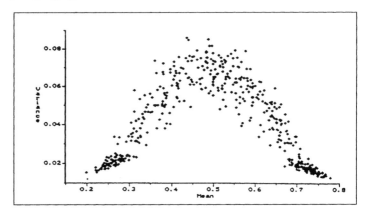

Figure 9.7. Estimated mean and variance for the Day–Huang model.

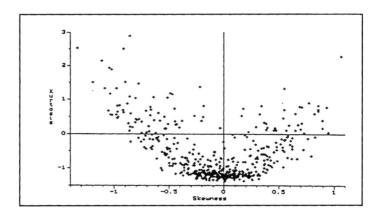

Figure 9.8. Estimated skewness and kurtosis for the Day–Huang model.

(see Figures 9.7 and 9.8, respectively). The mean-variance plot reveals that a substantial number of sample series reflect price movements around the low end and the high end of the market. Such series are associated by means around 0.25 and 0.75 as well as by small variance of about 0.02.

The skewness-and-excess-kurtosis plot indicates that the typical marginal distribution of the sample processes is almost symmetrical and bulkier than the normal distribution. Below, we give an example for the price dynamics generated by the stock-market model. We observe a transition from a bearish to a bullish market after time $t = 120$ (cf. Figures 9.9 and 9.10).

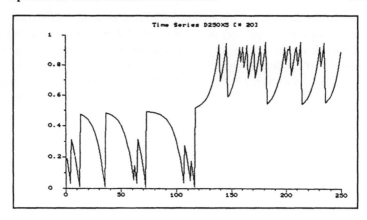

Figure 9.9. Typical trajectory from the Day–Huang model.

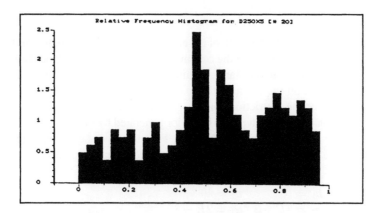

Figure 9.10. Marginal distribution of a typical trajectory.

3.4 *Model of interdependent consumer behavior*

So far, we have considered as data generators a model from macroeconomics as well as a model of a financial market. Our third model is taken from the sphere of dynamic microeconomics. Gaertner and Jungeilges (1988, 1993) discuss a model of interdependent consumer behavior. In this paper, it is postulated that an individual's demand pattern not only depends on her or his own past consumption but also on the past consumption of another individual. Using standard maximization techniques involving utility functions of the Cobb–Douglas type as well as a linear specification linking a consumer's elasticity of preference to his own past consumption as well as to his neighbor's past consumption, the authors derive a two-dimensional nonlinear system of difference equations describing the demand for consumer good x by two agents. The consumption of the other commodity, say y, can be computed using agent i's budget constraint. Let $x_{i,t}$ denote agent i's demand for good x at time t. In every period, individual i spends the budget b_i on the consumption of goods x and y. The prices of these goods, p_x and p_y, are assumed to be constant over time. Then, the consumption process of two individuals maximizing utility instantaneously is described by the following system:

$$\begin{pmatrix} x_{1,t+1} \\ x_{2,t+2} \end{pmatrix} = C_0 \begin{pmatrix} x_{1,t} \\ x_{2,t} \end{pmatrix} + C_1 \begin{pmatrix} x_{1,t}^2 \\ x_{2,t}^2 \end{pmatrix} \qquad (9.30)$$

where the coefficient matrices assume the form

$$C_0 = \frac{1}{p_x p_y} \begin{pmatrix} \alpha_1 b_1^2 & D_{12} b_1 b_2 \\ D_{21} b_1 b_2 & \alpha_2 b_2^2 \end{pmatrix} \qquad (9.31)$$

$$C_1 = \frac{1}{p_y} \begin{pmatrix} \alpha_1 b_1 & D_{12} b_1 \\ D_{21} b_2 & \alpha_2 b_2 \end{pmatrix}, \qquad (9.32)$$

where α_i reflects the strength of the effect of person i's experience and learning from past consumption on the consumption in the current period, and $D_{1,2}$ and $D_{2,1}$ are amalgamated distance parameters reflecting the influence of agent 1's consumption on the consumption pattern of consumer 2 and vice versa. The rationale for the restrictions on the parameters $\alpha_1, D_{12}, \alpha_2, D_{21}$, as well as a discussion of the rich dynamic behavior generated by system (9.30) is given by Gaertner and Jungeilges (1988, 1992). For the purpose of generating test data, we chose the following specification of the nonlinear map (9.30):

$$\begin{aligned} P_x &= 0.25 & p_y &= 1 \\ b_1 &= 10 & b_2 &= 20 \\ \alpha_1 &= 7E-3 & \alpha_2 &= 2E-3 \\ D_{12} &= 5E-4 & D_{21} &= 1.5E-3. \end{aligned} \qquad (9.33)$$

In the simulation experiments, we utilize time series of various lengths from the attractor depicted in Figure 9.11. The initial values are chosen from a neighborhood of $(x_0, y_0) = (25, 25)$. This neighborhood is designed such that the trajectories end up on the given attractor. After iterating the system 10,000 times, the last $T (T = 50, \ldots, 300)$ elements of the trajectory reflecting the consumption of commodity x by individual 1 is added to the database.

Following an approach discussed by Eckmann and Ruelle (1985), we computed the Lyapunov exponents for the map (9.33). The largest exponent was found to be positive (≈ 0.37), whereas the second exponent was negative (≈ -0.2). According to the Lyapunov exponent criterion, the series employed in the simulation experiments lie on an attractor that has sensitive dependence on initial conditions and are, in this sense, chaotic.

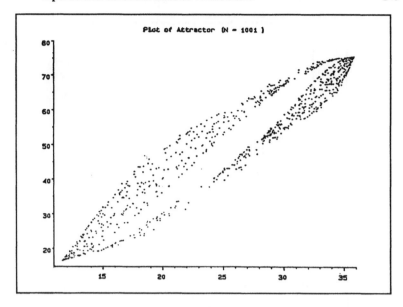

Figure 9.11. Attractor generated by map (9.30).

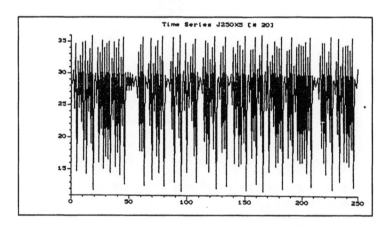

Figure 9.12. Typical trajectory from the consumption attractor.

Again, we characterize the sample of processes by plots of the moments of their associated marginal distributions for the sample size $T = 250$. The plots displayed in Figures 9.14 and 9.15 hint at a unique relationship between the moments. The estimates of mean and variance as well as those of skewness and kurtosis suggest a linear relationship between the moments. In contrast

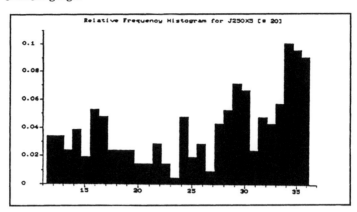

Figure 9.13. Marginal distribution of a typical consumer series.

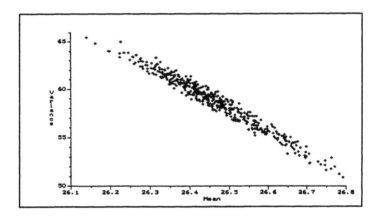

Figure 9.14. Estimated mean and variance for consumption processes.

to the map generated by Day and Huang, we cannot claim that a limiting distribution exists for map (9.33). If an invariant measure exists, then the plots characterizing the sample marginal distributions reveal that the moments of this underlying measure are linearly related. Both skewness and excess kurtosis are negative over the entire sample. Processes characterized by extreme (moderate) negative skewness of the marginal distribution exhibit moderate (extreme) excess kurtosis in the marginal distribution.

The three models discussed so far were utilized for the generation of a data basis. According to the experimental plan scrutinized above, the time series were subjected to White's NNT. A summary of the results from this experiment is given in the Section 4.

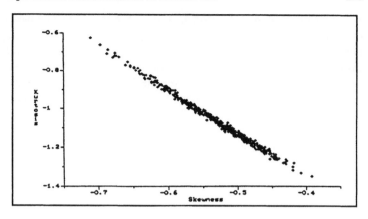

Figure 9.15. Estimated skewness and kurtosis for consumption processes.

4 Results

In this section, we discuss the simulation results obtained for each model.

4.1 Results concerning the size of the test

The first operational characteristic of White's test to be scrutinized reflects the test's ability to detect linearity in the mean if the true data-generating process is indeed linear. We present estimates of properties of the null distribution of White's test statistic based on 500 replications. Estimated 95 percent quantiles, rejection probabilities, and density estimates for the null distribution are related to their theoretical counterparts. In addition, we address the question concerning a possible effect of order estimation on the size of the test in the case in which the true data-generating process is a low-order autoregressive process.

Whereas earlier investigations concerned with the performance of White's test (see e.g., Lee et al. 1993), report simulation results for various values of the autoregressive parameter, we obtain results for different stable autoregressive specifications as well as for the unit root cases. In contrast to Lee et al. (1993), the current effort includes the application of a nonparametric test of fit providing evidence for the appropriateness of the theoretical null distribution. Another augmentation of the earlier evidence consists in the explicit treatment of the problems related to the fact that in application of the test, the true order of the underlying process cannot be known with certainty.

The analysis of the experiment considering the first block of problems was carried out according to the following scheme. At each point of the $6 \times 10 \times 3$ design, 500 realizations of White's test statistic were generated, that is, the test was carried out one time for each of 500 AR(1) time series. The resulting pseudorandom sample was stored. For each sample, we obtained estimates of the density function (conventional histogram together with the graph of the density of the null distribution, a box plot, and a stem-and-leaf plot) and the distribution function [Galton's Ogive with the graph of a chi-square (2 degrees of freedom) superimposed]. Moreover, the 95 percent confidence intervals for the 0.95 quantile and for the probability to reject the true null hypothesis are computed given that one uses the theoretical critical value 5.99.

Finally, a Kolmogorov–Smirnov test of fit is applied. We test the hypothesis that the realizations in the sample follow the theoretical null distribution $[\chi^2(2)]$.

Results concerning the aspect of unknown order of the true underlying data-generating process were obtained via a comparison of the estimated densities and distribution functions of the random samples associated with each selection criterion and the baseline case of known order.

The simulation results are reflected in Tables 9.1–9.6 and Figures 9.16–9.18. The evidence shown in Figure 9.16 is based on the content of columns 2, 3, and 4 of each of Tables 9.1–9.6. For the cases of the stable autoregressive data generators, the 95 percent confidence intervals for the 0.95 quantile of the distribution of White's statistic under the null hypothesis of linearity in the mean covers the theoretical value of 5.99. This statement holds for all sample sizes considered. The estimated 0.95 quantiles are fairly stable across the parameter space $(-1, 1)$, considering the fact that the estimates are based on only 500 replications. The same qualitative feature is displayed by the plots of the confidence intervals for the size of the test for stable autoregressions. With one exception ($\theta = 0.8$ and $T = 300$), the confidence intervals cover the theoretical value of 0.05. Focusing on the point estimates of the 0.95 quantile and the probability of rejecting the null hypothesis, although it is true, we see that for a sample size of 50, the estimates tend to be larger than their theoretical analogue. For the sample sizes of 100, 150, and 200, the estimates tend to be smaller than their theoretical counterparts, whereas the simulated quantiles and simulated rejection probabilities exceed the theoretical values almost as often as they do not exceed them for time series of length 250 and 300.

As explicated in Figures 9.18, it is hard to quantify an effect attributable to additional information. For all sample sizes, the absolute deviation of the estimated sizes from the theoretical value lies within a narrow band around $0(\pm 0.02)$ given $\theta \in (-1, 1)$.

If one uses 5.99 as a critical value and the true process has a negative unit root, then the probability for the rejection of H_0 is significantly higher than the nominal level of 0.05. The same might also happen in the cases in which the true generating process has a positive root (cf. $\theta = 1, T = 200$). Such reactions of the real size of the test to violations of a basic assumption – that of stability of the underlying process – reveals a lack of robustness of the test. The consequence of such an observation for the user of the test is immediate.

Table 9.1. *Distributional properties of $\widetilde{W}_n$ under $H_0(N = 50)$*

θ	95% Sample quantile			P (rejection)		
−1.0	(6.941)	7.585	(8.878)	(0.082)	0.110	(0.138)
−0.8	(5.659)	6.374	(7.294)	(0.042)	0.064	(0.086)
−0.6	(5.489)	6.224	(7.230)	(0.035)	0.056	(0.077)
−0.4	(5.903)	6.362	(7.223)	(0.049)	0.072	(0.095)
−0.2	(5.922)	6.012	(7.215)	(0.043)	0.062	(0.079)
0.2	(5.500)	6.131	(7.227)	(0.035)	0.056	(0.077)
0.4	(4.651)	5.258	(6.282)	(0.019)	0.036	(0.053)
0.6	(5.292)	6.013	(6.834)	(0.035)	0.056	(0.077)
0.8	(5.608)	6.198	(7.286)	(0.039)	0.060	(0.081)
0.1	(5.254)	5.729	(6.895)	(0.027)	0.046	(0.065)

Table 9.2. *Distributional properties of $\widetilde{W}_n$ under $H_0(N = 100)$*

θ	95% Sample quantile			P (rejection)		
−1.0	(7.093)	7.885	(9.021)	(0.087)	0.116	(0.145)
−0.8	(5.320)	5.957	(6.445)	(0.035)	0.056	(0.077)
−0.6	(5.730)	6.249	(7.334)	(0.039)	0.060	(0.081)
−0.4	(4.826)	5.453	(6.813)	(0.027)	0.046	(0.065)
−0.2	(6.223)	5.165	(6.878)	(0.034)	0.054	(0.074)
0.2	(5.516)	6.037	(6.744)	(0.034)	0.054	(0.074)
0.4	(5.487)	6.121	(6.754)	(0.037)	0.058	(0.079)
0.6	(5.652)	6.094	(7.483)	(0.037)	0.058	(0.079)
0.8	(4.886)	5.488	(6.314)	(0.022)	0.040	(0.058)
1.0	(5.057)	6.204	(7.823)	(0.037)	0.058	(0.079)

Table 9.3. *Distributional properties of $\widetilde{W}_n$ under $H_0(N = 150)$*

θ	95% Sample quantile			P (rejection)		
−1.0	(6.633)	7.220	(8.984)	(0.066)	0.092	(0.118)
−0.8	(4.953)	5.523	(7.078)	(0.021)	0.038	(0.055)
−0.6	(5.210)	5.731	(7.115)	(0.027)	0.046	(0.065)
−0.4	(5.604)	6.220	(7.157)	(0.040)	0.062	(0.084)
−0.2	(5.442)	6.347	(7.986)	(0.037)	0.058	(0.079)
0.2	(5.191)	5.607	(6.417)	(0.024)	0.042	(0.060)
0.4	(5.474)	5.852	(6.924)	(0.029)	0.048	(0.067)
0.6	(5.268)	6.078	(7.491)	(0.037)	0.058	(0.079)
0.8	(4.913)	5.281	(0.018)	(0.018)	0.034	(0.050)
1.0	(5.365)	5.764	(0.260)	(0.026)	0.044	(0.062)

Table 9.4. *Distributional properties of* $\widetilde{W}_n$ *under* $H_0(N = 200)$

θ	95% Sample quantile			P (rejection)		
−1.0	(7.587)	8.342	(9.802)	(0.118)	0.150	(0.182)
−0.8	(5.112)	5.790	(6.596)	(0.026)	0.044	(0.062)
−0.6	(4.914)	5.382	(6.015)	(0.019)	0.036	(0.053)
−0.4	(5.019)	5.449	(6.395)	(0.027)	0.046	(0.065)
−0.2	(5.554)	6.313	(7.476)	(0.040)	0.062	(0.084)
0.2	(5.324)	5.997	(7.031)	(0.034)	0.054	(0.074)
0.4	(5.060)	5.726	(6.679)	(0.031)	0.050	(0.069)
0.6	(5.278)	5.506	(6.259)	(0.018)	0.034	(0.050)
0.8	(5.053)	5.565	(6.871)	(0.026)	0.044	(0.062)
1.0	(8.135)	8.637	(8.135)	(0.118)	0.150	(0.182)

Table 9.5. *Distributional properties of* $\widetilde{W}_n$ *under* $H_0(N = 250)$

θ	95% Sample quantile			P (rejection)		
−1.0	(7.857)	8.654	(9.504)	(0.120)	0.152	(0.148)
−0.8	(5.627)	6.520	(7.649)	(0.037)	0.058	(0.079)
−0.6	(5.399)	6.013	(6.971)	(0.034)	0.054	(0.074)
−0.4	(5.259)	5.699	(6.691)	(0.026)	0.044	(0.062)
−0.2	(4.967)	5.707	(6.525)	(0.029)	0.048	(0.067)
0.2	(5.070)	5.540	(6.529)	(0.019)	0.036	(0.053)
0.4	(5.146)	6.053	(7.112)	(0.034)	0.054	(0.074)
0.6	(5.295)	5.742	(6.689)	(0.022)	0.040	(0.058)
0.8	(5.430)	6.030	(6.878)	(0.034)	0.054	(0.074)
1.0	(5.264)	5.750	(6.581)	(0.026)	0.044	(0.062)

Table 9.6. *Distributional properties of* $\widetilde{W}_n$ *under* $H_0(N = 300)$

θ	95% Sample quantile			P (rejection)		
−1.0	(7.547)	8.020	(9.718)	(0.100)	0.130	(0.160)
−0.8	(5.765)	6.475	(7.227)	(0.045)	0.068	(0.091)
−0.6	(4.971)	5.783	(6.573)	(0.027)	0.046	(0.065)
−0.4	(5.505)	6.078	(6.591)	(0.037)	0.058	(0.079)
−0.2	(5.422)	6.169	(7.529)	(0.034)	0.054	(0.074)
0.2	(5.755)	5.084	(6.823)	(0.027)	0.046	(0.065)
0.4	(5.597)	6.443	(7.325)	(0.039)	0.060	(0.081)
0.6	(5.118)	5.866	(7.507)	(0.031)	0.050	(0.069)
0.8	(4.339)	4.653	(5.809)	(0.013)	0.028	(0.043)
1.0	(5.024)	6.143	(6.963)	(0.034)	0.054	(0.074)

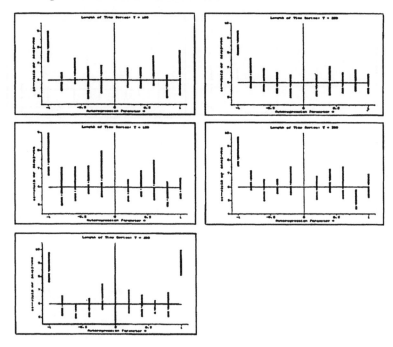

Figure 9.16. 95 percent confidence intervals for the 0.95 quantile versus θ for alternative T.

If there is prior evidence supporting the conjecture that the underlying process is indeed an AR(1), then it seems advisable to check for stability, for example, by testing for unit roots.

Apart from scrutinizing the upper tail of the null distribution of White's NNT statistic, we decided to subject the simulated realizations to a Kolmogorov–Smirnov test to fit. The hypothesis

$$H_0 : \mathcal{F}(\tilde{W}_n) = \chi^2_{1-\alpha}(q = 2)$$

is tested against the hypothesis

$$H_1 : \mathcal{F}(\tilde{W}_n) \neq \chi^2_{1-\alpha}(q = 2).$$

The p-values for this nonparametric test of fit are listed in Table 9.7. Apart from a single case, one cannot reject the null hypothesis for experiments involving stable autoregressions. Lower p-values are caused by one and the same phenomenon. There exists a lack of realizations near the origin, implying a large distance between the theoretical and the sample distribution function in a neighborhood of zero. Ample evidence against the null is found whenever

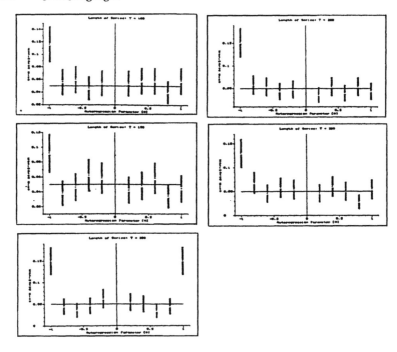

Figure 9.17. 95 percent confidence intervals for the size versus θ for alternative T.

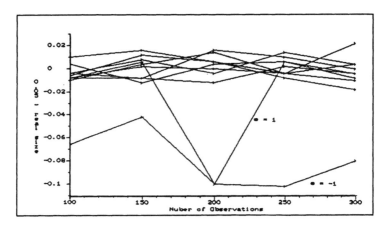

Figure 9.18. Estimated size for all θ values versus T.

Table 9.7. *p-Values for the Kolmogorov–Smirnov test of fit*

θ	T					
	50	100	150	200	250	300
−1.00	0.00	0.00	0.00	0.000	0.00	0.00
−0.80	0.64	0.31	0.11	0.211	0.38	0.59
−0.60	0.34	0.31	0.05	0.442	0.71	0.18
−0.40	0.00	0.88	0.05	0.659	0.06	0.39
−0.20	0.05	0.07	0.28	0.613	0.72	0.53
0.20	0.83	0.59	0.69	0.823	0.24	0.07
0.40	0.50	0.30	0.95	0.099	0.37	0.04
0.60	0.14	0.09	0.60	0.286	0.64	0.99
0.80	0.69	0.13	0.78	0.145	0.92	0.05
1.00	0.38	0.71	0.15	0.000	0.35	0.35

the true generating process has a negative unit root. The analogous statement for the case of a positive unit root only holds for time series of length $T = 200$.

For the domain of stable autoregressive processes of order 1, the size of the current version of the test seems to be appropriate even for the small sample sizes for which our experiment was carried out. But note again that estimates of sample quantiles and rejection probabilities were computed by an "omniscient" statistician – someone who knew the order of the underlying process! To see whether the uncertainty with respect to this characteristic of the data-generating process has an impact on the performance of the test, we ran the NNT again, 500 times of each case considered before. To avoid the introduction of an additional source of randomness, we used the same data basis as in the previous case. Unlike before, the order of the affine part of the network was now decided upon, utilizing three different order-selection criteria: Akaike's FPE criterion (Akaike 1969, 1970), the AIC (Akaike 1973, 1974), and the SBIC (Schwarz 1978). The first two criteria are designed to select optimal predictors, but the SBIC is tailored to select the true model. It is known that SBIC provides an asymptotically unbiased estimate of AR order, whereas the FPE criterion and the AIC tend to overestimate the order even in the asymptotic case.

Figures 9.19 and 9.20 are representative for the outcome of the experiment. For stable processes, one cannot reject the hypothesis that the empirical distributions for the sets of realizations of the test statistic under the four treatments [i.e., order known (batch 1), selection by FPE criterion (batch 2), selection by AIC (batch 3), and selection by SBIC (batch 4)] follow the same distribution. One typically finds differences only with respect to the spread in the extreme tails, as demonstrated in the comparative box plot of Figure 9.19. We did not

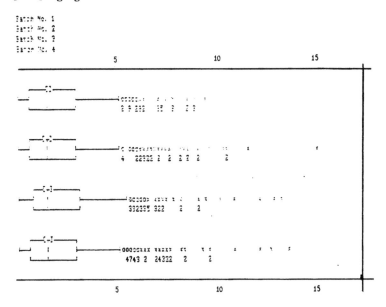

Figure 9.19. Comparative box plot ($T = 100$).

observe a single stable case in which there was sufficient evidence to support a hypothesis concerning differences in location or spread. In the presence of unit root cases, we observe that shifts in location and spread occur as one no longer assumes perfect knowledge of the underlying order. In the case explicated in Figure 9.20, choosing the order by a criterion leads to a lower probability for a wrong decision. Table 9.8 reveals that rejections of the null hypothesis occur in only 8 to 10 percent of the observed cases if one uses a selection criterion as opposed to committing an error 15 percent of the time when fixing the order at the true order of the unstable process. Scrutinizing Table 9.9, we notice that, in 24 percent of the cases, the FPE criterion as well as the AIC in fact overestimate the order of the process. What is left after this structure is removed is misidentified by White's test as being nonlinear less often than in those cases in which the SBIC is used as selection criterion. The SBIC only overestimates order in 4.2 percent of all observed cases.

Because there is no apparent decrease in the quality of the test if selection criteria are used in the presence of low-order stable autoregressive processes and there is an obvious advantage when the underlying process is of low order and unstable, it seems justifiable to advise users to rely on this technology. In a certain sense, the use of selection rules to determine the order of the affine part

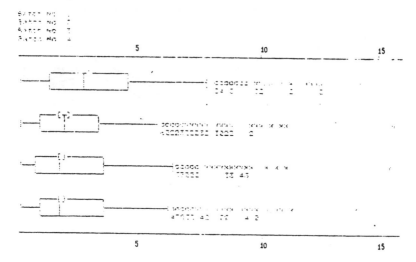

Figure 9.20. Comparative box plot ($T = 200$).

Table 9.8. *Probability for type-I error for alternative criteria*

Order	P (false rejection)
Known	0.150
FPE	0.082
AIC	0.096
SBIC	0.104

of the network may be looked upon as a strategy aimed at a robustification of White's test for nonlinearity with respect to the size of the test. Of course, such a strategy would only be adequate if it does not decrease the power of the test against certain types of nonlinearity. We turn to that question in the subsequent sections.

4.2   *Test's ability to detect Hicksian nonlinearities*

The time series generated by the stochastic multiplier–accelerator model were stored and then subjected to three versions of White's test. The versions differ only with respect to the criterion used to determine the order of the affine part of the network. That is, the treatment variable has three levels: FPE criterion, AIC, and SBIC. The realizations of the test statistic under each treatment were analyzed with respect to their distributional properties. Our findings indicate

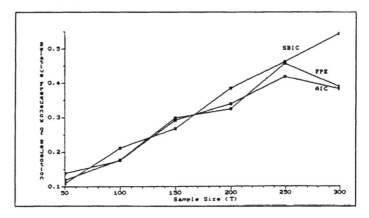

Figure 9.21. Estimated probability for rejection of linearity if the true underlying process is a nonlinear Hicksian process.

Table 9.9. *Estimated order of an AR(1) possessing
a negative unit root*

Criterion	Estimated order					
	0	1	2	3	4	≥ 5
FPE	0	0.760	0.190	0.038	0.010	0.010
AIC	0	0.760	0.190	0.038	0.010	0.010
SBIC	0	0.958	0.038	0.004	0.000	0.000

that if the noisy Hicksian economy, would be an adequate description of reality,
the chances of detecting the underlying nonlinearity would be moderate, at least
for the sample sizes considered in our experiment. For sample sizes larger than
150, the version of White's test utilizing the SBIC dominates the alternative
versions in terms of their ability to indicate the nonlinearity of the underlying
process.

Figure 9.21 summarizes the outcome of the experiment focusing on the
test's power against Hicksian-type nonlinearities. The point estimates and their
associated confidence intervals are given in Tables 9.10 and 9.11, respectively.

The plots indicates that an analyst trying to test for nonlinearity in economic
time series, representing output of a nonlinear economic system that is sensitive
to a noisy non-economic environment, will hardly be successful in revealing
the true state of nature if the time series available are not longer than 300. The
ability to detect the Hicksian nonlinearity is clearly a positive function of the
sample size, no matter which version of the test is used. For sample sizes

Table 9.10. *Estimated Probability of rejection for alternative selection criteria*

N	Fixed order	FPE	AIC	SBIC
50	0.116	0.120	0.138	0.110
100	0.174	0.178	0.176	0.212
150	0.016	0.298	0.292	0.268
200	0.398	0.324	0.338	0.384
250	0.008	0.456	0.418	0.462
300	0.812	0.388	0.382	0.544

Table 9.11. *95% Confidence intervals for probability of rejection*

N	White		FPE		AIC		SBIC	
50	0.087	0.145	0.091	0.149	0.107	0.169	0.082	0.138
100	0.140	0.208	0.144	0.212	0.142	0.210	0.175	0.249
150	0.005	0.027	0.257	0.339	0.251	0.333	0.228	0.308
200	0.354	0.443	0.282	0.366	0.296	0.380	0.340	0.428
250	0.000	0.016	0.411	0.501	0.374	0.462	0.417	0.507
300	0.777	0.847	0.344	0.432	0.339	0.425	0.499	0.589

larger then 150, the asymptotic properties of the SBIC seem to operate, and the FPE criterion as well as the AIC are dominated. Table 9.12 reveals that the SBIC's tendency to chose parsimonious filters seems to pay at least for T larger than 150.

In the case of the experiment at hand, there is clearly an optimal dimension for the autoregressive model used as a filter. Let us define the following conditional probability as our goal function:

$$P(\text{ rejection } | \text{ order } = p \wedge d.g.p = \text{Hicksian}).$$

The notion of an optimal dimension for the affine network could be defined in terms of this probability. Let p^* denote that dimension for which the conditional probability of rejection is maximized. We estimated the conditional rejection probabilities from the data generated in our simulation experiment. Three estimates – one for each version of the test – of the conditional probability are available for each order considered. As the sample size increases, these estimates converge and the level at which they are realized increases. Moreover, for each sample size, the estimated conditional rejection probability is maximized at $p = 2$. For an illustration of the point, turn to Figures 9.22 and 9.23.

In the case of $T = 150$, the conditional rejection probability is maximized at $p = 2$. The same is true if 300 data points constitute the series. In the former case, approximately 30 percent of all test runs indicate nonlinearity, whereas

Table 9.12. *Estimated order by the FPE criterion, the AIC, and the SBIC for the Hicks model*

		Estimated order of AR(p)							
N	Criterion	1	2	3	4	5	6	7	8
50	FPE	0.010	0.766	0.182	0.034	0.004	0.004	0.000	0.000
	AIC	0.010	0.766	0.182	0.034	0.004	0.004	0.000	0.000
	SBIC	0.024	0.892	0.076	0.006	0.000	0.002	0.000	0.000
100	FPE	0.000	0.770	0.174	0.046	0.008	0.002	0.000	0.000
	AIC	0.000	0.770	0.174	0.046	0.008	0.002	0.000	0.000
	SBIC	0.004	0.938	0.056	0.002	0.000	0.000	0.000	0.000
150	FPE	0.000	0.778	0.170	0.038	0.010	0.004	0.000	0.000
	AIC	0.000	0.778	0.170	0.038	0.010	0.004	0.000	0.000
	SBIC	0.000	0.950	0.044	0.006	0.000	0.000	0.000	0.000
200	FPE	0.000	0.732	0.202	0.050	0.016	0.000	0.000	0.000
	AIC	0.000	0.732	0.202	0.050	0.016	0.000	0.000	0.000
	SBIC	0.000	0.954	0.046	0.000	0.000	0.000	0.000	0.000
250	FPE	0.000	0.814	0.144	0.038	0.002	0.002	0.000	0.000
	AIC	0.000	0.812	0.146	0.038	0.002	0.002	0.000	0.000
	SBIC	0.000	0.978	0.022	0.000	0.000	0.000	0.000	0.000
300	FPE	0.000	0.350	0.232	0.182	0.156	0.052	0.026	0.002
	AIC	0.000	0.350	0.232	0.182	0.156	0.052	0.026	0.002
	SBIC	0.000	0.670	0.212	0.072	0.044	0.002	0.000	0.000

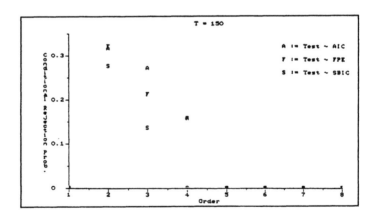

Figure 9.22. Conditional rejection probability versus order for $T = 150$.

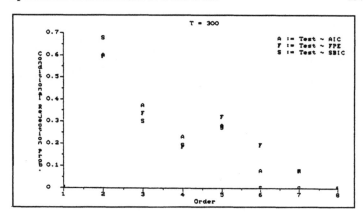

Figure 9.23. Conditional rejection probability versus order for $T = 300$.

linearity is correctly rejected in about 63 percent of the tests in the latter case. For the sample sizes scrutinized in the experiment, it is evident that a negative relationship prevails between the order of the linear filter and the conditional rejection probability. The plots for the remaining sample sizes basically display the same pattern.

Because we do not have any useful evidence for order 1, we decide to rerun the experiment, forcing an affine network of order 1. The results indicate that such a low-order linear filter proves useless in the presence of the Hicksian nonlinearity considered so far. From the evidence discussed above, we can conclude that it may not be a useful strategy to remove linearity in an *ad libitum* manner. As we see in the following sections, this insight is also relevant in the presence of noise-free chaotic data.

4.3   *Simulation results for the stock-market model*

The outcome of the simulation experiments implies that White's test detects the nonlinear nature of the process generating the chaotic, artificial stock-market data in a vast majority of the cases considered. Although the power of the test against this deterministic piecewise linear alternative is high, the test's ability to reject linearity correctly is negatively related to the available sample size. A third aspect concerns the effects of alternative methods for the determination of the order of the AR(p) process to be fitted on the power of the test against this specific type of nonlinearity. In the present case, the use of statistically motivated order-selection criteria enhances the test's ability to detect the nonlinearity manifested in the data.

258   J. A. Jungeilges

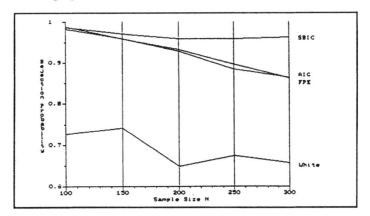

Figure 9.24. Rejection probabilities versus sample size for various selection criteria.

Table 9.13. *Point estimate of the probability of correct rejection for various methods of AR($\cdot$) order selection*

N	White	FPE	AIC	SBIC
50	0.710	0.979	0.981	0.980
100	0.726	0.988	0.982	0.986
150	0.742	0.958	0.958	0.970
200	0.648	0.932	0.928	0.958
250	0.674	0.896	0.884	0.958
300	0.656	0.862	0.864	0.962

The evidence concerning the high power of the test against the chaotic, deterministic motion is summarized in Figure 9.24. Even in the worst case, that is, the order of the AR(p) is fixed at 5 throughout the entire experiment, the estimated probability of rejecting linearity correctly exceeds 0.65 for all sample sizes considered. Figure 9.24 is based on information contained in Table 9.13. Table 9.14 gives the confidence limits for the point estimates presented in Table 9.13.

Irrespective of the strategy used to determine the order of the affine network, we observe that an increase in sample size does not necessarily increase the ability of the test to detect the nonlinearity present in the data. For the constant fitting of a higher-order process, for the FPE criterion and the AIC, the estimated power of the test deteriorates as N increases. This tendency is less pronounced for the strategy using the SBIC. We conjecture that an explanation for this phenomenon is provided by the nature of the data. As the time series become longer, there is more information available that is generated by a linear piece of the map under scrutiny. The trajectory moves around an unstable

Table 9.14. *95.4% Confidence intervals for the probability of a correct rejection under various methods of order selection*

N	White		FPE		AIC		SBIC	
50	0.655	0.726	0.942	0.998	0.954	0.990	0.940	0.997
100	0.686	0.766	0.978	0.998	0.970	0.994	0.975	0.997
150	0.703	0.781	0.940	0.976	0.940	0.976	0.955	0.985
200	0.605	0.691	0.909	0.955	0.905	0.951	0.940	0.976
250	0.632	0.716	0.869	0.923	0.855	0.913	0.940	0.976
300	0.614	0.698	0.831	0.893	0.833	0.895	0.945	0.979

equilibrium before it wanders off to the other source of the map. In longer time series, the evidence for linearity, that is, movement around the unstable equilibrium associated with a linear piece of the map, becomes a dominating type of information relative to the jumps, that is, the manifestation of the nonlinearity of the data-generating process.

The evidence displayed in Figure 9.24 suggests that, in the present case, the use of statistically motivated selection criteria to estimate the order of the affine part of the network implies a significant improvement of the test's performance. The more parsimonious the order-selection strategy, the higher the estimated power of the test against the type of the nonlinearity inherent in Day and Huang's stock-market model. It is evident that at least for the sample sizes considered, the application of a linear filter of arbitrary high order represents a suboptimal strategy. Even criteria known to be biased toward models being too large (PEE and AIC) seems to extract too much structure from the series. Only the parsimonious SBIC determines an order of the filter leaving enough structure in the data to be identified as evidence of nonlinearity by White's test. Detail on the order estimation by the three criteria are presented in Table 9.15.

So far, only the effect of order selection has been established by focusing on a shift of the percentage of correct rejections, given 500 replications of the experiment. The experiment was conducted such that it is possible to demonstrate the implications of parsimonious order selection on the distribution of White's test statistic. Various density estimates (box plot, stem-and-leaf plot, and the traditional histogram) were generated on the basis of 500 realizations of the test statistic. For the purpose of this exposition, histograms are sufficient. The density estimates for the test statistics generated under the four alternative order-selection strategies are shown in Figure 9.25. For the cases associated with the use of order-selection criteria, the distribution of White's statistic resembles a mixture of distributions. Note how the probability mass concentrated over the left-hand side of the domain for the constant-order case is reduced as one moves to FPE and AIC order selection. The domain increases and the mass shifts into the two humps with modes around 150 and 225. The mass over the

Table 9.15. *Estimated order by the FPE criterion, the AIC, and the SBIC*

N	Criterion	Estimated order of AR(p)							
		1	2	3	4	5	6	7	8
100	FPE	0.87	0.116	0.008	0.004	0.002	0	0	0
	AIC	0.87	0.116	0.008	0.004	0.002	0	0	0
	SBIC	0.882	0.114	0.004	0	0	0	0	0
150	FPE	0.868	0.118	0.01	0.003	0.002	0	0	0
	AIC	0.868	0.118	0.01	0.003	0.002	0	0	0
	SBIC	0.9	0.098	0.002	0	0	0	0	0
200	FPE	0.83	0.136	0.014	0.012	0.006	0.002	0	0
	AIC	0.83	0.136	0.014	0.012	0.006	0.002	0	0
	SBIC	0.888	0.11	0.002	0	0	0	0	0
250	FPE	0.784	0.152	0.048	0.012	0.002	0.002	0	0
	AIC	0.784	0.152	0.048	0.012	0.002	0.002	0	0
	SBIC	0.904	0.094	0.002	0	0	0	0	0
300	FPE	0.678	0.196	0.066	0.038	0.016	0.002	0.002	0.002
	AIC	0.678	0.196	0.066	0.038	0.016	0.002	0.002	0.002
	SBIC	0.876	0.12	0.004	0	0	0	0	0

interval [0, 25] is further reduced if one determines the order of the affine part of the network by SBIC.

4.4   *Power against a nonlinear consumption process exhibiting sensitive dependence on initial conditions*

The experiment involving idealized consumption processes exhibiting complex dynamics again provides evidence supporting the notion that White's test has high power against nonlinear process exhibiting intricate dynamic behavior. A glance at Table 9.16 shows that even for sample sizes of 50 and 100 the test is able to detect the underlying nonlinearity in each of the 500 cases, given that the order of the affine part of the network is chosen on the basis of the SBIC. As explicated in Table 9.17, this criterion chooses order 1 in approximately 99 percent of all cases. Order selection based on the alternative criteria tends to result in higher-dimensional affine parts of the network. As observed in the case of the artificial financial data, the power of the test drops slightly if those alternative selection criteria are utilized to determine the dimension of the linear filter.

A descriptive analysis of the realizations of $\tilde{W}_N$ under the different modes of order selection revealed a pattern that also was observed in the previous experiment. Instead of allowing for a detailed view of the densities of the test

Table 9.16. *Probability of correct rejection for various methods of AR(·) order selection*

N	FPE	AIC	SBIC
50	0.996	0.994	1.000
100	0.988	0.994	1.000
150	0.996	0.994	1.000
200	1.000	0.994	1.000
250	0.996	0.996	0.998
300	0.996	0.996	1.000

Table 9.17. *Estimated order by FPE, AIC, and SBIC*

		Estimated order of AR(p)							
N	Criterion	1	2	3	4	5	6	7	8
50	FPE	0.924	0.034	0.024	0.016	0.003	0.000	0.000	0.000
	AIC	0.924	0.034	0.024	0.016	0.003	0.000	0.000	0.000
	SBIC	0.988	0.010	0.003	0.000	0.000	0.000	0.000	0.000
100	FPE	0.908	0.018	0.044	0.022	0.006	0.002	0.000	0.000
	AIC	0.906	0.018	0.044	0.024	0.006	0.002	0.000	0.000
	SBIC	0.998	0.002	0.000	0.000	0.000	0.000	0.000	0.000
150	FPE	0.878	0.012	0.056	0.046	0.002	0.006	0.000	0.000
	AIC	0.878	0.012	0.056	0.046	0.002	0.006	0.000	0.000
	SBIC	0.998	0.002	0.000	0.000	0.000	0.000	0.000	0.000
200	FPE	0.840	0.010	0.072	0.060	0.006	0.010	0.002	0.000
	AIC	0.840	0.010	0.072	0.060	0.006	0.010	0.002	0.000
	SBIC	0.988	0.006	0.006	0.000	0.000	0.000	0.000	0.000
250	FPE	0.812	0.010	0.066	0.098	0.002	0.010	0.002	0.000
	AIC	0.812	0.010	0.066	0.098	0.002	0.010	0.002	0.000
	SBIC	0.994	0.002	0.004	0.000	0.000	0.000	0.000	0.000
300	FPE	0.810	0.000	0.038	0.126	0.006	0.018	0.000	0.002
	AIC	0.810	0.000	0.038	0.126	0.006	0.018	0.000	0.002
	SBIC	0.994	0.002	0.004	0.000	0.000	0.000	0.000	0.000

statistic under the various selection mechanisms, we summarize the evidence in Figure 9.26.

Each dotted line in Figure 9.26 is associated with a length of the simulated consumption series. As indicated for the cast $T = 300$, the lines connect points in the (mean, standard deviation)-space associated with FPE, AIC, and SBIC.

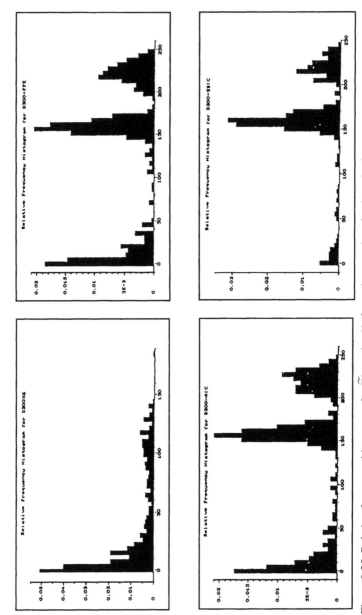

Figure 9.25. Relative-frequency histograms for $\widetilde{W}_N$ under H_1 for various modes of order selection.

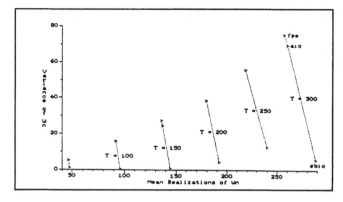

Figure 9.26. Standard deviation versus mean of $\widetilde{W}_N$ for alternative sample sizes.

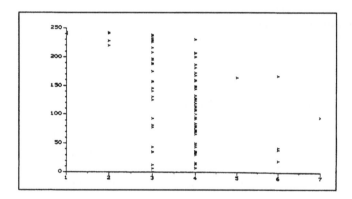

Figure 9.27. Realizations of $\widetilde{W}_N$ versus order selected by *AIC* ($T = 250$).

The negative slope of all lines suggests that in the SBIC case the average realization of White's test statistic will be larger than the average realizations based on the alternative selection criteria. The fact that the length of the lines grows with increasing T reflects the higher degree of concentration of realizations around the mean for the SBIC case. The inflation in the second moment of the sample distributions associated with the Akaike criteria is exclusively due to cases in which the linear filter was chosen to be of order three or higher. As an example, consider Figure 9.27.

The pattern shown in this plot is typical for the entire experiment. As soon as higher-dimensional filters are applied, the level of the realized test statistics tends to drop, that is, the evidence against linearity becomes less pronounced.

We conclude that in terms of its ability to generate evidence against linearity, the choice of the dimension of the affine part of the network matters and a strategy involving the SBIC would be preferred over strategies involving alternative criteria.

5   Concluding remarks

The present effort to study the operational characteristics of the NNT for sample sizes typical for economic applications certainly supports earlier claims of Lee et al. (1993) that the test has appropriate size and is characterized by power against certain forms of nonlinearities in the mean. In addition, we provide evidence for the significance of choosing the dimension of the affine network. The choice of the affine network's order matters. The power of the test depends on this order in a crucial manner. At the same time, the present exercise suggested a set of open problems, a set of future research questions. First of all, the performance of the test against noisy chaotic alternatives should be scrutinized. Controlling the degree of observer noise that is added to the already existing trajectories should allow us to establish the relationship between the probability for a correct rejection and the signal-to-noise ratio in the presence of nonlinearities being low dimensional and chaotic. Moreover, an inclusion of a wider range of nonlinear macroeconomic models would be of interest. A variety of alternative strategies for choosing the order of the linear filter are available (see Hannan and Deistler 1988, chap. 6). The array of selection criteria scrutinized should be extended. An interesting procedure from Rissanen (1988), referred to as the predictive least-squares criterion, has the practical advantage that all calculations can be done simultaneously using a single lattice filter instead of having to recompute everything for each model order being considered.

REFERENCES

Akaike, H. (1969). Fitting autoregressive models for prediction, *Ann. Inst. Stat. Math.*, **21**, 243–7.

—— (1970). Statistical predictor identification, *Ann. Inst. Stat. Math.*, **22**, 203–17.

Aaike, H. (1973). Information theory and an extension of the maximum likelihood principle. In *Second International Symposium on Information Theory*, eds. B. N. Petrov and F. Coaki, Budapest: Akedemiai Kido, 267–81.

—— (1974). A new look at the statistical identification model. *IEEE: Trans. Auto Control*, **198**, 716–23.

Ashley, R. A., and Patterson, D. M. (1988). Linear versus nonlinear macroeconomics: A statistical test, *Int. Econ. Rev.*, **30**, 685–704.

Bierens, H. (1990). A consistent conditional moment test of function form, *Econometrica* **58**, 1443–58.

Blatt, J. M. (1983). *Dynamic Economic Systems: A Post-Keynesian Approach*, Sharpe, New York.

Davies, R. B. (1977). Hypothesis testing when a nuisance parameter is present only under the alternative, *Biometrika* **64**, 247–54.

(1987). Hypothesis testing when a nuisance parameter is present only under the alternative, *Biometrika*, **74**, 33–43.

Doob, J. L. (1954). *Stochastic Processes.* New York: Wiley.

Eckmann, J.-P., and Ruelle, D. (1985). Ergodic theory and strange attractors, *Rev. Mod. Phys.*, **57**(3), 617–56.

Gaertner, W., and Jungeilges, J. A. (1988). A Nonlinear model of interdependent consumer behavior, *Econ. Lett.*, **27**, 145–50.

(1993). "Spindles" and coexisting attractors in a dynamic model of interdependent consumer behavior: A note, *J. Econ. Behav. Organ.*, **21**, 223–31.

Granger, C. W. (1966). the typical spectral shape of an economic variable, *Econometrica*, **34**, 150–61.

Hannan, E. J., and Deistler, M (1988). *The Statistical Theory of Linear Systems*, Wiley, New York.

Hemerly, and Davies (1991)

Hicks, J. R. (1950). *A Contribution to the Theory of the Trade Cycle*, (2nd ed., 1965). Clarendon press, Oxford, England.

Hiemstra, C., and Jones, J. (1992). Detection and description of linear and nonlinear dependence in daily Dow Jones stock returns and NYSE trading volume, mimeo. Office of Economic Analysis, U.S. Securities and Exchange Commission, Washington, DC.

Hommes, C. (1991). Chaotic dynamics in economic models, Ph.D. dissertation, University of Groningen.

Huang, W., and Day, R. (1993). Distributional Dynamics of Bull and Bear Markets. In *Evolutionary Dynamics and Nonlinear Economics*, ed. R. Day and P. Chen, Oxford: Oxford University Press.

Kuan, C., and White, H. (1991). Artificial neural networks: An econometric perspective, mimeo, Department of Economics and Institute for Neural Computation, University of California at San Diego.

Lee, T.-H., White, H., and Granger, C. (1989). Testing for neglected nonlinearities in time series models. *Journal of Economics*, **56**, 269–90.

McCaffrey, D. F., Ellner, S., Gallant, A. R., and Nychka, D. W. (1992). Estimating the Lyapunov exponent of a chaotic system with nonparametric regression, *J. Am. Stat. Assoc.*, **87**(419), 682–95.

Metzler, L. A. (1941). The nature and stability of inventory cycles, *Rev. Econ. Studies*, **23**, 113–29.

Rissanen, J. (1986). Stochastic Complexity and Modelling. *Annals of Statistics*, **14**, 1080–1100.

Samuelson, P. A. (1939). Interactions between the multiplier analysis and principle of acceleration, *Rev. Econ. Stat.*, **21**, 75–78.

Schuhr, R. (1991). *Lineare versus nichtlineare Modelle für univariate Zeitreihen: Diagnoseverfahren im Test*, Peter Lang, Frankfurt am Main, Germany.

Schwarz, G. (1978). Estimating the dimensions of a model, *Ann. Stat.*, **6**, 461–4.

Tong, H. (1990). *Non-linear Time Series: A Dynamical Approach.*, Oxford University Press, Oxford, England.

White, H. (1989a). An additional hidden unit test for neglected nonlinearity in multilayer feedforward networks, *Proceedings of the International Joint Conference on Neural Networks*, (Washington, DC) Vol. 2, IEEE Press, New York, pp. 451–5.

(1989b). Some asymptotic results for learning in single hidden-layer feedforward network models, *J. Am. Stat. Assoc.*, **84**(408), 1003–13.

CHAPTER 10

Time series, stochastic and chaotic

Thomas J. Taylor

1   Introduction

We consider two topics. The first, treated in Section 1, is the question of how
one can distinguish chaotic time series from stochastic time series, and why we
feel that this is the wrong question to ask. In addressing this topic, we describe
scenarios in which a chaotic time series also can be a stochastic time series,
and show that even when this is not the case that a chaotic time series may
be experimentally indistinguishable from a stochastic time series, even from
white noise. The second topic is a mathematically coherent description of a
problem that seemed to be a subject of much of the discussion of the workshop of
which this volume is the proceedings: the determination of nonlinear structures
in time series and their use for the purposes of prediction. In Section 3, we
discuss this topic from the viewpoint of the classic theory of prediction of
stochastic processes, incorporating the embedding method as a tool extending
this theory. In Section 4, we report briefly on new techniques and viewpoints
toward extending embedding methods to treat environments in which noise
affects the observation of the chaotic signals; our paradigm for treating this
problem takes much from the field of computer vision.

2   Stochastic versus chaotic structures?

Let $\{y_t\}_{t=0}^{\infty}$ be a time series; for simplicity, we assume, that each member y_t of
the time series is a real number and that t is a discrete parameter, $t \; \varepsilon \; \mathbf{Z}$, although
all results are equally valid when t is a continuous parameter or y_t is a vector
of real numbers. To analyze this time series we may wish to take advantage of
various idealized structures that may occur.

We are particularly interested in the case that $\{y_t\}_{t=0}^{\infty}$ has what we call a
dynamical structure. This is the case in which $\{y_t\}_{t=0}^{\infty}$ is generated by a dynamic
system, in other words, that there is a dynamic system $x_{t+1} = F(x_t)$, with initial

condition x_0, and an observation function $h(x)$ of the state of the dynamic system satisfying a particular relationship with y_t. The state x_t of the dynamic system that we suppose to be unobservable for all times t, the dynamics F, the observation function h, and even the dimension n may be unknown, but it is supposed that the observed values of the time series satisfy $y_t = h(x_t) = h(F^t x_0)$, that is, the time series represents partial observations of the state of the system. Note that we have used the common notation that $F^t x$ denotes the t-fold composition $F(F \dots F(x) \dots)(t\text{-times})$. We discuss here only the case that x_t takes values in some n-dimensional Euclidean space $\mathbf{R}^n$, although all results are valid also in the case that x_t takes value in some other manifold $\mathbf{M}$ of dimension n, or even in an attractor in $\mathbf{R}^n$. We assume that F is a smooth, smoothly invertible mapping, that is, diffeomorphism. A *chaotic structure* may then be defined as a dynamic structure for which the dynamics F are chaotic.

Another class of structures that is often useful in treating time series are stochastic structures. A stochastic structure is defined by a family of probability distributions that describes the probabilities of different kinds of events in the time series; a stochastic structure is given by a family of probability distributions

$$\{P(y_{t_1} \leq a_1, y_{t_2} \leq a_2, \dots, y_{t_k} \leq a_k, \dots, y_{t_p} \leq a_p) :$$

$$\text{for all } p \geq 0 \text{ and all } n\text{-tuples}(t_1, t_2, \dots, t_p)\},$$

where we $y_{t_1}, y_{t_2}, y_{t_3}, \dots, y_{t_p}$ are potential observed values of the time series at the times $t_1, t_2, \dots, t_p$. This collection of probability distributions must satisfy certain consistency conditions, in particular, in the limit that $a_k \to \infty$, we must have

$$P(y_{t_1} \leq a_1, \dots, y_{t_{k-1}} \leq a_{k-1}, y_{t_k} \leq a_k, y_{t_{k+1}} \leq a_{k+1}, \dots, y_{t_p} \leq a_p)$$

$$\to \quad P(y_{t_1} \leq a_1, \dots, y_{t_{k-1}} \leq a_{k-1}, y_{t_{k+1}} \leq a_{k+1}, \dots, y_{t_p} \leq a_p).$$

As usual, manipulations involving the distributions P may be treated equally well using probability densities $p(\xi_1, t_1; \xi_2, t_2; \dots \xi_p, t_p)$; these are related by

$$P(y_{t_1} \leq a_1, y_{t_2} \leq a_2, y_{t_3} \leq a_3, \dots, y_{t_p} \leq a_p) =$$

$$\int_{-\infty}^{a_1} \int_{-\infty}^{a_2} \dots \int_{-\infty}^{a_p} p(\xi_1, t_1; \xi_2, t_2; \dots \xi_p, t_p) d\xi_1 \dots d\xi_p.$$

It may be useful to consider an observed time series $\{y_t\}_{t=0}^{\infty}$ as having a particular stochastic structure $\{P\}$ if the time series satisfies properties consistent with those of generic samples of a stochastic process with finite dimensional distributions given by the $\{P\}$. One special type are the stationary stochastic structures; these are defined by the condition that the probability distributions $P(y_{s+t_1}, y_{s+t_2}, \dots, y_{s+t_p})$ are independent of s. In this case, one may require that the distributions $P(y_{t_1}, y_{t_2}, \dots, y_{t_p})$ of an assumed stochastic structure be consistent with the observed frequency of occurrence of the events

$\{y_{s+t_1} \leq a_1, y_{s+t_2} \leq a_2, \ldots, y_{s+t_k} \leq a_k, \ldots, y_{s+t_p} \leq a_p\}$; this is equivalent to assuming that the ergodic theorem is valid. In the nonstationary case, it is not easy to see how to proceed in general; often, a wide variety of nonstationary stochastic structures may be consistent. Usually, one hopes to describe the nonstationary observed time series in terms another which is described in terms of a stationary stochastic structure.

We note that the definitions of the dynamic structures and stochastic structures are not mutually exclusive. Indeed, as the following basic example illustrates, we may have both structures in a natural way. We consider digital observations of a smooth chaotic system, a consideration very much in touch with experiment. Consider the chaotic dynamic system given by the map F, which takes the unit circle, uniformly stretches it to twice its circumference, and then wraps it around twice to obtain the unit circle: this map can be characterized as the map $z \rightarrow z^2$ for $z = e^{i\theta}$, a unimodular complex number, or equally well in terms of the map $\theta \rightarrow 2\theta$ (mod 2π). In terms of the latter characterization, see Figure 10.1. Consider also the binary observation

$$h(\theta) = \begin{cases} 0 & 0 \leq \theta < \pi \\ 1 & \pi \leq \theta < 2\pi \end{cases}.$$

The graphs h and the compositions $h \circ F$ and $h \circ F^2$ are shown in Figure 10.2.

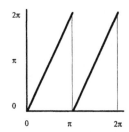

Figure 10.1. Graph of F in terms of the map $\theta \rightarrow 2\theta$ (mod 2π).

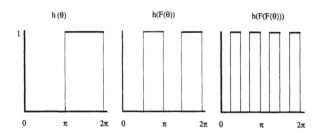

Figure 10.2.

Thus for every initial point θ_0 between 0 and 2π, we obtain a time series consisting of zeros and ones; in fact, the time series is a readout of the bits in the binary representation of the number $\theta_0/2\pi$. In the absence of information to suggest some particular value of θ_0, or some special class of values to which θ_0 must belong, it is natural to consider the behavior of the observation time series of values of θ_0 chosen at random, that is, to assume that θ_0 is a sample of a random variable uniformly distributed in the interval $[0, 2\pi]$. In other words, the probability of θ_0 taking a value in a given interval is simply the length of the interval divided by 2π. With respect to this probability, we see from Figures 10.1 and 10.2 that, for all t, the observations $y_t = h(F^t x)$ take the values 0 and 1, each with probability $\frac{1}{2}$. We also may evaluate conditional probabilities, for example, $P(y_1 = i | y_0 = j)$, where i and j can take the values 0 or 1. By definition of conditional probability, this is equal to the quotient

$$\frac{P(y_1 = i, y_0 = j)}{P(y_0 = j)},$$

which can be seen to be equal to $\frac{1}{2}$ for all choices of i, j. Thus, we see that y_0 and y_1 are independent, and similarly, y_0 and y_t for all t. Such considerations lead us to the conclusion that, for almost every initial condition, the observation time series is precisely as random as tossing a coin: quite random, in other words. This randomness in temporal behavior of the time series comes from the randomness of the initial conditions, from the unstable nature of the chaotic dynamics, and from the finite precision of the measurement function h.

A systematic discussion of the stochastic behavior of observation time series of dynamic systems requires some concepts regarding the statistical behavior of dynamic systems and also theory of prediction of stochastic processes. An attractor of a smooth dynamic system is a closed region Λ of the state space, which has the following properties:

(1) Λ is invariant under the action of the dynamics, that is, if x_0 is in Λ, then x_t is in Λ for all times t:

(2) Λ is irreducible, that is, there is some initial condition x_0 in Λ that has an orbit x_t that fills out Λ (is dense in Λ); and

(3)   there is an open neighborhood U_Λ of Λ (called the *basin of attraction* of Λ) in which almost all initial conditions have orbits x_t that converge to Λ as $t \to \infty$. This entails the existence of an orbit $\tilde{x}_t$ in Λ for which the distance between x_t and $\tilde{x}_t$ decreases to zero as $t \to \infty$.

In chaotic dynamic systems [e.g., the uniformly hyperbolic systems of Smale (1980)], once transient behavior has died out, the dynamic behavior of generic initial conditions is determined by the behavior on attractors. If there are no chaotic attractors, then generic behavior can exhibit only transient chaotic phenomena. On the other hand, if there are chaotic attractors, the behavior of a large set of initial conditions will be asymptotically chaotic. For a large class of chaotic attractors there is a natural probabilistic structure: This is given by a probability measure, μ, on the chaotic attractor Λ, that is, an assignment of probabilities $\mu(E)$ to sets E contained in or intersecting Λ. This is the unique probability measure with the property that for open sets, V, and generic initial conditions x_0 in U_Λ, $\mu(V)$ is the limiting relative frequency of the occurrence that $x_t = F^t(X_0)$ is contained in V, that is, $\mu(V) = \lim_{t\to 0} 1/t \#\{s \le t : x_s \varepsilon V\}$, where we use the notation $\#\{A\}$ to signify the cardinality of a set A. This is called the *natural measure*, or the *Sinai–Ruelle–Bowen measure*. The natural measure has the property of being invariant: $\mu(U) = \mu(F^{-1}U)$.

In particular, because the natural measure describes the asymptotic statistical behavior of most orbits, it is the natural choice to use in a statistical treatment of the behavior of generic initial conditions. Moreover, we can use this measure to obtain a natural (asymptotically) stationary stochastic structure for time series of observations of dynamic systems with chaotic attractors, as follows:

$$P(y_{t_1} \le a_1, y_{t_2} \le a_2, y_{t_3} \le a_3, \ldots, y_{t_p} \le a_p) =$$
$$\mu[\{x : h(F^{t_1}x) \le a_1, \ldots, h(F^{t_p}x) \le a_p\}].$$

In considering the nature of this stochastic structure, it is natural to recall some basic definitions. By definition, a *stochastic process* is family of functions on a probability space, indexed by a time parameter. A stochastic process y_t is said to be *purely deterministic* if it is possible to predict the future precisely on the basis of the past, that is, if there is a function $q(a_1, a_2, \ldots, a_k, \ldots)$ of a (possibly infinite) number of real valued parameters such that

$$y_{t+1} = q(y_t, y_{t-1}, \ldots, y_{t-k}, \ldots)$$

for all times t; one can show that this is essentially equivalent to the assertion that the conditional expectation $E(y_t | y_{t-n}, y_{t-n-1}, \ldots, y_{t-n-k}, \ldots) = y_t$ for all n. At the opposite extreme, a process is said to be *purely nondeterministic* $E(y_t | y_{t-n}, y_{t-n-1}, \ldots, y_{t-n-k}, \ldots)$ converges to Ey_t as $n \to \infty$. In other words, past observations lose their predictive value completely as the age of the observations increases. As an example of such a process, one can consider the transitive Markov chains. There are also processes intermediate between the two extremes of purely deterministic and purely nondeterministic processes, which have some, but not complete, predictability [see Rozanov (1967) for details]. We note that the possibility that a stochastic process may be purely deterministic is an eventuality allowed by the generality of our definition of stochastic structure. However, a purely deterministic process may be characterized by certain degeneracies of the probabilistic structure; in particular, the conditional distribution $P(y_t \le a | y_{t-n}, y_{t-n-1}, \ldots, y_{t-n-k}, \ldots)$ is degenerate in the same way that a known parameter is degenerate, namely that

$P(y_t \leq a \mid y_{t-n}, y_{t-n-1}, \ldots, y_{t-n-k}, \ldots)$ is equal to zero if a is less than the actual value of of y_t and equal to one if greater than or equal to the actual value of y_t.

Relative to the above characterization of stochastic processes, we have the following result, which is a composite of results of Kolmogorov and Sinai characterizing nondeterministic properties of "K-automorphisms" (see Walters 1982 p. 95), Bowen (1975), and others who establish the K-automorphism property for various chaotic dynamic system of interest. See Taylor (1988) for a proof.

Proposition 10.1: *Let the observation function h take discrete values only. Then, the observation time series is purely nondeterministic for a large class of chaotic dynamic systems, including uniformly hyperbolic systems as well as some nonuniformly hyperbolic cases.*

We remark that we have been unable to determine the validity of the analogous result for continuous-time chaotic systems, but every other formally stated result in this section has a natural extension to the continuous-time case.

On the other hand, when the observation function h is smooth, most (we conjecture all) observation time series of chaotic dynamic systems are purely deterministic. This follows from results of Aeyels (1981), and (independently) of Takens (1980), on the embedding of dynamic systems; Packard et al. (1980) used these methods prior to Aeyels and Takens, and quote a result of Ruelle as justification. These results show that, when a time series comes from a dynamic structure, it is almost always possible to use the time-series data to reconstruct a model of the observed dynamic system F, h. The idea is to regard a "window" of length k in the time series, that is, a finite subsequence of the time series of the form $(y_i, y_{i-1}, \ldots, y_{i-k+1})$, as defining a point in k-dimensional space $\mathbf{R}^k$. Then, because $y_t = h(x_t)$ and $x_{t+i} = F^t x_i$ $(=$ the tth iterate of F acting on $x_i)$, this point in $\mathbf{R}^k$ is the image of the map

$$\Phi_k(x_i) = [h(x_i), h(Fx_i), h(F^2 x_i) \ldots h(F^{k-1} x_i)].$$

Thus, by moving the window along the time series, one obtains the successive images of all points in the future orbit $\{x_t\}_{t \geq 0}$; the action of moving the window one position along the time series is a representation or model of the action of F on the points of the orbit.

Proposition 10.2: *For sufficiently smooth generic F and h, and for $k > 2n$, the mapping $\Phi_k(x)$ gives a topologically faithful, if possibly distorted, representation in $\mathbf{R}^k$ of points in $\mathbf{R}^n$ and of the action of F on these points.*

In conceptual terms, this means that our model of F is the composition map $\Phi_k \circ F \circ \Phi_k^{-1}$, which is defined on points in $\mathbf{R}^k$ that are actual windows in the observation time series of some initial condition x_0. For such a window we have

$$\Phi_k \circ F \circ \Phi_k^{-1}(y_i, y_{i-1}, \ldots, y_{i-k+1}) = (y_{i+1}, y_i, \ldots, y_{i-k+2})$$

for all i, so that y_{i+1} is a function $(y_i, y_{i-1}, \ldots, y_{i-k+1})$. Hence, because we may consider the time series y_t to be a sample of a stochastic process with probabilities given by the natural measure as described above, we have the following.

Corollary 10.1: *For generic smooth dynamic systems F and observation function h, the observation time series is purely deterministic.*

We may use this model of F as the basis of a practical method of predicting the future behavior of chaotic time series. If F has a chaotic attractor Λ so that generic orbits of F are dense in Λ, the sequence of windows $\{(y_i, y_{i-1}, \ldots, y_{i-k+1}) : i \geq 0\}$ fills out a picture of the attractor, and also tells us where points of the attractor go under the influence of F. When we have a sufficiently large number of values in the time series in some small region of the attractor, we may locally fit the data to obtain a polynomial approximation of F [see, e.g., Sidorowich and Farmer (1988) or Sauer, Yorke, and Casdagli (1991), as well as references contained therein; the latter reference also contains certain extensions of the embedding results quoted above]. These local approximations can be patched together to obtain a global approximation of F within some error. This global approximation can be iterated to obtain an approximation of F^t. However, as a consequence of the sensitive dependence of chaotic dynamics, the error of this approximation grows exponentially with time, up to some maximum. Thus, we may "predict the future" of our time series, but the accuracy of these predictions depends strongly on the number of data points that we have to work with, and deteriorates rapidly with increased length of time interval over which we wish to predict.

In other words, a consequence of the exponential growth of the error of prediction is that the purely deterministic observation time series have qualitatively the same kind of difficulty with respect to prediction that a purely nondeterministic observation time series has, when viewed with limited accuracy or on a long timescale. Thus, in practice, the distinctions between these ideal considerations of determinism and nondeterminism are blurred. We may analyze this qualitative similarity of behavior quantitatively, in several different ways. For example, suppose that observations are accurate only to $\pm \varepsilon$, for some positive ε. In this case, the time series from an observation function $h(x)$ is indistinguishable from that of a discrete observation function $\tilde{h}(x)$ with the property that $|h(x) - \tilde{h}(x)| < \varepsilon$. As we have seen above, when the dynamics are chaotic, the observation time series of $\tilde{h}(x)$ will be nondeterministic. Thus, the time series will be indistinguishable to some accuracy ε from a purely nondeterministic time series, with a consequent loss in the ability to predict the future behavior of the process to any useful accuracy. We also can consider the behavior of chaotic observation time series when viewed on a long timescale. The following proposition considers this situation, and can be proven as a special case of results discussed by Taylor (1993).

Proposition 10.3: *Let F be a uniformly hyperbolic map on $\mathbf{R}^n$, and let Λ be a chaotic attractor for F, with natural measure μ. Then, for generic initial conditions in the basin-of-attraction U_Λ and for generic smooth observation functions h, there is a $\sigma^2 > 0$ and a Brownian motion $B(t) = B(t, x_0, \omega)$ having sample paths parameterized in part by the initial condition x_0 [see Taylor (1993) for details], such that*

$$\left| \frac{1}{\sqrt{N}} \sum_{k=0}^{[N_t]} h(F^k x_0) - \frac{\sigma}{\sqrt{N}} B(N_t, x_0, \omega) \right| \leq \frac{K}{N^\varepsilon}$$

for a suitable choice of constant $\varepsilon > 0$, for t in any bounded interval, and for suitable constant $K > 0$ depending on this interval. In the above formula, we use the standard notation that $[b]$ denotes the integer part of a real number b, that is, the largest integer less than b.

To interpret this result, we recall that Brownian motion has a scaling invariance property: $(1/\sqrt{N})B(N_t)$ is again a Brownian motion with the same statistics as $B(t)$. When we also recall that continuous-time Gaussian white noise may be considered to be the time derivative of Brownian motion, we may rephrase the proposition as the statement: *The observation process $y_t = h(F^t x_0)$, when viewed on a timescale so long that a large number of increments of t occur during one unit of time, is indistinguishable from Gaussian white noise*

We stress that this proposition is stated for smooth observation functions, for which we expect the observation time series to be purely deterministic; it may seem surprising that a purely deterministic process can approximate white noise. We remark also that this proposition is valid for low-dimensional dynamic systems, for example, two- or three-dimensional; much of the literature seems to expect stochastic-like behavior for high-dimensional dynamic systems and regular behavior for low-dimensional systems. We may view these results as a statement that a chaotic time series, even a deterministic chaotic time series, which produces entropy, or information, at a rate too great for our processing equipment (computer or brain) to process, is essentially random.

As a consequence of these various mechanisms for random behavior of chaotic time series, it is our view that statistical test formulated to distinguish between chaotic time series and stochastic time series cannot, in fact, do so. The reason for this is that the class of chaotic time series contains a continuum of possible behaviors including purely nondeterministic time series and, even if one excludes such nondeterministic processes, has white noise as one type of limiting behavior. This is not to say that such statistical tests may not distinguish correctly between certain purely deterministic chaotic time series for which embedding methods may yield accurate predictions about the short-term future behavior of the time series, and those chaotic and/or stochastic time series for which embedding methods are not completely effective. We feel, however, that a proper conceptual foundation informed of the probabilistic structures of the problem can play an important part in the formulation of such tests.

3   Prediction

It is our view that some part of the interest in embedding methods in the context of chaos has more to do with an interest in predicting the future with sufficient accuracy (based on the past, because that is all we have experience with) rather than because the properties of chaos may be related to any observed properties of the time series of interest. Accordingly, we discuss some theoretical tools from the theory of prediction of nonlinear stochastic processes for the treatment of this problem; these tools have been relatively little discussed in an applied modeling context. Nonetheless, we feel that these tools may be usefully combined with the embedding method to characterize nonlinear regularities of time series, even when the time series is nondeterministic. Much of what is considered below is more or less well known from a probabilistic point of view (see, e.g., Rozanov 1967) although its application in the context discussed in the preceding section may have novel aspects.

We again restrict our consideration to stationary stochastic time series $\{y_t\}$ for which t takes all integer values. Suppose that $\{y_t\}$ is purely deterministic process and that $y_{t+1} = q(y_t, y_{t-1}, \ldots)$. We say that $\{y_t\}$ is k-step deterministic if q does not depend on more than the first k values of the past, that is, $q = q(y_t, y_{t-1}, \ldots, y_{t-k+1})$. We can call q the *one-step predictor* of $\{y_t\}$. By iteration of the one-step predictors, we obtain the j-step predictor for every j: We can predict the future behavior of the process arbitrarily far in the future.

One way to obtain a one-step predictor, at least in theory, is to search over the space of all functions $\hat{q}(y_t, y_{t-1}, y_{t-2}, \ldots)$ of the past values of y, for a function q that will minimize some function-space distance to y_{t+1}, such as the maximum over all t of $|y_{t+1} - \hat{q}(y_t, y_{t-1}, y_{t-2}, \ldots)|$, or the pth mean, which is

$$\sqrt[p]{\text{Mean}_t |y_{t+1} - \hat{q}(y_t, y_{t-1}, y_{t-2}, \ldots,)|^p}.$$

If the function-space distance between y_{t+1} and the minimizing function is zero, then this function provides a one-step predictor. If the minimal distance is not zero, then there is no one-step predictor; we can call the minimizing function the *optimal approximate one-step predictor*. In this case, the time series is nondeterministic. There may or may not be value in having an approximate one-step predictor: If the magnitude of the function-space distance between y_{t+1} and $q(y_t, y_{t-1}, y_{t-2}, \ldots)$ is small, then we can predict with great accuracy, at least for short time intervals. The pth mean distance may be small even for purely nondeterministic processes. Nevertheless, for purely nondeterministic processes, the approximate one-step predictor also will predict the wrong value some fixed percentage of time, and iteration of one-step predictors to obtain j-step predictors can yield rapidly decaying accuracy of prediction.

Given sufficient data, (sub)optimal nonlinear prediction of time series is not conceptually difficult. To take advantage of nonlinear correlations in the time series, on may pursue the embedding procedure describing above, for example, using the local singular value decomposition of Broomhead, Jones, and King (1987) to determine the embedding dimension. This method determines n, the topological dimension of the space or manifold in which the attractor lives (hence also the embedding dimension). The method constructs a local rectangular matrix $X(\xi)$, with rows consisting of time-series windows ξ' of some length p, sufficiently long, having the property of being close (closer than ε) to a particular window ξ (of length p), and computes the singular values $\{\lambda_1 \geq \lambda_2 \geq \lambda_3 \geq \ldots \geq \lambda_m \geq \ldots\}$ of these matrices. According to Broomhead et al. the embedding dimension $k = 2n + 1$ should be determined by the criteria that, for ε sufficiently small, the size of the singular values λ_m stabilizes for $m > n$ (i.e., reaches the noise floor no longer decrease). If the data are sufficiently clean and the time series has a low-dimensional dynamic structure, then for m sufficiently large the eigenvalues λ_m are essentially zero [i.e., to first order in ε, see Broomhead et al. (1987)]. In this case, the embedding produces an image of an attractor with well-defined geometric structures, and there is a smooth function of points in the embedded attractor Λ^* that describes the relationship between $\xi_i = (y_i, y_{i-1}, \ldots, y_{i-\ell}) \in \Lambda^*$ for any i and its successor $\xi_{i+1} = (y_{i+1}, y_i, y_{i-1}, \ldots, y_{i-\ell+1})$; in particular, the successors of a group of sufficiently nearby points are group of points that are also near each other.

In the more general case, however, the λ_m will not be zero even for large k, nor need there even be an obvious break of the size of the λ_m with which to determine a natural assignment of effects to structure versus noise, or which allows the determination of a natural embedding dimension. Here, the embedded attractor need not exhibit a well-defined geometric structure, and the relationship between a point of the embedding and the point that follows by moving the window one time step is not deterministic, that is, the one-step successors of a group of nearby points are not necessarily near each other and (hence) cannot be well described by a smooth function of the position in the embedded attractor.

It is well known that the optimal quadratic mean approximate predictor, that is, the least-squares predictor, of any function of the one-step-in-the-future embedded state $f(\xi_{i+1})$ (e.g., the next value of y_{i+1} of the time series itself) conditioned on the fact that the past values $\{\xi_i, \xi_{i-1}, \xi_{i-2}, \ldots, \xi_{i-k}, \ldots\}$ are given, is the conditional expectation of ζ on the past. Although there are optimal estimation criteria other than least squares, such as maximum likelihood, most of these may also, like the conditional expectation, obtained from the conditional probability distribution

$$P(\xi_{n+1} | \xi_n, \xi_{n-1}, \xi_{n-2}, \ldots).$$

Under certain continuity assumptions, a good approximation of the conditional distribution can be obtained from the embedding as an empirical distribution of a collection of points ξ_{i+1} in the embedded attractor having the property that their predecessors $\{\xi_i, \xi_{i-1}, \xi_{i-2}, \ldots\}$ all take values close to some particular set of values $\{\xi_n, \xi_{n-1}, \xi_{n-2}, \ldots\}$.

For example, the optimal least-squares approximate predictor of the statistic f, the conditional expectation of $f(x)$, is approximated as

$$E(f | \xi_n, \xi_{n-1}, \ldots \xi_{n-m}) = \frac{1}{N} \sum_j f(\xi_{j+1}),$$

where the sum is over all $(m+2)$-windows $\xi_{j+1}^{m+2} = \{\xi_{j+1}, \xi_j, \xi_{j-1}, \ldots, \xi_{j-m}\}$ of the attractor with the property that the subwindow $\xi_j^{m+1} = \{\xi_j, \xi_{j-1}, \ldots, \xi_{j-m}\}$ is uniformly close to the sequence $\{\xi_n, \xi_{n-1}, \ldots, \xi_{n-m}\}$ (closer than ε for some choice of ε), where N is the number of sequences ξ_{j+1}^{m+2} satisfying this property, and where f is evaluated on the last entry, ξ_{j+1}, of each of these sequences. This number N must be sufficiently large for this empirical conditional expectation to be taken as a statistically valid approximation; hence, there must be a sufficiently larger number of observed values of the time series to fill out the attractor near the points $\{\xi_n, \xi_{n-1}, \ldots, \xi_{n-m}\}$. We reemphasize that, in general, this conditional mean of f is *not* equal to f evaluated on the optimal estimate of x, that is, to $f[E(\xi_{n+1} | \xi_n, \xi_{n-1}, \ldots, \xi_{n-m})]$.

This procedure deserves several remarks.

(1)   Suboptimal predictors can be obtained by looking at the probabilities conditioned on less than the full set of past data; for chaotic time series and other approximately nondeterministic processes, these may be very close to optimal. Often the conditional-probability distribution will depend only weakly on the distant past, but strongly on some few values of the recent past. A simple but crude measure of this that is useful sometimes is the variance. However, the variance does not reflect any nonlinear geometric structures of the conditional probability;

such nonlinear structures contain information on nonlinear regularities of the process.

(2) A common modeling assumption is that the error of the approximate prediction is a Gaussian white noise independent of the past observed values of the time series. In actuality, the error process need be either Gaussian nor white nor independent: The distribution will be non-Gaussian and depend on the past values of the time series. Another assumption, sometimes distinct, is that the time series is Markovian, that is, $P(\xi_{i+1}|\xi_i, \xi_{i-1}, \xi_{i-2}, \ldots) = P(\xi_{i+1}|\xi_i)$ depends only on the most immediate past; an actual dependence on the more extended past may limit the accuracy of this assumption.

(3) Results obtained by conditioning on $\xi_i, \xi_{i-1}, \xi_{i-2}, \ldots \xi_{i-j}$ are conceptually and practically equivalent to dealing with an embedding into $(k \times j)$-dimensional space rather than k-dimensional space. Thus, taking account of dependence on the past imposes greater memory and CPU requirements. One would like to determine the optimal trade-off between accuracy and computational complexity, although there seems to be no obvious criteria with respect to which one may say precisely what this means.

(4) When the criteria of Broomhead et al. (1987) is strictly satisfied, in the sense that the singular values λ_k no longer decrease for k larger than the embedding dimension, a predictor with optimal variance is then obtained by conditioning on only the last observed state value. This amounts to a weak-sense Markovian situation, that is, a locally linear-Gaussian approximation. Again, this criterion cannot select for nonlinear regularities.

We remark that taking prediction as a fundamental concern suggests a new criterion for determining the embedding dimension. For a generic time series, of which we want to predict the future values, there is no reason to suppose that there are underlying geometric structures such as one has in the case that the time series comes from observing a low-entropy, finite-dimensional dynamic system. We should view the embedding procedure as a method of codifying nonlinear structure for the purposes of prediction. In this context, the embedding dimension may be chosen to optimize predictability of a particular Markov approximation scheme in the sense of remarks (2) and (3), above, or perhaps some convex function of predictability and computational cost: Both the accuracy of prediction and computational complexity may be strictly increasing with the number of past values taken into account. The term "predictability" may be taken as some numerical measure of the predictive value of a scheme: The pth means of the prediction error as defined above suggest themselves.

4 Embedding methods in the presence of noise

In this section, we give a brief synopsis of recent results reported by Taylor and DiMasi (1994); a full treatment is forthcoming. These results are valid in the case of time series generated by a finite-dimensional chaotic system, as distinct from the results of the preceding section, which are valid much more generally. We believe that these results represent an novel approach to reconstruction of dynamics in the presence of observational noise. The embedding method as originally developed was framed in the context of ideal dynamic systems with ideal observations, "ideal" meaning noise-free, in particular. Attempts to treat more realistic models have preceded by introducing additive noise, so that one obtains the following model of the time series $\{y_t\}_{t=0}^{\infty}$:

$$x_{t+1} = F(x_t) + u_t$$

$$y_t = h(x_t) + w_t$$

It has usually been assumed that the dynamic noise and the observational noise processes are each independent and identically distributed, as well as mutually independent. As with the classic embedding methods, x, F, and h are assumed to be unknown and inaccessible to observation.

A rigorous analysis of this problem can be performed in the simplified case that u_t is negligible (or identically equal to zero), as follows. Assume as above, that x, F, and h are unknown, but suppose (for now) that the distribution of w_t is known; the noise statistics of a measuring apparatus may be well documented, at least in some cases. Denote by z_t the value of $h(x_t)$ so that $y_t = z_t + w_t$. Let ξ_t be the k-window $(y_t, y_{t-1}, \ldots, y_{t-k+1})$, let $\zeta_t = (z_t, z_{t-1}, \ldots, z_{t-k+1})$, and let $W_t = (w_t, w_{t-1}, \ldots, w_{t-k+1})$. Note that ζ_t and W_t are accessible only through their sum, ξ_t, and that ξ_t and W_t are highly correlated.

The problem that we wish to solve is that of recovering the embedded attractor, Λ, as characterized by the points $\{\zeta_t\}_{t=0}^{N}$, from the noisy data consisting of the collection of points $\{\xi_t\}_{t=0}^{N}$. For example, one may wish to do this by smoothing on this data set; one may apply multiple iterations of Bayes' theorem to find the disappointing result that the optimal estimate of ζ_t is, in fact, ξ_t. The reason for this is simple. We can regard ζ_t as a sample of a k-dimensional random variable, call it ζ, that is, the $\mathbf{R}^k$-valued function on Λ that distributes points according to the probability distribution $\bar{\mu}$ induced on $\mathbf{R}^k$ from the natural measure μ by Φ_k. Likewise, W_t is the sample of a k-dimensional random variable W, which is independent of ζ; ξ_t can be regarded as a sample of the sum of the random variables $\xi = \zeta + W$. In these terms, our problem can be regarded as that of recovering ζ from $\zeta + W$. Thus formulated, the task is revealed to be a problem of inverse type of probability theory, more closely related to the problem of determining a initial temperature distribution from the distribution at some later time, for example, than to smoothing or filtering problems. In common with many inverse problems, it has the property of being ill posed: Very small errors in one's characterization of ξ can yield much larger errors in the solution obtained for ζ.

Nevertheless, the problem is susceptible to treatment using the body of techniques that have been developed for the solution of inverse-type problems. As is common for such problems, we are required reduce the complexity of the problem by incorporating information of the structure of allowable solutions into our solution algorithms, to make the computation feasible. In particular, the problem is closely related to problems of recovering visual images from blurred images in a low-light-intensity environment, and techniques developed to treat this problem are readily generalized to treat reconstruction of dynamics as well.

REFERENCES

Aeyels, D. (1981). Generic observability of differentiable systems, *SIAM J. Control Optim.* **19**, 595–603.

Bowen, R. (1975). *Equilibrium States and the Ergodic Theory of Axiom A Diffeomorphisms*, Lecture Notes in Mathematics No. 470, Springer–Verlag, Berlin.

Broomhead, D. S., Jones, R., and King, G. P. (1987). Topological dimension and local coordinates from time series data, *J. Phys. A: Math. Gen.* **20**, L563–9.

Packard, N. H., Crutchfield, J. P., Farmer, J. D., and Shaw, R. S. (1980). Geometry from time series, *Phys. Rev. Lett.* **45**, 712.

Rozanov, I. A. (1967). *Stationary Random Processes*, Holden-Day.

Sauer, T., Yorke, J., and Casdagli, M. (1991). Embedology, *J. Stat. Phys.*, **65**, 579–616.

Sidorowich, J. J., and Farmer, J. D. (1988). Exploiting chaos to predict the future and reduce noise. In *Evolution, Learning and Cognition*, ed. Y. C. Yee, World Scientific.

Smale, S. (1980). *The Mathematics of Time*, Springer–Verlag, Berlin.

Takens, F. (1980). Detecting strange attractors in turbulence. In *Dynamical Systems and Turbulence*, Lecture Notes in Mathematics No. 898, Warwick.

Taylor, T. J. (1988). Observations of chaotic dynamical systems and randomness, In *Analysis and Control of Nonlinear Systems*, North-Holland, pp. 493–8

(1993). On stochastic and chaotic motion. *Stochastics and Stochastics Reports*, pp. 179–97.

Taylor, T. J., and DiMasi, G. B. (1994). Reconstruction of dynamics from noisy observations, *Proceedings of the 33rd Conference on Decision and Control*, Institute of Electrical and Electronics Engineers.

Walters, P. (1982). *An Introduction to Ergodic Theory*, Springer–Verlag, Berlin.

CHAPTER 11

Linearity testing and nonlinear modeling of economic time series

Timo Teräsvirta

This paper reviews some recent developments in testing linearity of a model against well-specified nonlinear alternatives. Special attention is paid to the situations in which the nonlinear model is not identified under the null of linearity. A specification strategy for smooth transition regression models based on linearity tests is discussed and illuminated by an example.

1   Introduction

In many fields of science, such as physics, most theories are nonlinear rather than linear. There in nonlinear theory in economics as well, but a vast majority of applications have been based on linear theory or linear approximations to nonlinear theory. Such linear approximations seem to have served economists rather well, because otherwise they would have been given up long ago. A typical feature of many economic theories is that they may not imply an econometric model whose parameters can be estimated. Even if they do, the resulting model may not be fully specified; for example, the dynamic structure of the model may remain unspecified. Thus, a completely specified nonlinear model ready for estimation and hypothesis testing is more of an exception than a rule.

This state of affairs is bound to have implications for modeling nonlinear economic relationships. There in clearly a need for tests for testing linearity either within a family of nonlinear models or against unspecified alternatives. Because linear approximations have worked well in the past, they should not be given up without first empirically making sure that they indeed are inadequate for the purpose and data at hand. For situations in which economic theory does

The paper is based on a presentation at the Workshop on Nonlinear Dynamics in Economics, in Florence, Italy, July 6–17, 1992, organized by the European University Institute and Centre for Economic Policy Research (CEPR). I wish to thank the participants of the workshop for their comments and the organizers for their hospitality. Any errors and shortcomings are my sole responsibility.

281

not provide a completely parameterized nonlinear model, data-based modeling procedures are required to help the model builder find an appropriate model within a family of parametric models, estimate its parameters, and evaluate the estimated model. The modeling strategy of Box and Jenkins (1970) for constructing autoregressive moving-average models offers a convenient analogy.

The issues of linearity testing and data-based nonlinear model building in economic research are discussed. The starting-point is that the economic phenomena can be described adequately using stochastic models. The possibility that economic processes are deterministic is not considered here. Section 2 studies linearity testing against well-specified alternatives. Section 3 reviews a modeling strategy for constructing smooth transition regression (STR) and smooth transition autoregressive (STAR) models. Section 4 discusses an example of the specification, estimation, and evaluation cycle, and Section 5 contains final remarks.

2   Linearity tests against well-specified nonlinear alternatives

Linearity tests can be divided into two broad categories: the tests against a specific alternative and those against an unspecified alternative. I concentrate on the former category. For an overview of tests against an unspecified alternative, see Granger and Teräsvirta (1993, chap. 6). However, the dividing line between them is somewhat diffuse. Some tests originally presented as general linearity tests against an unspecified alternative also can be viewed as tests against a specific alternative. The linearity test of Tsay (1986) and RESET of Ramsey (1969) are examples of this. On the other hand, the specific alternative need not be unique. The same test can be derived starting from different nonlinear models; see, e.g., Granger and Teräsvirta (1993, chap. 6) for discussion.

Many linearity tests against parametric alternatives are Lagrange multiplier or score tests. The score principle is the natural one to use for deriving linearity tests because it does not require any parameter estimation under the alternative. The estimation of a linear auxiliary regression often suffices. Pagan (1978) already pointed this out. There is often another compelling reason for applying the score principle. A few nonlinear models are only identified under the null hypothesis of linearity. Neither the Wald nor the likelihood ratio test is directly applicable, because the model cannot be consistently estimated under the alternative if the null hypothesis happens to be true. The following exposition ignores the possibility that the nonlinear model has a nonconstant conditional variance. It is discussed by Granger and Teräsvirta (1993, chap. 6); see also Teräsvirta, Tjøstheim and Granger (1994).

Consider the following nonlinear model:

$$y_t = \varphi' w_t + f(\theta, w_t) + u_t \tag{11.1}$$

where $w_t = (1, y_{t-1}, \ldots, y_{t-p}, x_{t1}, \ldots, x_{tk})'$, u_t are independent and identically distributed errors, $E(u_t|I_t) = 0$, cov $(u_t|I_t) = \sigma_u^2$, with $I_t = \{y_{t-j}, j > 0, x_{t-i}, i \geq 0\}$. Assume that f is at least twice continuously differentiable with respect to the parameters $\theta = (\theta_1, \ldots, \theta_m)'$. Let $f(0, w_t) = 0$, so that the linearity hypothesis becomes $H_0 : \theta = 0$.

To test this hypothesis, write the conditional (pseudo) logarithmic likelihood function as

$$l(\theta, \varphi; y_T, w_T, w_{T-1}, \ldots, w_1|W_0) = \sum_1^T l_t(\theta, \varphi; y_t|w_t, \ldots, w_1, W_0)$$

$$= c - (T/2) \log \sigma_u^2 - (1/2\sigma_u^2) \sum_1^T u_t^2,$$

where W_0 contains the starting values that can be assumed to be fixed. The block corresponding to θ of the score vector scaled by $1/\sqrt{T}$ becomes

$$\frac{1}{\sqrt{T}} \frac{\partial l}{\partial \theta} = \left(1/\sqrt{T}\sigma_u^2\right) \sum u_t h_t, \quad h_t = \left(\frac{\partial u_t}{\partial \theta_1}, \ldots, \frac{\partial u_t}{\partial \theta_m}\right)'.$$

This is the block that obtains a nonzero value under the null hypothesis. The remaining part of the gradient vector (scaled) is $\frac{1}{\sqrt{T}}\frac{\partial l}{\partial \varphi} = \left(1/\sqrt{T}\sigma_u^2\right) \sum u_t w_t$. The information matrix is block diagonal such that the diagonal element conforming to σ^2 builds a separate block. Thus, the inverse of the block related to θ and evaluated at H_0 becomes

$$I_\theta = (T\sigma_u^2)^{-1} \left\{ \sum \tilde{h}_t \tilde{h}_t' - \sum \tilde{h}_t w_t' \left(\sum w_t w_t'\right)^{-1} \sum w_t \tilde{h}_t' \right\},$$

where $\tilde{h}_t$ is h_t evaluated at H_0. Setting $\tilde{u} = (\tilde{u}_1, \ldots, \tilde{u}_T)'$ where $\tilde{u}_t = y_t - \tilde{\varphi}'w_t$, $\tilde{\varphi}$ is a consistent [ordinary least squares (OLS)] estimator of φ under H_0, the test statistic, in obvious notation, has the form

$$LM = \tilde{\sigma}_u^{-2} \tilde{u}' H (H' M_W H)^{-1} H' \tilde{u} \tag{11.2}$$

where $M_W = I - W(W'W)^{-1}W'$. Under a set of assumptions that are moment conditions for equation (11.2) (see White 1984, Theorem 4.25), equation 11.2 has an asymptotic $\chi^2(m)$ distribution under H_0. A practical way of carrying out the test is by OLS, as follows:

(1) Regress y_t on w_t, compute the residuals $\tilde{u}_t$, and the sum of squared residuals SSR_0.
(2) Regress $\tilde{u}_t$ on w_t and $\tilde{h}_t$, compute the sum of squared residuals SSR_1.
(3) Compute

$$F(m, T - n - m) = \frac{(SSR_0 - SSR_1)/m}{SSR_1/(T - n - m)}$$

with $n = k + p + 1$, which has an approximate F distribution with m and $T - n - m$ degrees of freedom under H_0: $\theta = 0$.

The χ^2 test given by the asymptotic theory is likely to suffer from size problems in small samples if m is large. This is often the case in practice. The use of an F test is recommended instead because of its good size and power properties: see Harvey (1990, pp. 174–5) or Teräsvirta and Anderson (1992) for discussion.

An important special case is the one in which f in equation (11.1) factors as follows:

$$f(\theta, w_t) = (\theta_1' w_t) f_1(\theta_2, \theta_3, w_t) \tag{11.3}$$

and $f_1 (0, \theta_3, w_t) = 0$. Assume that θ_2 is a scalar whereas θ_3 may be a vector. This is the case for many nonlinear models such as smooth transition regression models (Chan and Tong 1986; Granger and Teräsvirta 1993). The linearity hypothesis can be expressed as H_{02}: $\theta_2 = 0$. Note that equation (11.1) with equation (11.3) is only identified under the alternative $\theta_2 \neq 0$ but not under $\theta_2 = 0$. If $\theta_2 = 0$, then θ_1 and θ_3 can take any value. Davies (1977, 1987) considered general solutions to testing problems in which the model is only identified under the alternative. I focus on a more specific technique that works when the model is of type (11.3). If we choose H_{02} as our starting point, we can use the Taylor expansion

$$f_1(\theta_2, \theta_3, w_t) = f_1(0, \theta_3, w_t) + b(0, \theta_3, w_t)\theta_2$$
$$+ R_2(\theta_2, \theta_3, w_t) \approx b_t \theta_2. \tag{11.4}$$

Assume furthermore that b_t has the form

$$b_t = \beta(\theta_3)' k(w_t), \tag{11.5}$$

where $\beta(\theta_3)$ and $k(w_t)$ are $r \times 1$ vectors. Next, replace f_1 in equation (11.3) with the first-order Taylor approximation at $\theta_2 = 0$:

$$t(0, \theta_3, w_t) = \beta(\theta_3)' k(w_t)\theta_2.$$

Then, equation (11.3) becomes

$$\overline{f}(\theta, w_t) = (\theta_1' w_t)[\beta(\theta_3)' k(w_t)]\theta_2$$
$$= \psi_1' w_t + \psi_2' g(w_t)$$

where $\psi_1 = \psi_1(\theta_1, \theta_2, \theta_3)$ and $\psi_2 = \psi_2(\theta_1, \theta_2, \theta_3)$ such that $\psi_2 (\theta_1, 0, \theta_3) = 0$. Vector $g(w_t)$ contains those elements of $k(w_t)w_t'$ that are of higher order than one. From this, it follows that equation (11.1) has the form:

$$y_t = \psi_1' w_t + \psi_2' g(w_t) + u_t^*. \tag{11.6}$$

The test can be carried out as before. After estimating equation (11.1) under H_0, $\tilde{u}_t$ is regressed on w_t and $g(w_t)$, and under H'_{01}: $\psi_2 = 0$, the test statistic has an asymptotic $\chi^2(s)$ distribution if ψ_2 is an $s \times 1$ vector.

From equation (11.6), it is seen that the original null hypothesis H_{02} has been transformed into H'_{01}: $\psi_2 = 0$. Approximating f_1 as in equation (11.4) and reparameterizing the model can be seen as a way of removing the identification problem. However, it also can be seen as a solution in the spirit of Davies (1977, 1987). Let u^* be the residual vector from the OLS regression (11.6). Then,

$$\tilde{u}^{*'} \tilde{u}^* = \inf_{\theta_2, \theta_3} u(\theta)' u(\theta),$$

and the test statistic

$$\overline{F} = \sup_{\theta_2, \theta_3} F(\theta_2, \theta_3) = \frac{[\tilde{u}'\tilde{u} - \inf u(\theta)' u(\theta)]/s}{\inf \tilde{u}(\tilde{\theta})'\tilde{u}(\tilde{\theta})/(T - n - s)}.$$

The price of the neat asymptotic null distribution with s degrees of freedom is that not all of the information about the parameter structure of equation (11.3) has been used, because the original null hypothesis contains only one parameter.

As an example, assume that $w_t = \overline{w}_t = (y_{t-1}, \ldots, y_{t-p})'$, and let $\beta(\theta_3) \equiv 1$ and $k(w_t) = y_{t-1}^2$. This gives $\psi_2 = \theta_2\theta_1$ and $g(w_t) = (y_{t-1}^3, y_{t-1}^2 y_{t-2}, \ldots, y_{t-1}^2 y_{t-p})'$. The resulting test is the linearity test against the univariate exponential autoregressive model of Saikkonen and Luukkonen (1988). In that model, $f_1 = 1 - \exp\{-\theta_2(y_{t-1} - \theta_3)^2\}$ with $\theta_3 = 0$, $\theta_2 > 0$. Take another example where

$$k(w_t) = w_t, \quad \psi'_2 g(w_t) = \sum_{i=1}^{p} \sum_{j=1}^{p} \varphi_{ij} y_{t-i} y_{t-j}$$

and H_{01}: $\varphi_{ij} = 0$, $i = 1, \ldots, p$; $j = i, \ldots, p$. The test is the first of the three linearity tests against smooth transition autoregression in Luukkonen, Saikkonen and Teräsvirta (1988) when the delay parameter d is unknown but it is assumed that $1 \leq d \leq p$. The number of degrees of freedom in the asymptotic null distribution equals $p(p + 1)/2$. If w_t also contains variables other than lags of y_t, the test is a linearity test against smooth transition regression; see Granger and Teräsvirta (1993, chap. 6). If the delay parameter is known, $k(w_t) = (1, y_{t-d})'$, so that $g(w_t) = (y_{t-1}y_{t-d}, \ldots, y_{t-d}^2, \ldots, y_{t-p}y_{t-d})'$ and the F test has p and $T - 2p - 1$ degrees of freedom.

In some cases, the first-order Taylor-series approximation is inadequate. For instance, let $\theta_1 = (\theta_{10}, 0, \ldots, 0)'$ in equation (11.3) so that the only nonlinearity is described by f_1 multiplied by a constant and, furthermore, let $k(w_t) = w_t$. Then, $\theta'_1 w_t \equiv \theta_{10}$ and $\beta(\theta_3)'k(w_t) = \beta(\theta_3)'w_t$. The LM-type test thus has no power against the alternative because the auxiliary regression (11.6) does not contain higher-order terms: $\psi_2 \equiv 0$. In such a situation, a higher-order

Taylor-series approximation of f_1 is needed for constructing a proper test; see Luukkonen et al. (1988) for discussion.

The aforementioned considerations are based on a suitable approximation of the original model. Recently, Hansen (1992) considered a situation with an additional complication. Not only is the model not identified, but the score vector is identically zero under the null hypothesis. Hansen's solution is to regard the likelihood function of the model as an empirical process of the unknown parameters. The distribution of a modification of this process under the null hypothesis can be obtained by simulation. In what follows, I do not use this theory but apply the results based on approximating the function f_1 in equation (11.3).

3   Building STAR models

3.1   Specification

Anyone fitting parametric models to economic data is regularly faced with the problem that economic theory does not provide a fully specified model. This is different from some other disciplines such as physics. Because the linear approximations have served economists reasonably well in the past, testing linearity before fitting nonlinear models is necessary. If linearity is rejected, the problem of selecting an appropriate nonlinear model emerges. Various specification techniques have been presented in the literature. So far, it seems that the most successful are the ones that are restricted to a rather narrow class of models such as the technique of Tsay (1989) for specifying threshold autoregressive models. Here, I concentrate on the specification, estimation, and evaluation cycle for STAR models described earlier (Teräsvirta 1994) and completed by Eitrheim and Teräsvirta (1996). Its generalization to multivariate STR models is straightforward and discussed by Granger and Teräsvirta (1993, chap. 7).

The STAR model can be defined as follows (see, e.g., Chan and Tong 1986; Luukkonen et al. 1988; or Teräsvirta 1994):

$$y_t = \pi_{10} + \pi_1' \overline{w}_t + (\pi_{20} + \pi_2' \overline{w}_t) F(y_{t-d}) + u_t, \tag{11.7}$$

where $u_t \sim \text{nid}(0, \sigma_u^2)$, $\pi_j = (\pi_{j1}, \cdots, \pi_{jp})'$, $j = 1, 2$, and $\overline{w}_t = (y_{t-1}, \ldots, y_{t-p})'$ as before. F is a bounded continuous function. Following Teräsvirta (1994), I consider two different STAR models. The first one is the logistic STAR (LSTAR) model in which

$$F(y_{t-d}) = (1 + \exp\{-\gamma(y_{t-d} - c)\})^{-1}, \gamma > 0. \tag{11.8}$$

The second one is the exponential STAR (ESTAR) model for which

$$F(y_{t-d}) = 1 - \exp\{-\gamma^*(y_{t-d} - c^*)^2\}, \gamma^* > 0.$$

Both models are locally linear autoregressive models. The local behavior of the STAR model is dependent on the transition variable y_{t-d}. The LSTAR and ESTAR models are contrived to characterize different types of nonlinear behavior. An LSTAR model can be used in situations where the local behavior changes monotonically from one extreme regime ($F = 0$) to the other ($F = 1$). An ESTAR model can be applied in cases where the local behavior is very similar for both high and low values of y_{t-d}, but different for the midrange of the transition variable. Examples can be found in Teräsvirta and Anderson (1992).

The data-based specification of STAR models was discussed in Teräsvirta (1994) and consists of several stages. First, specify a linear autoregressive model to form a base for linearity tests. This can be done by applying model selection criteria such as the Akaike information criterion (AIC, Akaike 1974). Second, test linearity against STAR. Any STAR model is of type (11.3) so that theory applied in Section 2 is available for deriving an LM-type test against STAR. Third, determine the delay parameter d, which is usually unknown. Next, select between an LSTAR and an ESTAR model. Finally, determine the lag structure of the selected model. For the second stage, an LM-type linearity test with power both against LSTAR and ESTAR alternatives is required. Applying the theory outlined in the previous section, this turns out to be the test of the null hypothesis H_0: $\beta_1 = \beta_2 = \beta_3 = 0$ in the auxiliary regression

$$\tilde{u}_t = \beta_0' w_t + \beta_1' \overline{w}_t y_{t-d} + \beta_2' \overline{w}_t y_{t-d}^2 + \beta_3' \overline{w}_t y_{t-d}^3 + \eta_t \tag{11.9}$$

where y_{t-d} is the transition variable and $\tilde{u}_t$ is the OLS residual from the linear regression $y_t = \beta' w_t + u_t$. Equation (11.9) is also used for determining the delay d. The test is carried out for $d = 1, \ldots, D$, and the value of d for which the test yields the smallest p-value is selected if that value is sufficiently small. If it is not, the model is taken to be linear. This procedure is motivated as follows. Suppose that there is a true STAR model with delay d that generated the data. Then, the LM-type test against that alternative has good power properties. If an inappropriate delay is selected for the test, the resulting test may still have power against the true alternative, but the average power is less than if the test is carried out for the correct d. Thus, the strongest rejection of the null hypothesis suggests that the corresponding delay be selected. For more discussion of this procedure see Teräsvirta (1994) and Granger and Teräsvirta (1993, chap. 7). If linearity is rejected and d is determined, then the next step is to choose between LSTAR and ESTAR models. This can be done by testing a set of nested null hypotheses within equation (11.9): they are H_{03}^*: $\beta_3 = 0$, H_{02}^*: $\beta_2 = 0 |$ $\beta_3 = 0$, and H_{01}^*: $\beta_1 = 0 | \beta_2 = \beta_3 = 0$. The strongest rejection of the three tests again provides the basis for the decision. If the test of H_{02}^* has the smallest p-value, select an ESTAR model; otherwise, choose an LSTAR model. The rationale for this rule and the numerical demonstration of its small-sample performance, which in the light of the examples seems satisfactory, was given previously (Teräsvirta 1994).

Specifying the lag structure of the selected STAR model can be done by estimating STAR models starting with a large number of parameters, omitting redundant ones and reestimating. Although, in principle, one moves from general to specific, it does not seem possible to have strict formal rules for carrying out the necessary reduction of the model.

3.2   Estimation and evaluation

The parameters of a STAR model can be estimated by nonlinear least squares. The general theory with the conditions for consistency and asymptotic normality is given by Klimko and Nelson (1978): These conditions are often difficult to verify in practice. For more discussion, see Tong (1990, chap. 5). The theory is limited to stationary models, but, in practice, many interesting STAR models may not satisfy the existing sufficient conditions for stationarity. On the other hand, no useful necessary conditions are available. Caution is thus required in interpreting the estimation results. The estimation of parameters also presents numerical difficulties. Local minima may abound so that several sets of starting values should be used. Estimating parameter γ in LSTAR models may present numerical problems when γ is large. If an estimate is obtained, it is bound to be rather uncertain; see Teräsvirta (1994) for discussion.

The next step after estimation is to evaluate the properties of the estimated model. Recently, Eitrheim and Teräsvirta (1996) considered an LM test for the hypothesis of no error autocorrelation in STAR models. The hypotheses of normality of errors and no autoregressive conditional heteroskedasticity (ARCH) in errors can be tested using standard procedures. The long-term properties of the model have to be checked. This can only be done numerically by generating solution paths for the nonlinear difference equation implied by the estimated model starting from different sets of starting values. If at least one of the paths diverges, the model is rejected. Postsample forecasting can be used as a check as well, and a linear model then is a natural benchmark.

Eitrheim and Teräsvirta (1996) also discussed a linearity test for checking whether the estimated STAR model explains all nonlinearity in the data. Their idea is to extend equation (11.1) with equation (11.3) by another additive component and define the following model:

$$y_t = \varphi' w_t + (\theta_1' w_t) f_1(\theta_2, \theta_3, w_t) + (\delta_1' w_t) f_2(\delta_2, \delta_3, w_t) + u_t \qquad (11.10)$$

where f_2 is bounded and $f_2(0, \delta_3, w_t) = 0$. The null hypothesis is H_0: $\delta_2 = 0$. An LM-type test statistic can be based on the third-order Taylor expansion of f_2 about $\delta_2 = 0$ and requires the estimation of equation (11.10) only under the null hypothesis. The Monte Carlo evidence in the paper indicates that the small-sample properties of the test are satisfactory.

As Eitrheim and Teräsvirta (1996) pointed out, the test of no remaining non-linearity against an additive STAR-type component can be carried out separately for different values of d and completed with the test sequence for selecting between model families similar to that discussed above. This can be used as a respecification device much like the original linearity test against STAR.

4   Application

To illustrate the above model selection strategy, I take a previous application as an example (Teräsvirta 1995). The series to be modeled is that of the first differences of the annual logarithmic real per capita U.S. gross national product, 1889–1987. A few authors (e.g., DeLong and Summers 1988; Durlauf 1989; and Harvey 1985) have argued that the parameters of the (linear) data-generating process have not remained constant over time. On the other hand, formal parameter constancy tests do not support this view. Thus, the possibility that the data-generating process is not linear has been considered (Teräsvirta 1995).

The first step of model specification is to select an autoregression (AR) model for linearity tests. AIC suggests an AR(4) model. Its estimated equation is

$$y_t = 0.018 + 0.37y_{t-1} - 0.083y_{t-2} - 0.031y_{t-3} - 0.22y_{t-4} + \hat{u}_t \quad (11.11)$$

$$(0.0056)(0.010) \quad (0.11) \quad (0.11) \quad (0.10)$$

$$R^2 = 0.20, \, s_L = 0.0466, \, F_{AR}^*(1, 88) = 0.13 \, (0.72),$$

$$F_{AR}^*(6, 83) = 1.88 \, (0.093), \, ML(2) = 8.0 \, (0.019),$$

$$sk = -0.66, \, ek = 1.56, \, LJB = 16.3(3 \times 10^{-4})$$

where the figures below the coefficient estimates are standard deviations, s_L is the residual standard error, $F_{AR}^*(p_1, p_2)$ is the F-version of the LM test of no error autocorrelation against autocorrelation of order p_1, $ML(k)$ is McLeod–Li tests with k degrees of freedom, sk is skewness, ek is excess kurtosis, and LJB is the Lomnicki–Jarque–Bera normality test of errors. The figures in parentheses following values of the test statistics are p-values. Note that the p-value of the ML test of no autoregressive conditional heteroskedasticity is small. This may tempt one to model the series by an AR(4) model with ARCH, but that is not done here. There is also excess kurtosis in the residuals as well as negative skewness, which indicates the presence of mainly negative outlines. The roots of the characteristic polynomial appear in Table 11.1 and indicate that the model is stationary. The dominating, but not very strong, cyclical component has a period of about 8.5 years.

The results of the linearity test of the GNP series are shown in Table 11.2. It is seen that linearity is strongly rejected for $d = 2$, which determines the delay. Testing down within equation (11.9) gives the result that only H_{02}^* is rejected at

Table 11.1. *Roots of the characteristic polynomials of the*
autoregressive (AR) model (11.11) and the ESTAR model (11.12)

Model	Root	Modulus	Period
AR	0.57 ±0.52i	0.77	8.6
	−0.39 ±0.47i	0.61	2.8
ESTAR			
$F = 0$	0.38 ±0.35i	0.52	8.4
	−0.51 ±0.66i	0.83	2.8
$F = 1$	1.09 ±0.64i	1.26	11.8
	−0.43		
	−0.27		

Table 11.2. *p-values of linearity tests of autoregressive model*
(11.11) against STAR and tests of no remaining nonlinearity in
ESTAR model (11.12)

	Delay			
Null hypothesis	1	2	3	4
Linearity tests, equation (11.8)				
$H_0(\beta_1 = \beta_2 = \beta_3 = 0)$	0.014	0.0018	0.30	0.22
$H_{03}^*(\beta_3 = 0)$		0.51		
$H_{02}^*(\beta_2 = 0\|\beta_3 = 0)$		3×10^{-5}		
$H_{01}^*(\beta_1 = 0\|\beta_2 = \beta_3 = 0)$		0.81		
Tests of no remaining nonlinearity, equation (11.10)				
$H_0(\delta_2 = 0)$	0.94	0.86	0.49	0.24

any conventional level of significance, but then the *p*-value is very small. The decision rule described above thus leads to choosing an ESTAR model.

The estimated ESTAR model is

$$y_t := 0.020 - 0.27y_{t-1} - 0.19y_{t-2} + 0.25y_{t-3} - 0.19y_{t-4} \quad (11.12)$$

$$(0.0053)(0.17) \quad (0.11) \quad (0.16) \quad (0.086)$$

$$+ (1.75y_{t-1} - 1.12y_{t-3})\{1 - \exp[-0.56 \times 394$$

$$(0.31) \quad (0.28) \quad (0.28)$$

$$\times (y_{t-2} - 0.0039)^2]\} + \hat{u}_t$$

$$(0.0040)$$

$R^2 = 0.46, s = 0.0394, s^2/s_L^2 = 0.72, F_{AR}(6, 72) = 1.1 \, (0.36), \text{ML}(2) = 0.17 \, (0.92), sk = -0.49, ek = 0.31, \text{LJB} = 4.2 \, (0.12).$

Note that $1/\hat{\sigma}^2(y) = 394 \, (\hat{\sigma}^2(y)$ is the sample variance of y; this standardization of the exponent in the transition function is useful for finding a proper starting value for γ). The residual variance of equation (11.12) is only 72 percent of that of equation (11.11), and R^2 has more than doubled. F_{AR} (6,72) is the above-mentioned Lagrange multiplier test of no error autocorrelation against AR(6) [or MA(6)] errors. The residuals cannot be considered nonnormal (LJB test), although there is negative skewness (more on this below). Note in particular that there is no trace of ARCH in the residuals. The results of the linearity test based on (11.10) for the estimated model are found in Table 11.2. The p-values are high at all lags considered, so that, according to that test, equation (11.12) seems an adequate description of the nonlinearity in the series. The numerical long-term solutions of equation (11.12) derived from different starting values all seem to converge to a stable stationary point $y_\infty = 0.015$, so that the process is not inherently cyclical.

An illuminating way of interpreting STAR equations is to consider characteristic polynomials at various values of F. The most interesting values are zero and unity, respectively. In ESTAR model (11.12), the former one corresponds to near-zero growth, whereas $F = 1$ is related both to strong expansion and deep recession.

Consider the roots of the characteristic polynomial of the mid regime $F = 0$. They are the roots of $g(z) = z^4 + 0.27z^3 + 0.19z^2 - 0.25z + 0.19$ and are stationary as shown in Table 11.1. The two complex pairs have the same periods as the roots of equation (11.11), but the 8.5-year cycle is now the less prominent of the two. On the other hand, the characteristic polynomial of the outer-regime $F = 1$ contains a complex pair of explosive roots with the period of 12 years. This means that the process is locally explosive at large values of $|y_{t-2}|$. Being a complex pair, these roots induce a cycle, and therefore the process tends to return toward the mid regime where it is locally stationary after first swinging out as a result of a large shock.

As explained previously (Teräsvirta 1995), this suggests the following interpretation. If the shocks to the economy remain small, the fluctuations in output on the average are small as well. There is nothing inherent in the system to generate large fluctuations. However, if the economy is hit by a very large shock, then a realization may leave the stationary domain and move to an explosive oscillatory path. Yet the process does not explode. The reason is that, because the mid regime is stationary, the cycle practically dies out upon return of the output growth, positive or negative, to the mid range. Another large shock or a sequence of small ones is needed to start another cyclical movement of the same kind. Because these shocks are exogenous, the large ones show up as large absolute residuals in the model. It turns out that the three large residuals of equation (11.12) in 1930, 1939, and 1946 all have a plausible interpretation. Most of the largest residuals in absolute value during the observation period are negative, which explains the negative skewness found in the residuals.

It is not possible to describe this kind of behavior with a univariate linear model. On the other hand, it is quite conceivable that the large variations in the series may be adequately described by a multivariate, perhaps multiequation, linear model.

5   Final remarks

I have stressed the importance of linearity testing before embarking upon the estimation of nonlinear models. I highlight a simple principle for deriving linearity tests against specific nonlinear alternatives in situations where the nonlinear model is not identified under the null of linearity. A typical model of this kind is the STAR model or its multivariate generalization, the STR model. These tests form the backbone of a modeling strategy for specifying the type of the STAR or STR model when it is not known from theory. Similar tests are available to check whether the specified and estimated model really explains all of the nonlinearity that seems present in the data.

The obvious success of this modeling strategy is based on the fact that the STAR or STR family of models is a rather restricted one. Similar strategies can be devised to specify nonlinear models of other types as well. However, it seems to me that an important precondition for a successful model selection technique is that the set of alternative models from which to choose be sufficiently restricted. This concerns selecting parametric models. Nonparametric modeling techniques have not been discussed here, and the reader is referred to Härdle (1990), Teräsvirta et al. (1994), and Tjøstheim (1994), who summarize recent developments in that area.

REFERENCES

Akaike, H. (1994). A new look at the statistical model identification, *IEEE Trans. Autom. Control*, **AC-19**, 716–23.

Box, G. E. P., and Jenkins, G. M. (1970). *Time Series Analysis. Forecasting and Control*, Holden-Day, San Francisco, CA.

Chan, K. S., and Tong, H. (1986). On estimating thresholds in autoregressive models, *J. Time Ser. Anal.*, **7**, 179–90.

Davies, R. B. (1977). Hypothesis testing when a nuisance parameter is present only under the alternative, *Biometrika*, **64**, 247–54.

    (1987). Hypothesis testing when a nuisance parameter is present only under the alternative, *Biometrika*, **73**, 33–43.

DeLong, J. B., and Summers, L. H. (1988). On the existence and interpretation of a "unit root" in U.S. GNP, Working Paper No. 2716, National Bureau of Economic Research, New York.

Durlauf, S. N. (1989). Output persistence, economic structure, and the choice of stabilization policy, *Brookings Pap. Econ. Act.*, **2/1989**, 69–116.

Eitrheim, Ø., and Teräsvirta, T. (1996). Testing the adequacy of smooth transition autoregressive models, *Journal of Econometrics*, **74** (forthcoming)

Granger, C. W. J., and Teräsvirta, T. (1993). *Modelling Nonlinear Economic Relationships*, Oxford University Press, Oxford, England.

Hansen, B. M. (1992). The likelihood ratio test under nonstandard conditions: Testing the Markov switching model of GNP, *J. Appl. Econ.*, **7**, S61–S82.

Härdle, W. (1990). *Applied Nonparametric Regression*. Cambridge University Press, Cambridge, England.

Harvey, A. C. (1985). Trends and cycles in macroeconomic times series, *J. Bus. Econ. Stat.*, **3**, 216–27.

(1990). *The Econometric Analysis of Time Series*, 2nd ed. MIT Press, Cambridge, MA.

Klimko, L. A., and Nelson, P. I. (1978). On conditional least squares estimation for stochastic processes, *Ann. of Stat.*, **6**, 629–42.

Luukkonen, R., Saikkonen, P., and Teräsvirta, T. (1988). Testing linearity against smooth transition autoregressive models, *Biometrika*, **75**, 491–9.

Pagan, A. (1978). Some simple tests for non-linear time series models, Discussion Paper No. 7812, Center for Operations Research and Econometrics (CORE), Louvain-la-Neuve, Belgium.

Ramsey, J. B. (1969). Tests for specification errors in classical linear least-squares regression analysis, *J. Roy. Stat. Soc., B*, **31**, 350–71.

Saikkonen, P., and Luukkonen, R. (1988). Lagrange Multiplier tests for testing nonlinearities in time series models, *Scand. J. of Stat.*, **15**, 55–68.

Teräsvirta, T. (1994). Specification, estimation, and evaluation of smooth transition autoregressive models, *J. Am. Stat. Assoc.*, **89**, 208–18.

(1995). Modelling nonlinearity in U.S. Gross National Product 1889–1987, *Empirical Economics*, **20**, 577–97.

Teräsvirta, T., and Anderson, H. M. (1992). Characterizing nonlinearities in business cycles using smooth transition autoregressive models, *J. Appl. Econ.*, **7**, S119–36.

Teräsvirta, T., Tjøstheim, D., and Granger, C. W. J. (1994). Aspects of modelling nonlinear time series. In *Handbook of Econometrics*, Vol. 4, eds. R. F. Engle and D. L. McFadden, North-Holland, Amsterdam, pp. 2919–57.

Tjøstheim, D. (1994). Nonlinear time series analysis: A selective review, *Scand. J. Stat.*, **21**, 97–130.

Tong, H. (1990). *Non-linear Time Series. A Dynamical System Approach*, Oxford University Press, Oxford, England.

Tsay, R. (1986). Non-linearity tests for time series, *Biometrika*, **73**, 461–6.

(1989). Testing and modeling threshold autoregressive processes. *J. Am. Stat. Assoc.*, **84**, 231–40.

White, H. (1984). *Asymptotic Theory for Econometricians*, Academic Press, Orlando, FL.

PART IV

Frequency domain methods and nonlinear business cycles

CHAPTER 12

The importance of being nonlinear: A frequency-domain approach to nonlinear model identification and estimation

Richard Ashley and Douglas Patterson

Tests for a nonlinear generating mechanism based on the estimated bispectrum strongly suggest that a number of important financial and economic time series are highly nonlinear and should be well represented by a quadratic generalization of the usual (linear) autoregressive (AR) process. But models for these data fitted to this quadratic AR specification appear overparameterized and do not forecast well, so it is not feasible to use the postsample forecasting performance of such models to quantify the importance of nonlinearity in the generating mechanisms for these time series..

We resolve this apparent paradox by deriving a frequency-domain representation for the quadratic generalization of the AR process. In particular, we demonstrate that a highly nonlinear time series with a simple frequency-domain representation will have a complicated time-domain representation characterized by a large number of mostly-small coefficients, many of the largest of which correspond to terms at apparently arbitrary lag pairs. Preliminary results indicate that this new class of nonlinear frequency-domain models will allow us to develop an identification/estimation/diagnostic-checking algorithm (in which the sample bispectrum plays a role analogous to that of the sample correlogram in the Box–Jenkins algorithm) that will provide a useful framework for modeling and forecasting a variety of economic and financial time series.

1   Introduction

Linear modeling methods (e.g., the Box–Jenkins approach) can be applied to any stationary time series, regardless of whether the mechanism that generated the data is linear or not. However, if the generating mechanism is substantially

Virginia Polytechnic Institute and State University, Economics Department Working Paper No. E93-22

297

nonlinear (and the linear modeling technique is properly applied), then the innovations (one-step-ahead forecasting errors) implied by the resulting (misspecified) linear model are serially uncorrelated (by construction) but they are not serially independent. Because they are serially dependent, the one-step-ahead forecasting errors made by the linear model are themselves forecastable, albeit not linearly forecastable. Thus, where the underlying generating mechanism is actually nonlinear, linear modeling methods not only provide a distorted representation of the mechanism that generated the data, they also yield suboptimal – in some cases highly suboptimal – forecasts.

These potentially serious inadequacies of the linear modeling framework motivated the development of statistical tests for whether or not the underlying generating mechanism of an observed time series is in fact nonlinear. Tests based on the sample bispectrum were proposed by Subba Rao and Gabr (1980) and by Hinich (1982); the Hinich bispectral test was further developed and applied by Hinich and Patterson (1985), Ashley, Patterson, and Hinich (1986), Ashley and Patterson (1989), and Ashley, Hinich and Patterson (1990). Tests for nonlinear generating mechanisms not based on the sample bispectrum include a test developed by Granger (1980) and Maravall (1983) based on the sample correlogram of the data squared and a test by Brock, Dechert, and Scheinkman (1986, BDS test) based on an estimate of the correlation dimension (Although the BDS test was originally put forth as a test for deterministic chaos, it has come to be viewed as a test for a nonlinear generating mechanism.) The Granger–Maravall and BDS tests are not emphasized here because the results below are more closely related to the Hinich bispectral test.

In Ashley et al. (1986) and Ashley and Patterson (1989), we found that the size of the Hinich bispectral test converges to the nominal value for sample sizes as low as $N = 256$ and that the test has substantial power, even in such "small" samples, to detect a wide variety (albeit not all varieties) of nonlinear generating mechanisms. Turning to "real" data, we found that the bispectral test often rejects the null hypothesis of a linear generating mechanism at extremely high significance levels. For example, with 456 monthly values of the U.S. index of industrial production (IP_t) the null hypothesis of a linear generating mechanism can be rejected at the 0.0001 percent level.

Does this test result imply that the generating mechanism (the U.S. economy) is highly nonlinear? Or does it merely imply that the test itself is extremely powerful with a sample period of this length? The only way to answer this question in a credible and satisfying way is to identify and estimate a statistically adequate model for IP_t – that is, a model whose fitting errors at least pass the bispectral test for serial independence – and examine its out-of-sample forecasting performance.

The bispectrum and the Hinich bispectral nonlinearity test are briefly described in Section 2. The basis for the bispectral test suggests that its power arises primarily from quadratic forms of nonlinearity. This observations strongly suggests that time series (such as IP_t) for which the bispectral test emphatically rejects a linear generating mechanism ought to be well represented by a quadratic generalization of the usual $AR(p)$ process:

$$x(t) = \mu + \sum_{j=1}^{p} a_j x(t-j) + \sum_{j=1}^{p} \sum_{k=1}^{p} b_{ij} x(t-j) x(t-k) + u(t), \quad (12.1)$$

where $u(t)$ is serially independent.[2] In practice, however, we find that models for times series, such as IP_t, based on equation (12.1) do not work well at all. The b_{ij} estimates are typically small; and the occasional sizable b_{ij} estimate is usually at some isolated lag (pair) that makes little sense. Moreover, the resulting fitted models forecast (out of sample) quite poorly, regardless of whether one eliminates some, none, or all of the terms with small estimated t ratios.

These results lead us to conjecture that the bispectrum is concentrating the information on the (approximately quadratic) nonlinear dynamics of series such as IP_t into a relative handful of peaks in the frequency domain. In contrast, this same information is spread over a large number of $b_{ij} x(t-i) x(t-j)$ terms in the time domain, resulting in highly overparameterized models.

In Section 3, we provide a frequency-domain representation for time series generated by nonlinear processes such as equation (12.1), in Section 4, we use this representation to explicitly demonstrate that a strong, simple model in the frequency domain typically implies a time-domain model with large numbers of small b_{ij} coefficients. In Section 5, we briefly indicate how the frequency-domain representation can be utilized to identify and estimate nonlinear forecasting models for economic and financial time series (such as IP_t) whose estimated bispectra strongly indicate a nonlinear generating mechanism, thereby allowing us to quantify the importance of nonlinear modeling for such time series.

2   Brief exposition of bispectrum-based nonlinearity test

The bispectral nonlinearity test is based on the observation that, if $x(t)$ is the result of a linear filter applied to a serially independent innovation series,

$$x(t) = \sum_{i=0}^{\infty} a_l u(t-i) \quad u(t) \sim \text{i.i.d.}[0, \sigma^2], \quad (12.2)$$

---

[2] This is a scalar $GAR(1,p)$ process in the notation of Mills and Mittnik (1993). We have not implemented their Bayesian estimation method, but we note that they present only within-sample fitting results.

then the squared skewness function for $x(t)$,

$$\Psi^2(f_1, f_2) = \frac{|B(f_1, f_2)|^2}{S^2(f_1)S^2(f_2)S^2(f_1 + f_2)} \tag{12.3}$$

is a constant for all frequency paris (f_1, f_2). $B(f_1, f_2)$ in equation (12.3) is the bispectrum of $x(t)$ at frequency pair (f_1, f_2). Assuming that $x(t)$ is third-order stationary with mean zero, $B(f_1, f_2)$ is defined as the double Fourier transform of the third-order cumulants of $x(t)$:

$$B(f_1, f_2) \equiv \sum_{j=0}^{N-1}\sum_{k=0}^{N-1} e^{-i2\pi(f_1 j + f_2 k)} E\{x(t)x(t-j)x(t-k)\} \tag{12.4}$$

and $S^2(f)$ is the ordinary spectrum of $x(t)$ at frequency f:

$$S^2(f) \equiv \sum_{j=0}^{N-1} e^{-i2\pi f j} E\{x(t)x(t-j)\}. \tag{12.5}$$

Thus, one can test whether or not the generating mechanism for $x(t)$ is linear [i.e., one can test whether or not equation (12.2) holds] by estimating $\Psi^2(f_1, f_2)$ over all frequency pairs (f_1, f_2) and testing whether the estimated values for $\Psi^2(f_1, f_2)$ vary across the frequency pairs more than one would expect from chance alone.

$\Psi^2(f_1, f_2)$ can be thought of as the squared magnitude of a "scaled" bispectrum for $x(t)$; this scaling makes $\Psi^2(f_1, f_2)$ invariant to the application of any linear filter to $x(t)$. (This is why prewhitening of $x(t)$ is unnecessary.) There is no loss of generality, then, in supposing that $x(t)$ is serially uncorrelated, implying that $S^2(f) = \sigma_x^2$. If $x(t)$ is serially independent as well as serially uncorrelated, then $E\{x(t)x(t-j)x(t-k)\} = 0$ for all nonzero values of j and k, in which case, equation (12.4) implies that $B(f_1, f_2) = E\{[x(t)]^3\} = \mu'_3$, so that $\Psi^2(f_1, f_2) = (\mu'_3)^2/\sigma_x^6$, a constant not depending on f_1 or f_2. In contrast, if $E\{x(t)x(t-j)x(t-k)\}$ is not zero for some $(j^*, k^*) \neq (0, 0)$, then

$$B(f_1, f_2) = E\{[x(t)]^3\} + e^{i2\pi(f_1 j^* + f_2 k^*)}$$
$$\times E\{x(t)x(t-j^*)x(t-k^*)\}, \tag{12.6}$$

so that $\Psi^2(f_1, f_2)$ clearly does depend on f_1 and f_2. Evidently, the degree to which $\Psi^2(f_1, f_2)$ varies across the frequency pairs (and hence, the power of the bispectral test) hinges crucially on the nonzeroness of the third-order cumulants, $E\{x(t)x(t-j)x(t-k)\}$, for various values of j and k.

The ordinary (linear) AR(p) model is characterized by second-order terms such as $E\{x(t)x(t-k)\}$. For example,

$$x(t) = \rho x(t-k) + u(t) \tag{12.7}$$

with serially uncorrelated, mean-zero, innovation $u(t)$, then

$$p \lim[\hat{\rho}^{\text{ols}}] = \frac{E\{x(t)x(t-k)\}}{\sigma_x^2}. \qquad (12.8)$$

Analogously, the observation that the power of the bispectral nonlinearity test arises from terms of the form $E\{x(t)x(t-j)x(t-k)\}$ strongly suggests that the bispectral test is, in fact, testing for nonlinearities that can be approximated by a quadratic generalization of the $AR(p)$ model:

$$x(t) = \mu + \sum_{j=1}^{p} a_j x(t-j) + \sum_{j=1}^{p} \sum_{k=1}^{p} b_{ij} x(t-j)x(t-k) + u(t) \qquad (12.9)$$

with one or more of the $b_{ij} \neq 0$.

3 Frequency-domain representation theorem for the quadratic $AR(p)$ model

Unfortunately, the specification given above as Equation (12.9) does not work well with actual time series for which the bispectral nonlinearity test emphatically rejects the null hypothesis of a linear generating mechanism. The estimated b_{ij} coefficients are typically quite small for such time series and the occasional sizable b_{ij} estimate is often at some isolated (i, j) pair that makes no sense. Unsurprisingly, the resulting fitted models provide out-of-sample forecasts which are inferior to those obtained using a linear model specification.

How can this be when the squared skewness function, $|\Omega(f_1, f_2)|^2$, is varying substantially over the (f_1, f_2) pairs? It is our conjecture that the bispectrum is concentrating the information on the nonlinear dynamics in such time series into a relative handful of peaks in the frequency domain, whereas the same information is spread out over a large number of b_{ij} coefficients in the time domain, resulting in over-parametrized time-domain models. This conjecture leads to the following theorem:

Frequency-Domain representation theorem: If

$$x(t) = \mu + \sum_{j=0}^{p-1} \sum_{k=0}^{p-1} \beta_{j,k} x(t+j-p)x(t+k-p) + \frac{u(t)}{\Phi(B)}, \qquad (12.10)$$

where $\phi(B)$ is a pth-order polynomial in the lag operator, and $u(t)$ is a serially independent innovation, then $X(m; t)$, the spectral representation at frequency m/p of a block of p observations on $x(t)$ beginning in period $t - p + 1$ and ending in period t, is:

$$X(m; t) = \sum_{s=0}^{p-1} \gamma_{m,s} X(-s; t-1)X(s+m; t-1) + \varepsilon(m; t) \qquad (12.11)$$

where $\varepsilon(m; t)$ is complex-valued innovation term; $X(m; t)$ is the Fourier transform (at frequency m/p) of the data block $x(t - p + 1) \cdots x(t)$,

$$X(m; t) = \sum_{\tau=0}^{p-1} e^{-i\frac{2\pi}{p}m\tau} x(t + 1 + \tau - p) \quad \text{for} \quad m \in [0, p - 1]; \quad (12.12)$$

and the nonlinearity coefficients in the two representations $\{\gamma_{m,s} \text{ and } \beta_{j,k}\}$ are simply related:

$$\beta_{j,k} = \frac{1}{p} \sum_{m=0}^{p-1} \sum_{s=0}^{p-1} \gamma_{m,s} \exp\left\{ -i\frac{2\pi}{p}[s(k - j) + m(k + 1)] \right\}$$

$$(12.13)$$

$$\gamma_{m,s} = \frac{1}{p} \sum_{j=0}^{p-1} \sum_{k=0}^{p-1} \beta_{j,k} \exp\left\{ i\frac{2\pi}{p}[s(k - j) + m(k + 1)] \right\}$$

Proof: Backtransforming equation (12.12) yields

$$x(t + 1 + \tau - p) = \frac{1}{p} \sum_{m=0}^{p-1} e^{i\frac{2\pi}{p}m\tau} X(m; t) \quad (12.14)$$

for $\tau \in [0, p - 1]$. Evaluating this expression at $\tau = p - 1$ yields

$$x(t) = \frac{1}{p} \sum_{m=0}^{p-1} e^{i\frac{2\pi}{p}m(p-1)} X(m; t) = \frac{1}{p} \sum_{m=0}^{p-1} e^{i\frac{2\pi}{p}m} X(m; t) \quad (12.15)$$

Substituting equation (12.11) into equation (12.15),

$$x(t) = \frac{1}{p} \sum_{m=0}^{p-1} \sum_{s=0}^{p-1} \gamma_{m,s} e^{-i\frac{2\pi}{p}m} X(-s; t - 1) X(s + m; t - 1)$$

$$+ \frac{1}{p} \sum_{m=0}^{p-1} e^{-i\frac{2\pi}{p}m} \varepsilon(m; t). \quad (12.16)$$

Identifying the error terms in equation (12.10) and (12.16) with one another,

$$\mu + \frac{u(t)}{\phi(B)} = \frac{1}{p} \sum_{m=0}^{p-1} e^{-i\frac{2\pi}{p}m} \varepsilon(m; t), \quad (12.17)$$

so that the two representations [equations (12.10) (12.11)] are equivalent if and only if

$$\sum_{j=0}^{p-1}\sum_{k=0}^{p-1}\beta_{j,k}x(t+j-p)x(t+k-p) = \frac{1}{p}\sum_{m=0}^{p-1}\sum_{s=0}^{p-1}\gamma_{m,s}e^{-i\frac{2\pi}{p}m}$$

$$\times X(-s;t-1)X(s+m;t-1). \qquad (12.18)$$

Replacing t with $t-1$ in equation (12.12) to obtain the Fourier transform of the data block $x(t-p)\dots x(t-1)$ at frequency $(-s/p)$ and at frequency $(s+m)/p$, the right-hand side of equation (12.18) becomes

$$\frac{1}{p}\sum_{m=0}^{p-1}\sum_{s=0}^{p-1}\gamma_{m,s}e^{-i\frac{2\pi}{p}m}\left[\sum_{j=0}^{p-1}e^{-i\frac{2\pi}{p}(-s)j}x(t+j-p)\right]$$

$$\times\left[\sum_{k=0}^{p-1}e^{-i\frac{2\pi}{p}(s+m)k}x(t+k-p)\right]. \qquad (12.19)$$

Thus, bringing the sums over j and k out and rearranging, the right-hand side of equation (12.19) can be written

$$\sum_{j=0}^{p-1}\sum_{k=0}^{p-1}\left\{\frac{1}{p}\sum_{m=0}^{p-1}\sum_{s=0}^{p-1}\gamma_{m,s}e^{-i\frac{2\pi}{p}[(m-sj+(s+m)k]}\right\}$$

$$\times x(t+k-p)x(t+j-p), \qquad (12.20)$$

so that the two representations are equivalent so long as the β_{jk} are related to the γ_{ms} as given by equation (12.13).

4   Example of a simple model in the frequency domain

For example, suppose that a third-order stationary time series $x(t)$ is generated by the quadratic generalization of usual (linear) AR(p) process given in equation (12.10) with $p = 12$, but in such a way that the spectral representation of its (nonlinear) generating mechanism has the simple form:

$$X(m;t) = \gamma_{3,4}X(-4;t-1)X(7;t-1)+\varepsilon_3 \quad (m=3)$$

$$= \gamma_{9,8}X(-8;t-1)X(5;t-1)+\varepsilon_9 \quad (m=9)$$

$$= \varepsilon_m \quad \text{(for all other values of } m), \qquad (12.21)$$

where $\gamma_{3,4} = (\gamma_{9,8})^* = (0.25, 0.80)$. [The $\gamma_{9,8}$ term is included to ensure that $X(m;t)$ is symmetric around the folding frequency $\{m/p = 1/2\}$ in such a way that it is the Fourier transform of a real-valued block of time-domain data.]

The magnitudes of the $\gamma_{m,s}$ specified in equation (12.21) are plotted in Figure 12.1; the magnitude of $\gamma_{3,4}$ and $\gamma_{9,8}$ is $(0.25^2 + 0.80^2)^{1/2} = 0.84$ the rest are

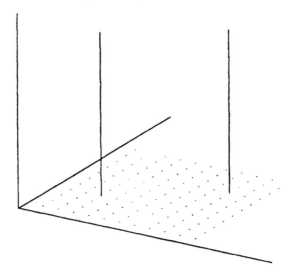

Figure 12.1. Plot of $|\gamma_{m,s}|$ (on vertical axis) versus $m \in [0, 11]$ and $s \in [0, 11]$.

all, of course, zero. The absolute values of the concomitant (real-valued) $\beta_{j,k}$ implied by equation (12.13) are plotted in Figure 12.2. The $\beta_{j,k}$ vary in a wave-like pattern over the range of j and k with a maximum height of only 0.14.

Clearly, a time-domain model for data generated in this way will typically contain lots of small $\beta_{j,k}$ estimates, many of the largest of which will occur at odd-looking (j, k) values. Yet, the $x(t)$ process implied by equation (12.21) is, in principle, forecastable.

We generated a large sample of data from this process by simulating equation (12.10) using the $\beta_{j,k}$ implied by equation (12.21) and setting: $\mu = 0$, $\phi(B) = 1$, and $u(t) \sim$ i.i.d. uniform $[0, 1]$. From the sample variance of the $x(t)$ generated in this way [and the known population variance of $u(t)$], we infer that this model has a potential $R^2 = 0.13$, which is quite respectable for what is essentially a one-term generating process.

A time plot of this generated data looks reasonably stationary. The sample correlogram, partial correlogram, and (smoothed) periodogram over 2,400 of these $x(t)$ observations indicate that $x(t)$ is not quite serially uncorrelated, but these serial correlations are so small that $x(t)$ is not linearly forecastable to any appreciable extent. [e.g., none of the first 25 sample serial correlations exceeds 0.07 in magnitude.] The sample bispectrum and squared skewness functions for $x(t)$, in contrast, both yield a single large peak. Moreover, when we estimate $\gamma_{3,4}$ and $\gamma_{9,8}$ by fitting the implied time-domain model to these data, we obtain a model whose postsample one-step-ahead errors are satisfyingly small [i.e., their

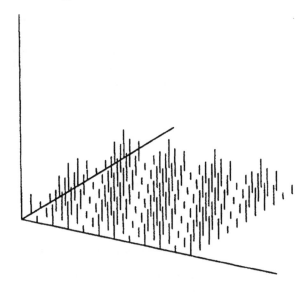

Figure 12.2. Plot of $|\beta_{j,k}|$ (on vertical axis) versus $j \in [0, 11]$ and $k \in [0, 11]$.

sample variance is close to the variance of $u(t)$] and whose squared skewness function is essentially flat across the frequency pairs.

5   Conclusions

The results in Sections 3 and 4 strongly suggest that the frequency-domain representation proposed here can, in principle, provide a practical framework for identifying and estimating a nonlinear model for a time series such as IP_t in which the bispectral nonlinearity test emphatically rejects a linear generating mechanism but for which a straightforward implementation of a time-domain quadratic model yields poor results. Our previous work with the bispectral test indicates that such behavior may be quite common among interesting economic and financial time series, and so, the ability to identify and estimate statistically adequate nonlinear models for time series exhibiting this kind of behavior is of practical importance. Moreover, the out-of-sample forecasting performance of the resulting nonlinear model, relative to that of a linear model, then can be used to quantify the importance of nonlinearity in the generating mechanism of time series such as IP_t.

Much work remains to be done, however. For example, it is our conjecture that the frequency domain representation will yield simple conditions for quadratic time-domain models such as equation (12.10) to be covariance stationary. Similarly, although our results indicate that, for many important financial and macroeconomic time series, the $\Psi^2(f_1, f_2)$ function contains in a concentrated form the crucial information needed to specify a quadratic nonlinear AR model, further work is necessary to determine which of several identification algorithms based on sample estimates of the $\Psi^2(f_1, f_2)$ function will provide the most reliable results with limited sample data.

REFERENCES

Ashley, R. A., and Patterson, D. M. (1989). Linear versus nonlinear macroeconomics: A statistical test, *Int. Econ. Rev.*, **30**, 685–704.

Ashley, R. A., Patterson, D. M., and Hinich, M. J. (1986). A diagnostic test for nonlinear serial dependence in time series fitting errors, *J. Time ser. Anal.* **7**, 165–78.

Ashley, R. A., Hinich, M. J., and Patterson, D. M. (1990). Nonlinear serial dependence in industrial stock returns, In *Advances in Mathematical Programming and Financial Planning*, Vol. 2, JAI Press, Inc.

Brock, W. A., Dechert, W. D., and Scheinkman, J. (1986). A test for independence based on correlation dimensin, unpublished manuscript, University of Wisconsin–Madison.

Granger, C. W. J. (1980). Forecasting white noise, Working Paper No. 80-31. San Diego, Economics Department, University of California.

Hinich, M. J. (1982). Testing for gaussianity and linearity of a stationary time series, *J. Time Ser. Anal.* **3**, 169–76.

Hinich, M. J., and Patterson, D. M. (1985). Evidence of nonlinearity in stock returns, *J. Bus. Econ. Stat.*, **3**, 69–77.

Maravall, A. (1983). An application of nonlinear time series forecasting, *J. Bus. Econ. Stat.* **1**, 66–74.

Mills, J. A., and Mittnik, S. (1993). Bayesian modelling of nonlinear vector autoregressive processes, unpublished manuscript.

Subba Rao, T. and Gabr, M. M. (1980). A test for linearity of stationary time series, *J. Time Ser. Anal.* **2**, 145–58.

CHAPTER 13

Trends, shocks, persistent cycles in evolving economy: Business-cycle measurement in time-frequency representation

Ping Chen

One basic problem in business-cycle studies is how to deal with nonstationary time series. Trend-cycle decomposition is critical for testing competing dynamic models, including deterministic and stochastic approaches in business-cycle theory. A new analytical tool of time-frequency analysis, based on the symmetry principle in frequency and time, is introduced for studies of business cycles. The Wigner–Gabor–Qian (WGQ) spectrogram shows a strong capability in revealing complex cycles from noisy and time-dependent time series. Traditionally, nonstationary process implies a stochastic one. By using the term of time-dependent time series, it implies either deterministic or stochastic process or a mix of the two. Competing detrending methods, including the first-difference (FD) and Hodrick–Prescott (HP) filter, are tested with the mixed case of cycles and noise. The FD filter does not produce a consistent picture of business cycles. The HP filter provides a good window for pattern recognition of business cycles. Existence of stable characteristic frequencies from economic aggregates provides strong evidence of endogenous cycles and valuable information about structural changes. Economic behavior is more like an organism rather than random walks. Remarkable stability and resilience of market economy can be seen from the insignificance of the oil price shocks and the stock-market crash. Surprising pattern changes occurred during wars, arm races, and the Reagan administration. Like microscopy for biology, time-dependent time-series analysis opens a new space for business-cycle studies and policy diagnostics. The role of timescale and preferred reference from economic observation is discussed. Fundamental constraints for Friedman's rational arbitrageurs are reexamined from the view of information ambiguity and dynamic instability. Nonlinear economic dynamics offers a new perspective in empirical measurement and theoretical analysis.

1   Introduction

An alternative title for econometric literature could be: "Business-cycle measurement without model specification."

One basic difficulty in business-cycle studies is that measurement is behind observation. We need analytical tools to characterize economic complexity. Hitherto, studies of business cycles are based on two alternative methods in time-series analysis. Correlation analysis measures mean, variance, and correlations based on the covariance-stationary model of the identical independent distribution (i.i.d.) process in the time domain. The Fourier spectral analysis measures frequency and amplitude based on the cycle-stationary harmonic oscillations in the frequency domain. However, all of these quantities are subject to changes in the timescale of business cycles. Real signals of economic movements contain both stochastic and deterministic components; therefore, we need new tools in time-series analysis and business-cycle modeling.

Economists realize the need to study nonlinearity and nonstationarity. There are two strategies to address the issue. One strategy is developing nonlinear and nonstationary versions of correlation analysis (Granger and Teräsvirta 1993). Another strategy is developing nonlinear and time-dependent representations of spectral analysis (Chen 1993a). We focus on the second approach in this paper, because it is still in its infancy.

To address time-dependent phenomena, we introduce a new tool of time-frequency analysis that originated in quantum mechanics and acoustic physics (Wigner 1932; Gabor 1946). A recent development in signal processing provides an efficient algorithm for calculating time-frequency distribution, which is a powerful tool to identify deterministic components from short and noisy signals (Chen and Qian 1993; Qian and Chen 1994a,b).

Most economic indicators have fluctuations around a growth trend. Different detrending methods lead to competing perspectives in business-cycle theory. Two detrending methods are tested by time-frequency analysis: the first differencing (FD) and the Hodrick–Prescott (HP) smoothing filter. We find that HP is much better than FD in revealing deterministic patterns from economic time series.

From a wide range of aggregate data, we find the existence of persistent cycles, in addition to color noise. Spectral analysis not only provides complementary evidence of comovements of business fluctuations (Lucas 1981; Kydland and Prescott 1990), but also reveals distinctive patterns of frequency evolution. It is found that characteristic frequencies of business indicators are remarkably stable. Only minor changes occurred under such events, for example, as the oil price shocks in 1973 and the stock-market crash in 1987. Surprisingly, more significant changes happened during the Vietnam War and the Reagan administration. The time lag between frequency responses of different indicators provides important information about the propagation mechanism in the real economy. A new approach of economic diagnostics and policy evaluation can be developed quantitatively.

The new perspective of time-frequency analysis indicates fundamental barriers for Friedman's rational arbitrageurs against market disequilibrium (Friedman, 1953). The roles of timescale, observation reference, dynamic instability, and information ambiguity in studies of business-cycle theory are discussed.

2 Time-frequency representation and complex economic dynamics

It is known that the deterministic and the stochastic approaches are complementary representations of dynamic systems. There are trade-offs in finite realizations of empirical signals. Which representation is useful in science is not a matter of philosophical debate, but a subject of empirical experiment.

Recent development of nonlinear economic dynamics demonstrates that business fluctuations can be explained by deterministic chaos (Benhabib 1992; Day and Chen 1993). Standard tests of deterministic chaos are based on the phase-space representation. The phase-space approach has limited applications in empirical analysis, because a large number of data points and a low level of noise are needed to calculate correlation dimension or to construct the Poincáre section (Chen 1988, 1993a,b). In contrast, time-frequency analysis has a much stronger power for dealing with noisy data.

Time-frequency analysis is a powerful tool in distinguishing white noise and complex cycles. Complex cycles are nonlinear chaotic cycles with irregular amplitudes and sophisticated frequency patterns that are generalizations of linear harmonic cycles with regular amplitudes and well-defined frequencies.

2.1 *Time-frequency distribution and the uncertainty principle*

The simplest time-frequency distribution is the short-time Fourier transform (STFT) by imposing a shifting time window in the conventional Fourier spectrum. STFT has poor resolution in the frequency domain caused by the finite square window in the time domain.

The Wiener–Khinchine theorem indicates that the autocorrelation and the power spectrum are Fourier pairs for a continuous-time stationary stochastic process (Priestley 1981). A natural generalization for the nonstationary process is introducing the instantaneous autocorrelation function $R_t(\tau)$ in the time-dependent power spectrum $P(t, \omega)$:

$$P(t, \omega) = \int R_t(\tau) \exp(-i\omega\tau)d\tau/(2\pi), \qquad (13.1)$$

where the angular frequency $\omega = 2\pi f$.

Considering a symmetric time window, $R_t(\tau)$ can be replaced by the kernel function $s[t + \frac{\tau}{2}]s^*[t - \frac{\tau}{2}]$ to produce a time-dependent power spectrum called the Wigner distribution (WD) (Wigner 1932):

$$\text{WD}(t, \omega) = \int s\left\{t + \frac{\tau}{2}\right\} s^*\left\{t - \frac{\tau}{2}\right\} \exp(-i\omega\tau) d\tau. \tag{13.2}$$

An important development in time-frequency analysis is the Gabor expansion (Gabor 1946). The best resolution in the frequency domain can be achieved by imposing a Gaussian window according to the uncertainty principle in signal processing (Gabor 1946; Papoulis 1977):

$$\Delta t \Delta f \geq (1/4\pi), \tag{13.3}$$

where the equality holds only for the Gaussian function.

Unfortunately, both the WD and the Gabor expansion are unorthogonal. The WD is hard to calculate in continuous time because cross-interference terms are generated by non-orthogonal bases.

A synthesis of these two approaches (WGQ hereafter) leads to a good resolution and an efficient algorithm (Qian and Chen 1994a,b, 1996).[1] The Wigner distribution can be decomposed via the orthogonal-like Gabor expansion in discrete time and frequency. The localized symmetric base function has the form:

$$\text{WD}_b(t, \omega) = 2\exp\{-[(t/\sigma)^2 + (\omega\sigma)^2]\}. \tag{13.4}$$

The time-frequency distribution series (TFDS) are constructed as approximations of the WD.

$$\text{TFDS}_D(t, \omega) = \sum_0^D P_d(t, \omega), \tag{13.5}$$

The zeroeth order of TFDS leads to STFT. The infinite order converges to the WD. For applied analysis, second or third order is a good compromise in characterizing frequency representation without severe cross-term interference.

The WGQ representation in time-frequency analysis has important properties in physics and economics. The WD ensures the conservation of energy density. This implies the conservation of variance in a time-series analysis that is a key constraint in statistical analysis. The Gabor expansion catches periodic components under local observation. The time-frequency distribution series

---

[1] The numerical algorithm has no specific name in the academic field. The originators call their approach the time-frequency distribution series from the view of mathematical formulation. The computer software is marketed by the National Instruments under the commercial name of Gabor spectrogram as a tool kit in the LabView System. The term WGQ representation is proposed by the author from the view of theoretical physics. Certainly, the author will take sole responsibility for this term. We will address this issue elsewhere.

retain leading terms in the energy distribution. These features are critical in analyzing complex dynamics.

2.2   *Time-frequency analysis of noise and chaos*

The development of nonlinear dynamics provides an alternative model of seemingly erratic movements: deterministic chaos, including white chaos (such as the logistic map and the Henon map) in discrete time and color chaos (such as the Rössler model) in continuous time (Rössler 1976; Hao 1990). The "color" of continuous-time chaos is characterized by its characteristic frequency f_c or characteristic period $P_c = 1/f_c$ observed in spectral analysis.

There are some limitations for spectral analysis in testing deterministic chaos. To avoid the aliasing effect, the standard frequency window in spectral analysis is one-half, or P_{min}, the lowest period observable, is two. The characteristic period and the characteristic frequency of white chaos are equal to one. Therefore, white chaos is outside the observational window. Spectral analysis alone is not sufficient to test the existence of color chaos; complementary measurements are needed (Chen 1993a). For studies of business cycles, the discovery of a characteristic frequency of erratic time series provides essential information about the components of deterministic cycles, regardless of whether they are pure-color chaos or mixed-color noise.

In testing deterministic chaos, the power spectrum plays an important role in studying color chaos in laboratory experiments (Swinney and Gollub 1978). In testing chaotic signals, thousands to hundreds of thousands of data points are required by the power spectrum. The noise level should be kept between 2 to 5 percent. The WGQ spectrogram has much stronger power to distinguish deterministic cycles from stochastic noise (Chen and Qian 1993a; Chen 1993c).

The strong power of time-frequency analysis can be understood from the energy distribution of signals. White noise is evenly distributed in time-frequency space whereas deterministic cycles are highly localized. The noise level in the power spectrum is an integration of the energy distribution in the time domain; therefore, the time-frequency distribution has a much higher signal/noise ratio than that of the power spectrum. For example, the autoregressive (AR) model can produce artificial cycles in the power spectrum. It cannot generate a stable frequency line in time-frequency representation (Chen and Qian 1993).

Econometric analysis assumes that all economic variables are random variables. From the view of signal processing and pattern recognition, testing mixed signals of cycles and noise is a more realistic task. Our investigation focuses in this direction. Typical WGQ representations of noise and chaos are shown in Figure 13.1.

Under WGQ representation, deterministic signals are characterized by a localized horizontal zone in the time-frequency space, whereas noise signals

312   **Ping Chen**

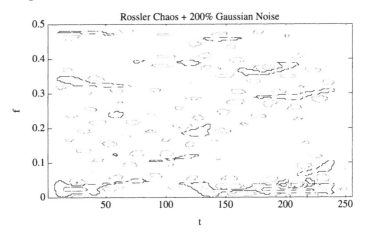

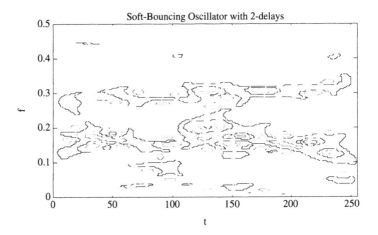

Figure 13.1. a. The WGQ spectrogram of color noise and color chaos ($N = 256$). Color noise modeled by Rössler chaos plus 200% noise. Rössler chaos is generated by three-dimensional differential equations: $dX/dt = -Y - Z, dY/dt = X + 0.2Y, dZ/dt = 0.2 - 5.7Z + XZ$ (Rössler 1976). The time unit is adjusted. b. Color chaos generated by the soft-bouncing oscillator with two time delays (Wen 1994). $dX/dt = 100X(t - 0.183)\exp[-200X(t - 0.183)^2] - 6X(t - 0.183) - Y(t - 0.048), dY/dt = X(t)$.

are featured by drop-like images distributed in wide time-frequency space. The patterns of color noise and color chaos are not easy to distinguish under numerical analysis, especially in the case of high-dimensional chaos (Wen 1993, 1994; Wen, Chen, and Turner 1994).

3   Trend-cycle decomposition and noise-cycles identification

The detrending problem in business-cycle studies is closely related to the observation reference in economic theory. Many controversial issues in macroeconomic studies, such as the oversmoothness of consumption, the excess volatility of stock prices, and the debate of chaos versus noise in economic aggregates, are closely related to competing detrending methods (Hall 1978; Barnett and Chen 1988; Brock and Sayers 1988; Chen 1988, 1993a; Shiller 1989).

Two most popular detrending methods are log-linear detrending and differencing detrending. Their theoretical frameworks are called trend-stationary (TS) and difference-stationary (DS) time series. The HP filter is a generalization of the log-linear detrending (Hodrick and Prescott 1981).

Econometric studies of detrending filters are based on a key assumption that economic time series can be characterized by linear stochastic processes (Nelson and Plosser 1982). The main analytical tools are correlation analysis and frequency analysis of stationary process (King and Rebelo 1993). The whole picture will be quite different, if testing signals are not generated by white noise, but by mixed signals of cycles and noise. In testing the performance of FD and HP filters, we use simulated time series of mixed signals of cycles and noise and a wide range of empirical data, including 16 economic aggregates.

3.1   *Correlation cancellor (FD) and trend-smoothing filter (HP)*

The differencing procedure can be considered as a linear filter $f(L)$ or $F(L)$, with L as the lag operator.

$$Y(t) = X(t) - X(t-1) = \Delta X(t)$$

$$= f(L)X(t) = (1-L)X(t) \tag{13.6}$$

$$X(t) = F(L)Y(t) = (1-L)^{-1}Y(t). \tag{13.7}$$

The differencing is a noninvertible filter with marginal stability. Its main function in econometric modeling is as a correlation cancellor. Actually, the differencing is not a whitening device but a "violeting" one, because it dampens low-frequency components but amplifies high-frequency components. Differencing generates an erratic time series when the time unit is not small compared with the length of serial correlations. The discontinuity caused by differencing can be described by a step function whose Fourier transform is a delta function (Papoulis 1977); therefore, differencing may introduce a zero-frequency or direct current (dc) component. This often happens with trendy time series.

An alternative way is to find a smooth trend by fitting log-linear or polynomial functions. A difficulty is its dependence on period boundaries in trend removal. This problem can be alleviated by the HP trend-smoothing algorithm (Hodrick and Prescott 1981).

The HP filter is a linear transformation of the original time series $\{X(i)\}$ into a smooth time series $\{G(i)\}$ by minimizing the following objective function

$$\Sigma[X(i) - G(i)]^2 + \lambda\Sigma\{[G(i+1) - G(i)] - [G(i) - G(i-1)]^2\}, \qquad (13.8)$$

Deviations from $\{S(i)\}$ are considered as the cyclic component

$$C(i) = X(i) - G(i). \qquad (13.9)$$

Empirical time series can be decomposed into smooth growth series $\{G(i)\}$ and cyclic series $\{C(i)\}$. The characteristic period of HP short cycles depends on the penalty parameter of λ; λ is chosen in such a way that the variance of the growth component is much less than that of the cyclic term (Hodrick and Prescott 1981). In practice, the recommended value of λ is 400 for annual data, 1,600 for quarterly data, and 14,400 for monthly data.

The penalty term in equation (13.8) is the second difference in the growth series. When λ goes to infinity, the growth trend is a linear function. For logarithmic data, log-linear detrending corresponds to the limiting case in HP decomposition. HP growth trends are less rigid than the log-linear function, and HP cycles are less erratic than differencing. Certainly, HP growth trends provide little information about growth cycles and long waves. A more generalized algorithm of multilevel symmetric decomposor is being further developed to analyze multiple frequencies in business cycles (Chen and Qian 1993).

A typical example of economic time series is showed in Figure 13.2. The erratic feature of FD series and the wavelike feature of TS cycles are visible from their autocorrelations.

3.2   *Correlation analysis of noise and cycles*

Correlation analysis is capable of revealing the existence of deterministic cycles when we examine cyclic movements in serial correlations. We may define the decorrelation time T measured by the lag length of the first zero in autocorrelations (Chen 1988, 1993a). In econometrics, the time lags in correlation analysis are integers. Here, the fractal length of decorrelation time is calculated from linear interpolation in the framework of continuous time.

The decorrelation period P_{dc} can be defined as follows:

$$P_{dc} = 4T\,\Delta t, \qquad (13.10)$$

where Δt is the sampling time unit of the time series.

For deterministic cycles, P_{dc} is close to the characteristic period P_c measured by the peak in the power spectrum. For random signals, T has no implication of cyclic movement.

We can see that the FD filtered time series have a shorter T or smaller P_{dc} than HP filtered series (Table 13.1).

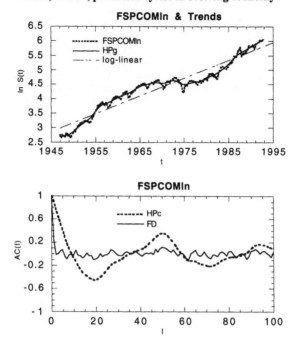

Figure 13.2. The logarithmic FSPCOM (the Standard & Poor 500 stock price index) ($N = 552$). a. Log-linear trend and HP growth trend. b. Autocorrelations of HP and FD cycles.

We should point out that the very long T_{FD} for FM1- and FM2 data is caused by residual trends in first-differenced data. These are good examples that multiple differencing may be needed to remove trends.

3.3   *Characterizing randomness and instability in the frequency domain*

In a time-series analysis, the degree of whiteness is often examined by its autocorrelations in the time domain. We introduce some useful indicators of randomness and instability in the frequency domain.

Given a time series $S(t), t = 1, 2, \ldots, T$, we can calculate its power spectrum $R_i, i = 1, 2, \ldots, M$. We define γ as the degree of randomness of a time series in terms of the discrete-time information entropy in the frequency domain:

$$\gamma = -\sum_{i=1}^{M} p_i \log_2 p_i / W \tag{13.11}$$

Table 13.1. *Correlation and variance analysis of filtered time series*

Series[a]	Δt[b]	Period	N[c]	λ[d]	σ_{HP}^e	T_{HP}^f	σ_{FD}^h	T_{FD}^k
GDPQ*	Q	1947–92	184	1,600	0.0180	4.83	0.0102	3.51
LBOUTU*	Q	1947–92	184	1,600	0.0104	4.22	0.0081	3.40
GCQ*	Q	1947–92	184	1,600	0.0117	4.93	0.0077	3.72
GCDQ*	Q	1947–92	184	1,600	0.0547	4.95	0.0416	2.58
GPIQ*	Q	1947–92	184	1,600	0.0822	3.73	0.0535	2.71
FSPCOM*	M	1947–92	552	14,400	0.0750	8.93	0.0340	1.95
FSDXP	M	1947–92	552	14,400	0.3420	8.41	0.1670	1.84
FYGT10	M	1953–92	480	14,400	0.6305	9.80	0.3198	1.73
FM1*	M	1959–92	408	14,400	0.0116	11.03	0.0049	20.84
FM2*	M	1959–92	408	14,400	0.0099	11.37	0.0034	24.87
GMYFM2*	M	1947–92	552	14,400	0.0154	10.3	0.0073	4.99
LHUR	M	1948–92	540	14,400	0.6398	9.38	0.2340	8.94
PZRNEW*	M	1947–92	552	14,400	0.0103	11.99	0.0040	88.82
FYFF	M	1955–92	456	14,400	1.2898	10.64	0.6377	1.98
FYCP90	M	1971–92	264	14,400	1.3860	10.5	2.4630	1.79
EXRJAN	M	1959–92	408	14,400	11.270	9.70	4.7500	5.68

Note: [b] Q = quarterly data, M = monthly data. [c] N = number of observations. [d] HP parameter. [e] the standard deviation in HP series. [f] decorrelation time (in Δt) in HP series. [h] the standard deviation in FD series. [k] decorrelation time (in Δt) in FD series. [a] GDPQ = real gross domestic products in 1987 US dollars; LBOUTU = nonfarm output/h; GCQ = total consumption; GCDQ = durable consumption; GPIQ = domestic investment; FSPCOM = Standard & Poor, 500 composite monthly index; FSDXP = S&P common-stock composite dividend yield; FYGT10 = 10-year Treasury Notes; FM1 = Federal Reserve monetary supply M1 index; FM2 = Federal Reserve monetary supply M2 index; GMYFM2 = velocity of money; LHUR = unemployment rate; PZRNEW = consumer price index for all items; FYFF = rate of Federal Funds; FYCP90 = 3-month commercial paper rate; and EXRJAN = exchange rate of Japanese Yen vs. U.S. dollar. All quantity data marked by the *symbol are in logarithm.
Source: Citibank Database.

$$p_i = R_i / \sum_{i=1}^{M} R_i \tag{13.12}$$

$$\psi = \log_2 M. \tag{13.13}$$

Here, R_i is the power intensity of frequency i calculated from the power spectrum; p_i is the probability of frequency i; M is the number of states in the frequency domain; ψ is the normalization factor, which is equal to the maximum entropy of white noise, whose $p_i = M^{-1}$. In ideal cases, γ is zero for periodic motion and 1 for white noise. The degree of randomness of color chaos or color noise will fall in between. In numerical tests, r is less than 0.3

for periodic cycles, and larger than 0.9 for the Gaussian noise, depending on the size of data.

From the time-frequency distribution $F(f, t)$, we can identify the peak frequency distribution $f(t)$ and calculate useful statistics to characterize peak frequency $f(t)$. For changing frequency of time-dependent time series, the characteristic frequency f_c is a function of time. The peak frequency $f(t)$ can be determined at each time intersection in a time-frequency representation. The characteristic frequency f_c can be measured by the mean value of the peak frequency. Its frequency instability can be defined by the standard deviation of the peak frequency.

We define ς as the degree of frequency instability measured by the percentage of white-noise frequency bandwidth:

$$\varsigma = \text{std}[f(t)]/W. \tag{13.14}$$

Here, $W = 0.5$ for the full band window in spectral analysis. For stable periodic cycles, ς is near zero. For random process, ς is close to one. The frequency instability can be considered as a measure of internal randomness caused by frequency evolution over time. For example, a harmonic oscillator with wandering frequency may appear as random signals in a Fourier spectrum, even though its deterministic nature can be seen from time-frequency analysis

Similarly, we may also define the frequency variability, v, as the percentage ratio of the standard deviation to the mean frequency:

$$v = \text{std}(f)/f_{\text{mean}^*}100\% \tag{13.15}$$

We use the above quantitative measures in studies of filter performance for mixed signals of noise and cycles.

3.4   *Color residuals and time-unit consistency*

We use the FSPCOM time series to demonstrate the performance of FD and HP filter in studies of business cycles. WGQ spectrograms are given in Figure 13.3. The residual statistics under time-frequency representation are given in Table 13.2. The residual statistics in the frequency domain under different time units are given in Table 13.3. We can see that these residuals are far from white noise in spectral analysis.

We can see that the FD filter does not provide a consistent picture of a detrended series. The frequency information entropy indicates that the FD residuals are not white. The bandwidth of the FD residuals is less than 20 percent of white noise. There is a strong component at near-zero frequency caused by the discontinuous nature of differencing time series. The FD filter fails to produce a consistent picture under the changing time unit. Changing the time unit will change the length of decorrelation time and the magnitude of

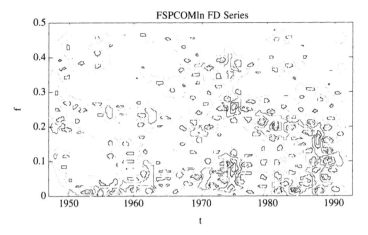

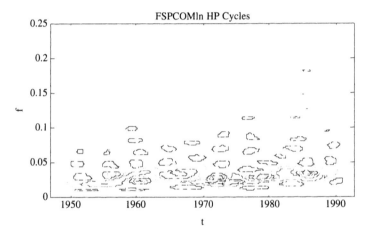

Figure 13.3. The WGQ spectrogram of logarithmic FSPCOM ($N = 552$). a. First differences. b. HP cycles ($\lambda = 14, 400$).

Table 13.2. *Time-frequency analysis of FSPCOM filtered cycles[a]*

Filter	f_{mean}	std(f)	ζ	v	P_{mean}	P_{min}	P_{max}
HP ($\lambda = 14, 400$)	0.0265	0.0057	0.0114	22	3.1	0.70	4.73
FD	0.0893	0.0886	0.1772	99	0.9	0.25	inf

Note: [a]The time unit of periods is a year. The sampling time interval, Δt, is 1/12 of a year; std(f) = the standard deviation of peak frequency over time; $f_c = f_{mean}$; $P_c = P_{mean} = \Delta t / f_{mean}$; P_{min} and P_{max} = the range of peak period over time; $\zeta =$ the degree of frequency instability; and $v =$ the frequency variability (%).

Table 13.3. *Spectral and correlation analysis of FSPCOM with changing time unit*

Δt^a	Filter	λ	γ^b	P_c^c (yrs)	$T^d(\Delta t)$	P_{dc}^e (yrs)	std$(t)^f$
M	FD		0.8895	inf	1.9	0.6	0.0338
Q_f	FD		0.8831	inf	1.4	1.4	0.0707
Q_v	FD		0.8384	inf	2.0	2.0	0.0578
A_f	FD		0.7075	inf	0.1	0.4	0.1136
A_v	FD		0.6475	inf	1.5	6.1	0.0895
M	HP	14,400	0.5501	3.6	8.9	3.6	0.0752
Q_f	HP	1,600	0.7366	4.0	3.5	3.5	0.0892
Q_v	HP	1,600	0.6659	3.8	3.5	3.5	0.0834
A_f	HP	400	0.7982	3.8	1.8	7.1	0.1161
A_v	HP	400	0.6592	5.1	1.7	6.7	0.0863

$^b\gamma$ = the frequency information entropy indicating the degree of randomness. ^cP_c = the characteristic period in power spectrum. ^dT = the decorrelation time. $^eP_{dc}$ = the decorrelation period. ^{f}std(t) = the standard deviation in time domain.
^{a}Two methods of constructing a time series in a larger time unit are used. $Q_f(A_f)$ series are constructed by picking up the figure of the final month (quarter) in the season (year). $Q_v(A_v)$ series are constructed by averaging value in the season (year).

variance. The FD filter plays a destructive role in testing the cyclic signals. The time-frequency representation shows that noisy signals of high frequencies are strongly amplified, whereas the deterministic cycles in the range of business cycles are hard to recognize from the FD-filtered series. The negative effects of the FD filter are not visible for pure deterministic or pure stochastic signals, but are quite severe for noisy data with growth trends.

In contrast, the HP filter provides a consistent picture of persistent cycles from an economic time series when the sampling rate is large enough to detect business cycles (quarterly or monthly, but not annual data). The characteristic periods for economic aggregates are highly stable, because they are slightly changing over time. The frequency variability of HP cycles is as low as less than 3 percent. The characteristic period, P_c, from spectral analysis and decorrelation period, P_{dc}, from correlation analysis are remarkably close. This is strong evidence of deterministic cycles. The magnitude of the characteristic period P_c is essentially invariant under the changing time unit. Time-unit consistency paves the way for refined measurement and generalized theory.

Previous claims of unit roots in aggregate data are produced from fitting annual or quarterly data to low-order autoregressive and moving average (ARMA) models (Nelson and Plosser 1982; Campbell and Mankiw 1987). There is no evidence of the unit root process because FD-filtered quarterly and monthly data are far from white under spectral representation (Chen 1993c).

Table 13.4. *Frequency stability and variability of HP short cycles*

Series	Δt	Period	N	P_{dc}^a	P_c^b (yrs)	v^c (%)
GDPQ	Q	1947–92	184	4.8	5.4	23
LBOUTU	Q	1947–92	184	5.1	4.2	26
GCQ	Q	1947–92	184	4.4	4.9	47
GCDQ	Q	1947–92	184	4.4	5.0	49
GPIQ	Q	1947–92	184	4.4	3.7	34
FSPCOM	M	1947–92	552	3.1	3.0	22
FSDXP	M	1947–92	552	2.9	2.8	37
FYGT10	M	1953–92	480	3.1	3.3	37
FM1	M	1959–92	408	3.7	3.6	46
FM2	M	1959–92	408	3.9	3.3	46
GMYFM2	M	1947–92	552	3.8	3.4	32
LHUR	M	1948–92	540	3.9	3.1	23
PZRNEW	M	1947–92	552	4.0	4.0	27
FYFF	M	1955–92	456	3.6	3.5	51
FYCP90	M	1971–92	264	3.1	3.5	73
EXRJAN	M	1959–92	408	3.0	3.2	57

[a] Decorrelation period from correlation analysis. [b] characteristic period from time-frequency analysis. [c] frequency variability (see Figures 5 and 6).

4   Frequency patterns and dynamic changes in business cycles

The HP-filtered economic time series show clear evidence of persistent cycles in the timescale of business cycles defined by National Bureau of Economic Research (NBER) documentation (Zarnowitz 1992). We further examine their frequency patterns and structural changes by time-frequency analysis.

In econometric modeling and business-cycle theory, variance-correlation analysis is the main tool in characterizing volatility and propagation mechanisms (Kydland and Prescott 1990). Structural changes are described by parameter changes in parametric models (Perron 1989; Friedman and Kuttner 1992). The time-frequency representation provides a new tool in observing dynamic patterns in business cycles.

4.1   *Frequency stability and structural flexibility*

We tested a wide range of aggregate data. Most of them have distinct color, or characteristic frequency. The empirical results of 16 economic aggregates from time-frequency analysis are given in Table 13.4. The period evolution for general indicators, such as GDPQ, LHUR, and LBOUTU are shown in Figure 13.4.

We find that the only frequency break of GDPQ HP cycles was caused by the first oil price shock in 1973. This observation provides complementary support to trend-shifting argument based on the parametric test (Perron 1989).

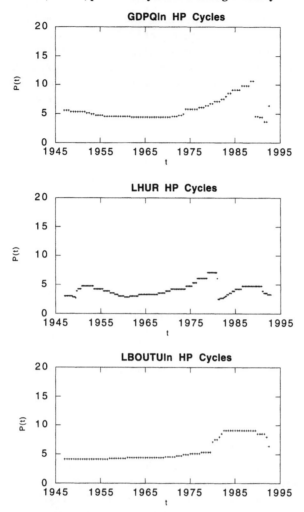

Figure 13.4. Period evolution of general indicators a. GDPQ (real gross domestic products) HP cycles ($N = 184$). b. LHUR (the unemployment rate) HP cycles ($N = 540$). c. LBOUTU (labor productivity) HP cycles ($N = 184$).

However, the oil price shock only had a minor impact on most macroeconomic indicators. For LHUR HP cycles, the first frequency shift occurred within the Korean War; the second and more drastic change appeared in early 1980s. For LBOUTU, a significant change happened in the early 1980s. Most economic indicators show more complex patterns of frequency evolution in history.

Examining the frequency stability of HP cycles under a time-frequency representation, the characteristic frequency of LBOUTU is most stable, whereas those of FYFF and FYCP90 are most variable. The other aggregates are in between. There are several interesting observations to business-cycle studies.

First, the frequency stability of economic indicators is remarkable. The variability of frequency is less than 80 percent. The bandwidth is only about 1 to 5 percent of white noise. Specifically, monetary movements cannot be oversimplified as external shocks because money indicators also have stable characteristic frequencies. The monetary velocity is more stable than FM2 and the long-term interest rate is more stable than the short-term interest rate.

Second, these characteristic frequencies have the similar range of magnitudes, but a distinctive pattern; therefore, they are nonlinear oscillators in nature, because a linear combination cannot change the characteristic frequencies.

Third, the stability and flexibility of the characteristic frequency under constant shocks cannot be explained by the Frisch-type linear oscillators (Frisch 1933). High-dimensional nonlinear oscillators are needed to describe persistent cycles observed from economic data.

4.2   *Frequency evolution and pattern classification*

Econometric modeling is used to treat economic aggregates as homogenous random variables. Under time-frequency representation, we find hard and soft cycles from their distinct patterns of frequency evolution (Figure 13.5).

Consumption, investment, and productivity are examples of hard cycles. They have piecewise flat regimes, a reflection of stability and rigidity in frequency domain. Hard cycles are more stable against small changes but vulnerable under dramatic shocks. Hard cycles behave like an autonomous subsystem such as the circulatory system and digestive system in animals. It is conceivable that consumption, investment, and technology have their own dynamics.

Stock-market indexes, monetary velocity, money supply, the consumer price index, interest rate, and exchange rate are examples of soft cycles. Soft cycles tend to move together since they have similar patterns in time-frequency space. A new kind of frequency comovements reveals a close interaction between stock market, money market, and economic performance.

We can further identify subgroups of economic indicators based on their pattern of similarity in frequency evolution. For example, both GDPQ and LBOUTU are insensitive to most historical events. GCQ, GDPQ, and GPIQ have similar rigidity and stability. Two stock-market indicators – FSPCOM and FSDXP – and the long-term interest rate FYGT10 have almost the same pattern, even though their frequencies are not the same. The pairs of FYFF and FYCP90 also move together during frequency shifting. These observations provide useful information about the interacting mechanism and propagation dynamics.

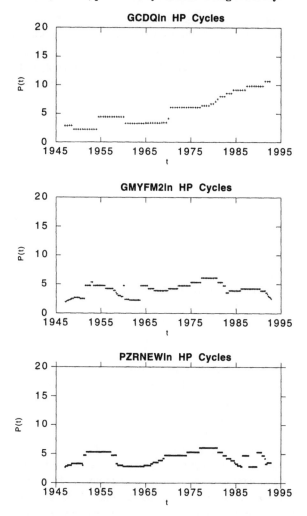

Figure 13.5. Period evolution of hard and soft cycles a. GCDQ (the real durable consumption) HP cycles ($N = 184$). b. GMYFM2 (the monetary velocity) HP cycles ($N = 552$). c. PZRNEW (the consumer price index) HP cycles ($N = 552$).

Examination of the time frequency pattern will provide a valuable guidance for business cycle modeling. For example, consumption and investment have closer interactions than income and price. Monetary movements have less of an impact on the stock market and the long-term interest rate than on the short-term interest rate.

The role of money is not neutral in business cycles. The frequency pattern of monetary indicators is similar to that of the consumer price index and the unemployment rate but more variable than real income, investment, and consumption. Unlike seasonal changes in weather, government, and monetary authority are integrated players in economic dynamics. Monetary movements have complex structures.

The real GNP serves as an anchor in real business-cycle modeling (Kydland and Prescott 1990). However, real GNP is not a sensitive indicator for structural changes. The monthly data of the unemployment rate can be a better barometer of business cycles and structural changes.

4.3   *Breaking points and propagation mechanism*

The breaking points in frequency evolution provide explicit information about the propagation mechanism. We can observe propagation speed and delay process by reviewing historical events.

In econometric exercises, the issue of persistent shocks is not clear under regression analysis (Christiano and Eichenbaum 1990). Impacts of historical shocks vary greatly under time-frequency representation. For example, two pairs of economic aggregates, stock-market indexes of FSPCOM and FSDXP, the Federal fund rate FYFF, and the short-term interest rate FYCP90, behave like synchronous cycles. In contrast, the frequency pattern of the long-term interest rate FYGT10 almost duplicates the pattern of stock-market indicators. But the frequency hysteresis lasted about six years during the Vietnam War and oil price shocks (Figure 13.6).

Exceptional variability in Federal Fund rates and short-term interest rates are visible in Figure 13.6. It is known that the pattern of monetary movements had changed greatly in 1980's (Friedman and Kuttner 1992). The puzzling issue of "missing money" and other anomalies can be explained away by adding more variables, such as long-term and short-term interest rates, in the error-correction model (Baba, Hendry, and Starr 1992). This approach is skeptical under time-frequency analysis because variables with different frequency responses cannot be easily put together in linear models.

4.4   *Oil shocks, stock-market crash, and the Vietnam War*

The extraordinary resilience of market economies can be revealed from the insignificance of the first oil price shock in October 1973 and the stock-market crash in October 1987. Both events generated only slight changes of characteristic frequencies for most economic aggregates.

We may have a closer look at frequency evolution in observing historical events (Figures 13.6(a,b)). Before the oil price shock in October 1973, the

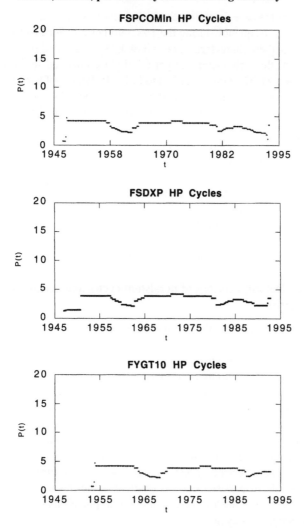

Figure 13.6. Synchronous cycles and frequency hysteresis a. FSPCOM (the S & P 500 stock index) HP cycles ($N = 552$). b. FSDXP (the S & P stock dividend yield) HP cycles ($N = 552$). c. FYGT10 (the 10-year treasure notes) HP cycles ($N = 480$).

characteristic period of stock market indicators was stabilized at the level of 4.26 years since 1971. After the oil price shock, the characteristic period of HP cycles changed to 3.86 years. Obviously, the oil price shock was the external cause of frequency change in the stock market.

This may not be the case for the stock-market crash in October 1987. There was a long swing of frequency during the 1981–90 period. For FSPCOM and FSDXP HP cycles, their characteristic period of 3.28 years lasted for two years (1985–86). Then, their characteristic period slightly changed to 3.05 years for FSPCOM (January–December 1987) and FSDXP (January–October 1987), and 2.84 years thereafter. The stock-market crash happened at the end of the 10-month "frequency shift." There was a two-month delay for FSPCOM after the stock–market crash. This suggests that the stock-market crash is the end of an internal bubble instead of external shocks.

The interesting thing is that the political economy of wars and arm races left a much stronger fingerprint in the time-frequency representation. The most significant changes of the frequency pattern happened in three periods: U.S.–Soviet arms and space races during 1958–62, the escalation of the Vietnam War during 1965–72, and the so-called Reagan revolution in the 1980s. Not only fiscal and monetary policy, but also industrial policy, tax policy, and military programs, may have notable impacts on structural changes of U.S. economy.

5   Theoretical implications of persistent cycles and economic instabilities

There is no question that external noise and measurement errors widely exist in economic data. The question is whether some regularities are observable from an empirical time series. The answer is yes.

Like a telescope in astronomy or a microscope in biology, time-frequency analysis opens a new window of observing evolving economies. The most enlightening result in business-cycle studies is the discovery of persistent cycles, i.e., self-generating cycles from economic aggregates. These cycles are nonlinear in nature with remarkable resilience and flexibility like living beings. This discovery provides a new perspective to business cycles. Traditionally, the economic order is characterized by negative feedback and equilibrium (steady) states. The new role of persistent cycles challenges the linear framework of economic dynamics. We need to re-examine the implications of complexity and instability in business cycles.

5.1   *Characteristic frequencies and endogenous cycles*

The existence of characteristic frequencies in economic movements has profound implications in business-cycle theory.

Economic movements, like organisms, have their distinct time rhythms. Different economic factors move with different speeds and different frequencies. In this sense, economic aggregates have their "personalities," and they are not all alike in frequency patterns. The pattern recognition in economic dynamics will pave the way for economic diagnostics and policy valuation.

Changing patterns of characteristic frequencies of business cycles reveal internal sources of economic shocks, such as military expenditures and tax policies. Economic interactions are highly correlated and are an essential nature of collective phenomena. The impact of monetary shocks and technology shocks can be better understood if we know their own dynamics. There is no absolute dividing line between internal and external shocks. Nonlinear interaction, rather than linear causality, provides a better picture for understanding the historical experience of economic evolution.

We should point out that the popular name of "chaos" is somewhat misleading because of its negative image of irregularity and disorder. That is why we suggest the term "complex cycles" for deterministic chaos. We also prefer the name "color chaos" to white noise. Unlike controlled experiments in natural science, complex chaotic cycles cannot be "verified" in economic dynamics, but can be observed through empirical patterns, such as time-frequency representation. Like calculus for classic mechanics, Riemann geometry for gravitation theory, new mathematical tools, such as nonlinear dynamics and time-dependent time-series analysis, are critical to the advancement of economic dynamics.

5.2   *Timescale and observation reference in measurement and theory*

Econometricians often argue that the measurement method of economic indicators (such as annual or daily data) demands the discrete-time algorithm (Granger and Teräsvirta 1993). These technical arguments ignore fundamental issues of timescale in any dynamic theory (Chen 1993a,b).

In the history of empirical science, many theoretical controversies can be settled by refining measurements. Whether economic laws of motion (if they exist) are invariant under changes of time units is a fundamental issue in economic dynamics. For example, if econometric tests of long-run economic relationships, such as unit roots or linear causality, succeed for annual or quarterly data but fail for monthly data, the validity of underlying economic theory would be questionable (Lütkepohl 1991).

The most visible pattern of economic movements is the recurrent feature of business cycles in the timescale of several years. Regression analysis is more comfortable with annual data than monthly data, because serial correlations can be easily explained by stochastic models with few lags. However, annual data are helpless for spectral analysis. Measurement precision does matter in empirical economic studies. If dynamic patterns change with the timescale, such as the patterns of the stock-market movements during a trading day may differ from the patterns during a business-cycle, we should change the dynamic model and not just the time unit.

The degree of mathematical complexity is associated with computational reliability. Conventional discrete-time ARMA models have poor resolution because of the extremely low computational degree of freedom. A better resolution of the WGQ spectrogram comes from new representation reconstruction in terms of a two-dimensional Gaussian lattice instead of a one-dimensional polynomial fitting.

The differencing operator serves a poor reference base in business-cycle studies. From the view of resource constraints, the DS framework implies unlimited resources in economic dynamics, if level information is not relevant to economic dynamics. Most economic variables, including the government budget, credit limits, wealth, capital stock, savings, inventory, consumption, and production, are measured by levels. Rich patterns in HP cycles indicate that both flow and level variables matter in economic dynamics.

We recommend the HP filter as a better device in trend-cycle decomposition, because it produces consistent measurement and historical patterns through time-frequency analysis. We may consider HP long cycles as a long-run evolving equilibrium and model HP short cycles by strange attractors.

5.3   *Dynamic instability and information ambiguity*

In the history of science, some thought experiments once dramatically shaped theoretical thinking in fundamental issues. Notable examples are Maxwell's demon in thermodynamics, the uncertainty principle in quantum mechanics, and the Friedman paradox on the non-existence of destabilizing patterns in speculative dynamics.

Friedman asserts that no predictable pattern can exist in the market beyond a short time horizon because rational arbitrageurs (Friedman's spirits) will rapidly wipe out any destabilizing traders from the market (Friedman 1953). This is the essence of the efficient-market hypothesis and the main argument against the possible existence of market regularity. Actually, Friedman's spirits behave much like Maxwell's demon in equilibrium thermodynamics, although their purposes are just the opposite (Brillouin 1962; Chen 1993b).

In addition to information costs and financial constraints (Grossman and Stiglitz 1980, De Long et al. 1990), there are more serious barriers for arbitrageurs' action.

First, the observational reference for economic equilibrium and market fundamentals are simply not well defined operationally. Friedman's argument may be valid for an island economy without growth and nonlinear interactions among residents, but not valid for an open economy with growth and collective actions.

Second, the problem of information ambiguity is more fundamental than information scarcity from the point of view of time-frequency analysis. The implications of the information flow can only be understood in terms of a historical context, such as the case of linguistic analysis. It is impossible to judge economic trends from uncorrelated shocks. Investment hysteresis in the range of two to four years can be understood by the value of waiting under uncertainty (Dixit 1992). The time delay in information analysis and decision making is a main source of overshooting and inertia.

Third, dynamic instability and bounded rationality set fundamental limits to economic forecasting. Nonlinearity, nonstationarity, and the uncertainty principle in information analysis all contribute to complexity and indeterminacy in economic forecasting (Chen 1993a,b; Prigogine 1993). Friedman's argument implies that irrational speculators are sure losers. This would be true only for simple dynamic systems when market movements could be perfectly predictable. The extreme cases of complete unpredictability of random walks and perfect predictability of harmonic cycles are unrealistic features of linear dynamics. The modest behavior of nonlinear oscillators fills in the gap between the two extremes.

In short, rational arbitrageurs, on average, cannot eliminate cyclic patterns, even in the long run. We can forecast general economic trends including their mean period and variance, but we cannot predict time path and turning points even when we know of some pattern of economic dynamics. There are no sure winners or losers on the speculative market because of the complex nature of business cycles.

6   Brief conclusion: evolving economy and complex dynamics

Now, we have a better understanding of why business cycles have been well documented by the NBER approach, but are hard to characterize by statistical analysis on the basis of a stationary process (Zarnowitz 1992). The existence of growing economic trends and structural changes needs new analytical tools for nonlinear and nonstationary process. Time-frequency representation and the HP trend-cycle decomposition pave the way for study of persistent cycles from empirical economic data.

The characteristic frequencies of economic variables provide rich information about internal dynamics and structural changes. Our integrated approach in empirical analysis and theoretical framework reveals the important roles of timescale, observation reference, and pattern recognition in business-cycle studies.

The software of time-frequency distribution is developed and modified by Shie Qian and Dapang Chen. Their contributions are indispensable to our progress in empirical analysis. The Hodrick-Prescott algorithm used here is provided by Finn Kydland. Our interdisciplinary research in nonlinear economic dynamics is a long-term effort in the studies of complex systems supported by Ilya Prigogine. The author wants to thank Heather Anderson, William Barnett, Clive Granger, Finn Kydland, Paul Samuelson, Kehong Wen, Michael

330 **Ping Chen**

Woodford, Vicor Zarnowiz, and Arnold Zellner for their stimulating discussions and valuable suggestions. Financial support from the Welch Foundation and IC^2 Institute is gratefully acknowledged.

REFERENCESREFERENCES

Baba,Baba, Y., Hendry, D. F., and Starr, R. M. (1992). The demand for M1 in the U.S.A., *Rev. Econ. Studies* **59**, 25–61.
Barnett, W. A., and Chen, P. (1988). The aggregation – theoretic monetary aggregates are chaotic and have strange attractors: an econometric application of mathematical chaos. In *Dynamic Econometric Modeling*, eds. W. Barnett, E. Berndt, and H. White, Cambridge University Press, Cambridge, England, pp. 199–246.
Benhabib, J. (1992). *Cycle and Chaos in Economic Equilibrium*. Princeton University Press, Princeton; NJ.
Brillouin, L. (1962). *Science and Information Theory*, 2nd ed., Academic Press, New York.
Brock, W. A., and Sayers, C. (1988). Is the business cycles characterized by deterministic chaos? *J. Monetary Econ.* **22**, 71–80.
Campbell, J. Y., and Mankiw, N. G. (1987). Permanent and transitory components in macroeconomic fluctuations, *Am. Econ. Rev.* **77**, 111–17.
Chen, P. (1988). Empirical and theoretical evidence of monetary chaos, *Sys. Dynam. Rev.* **4**, 81–108.
    (1993a). Searching for economic chaos: a challenge to econometric practice and nonlinear tests. In *Nonlinear Dynamics and Evolutionary Economics*, eds. R. Day and P. Chen, Oxford University Press, Oxford, England.
    (1993b). Complexity, instability, and business Cycles, IC^2 Working Paper No. 93-05-03, University of Texas at Austin.
    (1993c). Symmetry principle and coherent pattern in time-frequency representation and trend-cycle decomposition: a new perspective in business cycles analysis, IC^2 Institute Working Paper No. 93-12-01, University of Texas at Austin.
Chen, P., and Qian, S. (1993). Time-frequency distribution analysis of complex dynamic systems, IC^2 Working Paper No. 93-05-03, University of Texas at Austin.
Christiano, L. J., and Eichenbaum, M. (1990). Unit roots in real GNP: do we know and do we care? In *Unit Roots, Investment Measures and Other Essays*, ed. A. H. Meltzer, Carnegie-Rochester Conference Series on Public Policy, Vol. 32, North-Holland, Amsterdam.
Day, R., and Chen, P. (1993). *Nonlinear Dynamics and Evolutionary Economics*, Oxford University Press, Oxford, England.
De Long, J. B., Shleifer, A., Summers, L. H., and Waldmann, R. J. (1990). Positive feedback investment strategies and destabilizing rational speculation, *J. Finance* **45**(2); 379–395.
Dixit, A. (1992). Investment and hysteresis, *J. Econ. Perspect.* **6**, 107–32.
Friedman, B. M., and Kuttner, K. N. (1992). Money, income, prices, and interest rates, *Am. Econ. Rev.* **82**, 472–92.
Friedman, M. (1953). The case of flexible exchange rates. In *Essays in Positive Economics*, M. Friedman, University of Chicago Press, Chicago, IL.
    (1969). *The Optimum Quantity of Money and Other Essays*, Aldine, Chicago, IL.
Frisch, R. (1933). Propagation problems and impulse problems in dynamic economics. In *Economic Essays in Honour of Gustav Cassel*, Allen & Unwin, London.

Gabor, D. (1946). Theory of communication, *J. Inst. Electr. Eng.* (London), *Part 1*, **93**(3), 429–57.

Granger, C. W., and Teräsvirta, T. (1993). *Modeling Nonlinear Economic Relationship*, Oxford University Press, Oxford, England.

Grossman, S. J., and Stiglitz, J. E. (1980). On the impossibility of informationally efficient markets, *Am. Econ. Rev.* **70**(3), 393–408.

Hall, R. E. (1978). Stochastic implications of the life cycle-permanent income hypothesis: theory and evidence, *J. Polit. Econ.* **86**, 971–87.

Hao, B. L. (1990). *Chaos II*, World Scientific, Singapore.

Hodrick, R. J., and Prescott, E. C. (1981). Post-war US. business cycles: an empirical investigation, Discussion Paper No. 451, Carnegie-Mellon University, Pittsburgh, PA.

King, R. G., and Rebelo, S. T. (1993). Low frequency filtering and real business cycles, *J. Econ. Dynam. Control* **17**, 207–31.

Kydland, F. E., and Prescott, E. C. (1990). Business cycles: real facts and a monetary myth, *Fed. Reserve Bank of Minneapolis Q. Rev.* **14**, 3–18.

Lucas, R. E., Jr.. (1981). *Studies in Business-Cycle Theory*, MIT Press, Cambridge: MA.

Lütkepohl, H. (1991). *Introduction to Multiple Time Series Analysis*, Springer–Verlag, Berlin.

Nelson, C. R., and Plosser, C. I. (1982). Trends and random walks in macroeconomic time series, some evidence and implications, *J. Monetary Econ.* **10**, 139–62.

Papoulis, A. (1977). *Signal Analysis*, McGraw-Hill, New York.

Perron, P. (1989). The great crash, the oil price shock and the unit root hypothesis, *Econometrica*, **57**, 1361–401.

Priestley, M. B. (1981). *Spectral Analysis and Time Series*, Academic, New York.

Prigogine, I. (1993). Bounded rationality: from dynamical systems to socio-economic models. In *Nonlinear Dynamics and Evolutionary Economics*, eds. R. Day and D. Chen, Oxford University Press, Oxford, England.

Qian, S., and Chen, D. (1994a). Discrete Gabor Transform, *IEEE Trans. Signal Processing*, **41**(7), 2429–2439.

(1994b). Decomposition of the Wigner distribution and time-frequency distribution series, *IEEE Trans. Signal Processing.* **42**(10); 2836–2842.

(1996). *Joint Time-Frequency Analysis*, Prentice Hall, Apper Saddle River, NJ.

Rössler, O. E. (1976). An equation for continuous chaos, *Phys. Lett. A*, **57**, 397–98.

Shiller, R. J. (1989). *Market Volatility*, MIT Press, Cambridge, MA.

Swinney, H. L., and Gollub, J. P. (1978). The transition to turbulence, *Phys. Today* **31**(8), 41–49.

Wen, K. H. (1993). *Complex Dynamics in Nonequilibrium Economics and Chemistry*, Ph.D. Dissertation, University of Texas at Austin.

(1994). Continuous-time chaos in stock market dynamics, chapter 5, in this volume.

Wen, K. H., Chen, P., and Turner, J. S. (1994). Bifurcation and chaos in a Lienard equation with two delays. In *Proceedings of Dynamic Systems and Applications*, ed. M. Sambandham, **I**, 377–384, Dynamic Publishers, Atlanta: GA.

Wigner, E. P. (1932). On the quantum correction for thermodynamic equilibrium, *Phys. Rev.* **40**, 749–59.

Zarnowitz, V. (1992). *Business Cycles, Theory, History, Indicators, and Forecasting*, University of Chicago Press, Chicago, pp. 196–98.

CHAPTER 14

International evidence of business-cycle nonlinearity

Philip Rothman

Lagrangian multiplier linearity tests are applied to an international dataset of long-run business-cycle time series. In so far as business-cycle asymmetry is thought to be consistent with only smooth-transition autoregressive-type non-linearity, the results presented here do not offer very strong evidence of such asymmetry. However, there is substantial evidence of nonlinearity for most of the time series examined.

1   Introduction

The idea that the business cycle is asymmetric can be traced back at least 60 years to the work of Mitchell (1927) and Keynes (1936). The conventional asymmetry hypothesis is that economic expansions are longer but less sharp than downturns. With respect to a countercyclical series such as the unemployment rate, this would imply that the unemployment rate increases quickly in recessions but declines relatively slowly during expansions.

Given the dominance of linear time-series techniques in applied business-cycle analysis, the significance of cyclical asymmetry is quite clear. Assuming that the underlying innovations are drawn from a symmetric probability distribution, cyclical asymmetry is simply incompatible with linear time-series methods. Nonlinear approaches must be considered if formal testing shows that asymmetry is the rule, rather than the exception, as a characterization of business-cycle dynamics.

Following the seminal article by Neftci (1984), researchers in the business-cycle asymmetry literature have indeed documented substantial evidence in favor of business cycle asymmetry. Given that the asymmetry phenomenon

I wish to thank David Backus for kindly providing the data used in this paper.

333

was initially observed in the pre-World War II period by Mitchell and Keynes, there is a conspicuous absence, with just two exceptions, of work in the modern literature that analyzes any data from that time period. That is, practically all of the recent work on this problem has focused solely on data from the post-World War II period.

The two exceptions are DeLong and Summers (1986) and Ramsey and Rothman (1996). First, DeLong and Summers examined skewness coefficients for different pre- and post-World War II epochs, arguing that evidence of skewness would suggest asymmetry. They did not find any substantial evidence of asymmetry for the production series examined. The simulation results of Welsh and Jernigan (1983) however, suggest that the approach of DeLong and Summers has very low power against asymmetric alternatives.

Second, Ramsey and Rothman applied their time reversibility (TR) test to test for business-cycle asymmetry. Their TR test results provide very strong evidence of time irreversibility, and therefore of asymmetric behavior, for practically all of the time series examined.

Both testing procedures used in those two papers – the skewness and TR tests – are set up to be run against a general unspecified alternative hypothesis. In contrast, in their investigation of cyclical asymmetry, Luukkonen and Teräsvirta (1991) consider tests designed to have power against specific nonlinear alternatives. They apply Lagrangian multiplier (LM) tests set up to test the null hypothesis of linearity against threshold autoregressive and bilinear alternatives. Both the threshold autoregressive and bilinear classes of models have been used successfully in the nonlinear time-series literature to capture seemingly asymmetric cyclical behavior deemed inconsistent with conventional linear time-series techniques; see, for example, Subba Rao and Gabr (1984) and Tong (1990) for nonlinear analysis of the famous asymmetric sunspot and Canadian lynx data.

This paper tests for long-run evidence of cyclical asymmetry with the LM tests applied by Luukkonen and Teräsvirta. The primary contributions of the paper are twofold. First, an important gap in the literature is filled because, in contrast to most of the work done so far, this paper considers time-series data from both the pre- and the post-World War II periods. The data examined are from the international dataset recently analyzed by Backus and Kehoe (1992). Second, the LM testing approach can potentially point in the direction of a particular alternative nonlinear time-series model for these time series. This offers the possibility of learning more than simply that a particular long-run time series is inconsistent with a linear data-generating mechanism.

The paper proceeds as follows: Section 2 describes the LM tests. The LM tests are applied to the international long-run dataset in Section 3. Section 4 concludes.

2   LM tests against nonlinear alternatives

Assume that (X_t) is a stationary time series. (X_t) is generated by a pure linear autoregressive (AR) model if

$$\sum_{j=0}^{p} \phi_j X_{t-j} = u_t, \tag{14.1}$$

where $p < \infty$, (u_t) is a sequence of independently and identically distributed (i.i.d.) random variables, and the roots of

$$\sum_{j=0}^{p} \phi_j z^j = 0 \tag{14.2}$$

lie outside the unit circle. If the innovations sequence (u_t) is assumed to be drawn from a symmetric probability distribution, then the AR(p) model given by equation (14.1) is not an adequate representation for a cyclically asymmetric time series. More specifically, if the innovations are symmetrically distributed, then a nonlinear alternative must be considered to model cyclically asymmetric behavior.

One such class of nonlinear time-series models that is designed to capture asymmetric cyclical behavior is the set of self-exciting threshold autoregressive (SETAR) models. A time series is said to be generated by a SETAR (2; p, p) model if

$$X_t = \pi_0 + \sum_{j=1}^{p} \pi_j X_{t-j} + \left(\theta_0 + \sum_{j=1}^{p} \theta_j X_{t-j} \right) \cdot F(z_t) + \varepsilon_t, \tag{14.3}$$

where $(\varepsilon_t) = $ i.i.d. $(0, \sigma^2)$, and $F(\cdot)$ is the Heaviside function

$$F(z_t) = \begin{pmatrix} 1, & \text{if } z_t > 0 \\ 0, & \text{if } z_t \le 0, \end{pmatrix}, \tag{14.4}$$

where $z_t = (X_{t-d} - c)$, with c and d fixed but unknown parameters. If $\theta_j = 0$, $j = 0, 1, \ldots, p$, equation (14.3) reduces to an AR(p) model.

The SETAR model generalizes to the class of smooth-transition autoregressive (STAR) models. Instead of equation (14.4), assume:

(1) $F: \mathbf{R} \to \mathbf{R}$ is an odd, monotonically increasing function possessing a nonzero derivative of order $(2s + 1)$ in an open interval $(-a, a)$, $a > 0$, $s \ge 0$;
(2) $d^k F(z_t)/dz_t^k|_{z_t} \ne 0$ for k odd and $1 < k < 2s + 1$;
(3) $z_t = \gamma_t (X_{t-d} - c)$, $\gamma > 0$.

Compared to the discrete shifts between regimes in the SETAR model, assumptions (1)–(3) allow for relatively smooth transitions. Model (14.3) with $F(\cdot)$

defined by (1)–(3) is called a STAR $(2; p, p)$ model. Suitable candidates for $F(\cdot)$ are cumulative distribution functions of continuous random variables, e.g., the standard normal, exponential, or logistic distribution.

If one prefers not to impose the abrupt changes over states as dictated by equation (14.4), then the STAR model should be chosen over the SETAR model. As is the case for the SETAR model, the STAR model can generate asymmetric fluctuations.

Luukkonen et al. (1988a) developed LM-type tests for testing the null hypothesis of linearity against STAR, assuming that the delay parameter d, is unknown. Because equation (14.3) is identified only under the alternative and not under the null hypothesis,

$$H_0 : \theta_j = 0, \tag{14.5}$$

$j = 0, 1, \ldots, p$, this leads to a nonstandard testing problem of the type discussed initially by Davies (1977). Luukkonen et al. (1988a) replaced $F(\cdot)$ in assumption (1) by its first-order Taylor expansion about the origin. This leads to an auxiliary regression with $P(p + 1)/2$ quadratic terms. For an observed time series $X_{p+1}, \ldots, X_0, X_1, \ldots, X_T$, the test of equation (14.5) can be carried out as follows:

(1)   Regress X_t on 1, $X_{t-j}, j = 1, \ldots, p$, using ordinary least squares, and form the residuals $\hat{\varepsilon}_t$ and residual sum of squares SSE_0;
(2)   Regress $\hat{\varepsilon}_t$ on 1, $X_{t-i}, X_{t-i}X_{t-j}, i = 1, \ldots, p, j = i, \ldots, p$, and form the residuals $\hat{\eta}_t$ and residual sum of squares SSE_1;
(3)   Compute the test statistic

$$S1 = T(\text{SSE}_0 - \text{SSE}_1)/\text{SSE}_0.$$

Under equation (14.5), $S1$ has an asymptotic χ^2 distribution with $p(p+1)/2$ degrees of freedom. If $\theta_1, \ldots, \theta_p$ are zero or small in absolute value, so that the main source of nonlinearity equation (14.3) is θ_0, then $S1$ lacks power. In light of this possibility, Luukkonen et al. (1988a) developed two other LM-type tests. Both are based on using the third-order Taylor expansion of $F(\cdot)$. The following is the more parsimonious of the two:

(1)   Same step as before;
(2)   Regress $\hat{\varepsilon}_t$ on 1, $X_{t-i}, X_{t-i}X_{t-j}, X_{t-i}^3, i = 1, \cdots, p, j = 1, \cdots, p$, and form the residuals $\hat{v}_t, t = 1, \cdots, T$, and the residual sum of squares SEE_3;
(3)   Compute the test statistic

$$S3 = T(\text{SSE}_0 - \text{SSE}_3)/\text{SSE}_0.$$

Under equation (14.5), $S3$ has an asymptotic χ^2 distribution with $p(p + 1)/2 + p$ degrees of freedom. Both $S1$ and $S3$ are used below.

Because both $S1$ and $S3$ have power against non-STAR nonlinearity (see Luukkonen et al. 1988b), rejection of linearity via $S1$ and/or $S3$ does not necessarily imply cyclical asymmetry of the STAR type. It is necessary, then, to test linearity against more than one type of nonlinearity.

The simulations of Luukkonen et al. (1988b) showed that the $S1$ and $S3$ STAR tests have power against autoregressive conditional heteroskedasticity (ARCH). The same simulations demonstrated that the McLeod and Li (1983) squared residuals test, which is asymptotically equivalent to Engle's (1982) ARCH test, has little power against STAR. Thus, if the McLeod–Li ARCH test fails to reject linearity while the STAR tests do reject linearity, then ARCH can be excluded as a possible alternative to linearity.

Another interesting nonlinear alternative to consider is the bilinear model. The $BL(p; m, k)$ model is defined as

$$X_t = \mu + \sum_{j=1}^{p} a_j X_{t-j} + \sum_{i=1}^{m}\sum_{j=1}^{k} c_{ij}\varepsilon_{t-i} X_{t-j} + \varepsilon_t, \qquad (14.6)$$

where $\varepsilon_t = \text{i.i.d}(0, \sigma^2)$. Addition of the bilinear terms $\{\varepsilon_{t-i} X_{t-j}\}$ to the pure $AR(p)$ model yields a parsimonious and powerful nonlinear model. It is particularly well suited for capturing large amplitude changes. In the business-cycle context, this corresponds to sharp peaks and troughs. In contrast to SETAR and STAR models, however, the bilinear model is incapable of generating limit-cycle behavior.

Saikkonen and Luukkonen (1988) developed an LM test of linearity against bilinearity. The null hypothesis is

$$H_0 : c_{ij} = 0. \qquad (14.7)$$

$i = 1, \ldots, m, j = 1, \ldots, k$, in equation (14.6). This test can be carried out in three steps as follows:

(1) Same step as before;
(2) Regress $\hat{\varepsilon}_t$ on 1, $X_{t-i}, i = 1, \ldots, p, \hat{\varepsilon}_{t-i} X_{t-j}, i = 1, \ldots, m, j = 1, \ldots, k$, and form the residuals $\hat{\gamma}_t, t = 1, \ldots, T$, and the residual sums of squares SSE_4;
(3) Compute the test statistic

$$B = T(SSE_0 - SSE_4)/SSE_0. \qquad (14.8)$$

Under equation (14.7), B has an asymptotic χ^2 distribution with mk degrees of freedom. Two bilinear models are considered below as possible alternatives: the $BL(p; 1, 1)$ and the $BL(p; 2, 2)$. The corresponding LM statistics are called B1 and B2, respectively.

3   Linearity test results

The $S1$ and $S3$ STAR statistics, $B1$ and $B2$ bilinear statistics, and McLeod–Li ARCH statistic (here called Q), were calculated for 24 series from the Backus and Kehoe (1992) long-run international dataset. The same four business-cycle indicators for six different countries were examined. The four indicators chosen were output, prices, investment, and the money supply. The countries selected were Australia, Canada, Italy, Sweden, the United Kingdom, and the United States. Most of the series run for roughly 100 years, from the last quarter of the nineteenth century to either the 1970s or 1980s. For all of the 24 series, the growth rates, or log first differences, were analyzed.

The first stage of the analysis involved identification of the order p of a pure AR(p) model for each of the 24 series. Such lag-length identification was carried out using both the Akaike information criterion (AIC) and the Schwarzian Bayesian information criterion (SBIC). For all series except one – the growth rates of Australian real output – use of the AIC and SIC led to the same choice of the lag length p. For the growth rates of Australian real output, the results of the hypothesis tests were robust to use of both the AIC-identified and SIC-identified values of p. The results reported below for this series are those for the SIC-selected lag length.

Observed p-values of the linearity test statistics for the international growth rates of real output appear in Table 4.1. One feature that stands out is that all of the p-values for the ARCH Q test are above 0.05. Thus, any evidence of nonlinearity for these series is most likely not due to ARCH effects. For two output series – those for Canada and Sweden – the linearity null hypothesis can be rejected only at very high significance levels. There is strong evidence of bilinear-type nonlinearity for Australian, Italian, UK, and U.S. real output. Only Australian and UK real output show evidence of STAR-type nonlinearity. The clearest conclusion from analysis of the real output growth rates is that the Italian and U.S. real output series are consistent with only bilinear-type nonlinearity. The test statistics for the Australian and UK real output series suggest both STAR-type and bilinear-type nonlinearity.

Table 14.2 presents the observed p-values of the same linearity statistics for the aggregate price-level growth rates for each country. Only two series, the Canadian and the UK inflation rates, suggest STAR-type nonlinearity. There is strong evidence of bilinear-type nonlinearity for five out of the six series, the one exception being the growth rates of the UK price level. Only the Italian inflation-rate series suggests ARCH effects. Thus, for Italy, the data-generating mechanism for the inflation rate may be of either the bilinear or ARCH class. The UK inflation rate is consistent with only STAR-type nonlinearity. The Australian, Swedish, and U.S. inflation-rate series are consistent with only bilinear-type nonlinearity. The test statistics for the Canadian inflation rate suggest both STAR-type and bilinear-type nonlinearity.

Table 14.1. *p-Values of linearity statistics for output* [a]

Country	$S1$	$S3$	$B1$	$B2$	Q
Australia	0.22	0.03	0.13	0.04	0.71
Canada	0.73	0.38	0.34	0.57	0.33
Italy	0.16	0.06	0.15	0.01	0.09
Sweden	0.66	0.71	0.64	0.33	0.42
United Kingdom	0.04	0.03	0.03	0.19	0.18
United States	0.32	0.58	0.13	0.01	0.60

[a] *p*-Values of the $S1$ and $S3$ STAR, $B1$ and $B2$ bilinear, and Q ARCH test statistics for the Backus–Kehoe output growth rates.

Table 14.2. *p-Values of linearity statistics for prices* [a]

Country	$S1$	$S3$	$B1$	$B2$	Q
Australia	0.45	0.23	0.00	0.00	0.38
Canada	0.99	0.04	0.10	0.00	0.14
Italy	0.38	0.43	0.40	0.00	0.00
Sweden	0.52	0.63	0.29	0.02	0.13
United Kingdom	0.25	0.04	0.06	0.11	0.17
United States	0.65	0.47	0.46	0.01	0.05

[a] *p*-Values of the $S1$ and $S3$ STAR, $B1$ and $B2$ bilinear, and Q ARCH test statistics for the Backus–Kehoe price growth rates.

The observed *p*-values of the linearity test statistics for the international investment-growth-rate series are listed in Table 14.3. The Canadian investment-growth-rate series exhibits no departure from nonlinearity. The Australian Italian investment series suggest only ARCH-type nonlinearity. The UK series is consistent with both STAR-type and bilinear-type nonlinearity, whereas the U.S. series is consistent with both bilinearity and ARCH-type nonlinearity. The investment-growth-rate series for Sweden exhibits the strongest departure from linearity. The observed *p*-values for all of the linearity test statistics for this series are below 0.01. It is thus impossible to isolate the source of nonlinearity for this series with the statistics used.

Table 14.4 reports the observed *p*-values of the linearity statistics for the monetary growth rates for each country. Two monetary-growth-rate series, those for Canada and the United States, exhibit no departure from linearity. The Australian monetary growth rate suggests only ARCH-type nonlinearity. The UK monetary growth rate is consistent with only bilinear-type nonlinearity. The Italian money growth rate exhibits both STAR and bilinear nonlinearity. Once again, the Swedish series exhibits the most robust evidence of

Table 14.3. *p-Values of linearity statistics for investment* [a]

Country	S1	S3	B1	B2	Q
Australia	0.79	0.08	0.05	0.17	0.00
Canada	0.39	0.46	0.19	0.12	0.27
Italy	0.37	0.14	0.33	0.18	0.01
Sweden	0.00	0.00	0.00	0.00	0.00
United Kingdom	0.04	0.09	0.03	0.22	0.75
United States	0.49	0.18	0.18	0.01	0.00

[a] *p*-Values of the $S1$ and $S3$ STAR, $B1$ and $B2$ bilinear, and Q ARCH test statistics for the Backus–Kehoe investment growth rates.

Table 14.4. *p-Values of linearity statistics for money* [a]

Country	S1	S3	B1	B2	Q
Australia	0.66	0.65	0.16	0.12	0.00
Canada	0.31	0.59	0.19	0.12	0.29
Italy	0.78	0.00	0.47	0.02	0.13
Sweden	0.00	0.02	0.00	0.00	0.00
United Kingdom	0.92	0.54	0.00	0.00	0.10
United States	0.90	0.90	0.43	0.09	0.89

[a] *p*-Values of the $S1$ and $S3$ STAR, $B1$ and $B2$ bilinear, and Q ARCH test statistics for the Backus–Kehoe money growth rates.

nonlinearity, with the same result that it is impossible to isolate the source of nonlinearity for this country's series via the linearity statistics used in this paper.

4   Conclusions

Of the 24 series examined, 19 exhibit some form of nonlinearity. For seven out of these nineteen rejections of linearity, there is evidence of ARCH-type nonlinearity. Eight series exhibit STAR-type nonlinearity and ten series exhibit bilinear-type nonlinearity. The UK inflation rate is the only series that is consistent with only STAR-type nonlinearity. Five series are consistent with only bilinear-type nonlinearity. The test statistics for the U.S. long-run business-cycle indicators primarily suggest bilinear nonlinear dynamics.

Thus, if asymmetric business-cycle behavior is thought to be consistent with only STAR-type nonlinearity, then the results presented in this paper offer extremely weak evidence in favor of the asymmetry business-cycle hypothesis. It is interesting to contrast these results with the TR test results reported by Ramsey and Rothman (1996).

Ramsey and Rothman (1996) cast the question of business-cycle asymmetry within the context of time reversibility. That is, they argue that business-cycle symmetry implies time-reversible behavior in the dynamics of macroeconomic time series. Analyzing the same international dataset, their TR test statistics rejected the null of business-cycle symmetry for most of these series. The TR test results are not due to either ARCH or GARCH effects, because the TR test does not have power against these stochastic processes. Further, to the extent that the STAR LM statistics indeed have good power against STAR alternatives, then the results of this paper imply that the strong evidence of business-cycle asymmetry reported by Ramsey and Rothman (1993) is not of the STAR type. Consequently, it may be inappropriate to focus on testing the business-cycle asymmetry hypothesis within the context of STAR-type LM tests.

REFERENCES

Backus, D. K., and Kehoe, P. J. (1992). International evidence on the historical properties of business cycles. *American Economic Review*, **82**, 846–88.

Davies, R. B. (1977). Hypothesis testing when a nuisance parameter is present only under the alternative, *Biometrika*, **64**, 247–54.

DeLong, J. B., and Summers, L. H. (1986). Are business cycles symmetrical? In *The American Business Cycle*, ed. R. J. Gordon, National Bureau Economic Research and University of Chicago Press, Chicago.

Engle, R. F. (1982). Autoregressive conditional heteroskedasticity with estimates of the variance of U.K. inflation, *Econometrica*, **50**, 987–1008.

Keynes, J. M. (1936). *The General Theory of Employment, Interest, and Money*, Macmillan, London.

Luukkonen, R., Saikkonen, P., and Teräsvirta, T. (1988a). Testing linearity against smooth transition autoregressive models, *Biometrika*, **75**, 491–9.

(1988b). Testing linearity in Univariate time series models, *Scand. J. Stat.* **15**, 161–75.

Luukkonen, R., and Teräsvirta, T. (1991). Testing linearity of economics time series against cyclical asymmetry, *Ann. Econ. Stat.*, **20/21**, 125–42.

McLeod, A. I., and Li, W. K. (1983). Diagnostic checking ARMA time series models using squared-residual autocorrelations, *Journal of Time Series Analysis*, **4**, 269–73.

Mitchell, W. (1927). *Business Cycles: The Problem and Its Setting*, National Bureau of Economic Research, New York.

Neftci, S. (1984). Are economic time series asymmetric over the business cycle? *J. Polit. Econ.* **92**, 307–28.

Ramsey, J. B., and Rothman, P. (1996). Time irreversibility and business cycle asymmetry. *Journal of Money, Credit, and Banking*, **28**, 1–21.

Saikkonen, P., and Luukkonen, R. (1988). Lagrange multiplier tests for testing nonlinearities in time-series models, *Scand. J. Stat.*, **15**, 55–68.

Subba Rao, T., and Gabr, M. M. (1984). *An Introduction to Bispectral Analysis and Bilinear Time Series Models*, Springer–Verlag, New York.

Tong, H. (1990). *Nonlinear Time Series: A Dynamical System Approach*, Oxford University Press, New York.

Welsh, A., and Jernigan, R. (1983). A statistic to identify asymmetric time series, *American Statistical Association 1983 Proceedings of the Business and Economics Statistics Section*, pp. 390–5.

PART V

Nonlinear prediction and forecasting

Local Lyapunov exponents: Predictability depends on where you are

Barbara A. Bailey

The dominant Lyapunov exponent of a dynamic system measures the average rate at which nearby trajectories of a system diverge. Even though a positive exponent provides evidence for chaotic dynamics and unpredictability, there may predictability of the time series over some finite time periods. In this paper, one version of a local Lyapunov exponent is defined for a dynamic system perturbed by noise. These local Lyapunov exponents are used to detect the parts of the time series that may be more predictable than others. An examination of the fluctuations of the local Lyapunov exponents about the average exponent may provide important information in understanding the heterogeneity of a system. The theoretical properties of these local exponents are discussed and a method of estimating these quantities, using nonparametric regression, is proposed. An application of local exponents for interpreting surface-pressure data is presented.

1   Introduction

The characteristic feature of a chaotic system is that initially nearby trajectories diverge in time (Eckmann and Ruelle, 1985). This feature may be seen by imagining the system to be started twice, but from slightly different initial conditions. For a chaotic system, this difference or error grows exponentially in time, so that the state of this system is essentially unknown after a "short" time. Initially small perturbations that grow exponentially over time indicate sensitive dependence on initial conditions and is responsible for the unpredictability of a chaotic system. This unpredictable time evolution of nonlinear systems occurs in a variety of fields such as physics, meteorology, and epidemiology (see, e.g., ref. Gollub and Benson, 1980; Abarbanel, Levine, MacDonald, and Rothaus, 1990; and Olsen and Schaffer, 1990).

The Lyapunov exponent measures the asymptotic average exponential divergence (or convergence) of nearby trajectories in phase space and has proven

345

to be a useful diagnostic to detect and quantify chaos (Eckmann, and Ruelle 1985). A positive Lyapunov exponent or exponential divergence implies that the system is unpredictable. The predictability of a system is an important feature of its dynamics. Predictability, not only quantified by the Lyapunov exponent, which by definition is a global quantity, but by the identification of regions locally in the phase space that have different short-term sensitivity to small perturbations. This paper discusses local Lyapunov exponents (LLEs), a finite-time version of the Lyapunov exponent, and describes useful information that can be obtained from the analysis of these local exponents. The identification of regions in phase space that may be more predictable than others and the examinations of the fluctuations of these local exponents about the average exponent may be useful in describing the dynamics and heterogeneity of a system.

The paper is organized as follows: Section 2 reviews the mathematical ideas and basic properties of Lyapunov exponents of a system. In Section 3, a definition for LLEs is presented. Some technical details on the computational methods also are included. The statistical properties of local Lyapunov exponents are discussed, using Markov process theory. In Section 4, results for two examples – the Rossler system and surface-pressure data – are presented, showing how LLEs can be used to gain useful information about the system. Finally, Section 5 contains a discussion that concludes the paper.

2   Background and assumptions

We assume that the data $\{x_t\}$ are a time series generated by a nonlinear autoregressive model

$$x_t = f(x_{t-1}, x_{t-2}, \ldots, x_{t-d}) + e_t, \qquad (15.1)$$

where $x_t \in R$ and $\{e_t\}$ is a sequence of independent random variables or perturbations with $E(e_t) = 0$ and $\mathrm{Var}(e_t) = \sigma^2$. Note that the error in equation (15.1) is not measurement error, but dynamic noise, an inherent part of the dynamics of the system.

It is useful to express system (15.1) in terms of a state vector $\mathbf{X}_t = (x_t, \ldots, x_{t-d+1})^T$, an error vector $\mathbf{E}_t = (e_t, 0, \ldots, 0)^T$, and a function $F : R^d \to R^d$ such that

$$\mathbf{X}_t = F(\mathbf{X}_{t-1}) + \mathbf{E}_t, \qquad (15.2)$$

where $\{\mathbf{X}_t\}$ is the systems trajectory.

The state-space representation (15.2) is motivated by Takens (1981) method of reconstruction in time-delay coordinates for a deterministic system [$e_t = 0$ in equation (15.1)]. Intuitively, the data $\{x_t\}$ are observed from a system of unknown dimension, so that the idea of state-space reconstruction is to incorporate enough lags into the state vector that the dynamics of $\mathbf{X}_t$ are qualitatively the same as the full system. The time lags of a single variable x are a surrogate for the unobserved variables of the real system.

To approximate the action of the map F on two initial state vectors $\mathbf{X}_0$ and $\mathbf{Y}_0$, use a Taylor-series expansion:

$$\mathbf{X}_n - \mathbf{Y}_n = F(\mathbf{X}_0) - F(\mathbf{Y}_0)$$
$$\approx DF(\mathbf{X}_0)(\mathbf{X}_0 - \mathbf{Y}_0).$$

The difference at time n between these two initial state vectors is

$$\mathbf{X}_1 - \mathbf{Y}_1 = F^n(\mathbf{X}_0) - F^n(\mathbf{Y}_0)$$
$$\approx DF^n(\mathbf{X}_0)(\mathbf{X}_0 - \mathbf{Y}_0).$$

Let $J_t = DF(\mathbf{X}_t)$, the Jacobian matrix of F evaluated at $\mathbf{X}_t$. By the chain rule for differentiation,

$$\mathbf{X}_n - \mathbf{Y}_n \approx J_{n-1} \cdot J_{n-2} \ldots J_0(\mathbf{X}_0 - \mathbf{Y}_0).$$

Let $\mathbf{u}_0 = \mathbf{X}_0 - \mathbf{Y}_0$. Then, the above equation becomes

$$\mathbf{u}_n \approx DF^n(\mathbf{X}_0)\mathbf{u}_0$$
$$\approx J_0^n \mathbf{u}_0.$$

Therefore, the evolution of initially small differences in initial conditions behave approximately like the solution to the linear system.

One way of defining the global Lyapunov exponent for equation (15.2) is

$$\lambda = \lim_{n \to \infty} \frac{1}{n} \ln \left[\sup_{\mathbf{u} \in R^d, ||\mathbf{u}||=1} ||(J_{n-1} J_{n-2} \ldots J_0)\mathbf{u}|| \right]. \tag{15.3}$$

By the Multiplicative Ergodic Theorem of Oseledec (1968) if $\mathbf{X}_t$ is ergodic, stationary, and $\max(0, \ln||J_t||)$ has finite expectation, then λ exists, is constant, and is independent of the trajectory. The Multiplicative Ergodic Theorem also implies that for almost all $\mathbf{u} \in R^d$ (with respect to Lebesgue measure), the supremum over all directions in equation (15.3) can be omitted and

$$\lambda = \lim_{n \to \infty} \frac{1}{n} \ln ||J_{n-1} J_{n-2} \ldots J_0\mathbf{u}||. \tag{15.4}$$

The examples in Section 4 use $\mathbf{u} = (1, 0, \ldots, 0)^T$ and, in both equations (15.3) and (15.4), $|| \cdot ||$ is a vector norm. The global Lyapunov exponent measures sensitive dependence on initial conditions, that is, if λ is positive then initially close trajectories will diverge exponentially over time.

The concept of an attractor or attracting set in dynamic systems theory is to ensure that trajectories starting near this set converge onto it and their motion is confined to the set. In studies of the behavior of the evolution of trajectories of system (15.2), the physical long-term behavior is observed to settle near a subset of R^n. It is necessary to require bounded fluctuations of the state vector to ensure the existence of this attractor. For a system such as equation (15.2), an operational definition of chaos is bounded fluctuations in the state variable X_t with sensitive dependence on initial conditions (Eckmann and Ruelle, 1985).

3   Local Lyapunov exponents

3.1   *Definition*

The concept of an LLE was first examined in the area of chemical physics (Kosloff and Rice, 1981). The authors proposed a local criterion for the transition from quasiperiodic to chaotic motion in classic mechanical Hamiltonian systems based on geodesic flow on a manifold.

There has been renewed interest in LLEs (Sepulveda, Badii, and Pollak, 1989; and Abarbanel, Brown, Kennel, and Wolff, 1992), where the approach is to average the exponential divergence of nearby trajectories of the system over short time periods. Abarbanel et al. (1992) define a local Lyapunov exponent as a finite-time version of the global Lyapunov exponent, which provides information on how a perturbation to a system's orbit will exponentially increase or decrease in finite time. The experimental data are assumed to come from a system without noise and the method of attractor reconstruction using time delays was implemented. The estimation of Jacobians from observed data involved using the time evolution of the trajectories to construct an approximate neighborhood-to-neighborhood map using local polynomials. To describe the variation of the local exponents over the attractor, the mean value of the LLE weighted with the density of the points on the attractor was introduced. This phase-space average of the LLEs defined the average LLE and the moments about this average were defined in a similar manner.

Wolff (1992) defines LLEs by choosing trajectories starting at a certain distance from a trajectory and averages across all such trajectories after n time steps. The goal was to quantify the divergence of initially nearby trajectories originating in a small region in phase space. The analysis was applied to data arising from one-dimensional chaotic systems and examples with observational and system noise were examined. The local Lyapunov exponent as defined by Wolff was very sensitive to the bandwidth parameter or the distance chosen to average across.

Because Wolff's definition of LLE is sensitive to the choice of the bandwidth, the finite-time definition based on the approach by Abarbanel et al. (1992) is chosen for the definition [see equation (15.5)]. However, because of the assumption of noise in the system, the method of Jacobian estimation discussed in Section 3.2 is quite different from the method used by Abarbanel et al. Also, the variation of the local exponents about their mean are described in a different manner in Section 3.3.

The local Lyapunov exponent, a finite-time version of the global Lyapunov exponent (15.4), is defined as

$$\lambda_n(t) = \frac{1}{n} \ln ||J_{n+t-1} J_{n+t-2} \ldots J_t \mathbf{u}||, \tag{15.5}$$

where $|| \cdot ||$ and $\mathbf{u}$ are as described in equation (15.4). Because $\lambda_n(t)$ is a function of time, the LLE depends on the trajectory and can be thought of as an "n-step-ahead" LLE process.

3.2 *Computational aspects*

The calculation of LLEs in equation (15.5) requires an estimation of the Jacobian matrix J_t. LENNS, a neural-network program to estimate the dominant Lyapunov exponent of a noisy nonlinear system from a time series was used to estimate the map f of equation (15.1) (Ellner, Nychka, and Gallant, 1992). Neural networks have been shown to be successful in the modeling of time-series data (Casdagli, 1992). LENNS uses nonlinear regression to generate the estimate of f and its partial derivatives that are used to compute the LLE. In LENNS, the map f is approximated by a single hidden-layer feedforward network with a single output. The form of this model is

$$f(x_1, x_2, \ldots, x_d) = \beta_0 + \sum_{j=1}^{k} \beta_j \varphi(\mathbf{X}^T \gamma_j + \mu_j), \tag{15.6}$$

where $\gamma_j = (\gamma_{j1}, \gamma_{j2}, \ldots, \gamma_{jd})^T$ and φ is a sigmoid function $\varphi(u) = e^u/(1 + e^u)$. The model consists of d inputs, where $\mathbf{X}$ is the vector of inputs; and k hidden units.

The complexity of the model, that is, the embedding dimension and the number of hidden units, was chosen on the basis of generalized cross validation (GCV). Cross validation is a standard approach for selecting smoothing parameters in nonparametric regression (Wahba, 1990). Prediction accuracy is determined by deleting each point from the dataset, one at a time, and fitting the model to the reduced dataset and predicting the omitted point. The modified GCV function is

$$V_c = \frac{\frac{1}{n} \text{RSS}}{\left(1 - p\frac{c}{n}\right)^2} \tag{15.7}$$

where RSS is the residual sum of squares, n is the number of data points used to fit the model, and p is the effective number of parameters. The cost parameter,

c gives larger weight to the larger values of p. The standard GCV function is V_c with $c = 1$.

3.3   *Statistical properties*

In this section the asymptotic theory and limiting distribution of $\lambda_n(t)$ is investigated. Because LLEs involve the products of Jacobians, the analysis using products of random matrices may appear to be quite reasonable. However, convergence in distribution of products of random matrices requires conditions on nonnegativity of the entries (see, e.g., Furstenberg and Kesten, 1960; Lo and Mukherjea, 1991). For Jacobians, this assumption is not possible. The use of Markov process theory will make for a richer analysis. Let $\mathbf{X}_k$ be a stationary Markov process. Consider the vector Markov process

$$\mathbf{W}_k = \begin{bmatrix} \mathbf{X}_k \\ \cdots \\ \mathbf{u}_k \end{bmatrix},$$

where $\mathbf{X}_k$ is the state vector and

$$\mathbf{u}_k = \frac{J_k \mathbf{u}_{k-1}}{||\mathbf{u}_{k-1}||}.$$

The information needed to compute an n-step-ahead LLE is the product of n Jacobians. To describe this process, it is useful to think of $\mathbf{u}_k$ as a one-step action of the map F.

The motivation for the construction of the vector Markov process $\mathbf{W}_k$ is to write λ_n as the sum of random variables, that is, λ_n can be written as $\frac{1}{n}\sum_{k=1}^{n} g(\mathbf{W}_k)$. This can be seen more clearly by working backward from the definition of λ_n. In this derivation, $\frac{\mathbf{u}_0}{||\mathbf{u}_0||} = \mathbf{u}$ in equation 15.5.

$$\lambda_n = \frac{1}{n} \ln \left|\left| J_n J_{n-1} \ldots J_1 \frac{\mathbf{u}_0}{||\mathbf{u}_0||} \right|\right|$$

$$= \frac{1}{n} \ln \left(\frac{||J_n J_{n-1} \ldots J_1 \frac{\mathbf{u}_0}{||\mathbf{u}_0||}|| \ldots ||J_1 \frac{\mathbf{u}_0}{||\mathbf{u}_0||}||}{||J_{n-1} \ldots J_1 \frac{\mathbf{u}_0}{||\mathbf{u}_0||}|| \ldots ||J_1 \frac{\mathbf{u}_0}{||\mathbf{u}_0||}||} \right)$$

$$= \frac{1}{n} \left(\ln \left|\left| \frac{J_n J_{n-1} \ldots J_1 \frac{\mathbf{u}_0}{||\mathbf{u}_0||}}{||J_{n-1} \ldots J_1 \frac{\mathbf{u}_0}{||\mathbf{u}_0||}||} \right|\right| + \cdots + \ln \left|\left| J_1 \frac{\mathbf{u}_0}{||\mathbf{u}_0||} \right|\right| \right)$$

$$= \frac{1}{n} \sum_{k=1}^{n} \ln ||\mathbf{u}_k||$$

$$= \frac{1}{n} \sum_{k=1}^{n} g(\mathbf{W}_k)$$

The LLE now can be defined as

$$\lambda_n = \frac{1}{n} \sum_{k=1}^{n} \ln \|\mathbf{u}_k\| \tag{15.8}$$

$$= \frac{1}{n} \sum_{k=1}^{n} g(\mathbf{W}_k). \tag{15.9}$$

There are assumptions that need to be made on $\mathbf{W}_k$ and g to obtain distributional results. Suitable mixing conditions need to be assumed for the vector Markov process $\mathbf{W}_k$. Relaxation of a uniform mixing condition (stronger than strongly mixing) maybe difficult to show. The function g is assumed to be square integrable.

The mean of $\lambda_n(t)$ (as $n \to \infty$) converges to the global Lyapunov exponent, λ, as shown by Furstenberg and Kesten (1960), that

$$\lambda = \lim_{n \to \infty} \frac{1}{n} E\{\ln \|J_n J_{n-1} \ldots J_1\|\}. \tag{15.10}$$

A central limit theorem for LLEs based on a central limit theorem for Markov processes can now be applied to equation (15.9) (Rosenblatt, 1971).

Theorem 15.1: *Let $\{\mathbf{W}_k\}$ be a stationary Markov process. Assume that the processes W_k is uniformly mixing. If the function g is uniformly square integrable, then*

$$\frac{\sqrt{n}(\lambda_n - \lambda)}{\sqrt{\mathrm{Var}\,(\lambda_n)}} \to N\,(0,\,1) \quad \text{as} \quad n \to \infty.$$

An alternative CLT for any initial distribution of $\mathbf{u}_k$ and not just the stationary probability distribution is presented in Bailey et al. (1996). The CLT result can make it possible, to investigate the variance of the mean of the LLEs about the global Lyapunov exponent. To characterize the pattern of fluctuation in LLEs, their variance and autocorrelation may be useful. For example, to calculate standard errors of the variance about the mean, a moving-average process could be used to model on the local Lyapunov process, and the sample autocovariance function could be used to estimate the variance.

4   Examples

In this section, the LLEs of two systems are examined. The Rossler system is an example of a chaotic system and is a set of three first-order differential equations. Reconstruction in three-dimensional space using time delays make it possible to graph the local regions in space that are most unpredictable. Surface-pressure data are from a higher-dimensional nonchaotic system. However, the

LLEs still provide information about the predictability of the system as related to the seasons.

4.1   Rossler system

The Rossler system is a coupled, nonlinear system of three first-order differential equations:

$$\frac{da}{dt} = -(b + c)$$

$$\frac{db}{dt} = a + 0.5b$$

$$\frac{dc}{dt} = 0.2 + c(a - 10).$$

The data $\{x_t\}$ are a series of 400 points generated by sampling one of the variables, say $a(t)$, at equally spaced time steps. The Rossler equations were numerically integrated with a fixed time step, $\Delta t = 0.01$, and a_t was sampled at every 50 time steps. A noise of 5 percent was added to this system at each sampling time. Because the maximum of the range of $a(t)$ is about 20, a $\sigma = 0.1$ was chosen for the variance of $\{e_t\}$. The Rossler time series $\{x_t\}$ is in the form of equation (15.1).

The time series of the Rossler system with 5 percent noise can be seen in Figure 15.1. The Rossler system is an example of a very simple nonlinear system that produces very complicated dynamics. A three-dimensional phase space is needed to reconstruct the dynamics of the system. Figure 15.2, as a two-dimensional phase-space portrait of the system, where the third dimension is projected onto a plane. The system evolves in a clockwise direction.

In this example, the five-step-ahead LLEs were chosen for further analysis. There are 396 products of 5 Jacobians possible. Figure 15.3(a) shows the range of these exponents divided into five equally spaced groups. The smallest local exponents are labeled 1 and the largest are labeled 5. The largest local exponents are of interest because they represent the times when the series is most unpredictable. The size of the exponents are labeled on the time series in Figure 15.3(b). The fives often appear just before a large peak in the series. In Figure 15.4, the largest exponents are labeled 5 in their two-dimensional phase-space location. Here, it can be noticed that the largest exponents are found in the areas where complicated dynamics occur, that is, it is not certain whether nearby trajectories will continue to evolve in a smooth elliptical motion in the $X(t) - X(t-1)$ plane or bend into the third dimension, the $X(t-2)$ plane. This example demonstrates that LLEs may be able to detect unpredictable behavior locally in a system.

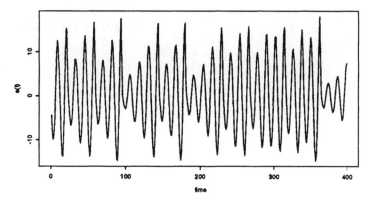

Figure 15.1. Rossler series: 5% noise.

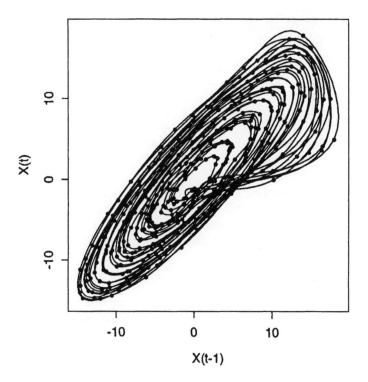

Figure 15.2. Two-dimensional phase space for the 5% noise Rossler system.

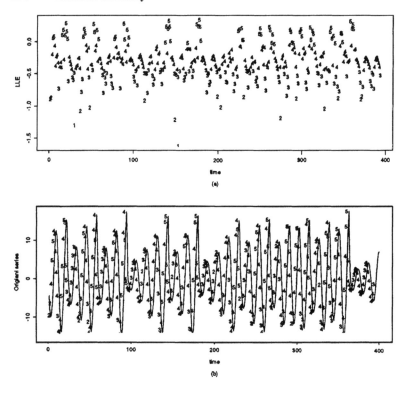

Figure 15.3. (a) Five-step-ahead LLEs for the 5% noise Rossler system. (b) Series coded by size of the five-step-ahead LLEs.

Figure 15.5 shows the distribution of LLEs as products of Jacobians increase from 5, 10, 20, 50, to 100. As n increase, the mean of the LLEs appear to converge to the global Lyapunov exponent, $\lambda = 0.045$. This is consistent with the asymptotics of the mean of the LLEs in equation (15.10).

4.2   Surface-pressure data

Ten years of daily surface-pressure data were taken from four European cities–Postdam, Fanoe, Uccle, and Prague. A principal component analysis showed the largest eigenvalue to be three orders of magnitude larger than the remaining ones, and so, the principal component was used as the data series $\{x_t\}$.

Figure 15.6 is the distribution of LLEs for the pressure data. The global exponent for the system is $\lambda = -0.38$. Because $\lambda > 0$, this is not a chaotic system. However, the examination of the largest five-step-ahead LLEs reveals that they occur primarily in the winter months. Figure 15.7 shows the 100 largest of the five-step-ahead LLEs on a yearly cycle between 0 and 1. The

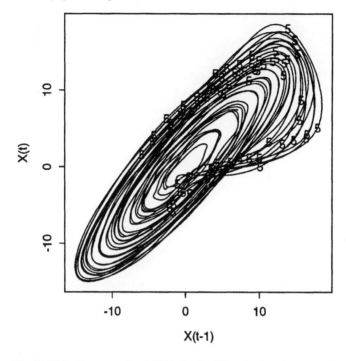

Figure 15.4. Five-step-ahead LLEs for the 5% noise Rossler system in phase space.

largest exponents are concentrated between 0–0.2 and 0.8–1. This finding is consistent with the observation of meteorologists that winter is inherently more variable than the other seasons.

5   Conclusion

This paper proposes a finite-time version of the global Lyapunov exponent, the LLE. The global exponent measures the long-term average response to perturbations of the system, in contrast to the local exponent that measures short-term responses to perturbations at different locations in the state space. Instead of an invariant quantity of the system, the LLE is a time-dependent process. Convergence in distribution results presented for the process make the characterization of the fluctuations of these local Lyapunov exponents about their mean possible.

The two examples presented, the Rossler system and surface-pressure data show that LLEs can be used to identify regions in the state space that are most unpredictable and the places in the times series where n-step-ahead prediction may be difficult.

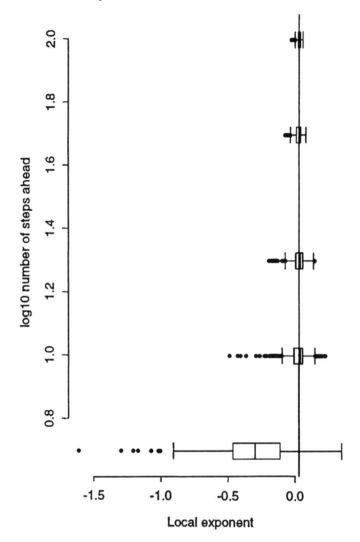

Figure 15.5.   Distribution of the five-step-ahead LLEs for the 5% noise Rossler system.

Systems that are identified as being near the transition to chaos, that is, a global Lyapunov exponent near 0, such as measles (Ellner, Gallant, and Theiler 1993), may vary between periods when there is finite-time "sensitive dependence" on initial conditions and when there is not. LLEs are one way to quantify this behavior. This fluctuation of the local exponents about the global exponent

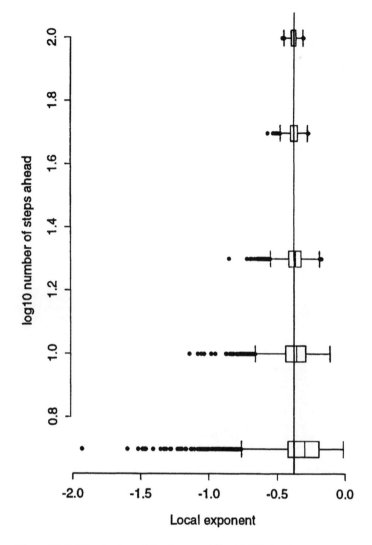

Figure 15.6. Distribution of the five-step-ahead LLEs for the pressure data.

may provide important information in understanding the heterogeneity of the system. The characterization of the patterns of fluctuation in LLEs, such as their variance and autocorrelation, is an important area for future research.

LLEs can be used to determine the parts of the state space that may be more predictable or less predictable than others. They also may detect the places in

358   **Barbara A. Bailey**

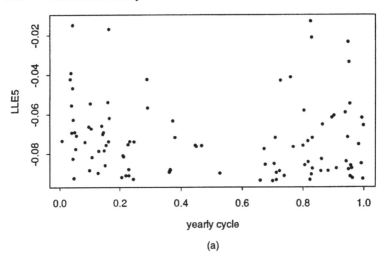

(a)

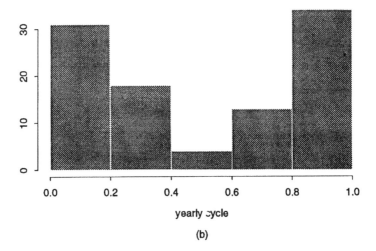

(b)

Figure 15.7. (a) The 100 largest five-step-ahead LLEs for the pressure data over the yearly cycle. (b) Histogram of (a).

the time series where short-term predictability is highest and lowest. Thus, the concept of predictability of a time series can be extended to the local behavior of a system and may depend on "where in the time series" or "where in the state space" the area of interest is.

REFERENCES

Abarbanel, H. D. I., Brown, R., and Kennel, B. (1992). Local Lyapunov exponents computed from observed data, *J. Nonlinear Sci.*, **2**, 343–65.

Abarbanel, H. D. I., Levine, H., MacDonald, G., and Rothaus, O. (1990). Statistics of extreme events with application to climate, Tech. Rept. JSR-90-305, MITRE Corp., McLean, VA.

Bailey, B. A., Ellner, S., and Nychka, D. W. (1991). *Chaos with confidence: Asymptotics and Applications of Local Lyapunov Exponents*, Fields Institute Communication. American Mathematical Association, Providence, RI, in press.

Casdagli, M. (1992). A dynamical systems approach to modeling input-output systems, *Nonlinear Modeling and Forecasting, SFI Studies in the Sciences of Complexity Proceedings*, Vol. 12, Addison Wesley, New York, pp. 265–81.

Eckmann, J.-P., and Ruelle, D. (1985). Ergodic theory of chaos and strange attractors, *Rev. Mod. Phys.*, **57**, 617–56.

Ellner, S., Gallant, A. R., and Theiler, J. (1993). Detecting nonlinearity and chaos in epidemic data, Tech. Rept., North Carolina State University, Raleigh, NC, Santa Fe Institute, Santa Fe, NM, Los Alamos National Lab., Los Alamos, NM. Preprint.

Ellner, S., Nychka, D. W., and Gallant, A. R. (1992). LENNS, a program to estimate the dominant Lyapunov exponent of noisy nonlinear systems from time series data, Institute of Statistics Mimeo Series 2235, Statistics Department, North Carolina State University, Raleigh, NC.

Furstenberg, H., and Kesten, H. (1960). Products of random matrices, *Ann. Math. Stat.*, **31**, 457–69.

Gollub, J. P., and Benson, S. V. (1980). Many routes to turbulent convection, *J. Fluid Mech.*, **100**, 449–70.

Kosloff, R., and Rice, S. A. (1981). Dynamical correlations and chaos in classical Hamiltonian systems, *J. Chem. Phy.*, **74**, 1947–56.

Lo, C., and Mukherjea, A. (1991). Convergence in distribution of products of d by d random matrices, *J. Math. Anal. App.*, **162**, 71–91.

Olsen, L. F., and Schaffer, W. M. (1990). Chaos versus noisy periodicity: Alternative hypotheses for childhood epidemics, *Science*, **249**, 499–504.

Oseledec, V. I. (1968). A multiplicative ergodic theorem. Lyapunov characteristic numbers for dynamical systems, *Moscow Math. Soc.*, **19** 197.

Rosenblatt, M. (1971). Markov processes structures and asymptotic behavior, Springer–Verlag, New York.

Sepulveda, M. A., Badii, R., and Pollak, E. (1989). Spectral analysis of concervative dynamical systems, *Phys. Rev. Lett.*, **63**(12), 1226–29.

Takens, F. (1981). *Lecture Notes in Mathematics, Dynamical Systems and Turbulence*, Vol. 898, Springer, Berlin.

Wahba, G. (1990). *Spline Models for Observational Data*, SIAM, Philadelphia, PA.

Wolff, R. C. L. (1992). Local Lyapunov exponents: Looking closely at chaos, *J. Roy. Stat. Soc. B*, **54**(2), 353–71.

CHAPTER 16

Forecasting realignments: The case of the French franc in the exchange-rate mechanism

Bruce Mizrach

I utilize a new model of Markov switching with probit transitions to characterize exchange-rate mechanism. For the French franc, I show that the probit model accurately anticipates realignments of the central parity. Used as a risk measure, the probit model also is a good proxy for volatility. When risk is high, we make less accurate forecasts. Adopting a rule of thumb, not to predict when the probit risk estimate is more than two standard deviations above the mean, we can dramatically improve forecast accuracy.

Our knowledge concerning exchange rates does not seem proportional to the effort. Despite being one of the most widely studied financial variables, very little is known about the behavior of the spot exchange rate. Foreign exchange rates seem to defy simple equilibrium relationships such as interest parity.[1] Atheoretical models have fared no better. Once estimated, the data quickly expose models to be nothing more than curve-fitting exercises.[2] Nonlinear modeling has emerged as a possible solution to this conundrum.

One branch of this new literature has adopted empirical models for the higher moments of exchange rates. Exchange-rate returns are generally nonnormal (in the Gaussian sense).[3] Leptokurtic (fat-tailed) distributions, with clustering of the large errors, has motivated the application of the generalized autoregressive conditional heteroscedasticity (GARCH) model of Engle (1982) and Bollerslev (1986) to exchange rates. The GARCH models have faltered largely on two grounds. A compelling theoretical explanation for the volatility clustering is

An earlier version of this paper was presented at the American Statistical Association Meetings in San Francisco, August 8–12, 1993. I would like to thank Doug Patterson for helpful comments.
[1] See, e.g., Froot and Thaler (1990) and the resolution proposed in Mizrach (1995c).
[2] An exhaustive survey of models from the 1970s can be found in Meese and Rogoff (1983).
[3] See, e.g., Hsieh (1988).

361

needed.[4] The GARCH effects seem also not to be present in the mean, and therefore are of little use for forecasting.

Nonlinear modeling also has been motivated by institutional changes. Since March 1979, nearly all major European currencies have been traded within target zones. Krugman (1991) has shown that target zones will introduce non-linearities into exchange rates even if the bands never change.

Several researchers have tried to make sense of the nonlinearities using time-series techniques. Engel and Hamilton (1990) used a Markov-switching model. Meese and Rose (1990, 1991), Diebold and Nason (1990), and Mizrach (1992) used nonparametric techniques. None of these papers has produced robust out-of-sample forecast improvements. The random walk is often a better predictor than sophisticated nonlinear technology.

This paper tries to get a better understanding of the failures of the nonlinear models. I show that the spot exchange rate is indeed predictable most of the time. At a few crucial junctures, coinciding with exchange-rate realignments, all models, linear and nonlinear, forecast poorly. I show that a new class of model introduced previously (Mizrach 1995a) can help us understand when forecasting is likely to be difficult. The Mizrach model produces a daily time series of the probability of realignment. Adopting a rule of thumb, not to forecast when the risk is more than two standard deviations above average, we can dramatically improve our overall accuracy.

The paper is organized as follows. I begin with the naive benchmark for the exchange rate, the unit root. I then turn to linear and nonlinear time-series models, including Mizrach's probit-Markov model. Using the probit's risk estimates, I repeat the modeling exercise using the rule of thumb. A summary and conclusion follow.

1   The random walk

This section is devoted to the benchmark model for all exchange-rate forecasting exercises – the random walk. I begin by describing the data used in the analysis of the unit root.

1.1   *Data*

For purposes of empirical illustration, I look at the French franc, German deutsche mark (Fr/DM) exchange rate over the period March, 13, 1979, to September, 11, 1992. This spans the creation of the exchange-rate mechanism (ERM) in Europe to the suspension of the Italian lira and the British pound from the ERM. I have 3,417 daily observations on European Currency Unit exchange rates from the 14:30 fix in Basle, which I convert into a cross rate.

---

[4] See Mizrach (1996) for some work along these lines.

Table 16.1. *Unit-root tests*

	Mar. 13, 1979 to Sept. 11, 1992	No. of observations
Coefficient	−5.002E-04	3,416
t-Statistic	(2.06)	

Table 16.2. *Descriptive statistics*

Δs_t	Full sample	Omit regime changes
Mean	11.4573-05	5.935E-05
SD	1.997E-03	1.253E-03
Kurtosis	324.694	26.916

ERM exchange rates float in 2.25 percent bands around a central parity. The central parity is occasionally realigned. With the franc, the parity has been rest on seven occasions.[5]

1.2   *Unit-root tests*

Let s_t denote the log of the spot exchange rate, and let Δs_t be the log difference. I regress the difference on the lag of the level. A coefficient significantly less than zero would reject the null hypothesis of a unit root.

The relevant critical values are the Dickey-Fuller statistics, not the usual t-statistics.[6] In a large sample, a 5 percent one-sided critical value is 2.86, and a 1 percent critical value is 3.43. Despite a t-ratio of 2.06, the coefficient is not significantly different from zero. This evidence supports the conventional wisdom that it is hard to reject the random walk as a statistical description for the spot exchange rate.

1.3   *Analysis of unconditional moments across regimes*

I next looked at the unconditional moments of the first differences of the Fr/DM exchange rate. The daily movements are quite small, but rates can still be quite volatile. The kurtosis for the sample as a whole is over 300.

I wanted to examine whether the regime changes were influencing these results. I omitted 66 influential data points, five days around either side of a

---

[5] On August, 4, 1993, the franc passed below its old ERM floor of 3.4305 Fr/DM. Bands of 15 percent have been introduced around the old parity, so technically, the franc has not devalued.

[6] For more discussion on this issue, see Mizrach (1993) in which the critical values is bootstrapped because of the nonnormality and serial correlation in the data. In an experimental design a bit different from this one, the appropriate critical values are found to be 3.43 and 5.06.

devaluation. These results appear in the second column of Table 16.2. The daily changes are much smaller because I have removed the large devaluations. Even more notable is that the kurtosis falls by a factor of more than 10, to 26.916.

2   Alternative models for the exchange rate

I turn next to several different approaches to model the exchange rate. I then analyze the residuals to see which, if any, of the models does the best job of depicting the important devaluation episodes.

2.1   *Linear time series*

The most straightforward time-series approach is a Box-Jenkins model. Using the Akaike information criterion, I fit an AR(3) model to the first differences.

2.2   *Near-neighbor models*

Nonparametric approaches are appealing because they can provide meaningful statistical inference when very little is known about the series' fundamentals or distribution. Recent efforts at nonparametric modeling include Meese and Rose (1990, 1991), Diebold and Nason (1990), and Mizrach (1992).

A technique that is amenable to our application is nearest-neighbor methods. The idea is to find neighbors near the current realization of the independent variables. With locally weighted regression, one then fits a regression surface to the neighboring dependent variables. I selected a model with five neighbors and used least-squares weights to estimate the exchange-rate changes. I denote this model as 5-NN.

3   Analysis of the residuals

In this section, I analyze the residuals of the two models to evaluate their performance in explaining the critical devaluation episodes.

The first column of Table 16.3 lists the dates of the six devaluation episodes. The next column is the percentage of the variance in the raw data due to the 66 realignment observations. Under the columns for the two models, AR(3) and 5-NN, are the percentages of the sum of squared residuals for the same dates. Even though they comprise only 66 observations out of 3,416, or less than 2 percent of the total, the six devaluation episodes explain 61 percent of the variance.

The AR(3) model does not explain these sudden devaluations. In the residuals of the AR(3) model, 58 percent of the sum of squared residuals is due to the six episodes.

Table 16.3. *Analysis of variance*

Date	%Variance	Percentage of sum of squared residuals	
		AR(3)	5-NN
9/17-10/1/179	0.37	0.39	0.20
9/24-10/8/81	13.81	14.35	13.93
6/7-6/21/82	25.24	25.16	24.79
3/15-3/30/83	12.54	8.73	12.59
3/24-4/10/86	8.63	8.81	8.49
1/5-1/19/87	0.83	0.83	0.73

The NN-model leaves just as much information behind in the residuals as do the linear AR models. Sixty-one percent of the sum of squared residuals is in these devaluation episodes.

It seems that if we are to make much progress, we need to uncover something that helps us predict realignments.

4 A probit-Markov model of devaluation risk

In Mizrach (1995a), I introduce a new type of Markov-switching model. Unlike conventional switching models, the probability of a change in regime varies smoothly throughout the sample.

The model has two parts. In the first part, as with conventional switching models, one specifies models for the conditional mean in both regimes. In our exchange-rate context, they are the within band and devaluation regimes. Within the band, the exchange rate is mean reverting. Outside of the band, I find that devaluations are proportional to the cumulative departure from purchasing-power parity.

I describe the probit part of the model in greater detail because that is what I will use in this section. I link the devaluation risk to a constant term, z_{1t}, and two state variables. The first is the position of the exchange rate within the band. Define

$$z_{2t} = (s_t - \underline{s})/(\bar{s} - \underline{s}), \qquad (16.1)$$

where $[\underline{s}, \bar{s}]$ are the lower and upper bounds of the target zone.

The second variable is based on the yield curve. During several devaluation crises, the term structure has become steeply negatively sloped. For example, on March, 15, 1983, five days prior to a realignment of the franc, the French 3-month $i_i^{3/12}$, 1-month $i_i^{1/12}$ spread, denoted here as

$$z_{3t} = \log(1 + i_t^{3/12}) - \log(1 + i_t^{1/12}) \qquad (16.2)$$

was -46.00. I also add a constant term, defining $z_t = (1, z_{2t}, z_{3t})$.

Table 16.4. *Risk estimates prior to realignment*

Date	Average risk	Peak risk
Sept. 24, 1979	8.56	9.11
Oct. 5, 1981	32.11	37.80
June 14, 1982	35.31	43.70
March 21, 1983	99.99	99.99
April 7, 1986	19.67	25.91
Jan. 12, 1987	14.72	19.75

To ensure that the risk remains on [0, 1], I make a probit transformation

$$p_t = \int_{-\infty}^{\gamma z_t} \left(\sqrt{2\pi}\right)^{-1} \exp(-t^2/2)dt \equiv \Phi(\gamma z_t). \tag{16.3}$$

In a fully specified model for the French-German interest differential, I obtain implicit market estimates of the potential devaluation risk. I find $\hat{\gamma} = (-1.563, 0.367, -17.177)$. I then compute a risk measure series, $\hat{p}_t$.

In Table 16.4, I look at the risk just prior to realignment. The first column contains the average risk in the five days prior to realignment. In the second column, I have the peak risk, which is almost always the day before the devaluation.

These risks should be compared relative to a mean risk of devaluation of 8.3 percent with a standard deviation of 6.2 percent. In five of the seven realignments, a risk two standard deviations above the mean (20.7 percent) was observed prior to a devaluation.[7]

Now we'll see whether this risk model can be useful in fitting the exchange-rate data.

5   Model evaluation

In regression exercises, I discovered that the risk model was not very precise in detecting the exact day of realignment. If you predicted a large change in the spot rate every day in which the risk was significantly above its mean, you would forecast very poorly. I chose instead to look at a rule of thumb where the risk measure provided information on when *not* to forecast.

In Table 16.5, I look at the sample mean squared errors (MSE) for the linear and nonparametric models. The random walk (a no-change forecast) is included as a benchmark. Note that the MSE for the nonlinear 5-NN model is less than 0.2 percent better than the random walk.

---

[7] On July, 30, 1993, prior to the widening of the bands, the franc's risk estimate was at 24.5%.

Table 16.5. *Model evaluation*

Model	MSE	*M*-stat
Random walk	4.01E-06	
5-NN	3.97E-06	0.03
AR(3)	3.95E-06	1.16
Risk AR(3)	1.37E-06	2.14

To make a formal comparison, I use the robust forecast comparison intro-duced previously (Mizrach 1995b), which I designate the *M*-stat in the table. This statistic has very weak population assumptions that can readily handle the kurtosis I found in Section 1. It has an asymptotic normal distribution, which is a good approximation in a sample of this size.

The last line of the table is a forecast rule of making no prediction when risk is more than two standard deviations above its mean (20.7 percent in our sample). Using this rule of thumb, 56 observations are eliminated, but the MSE improves almost threefold. The *M*-stat shows that the improvement is statistically significant.

6   Conclusion

The idea that exchange rates are unpredictable needs to be qualified. The fixed exchange rates of the ERM are difficult to predict only at times of realignment. These regime changes, which contribute to the characteristic GARCH effects, are also predictable. We were able to improve our forecast accuracy almost 300 percent by limiting our predictions to those days in which the risk of realignment was not significantly higher than average.

REFERENCES

Bollerslev, T. (1986). Generalized autoregressive conditional heteroscedasticity, *J. Econ.* **31**, 307–27.
Diebold, F. X., and Nason, J. (1990). Nonparametric exchange rate prediction? *J. Int. Econ.* **28**, 315–32.
Engle, R. (1982). Autoregressive conditional heteroscedasticity with estimates of the variance of U.K. inflation, *Econometrica* **50**, 987–1008.
Engel, C., and Hamilton, J. D. (1990). Long swings in the dollar: are they in the data and do Markets know it? *Am. Econ. Rev.* **80**, 689–713.
Froot, K., and Thaler, R. (1990). Anomalies: Foreign Exchange, *J. Econ. Perspect.* **3**, 179–92.
Hsieh, D. (1988). The statistical properties of daily foreign exchange rates: 1974–83, *J. Int. Econ.* **24**, 129–45.
Krugman, P. (1991). Target zones and exchange rate dynamics, *Q. J. Econ.* **56**, 669–82.

Meese, R., and Rogoff, K. (1983). Empirical exchange rate models of the seventies: Do they fit out of sample? *J. Int. Econ.* **14**, 3–24.

Meese, R., and Rose, A. (1990). Nonlinear, nonparametric, nonessential exchange rate estimation, *Am. Econ. Rev. Pap. Proc.* **80**, 192–96.

(1991). An empirical assessment of nonlinearities in models of exchange rate determination. *Rev. Econ. Stud.* **80**, 608–19.

Mizrach, B. (1996), Mimeo, Rutgers University. Learning and conditional heteroscedasticity in asset returns, Working Paper, The Wharton School,

(1992). Multivariate nearest-neighbour forecasts of EMS exchange rates, *J. Appl. Econ.* **7** (Supp.), S151–63.

(1993). Mean reversion in EMS exchange rates, Working Paper No. 93-01, Federal Reserve Bank of New York.

(1995a). *J. of International Money and Finance* **14**, 641–57. Target zones models with stochastic realignments: An econometric evaluation, Working Paper No. 93-02. Federal Reserve Bank of New York.

(1995b). Rutgers U. Working Paper 95-24. Forecast comparison in L_2, Working Paper, The Wharton School.

(1995c). Mimeo, Rutgers University. Uncovering interest parity in the ERM, Working Paper, Federal Reserve Bank of New York.

CHAPTER 17

Daily returns in international stock markets: Predictability, nonlinearity, and transaction costs

Steve Satchell and Allan Timmermann

Evidence of nonlinear components in daily returns is compared across 12 national stock-market indexes and a world index over the period 1980–92. A nonparametric nearest-neighbor algorithm is applied to identify nonlinear patterns in the daily returns and update embedding vectors one step ahead to generate recursive forecasts. The economic value of these nonparametric recursive forecasts is measured by using the forecasts in a simple trading strategy that explicitly accounts for transaction costs. The transaction costs are important factors in determining the stochastic properties of the daily returns series in the markets under consideration and probably are sufficiently large to rule out economic profits from trading on the basis of nonparametric forecasts.

1   Introduction

Nonlinear analysis is now securely placed as an important technique in applied economics. A possible procedure, and the one taken in this paper, is to test if a time series is independent and identically distributed, and, if this state is rejected, to investigate whether the series is chaotic.[1] The latter analysis can be based on an examination of the correlation integral as a function of the embedding dimension. In some cases, indications of chaos have been found although the statistical methodology is weakened by small sample problems (Ramsey, Sayers, and Rothman 1990).

What has not been done in most of these analyses is to link the identification of nonlinear patterns with the short-term predictability of the series and assess

Comments from two anonymous referees and from participants at the conference on nonlinear dynamics and economics at the European University Institute in Florence are gratefully acknowledged.
[1] See Brock et al. (1991), Frank, Gencay, and Stengos (1988), Frank and Stengos (1988), Hsieh (1989, 1991), and Sheinkman and LeBaron (1989). Alternatively, one could test for linearity and, if rejected, proceed to model the detected nonlinearity as a nonlinear stochastic process.

the economic significance of predictable components in daily stock returns.[2] We follow such a procedure in this paper and also investigate whether transaction costs are sufficiently large to eliminate possible profits based on a daily trading strategy that uses nonparametric forecasts. This brings some realism into the interpretation of the presence of predictable patterns in daily stock prices as a profitmaking opportunity.

From the very definition of a chaotic process, any series that exhibits chaos of low order should be highly predictable in the very short run. We apply a simple nonparametric approach to the statistical analysis of daily returns in 10 European stock markets as well as in Japan, the United States, and for the Morgan Stanley World Index over the period 1980–92. The method builds on a nearest-neighbor principle and attempts to recognize repeated patterns in the time series. Compared to standard chaos methods, our approach has the advantage that it can identify patterns in the data of a stochastic nature (such as serial correlation) as well as truly chaotic components.

To test the existence of chaotic components in stock returns, we compute correlation integrals for each of the daily returns series. In a white-noise time series, the correlation integral increases in proportion with the embedding dimension, whereas it tends to reach an early saturation point in a chaotic system of low order. Although we find that, for almost all of the international returns series, the correlation integral is an increasing function of the embedding dimension, the correlation integral does not increase in proportion with the embedding dimension. Hence, it seems possible that there may exist chaotic components of a sufficiently low order to be useful in forecasting the daily returns.

We also compare the correlation between the one-step-ahead forecasts from our nonparametric recursive procedure and the realized daily returns to the correlation between recursive linear forecasts from an autoregressive model and the realized returns. The criteria adopted in this comparison of the two sets of forecasts are the proportion of cases where the sign of the realized daily stock return is correctly forecast as well as the size of the correlation between realized and predicted stock returns. For 9 of the 13 investigated stock indexes, the recursive forecasts based on the nonparametric approach perform better than the recursive forecasts from the linear model.

To get a more precise notion of the economic significance of predictable patterns in the daily returns series, we use the nonparametric forecasts in a

---

[2] Diebold and Nason (1990) applied a nonlinear nearest-neighbor algorithm similar to ours to analyze weekly dollar spot exchange rates. They found that their out-of-sample predictions produced higher mean squared errors and mean absolute errors than a simple random-walk model and that nonlinear patterns in the exchange-rate series were not exploitable for improved point prediction.

trading strategy that switches the invested funds between any given stock index and cash. The switching strategy applies a simple investment criterion: Hold stocks if the forecasted value of the next-period stock return is positive; otherwise, hold cash. We characterize the turnover on the switching portfolio and the break-even transaction costs that imply that the mean return on the buy-and-hold strategy in the market index equals the mean return on the switching portfolio. This exercise provides information about the magnitude of the transaction costs, which will suffice to rule out a higher mean return on the switching portfolio than on a passive stragety of holding the market portfolio.

The main conclusion of the paper is that, although there appear to be detectable nonlinear components in daily stock prices, their magnitude is not sufficiently large to enable investors to generate profits that exceed returns from a buy-and-hold strategy once trading costs are considered. This highlights an inherent problem associated with predicting nonlinearities in asset prices: Detection of nonlinearities requires a large sample and, in practice, this means use of high-frequency data. But any investment strategy based on signals generated at a high frequency easily encounters the problems associated with a high turnover rate and the resulting high transaction costs.

The plan of the paper is as follows. Section 2 describes the statistical properties of the data sets. Section 3 introduces the nonparametric methods used in the paper and presents results on the evidence of nonlinearities in the investigated time series. In Section 4, we compute nonparametric forecasts of daily returns for the 13 stock indexes under consideration. These recursive, nonparametric one-step-ahead forecasts are compared to recursive forecasts from a linear model, and we further compare the market timing capacities of the two approaches in Section 5. The forecasts are used for investment purposes, and we compute payoffs and break-even transaction costs for a switching strategy to derive the economic significance of the two sets of forecasts. Some concluding remarks are offered in Section 6.

2   Statistical properties of the daily-returns series

It is well established in the empirical finance literature that daily stock returns follow a leptokurtic and skewed distribution that is incompatible with the normal distribution of returns assumed in much of the theoretical finance literature.[3] The use of the Paretian distribution has motivated an interest in applying chaos or nonlinear models to analyze daily stock returns (Fama 1964; Mandelbrot 1964). However, most investigations have concentrated on the U.S. stock market, and it is not clear how the identified properties of the daily-stock-returns series relate to such issues as the liquidity and the size of a stock market as reflected,

---

[3] See, for example, Blattberg and Gonedes (1974) and Kon (1984).

for instance, in the transaction costs of the market. By comparing evidence of nonlinear components and predictability of daily returns across a number of international stock markets, it becomes possible to address these issues.

Using DataStream as our source, we obtained daily stock prices for indexes in ten European countries (Belgium, Denmark, France, Italy, Norway, Spain, Sweden, Switzerland, the United Kingdom, and West Germany) as well as for Japan, the United States, and Morgan Stanley's World Index. The World Index was investigated to see whether common factors in stock prices are more chaotic than the country-specific series and whether international components are easier to predict than national ones. The Appendix gives details of the adopted indexes and of the data samples, which vary from 2,758 to 3,116 observations. The period under investigation is Jan. 1, 1980, to April 30, 1992. Daily returns were computed as the log-difference between the closing price of an index on two consecutive days with trading. Table 17.1 presents statistical information on autocorrelation, skewness, and kurtosis for the 13-return series.

In light of the problem associated with nonsynchronous trading of the shares included in any given index (Atchison, Butler, and Simonds 1987), it comes as no surprise that all of the daily data series contain at least one autocorrelation coefficient that is statistically significant at the 5 percent critical level.[4] However, some of the fiest-order autocorrelation coefficients are surprisingly large. In particular, we note, this holds for Belgium (0.22), Italy (0.20), Spain (0.30) and the World Index (0.16). The evidence of autocorrelation in the daily returns was weakest for Norway, Switzerland, the United States, and West Germany. Thus, there seems to be no systematic relationship between the degree of serial correlation in a market's daily returns and the size of the market, as measured, for example, by the market capitalization. This does not, however, exclude a systematic relationship between serial correlation and the proportion of stocks turned over on a daily basis or the level of transaction costs. Indeed, as is shown in Section 5, a significant part of the serial correlation in the stock indexes can be explained by the level of transaction costs in the markets.

Compared to the normal distribution, all of the daily-returns series were skewed to the left, and the series also proved to be strongly leptokurtic. Similar findings have been reported throughout the finance literature. The strong evidence of serial correlation in most of the daily-stock-returns series means that these are not independent and identically distributed. However, it is still of interest to see whether, apart from the autocorrelations, there is evidence of deviations from the null hypothesis of independent and identically distributed returns. To investigate this, we applied the BDS statistic (Brock, Dechert, and Scheinkman 1986) to the residuals from an AR(10) model fitted to the

---

[4] The standard errors are computed under the null of no heteroskedasticity. Alternatively, heteroskedasticity-consistent standard errors can be computed as suggested by Diebold (1986).

Table 17.1 Statistical properties of the daily returns on the stock indexes (1980–92)

	Belgium	Denmark	France	Italy	Japan	Norway	Spain	Sweden	Switzerland	UK	USA	West Germany	World
Mean	0.39 E-3	0.55 E-3	0.55 E-3	0.65 E-3	0.33 E-3	0.59 E-3	0.63 E-3	0.86 E-3	0.20 E-3	0.55 E-3	0.44 E-3	0.33 E-3	0.48 E-3
S.D.	0.0083	0.0085	0.0107	0.0141	0.0112	0.0140	0.0105	0.0118	0.0090	0.0091	0.0108	0.0116	0.0091
Skewness	-0.63	-0.65	-1.29	-0.38	-0.55	-1.57	-0.44	-0.34	-2.57	-1.42	-3.20	-1.12	-1.34
Kurtosis	25.17	10.50	17.32	9.89	27.94	54.85	12.31	11.90	36.42	20.97	71.37	17.76	30.49
Autocorrelation coefficients													
1	0.223	0.153	0.127	0.200	0.045	0.078	0.305	0.135	0.0564	0.132	0.048	0.028	0.158
2	0.001	0.018	0.026	-0.052	-0.117	-0.013	0.082	0.026	0.0357	0.045	-0.039	-0.060	-0.029
3	0.014	0.034	0.036	0.035	0.007	-0.021	0.057	0.000	-0.007	0.039	-0.020	0.011	0.008
4	0.042	0.031	0.045	0.040	0.043	-0.014	0.042	0.052	0.011	0.059	-0.047	0.024	0.064
5	0.051	0.015	-0.027	0.003	-0.043	0.010	0.010	0.033	0.087	0.017	0.042	0.004	-0.015
6	0.086	0.028	0.036	-0.024	-0.052	0.005	-0.002	-0.028	-0.012	0.016	0.015	-0.012	0.002
7	0.108	0.026	0.090	-0.005	0.035	0.080	0.087	0.076	0.031	0.018	-0.004	0.058	-0.016
8	0.028	0.039	0.059	0.037	0.045	0.057	0.056	0.030	0.056	0.023	-0.014	0.021	-0.010
9	0.030	0.049	0.067	0.026	0.050	0.037	0.014	0.047	0.014	0.043	-0.010	0.027	-0.001
10	0.085	0.054	0.056	0.033	0.028	0.042	0.042	-0.011	0.023	0.036	-0.026	0.018	-0.006
15	0.040	-0.019	0.043	0.001	0.031	0.071	0.027	0.021	-0.010	0.004	0.002	-0.009	-0.008
20	0.011	0.009	0.006	0.034	-0.018	0.025	0.039	-0.005	-0.015	0.023	0.014	0.005	0.007
Standard error	0.020	0.019	0.019	0.019	0.019	0.019	0.021	0.020	0.019	0.019	0.018	0.018	0.020

Notes: The skewness and kurtosis measures are given by skewness $= [m(3)/m(2)]\hat{}(3/2)$, Kurtosis $= m(4)/m(2)\hat{}2$ where $m(k)$ is the centered moment.

daily-returns series. The null hypothesis of the BDS test is that the observations are independent and identically distributed, such that a rejection of the null can either mean that the daily returns contain nonlinearities or that they follow a nonstationary distribution. The finite-sample distribution of the BDS statistic is well approximated by its asymptotic distribution – which is a standard normal distribution – provided that the embedding dimension is smaller than 10 and the sample size is reasonably large (well above 1,000 data points, cf. Brock, Hsieh, and LeBaron 1991). To compute the BDS statistic, we followed Brock et al. (1991) in setting the distance meausre, r, equal to one standard deviation of the data.[5] The results, reported in Table 17.2, clearly show that there is strong evidence suggesting a rejection of the null of independent and identically distributed daily returns.

3   Testing for the existence of nonlinearities in daily stock returns

We follow the procedure for tests of deterministic components in time series applied by Linden, Satchell, and Yoon (1993). Assume that the economic model under consideration depends on n factors that may not be observable. Suppose that these factors are stacked in an n-dimensional vector, $\mathbf{v}_t$, and that the (deterministic) law of motion of the system can be represented by the function f:

$$f : R^n \rightarrow R^n : \mathbf{v}_{t+1} = f(\mathbf{v}_t), \tag{17.1}$$

where t is the period under consideration and $t + 1$ is the next period.

The essential problem facing an investigator trying to forecast $\mathbf{v}_{t+1}$ is, of course, that the true economic system (law of motion) may not be known and, hence, the dimension of the system, n, or the identity of the components of $\mathbf{v}_t$ may not be known. In this situation, a possible strategy is to consider a vector, $\mathbf{x}_t$, that consists of N observable economic factors that depend on the economic system through a function, g:

$$g : R^n \rightarrow R^N : \mathbf{x}_t = g(\mathbf{v}_t). \tag{17.2}$$

N is known as the embedding dimension of the system. The principle of the analysis is that we can learn about the underlying economic system, $\mathbf{v}_t$, through the observable components in $\mathbf{x}_t$. For each value of the embedding dimension N, we can define an N-history of the observable vector

$$\Phi_N(\mathbf{v}) = \left\{ g(\mathbf{v}), g[f(\mathbf{v})], \ldots, g\left[f^{N-1}(\mathbf{v})\right] \right\}, \tag{17.3}$$

where Φ_N is a function from $R^n \rightarrow R^N$. The main result linking the underlying process $\mathbf{v}_t$ to the observed series $\mathbf{x}_t$ is known as Takens' Embedding Theorem, which, loosely speaking, states that $\mathbf{v}_t$ and the N-history of $\mathbf{x}_t$ are observationally

---

[5] For calculation of the BDS statistic, we used the C-program provided by Brock et al. (1991).

Table 17.2 Values of the BDS statistic for the daily stock returns (1980–92)

N	Belgium	Denmark	France	Italy	Japan	Norway	Spain	Sweden	Switzerland	UK	USA	West Germany	World
2	2.11	2.20	1.71	1.45	2.61	1.46	2.37	1.30	1.90	0.63	0.35	1.54	1.16
3	2.57	2.91	2.51	2.14	3.90	2.01	3.16	1.92	2.46	1.01	0.51	2.23	1.60
4	3.11	3.64	3.17	2.82	5.00	2.44	4.10	2.58	3.17	1.29	0.68	2.92	1.99
5	3.66	4.43	3.89	3.46	6.11	2.83	5.08	3.32	3.93	1.63	0.88	3.72	2.45
6	4.32	5.39	4.62	4.18	7.39	3.33	6.24	4.15	4.77	1.94	1.09	4.58	2.94
7	5.05	6.43	5.45	5.02	8.84	3.89	7.61	5.14	5.72	2.28	1.28	5.58	3.46
8	5.91	7.62	6.45	6.00	10.55	4.52	9.26	6.26	6.85	2.62	1.43	6.76	4.06
9	6.86	8.97	7.65	7.07	12.57	5.23	11.29	7.61	8.27	3.00	1.62	8.24	4.68
10	7.90	10.57	9.11	8.31	14.97	6.04	13.73	9.25	9.99	3.41	1.86	9.99	5.36

Note: One standard deviation of the daily returns was used as our measure of distance between the points. The returns series were filtered for tenth-order autocorrelation prior to the calculation of the BDS statistic. For a double-sided hypothesis test, the critical values are 1.96 (5%) and 2.58 (1%).

equivalent, provided that $N \geq 2n + 1$ (Takens 1981). In other words, the cost of not knowing the identity of $\mathbf{v}_t$ is that we have to include roughly twice as many historical points in the analysis based on the observable data. In practice, this means that we can still extract valuable information from the observed economic system as long as the dimension of the true economy, n, is low.

Suppose that $X_1, X_2, \ldots, X_T$ is a time series of length T. We construct N-dimensional vectors $\mathbf{Y}_i = (X_i, \ldots, X_{i+N-1})(i = 1, \ldots, T - N + 1)$. The correlation integral is a sample statistic $C_T(r, N)$ and is defined to be the proportion of pairs of $\mathbf{Y}_i, \mathbf{Y}_j$ lying within a distance r of each other. We define an indicator variable.

$$X^{ij} = 1 \text{ if } ||Y_i - Y_j|| < r,$$

$$= 0 \text{ if } ||Y_i - Y_j|| \geq r. \tag{17.4}$$

The distance measure $|| \cdot ||$ is Euclidian distance in our case, but could be any metric. Then, the correlation integral is given by

$$C_T(r, N) = \frac{2}{(T - N)(T - N + 1)} \sum_{i=1}^{T-N} \sum_{j=i+1}^{T-N+1} X_{ij}. \tag{17.5}$$

Define $C(r) \lim_{T \to \infty} C_T(r, N)$. This definition is motivated by the fact that for some chaotic processes and for smaller r.

$$C(r) = \mathcal{O}(r^{\alpha}), \tag{17.6}$$

where α, which is known as the correlation dimension, is a finite-valued positive number that is independent of N.[6] $C(r)$ measures the proportion of the total number of pairs whose distance is smaller than r; r is a filter in the sense that all distances smaller than r counted as neighbors and contribute to the correlation integral, whereas pairs of points whose distances are larger than r are ignored. It is clear that the correlation integral is based on a measure of closeness between the data points. This makes the correlation integral a particularly interesting statistic in economic applications where the focus is on the closeness between predicted and realized values of returns.

To estimate the correlation integral, α, we use the estimator α_N (see Satchell and Yoon 1991)

$$\alpha_N = \alpha(T, r, N) = \frac{\ln [C_T(r, N)]}{\ln (r)}. \tag{17.7}$$

If the data are generated by a white-noise process, we get

$$C_T(r, N) = \mathcal{O}(r^N). \tag{17.8}$$

---

[6] The correlation dimension is independent of the selected norm for the distance measure (Brock 1986).

It is this distinction that motivates the calculation of the correlation integral: If a plot of N against α_N flattens out as N increases, it can be interpreted as evidence in favor of the existence of a chaotic process with a finite correlation dimension. There are many problems associated with the estimation of the correlation integral: Autocorrelation drives down $C_T(r, N)$ (Wolff 1990); the obtained estimates may be very sensitive to the choice of r (Grassberger and Procaccia 1983; Brock et al. 1991); and lack of sufficient observations may lead to inaccurate measurement (Ramsey et al. 1990), to name a few difficulties.

The estimation procedure that we use is based on the maximum likelihood approach of Takens (1984). For some fixed value of the cutoff point $r > 0$, we assume that the distribution of distances follows a power law, that is, $C(d) = d^\alpha$ holds exactly for $d < r$. In a similar way as before, all distances larger than r are removed and the remaining distances are divided by r to produce a new set of distances $d_i \in (0,1]$. Again, this definition holds for arbitrary norms; in our calculations, we use the Euclidian norm. Letting $d_1, \ldots, d_m \in (0,1]$ be a sample so measured, we pretend, that it is a random sample from a probability distribution. For a given α, and under the simplifying assumption that the d_i are independent and identically distributed, the probability of finding a sample $(d_1, d_1 + \Delta d_1), \ldots, (d_m, d_m + \Delta d_m)$ equals $\prod_{i=1}^{m} \alpha d_i^{\alpha-1}$. By the maximum likelihood rule, we obtain the following estimator for α:

$$\hat{\alpha} = \frac{-m}{\sum \ln(d_i)}. \tag{17.9}$$

This example provides us with a simple rule for estimating α, but can be criticized because of the assumed independence across observations.[7,8]

For the 13-daily-returns series included in the investigation, Table 17.3 presents estimates of the correlation integral based on Takens' estimation procedure. The embedding dimension was varied from 1 to 10 and in all cases we adopted a filter (r_0) with a size equal to the standard deviation times the square root of the embedding dimension. This filter size was chosen after some experiments across various filters. The proportionality factor was chosen on the grounds that we used the Euclidian norm, which will grow with the square root of the number of points used in the distance computations. A number of researchers have found the estimated integral is quite sensitive with respect to the adopted filter size (Scheinkman and LeBaron 1989; Linden et al. 1993). We emphasize the necessity of reporting the exact procedure used to compute the correlation integrals such that the results can be replicated.

---

[7] Theiler (1990) investigates problems associated with estimating α under the assumption that the differenced data satisfy the independent distance hypothesis

[8] See also the alternative procedure for computation of the correlation integrals suggested by Grassberger and Procaccia (1983).

Table 17.3 Takens' measure of the correlation integral applied to daily stock returns (1980–92)

N	Belgium	Denmark	France	Italy	Japan	Norway	Spain	Sweden	Switzerland	UK	USA	West Germany	World
1	0.91	0.96	0.98	0.95	0.93	0.95	0.95	0.89	0.98	0.96	0.97	0.97	0.99
2	1.11	1.22	1.18	1.28	1.13	1.16	1.14	1.11	1.21	1.28	1.29	1.23	1.26
3	1.22	1.39	1.30	1.46	1.22	1.28	1.23	1.21	1.36	1.45	1.48	1.35	1.42
4	1.30	1.50	1.37	1.58	1.27	1.33	1.30	1.30	1.46	1.60	1.62	1.43	1.54
5	1.38	1.61	1.45	1.65	1.33	1.41	1.37	1.35	1.54	1.69	1.78	1.52	1.65
6	1.42	1.67	1.52	1.73	1.37	1.47	1.39	1.42	1.61	1.79	1.84	1.58	1.71
7	1.48	1.76	1.56	1.80	1.39	1.52	1.46	1.45	1.68	1.94	1.93	1.63	1.80
8	1.56	1.77	1.62	1.92	1.42	1.83	1.47	1.48	1.73	1.98	2.03	1.67	1.85
9	1.57	1.87	1.64	1.96	1.48	1.56	1.53	1.50	1.82	2.04	2.14	1.72	1.87
10	1.60	1.93	1.75	1.97	1.52	1.61	1.54	1.36	1.78	2.02	2.26	1.72	1.97

Note: A cutoff point equal to the standard deviation of daily returns times the square root of the embedding dimension was used in the computations. N is the embedding dimension.

It is clear from the estimates in Table 17.3 that the correlation integrals typically do not reach a saturation point after which they level off. This seems to indicate that at least some of the daily-returns series do not contain chaotic components of a sufficiently low order to be detected. If the time series had been white noise, then, as r tends to zero, the correlation integral would have increased in proportion with the embedding dimension. On the other hand, it is not clear that the estimated correlation integrals are different from those generated by a nonlinear stochastic series displaying the same degree of serial correlation, skewness, and leptokurtosis that is present in the series under consideration.

Most of the estimated correlation integrals in Table 17.3 take quite small absolute values, which are concentrated in the range between 1.4 and 2.3 for an embedding dimension of 10. Thus, it is possible that the correlation dimension may be sufficiently low to be used in a procedure that aims at identifying chaotic components for the purpose of predicting daily returns. However, we emphasize once again the sensitivity of the estimated correlation integrals with respect to the choice of the filter size.

4   Predictability of daily stock returns

Intuitively, a chaotic series of low order should, by definition, given accurate predictions over a very short period and poor ones over a longer horizon. It is obviously a complex task to predict chaotic time series from empirical data because we do not know the true model and because of the sensitivity to initial conditions associated with chaos. Attempts to use chaos to predict time series by estimating a specific model (such as the logistic equation) may fail as a result of such parameter sensitivity. To get around this problem, we used the nonparametric nearest-neighbor procedure suggested by Linden et al. (1993) and Sugihara and May (1990).

The procedure is to consider all vectors of length N (the embedding dimension) as defined in the Section 3. For the vector of the N most recent historical returns, we consider some number, say P, of vectors that are closest to Y. Our predictor of the next observation consists of a weighted sum of the P closest vectors. The positive weights are chosen such that they add to one and are inversely related to the distance between the vector of interest and its nearest neighbors. Hence, the closer that a historical sequence of returns is to the most recent history of returns, the larger a weight this sequence of returns will obtain. The search for the nearest neighbors was conducted across a library consisting of the previous 500 data points.

Let $x(i)(i = 1, \ldots, P)$ be the P nearest vectors to the vector of interest, $\mathbf{x}$, and let S represent the operator that moves the vector one period forward. Our forecast of the daily stock returns will be the last element of the vector:

$$\mathbf{x}^* = \sum_{i=1}^{P} \lambda_i S[(\mathbf{x}(i)], \tag{17.10}$$

where

$$\lambda_i = \exp(-d_i) / \sum_{i=1}^{P} \exp(-d_i) \tag{17.11}$$

The d_i' are the distances between $\mathbf{x}(i)$ and $\mathbf{x}$, and the λ_i have been chosen to have the abovementioned properties. It is possible to use different formulas in place of λ_i in equation (17.10) and to vary P in equations (17.10) and (17.11). However, our experience is that the method is fairly robust with respect to changes in both parameters. The main difference between our procedure and the estimation method adopted by Diebold and Nason (1990) to analyze foreign-exchange rates is that they used a tricubic neighborhood weighting function in place of our exponential weights, and their mean function depends upon a fixed number of lags (1, 3, and 5).

Our nonparametric forecasting procedure is attractive because it will work very well for chaotic processes of low order as well as for nonchaotic deterministic processes such as a sine function. For stochastic processes, we would expect to do as well as linear autoregressive models. For some details on the performance of the procedure, see Linden et al. (1993). We emphasize the necessity of using a forecasting procedure that will work well for different types of time series because, as shown in Sections 2 and 3, we do not have conclusive evidence as to whether the nonlinear components in the daily returns are of a chaotic nature or whether they are of a stochastic nature, or both.

The estimate of the correlation between the nonparametric recursive one-step-ahead forecasts based on a rolling window if past observations and the realized daily returns and their associated t-values are given in Table 17.4. It is clear that for all countries, possibly with the exception fo the United States and Germany, there are strong indications of predictability of daily stock returns. For most of the time series, the highest correlation between predicted and realized values occurs at a low value of the embedding dimension, and it decreases smoothly afterward. This fits well in line with the pattern of correlations that we would expect for a mixed stochastic-chaotic series with serial dependencies of a low order. It also comes as no surprise that the correlation between predicted and realized daily returns is highest for the countries with stock indexes that display strong serial correlation in their daily returns. This follows because the applied algorithm allows for stochastic as well as chaotic patterns in the daily-returns series.

Table 17.4 Correlation between forecasts and realised values of the n day daily changes in stock indexes and the associated t-values (1980–92)

	Belgium	Denmark	France	Italy	Japan	Norway	Spain	Sweden	Switzerland	UK	USA	West Germany	World
Non-parametric Forecasts													
1	0.215 (13.60)	0.140 (8.51)	0.089 (4.80)	9.137 (8.07)	0.025 (1.27)	0.080 (4.36)	0.275 (18.83)	0.102 (5.44)	0.020 (0.99)	-0.011 (-0.53)	-0.14 (-0.71)	0.037 (1.93)	0.124 (6.69)
2	0.170 (10.19)	0.204 (12.45)	0.059 (3.06)	0.116 (6.66)	0.090 (4.90)	0.111 (6.26)	0.274 (18.06)	0.104 (5.60)	0.056 (2.91)	0.083 (4.59)	0.020 (-1.01)	0.042 (2.19)	0.104 (5.52)
3	0.160 (9.44)	0.170 (9.99)	0.041 (4.34)	0.112 (6.44)	0.082 (4.43)	0.106 (6.02)	0.291 (19.56)	0.110 (5.94)	0.077 (4.14)	0.070 (3.82)	-0.016 (-0.79)	0.027 (1.40)	0.082 (4.22)
4	0.176 (10.59)	0.161 (9.35)	0.114 (6.43)	0.092 (5.17)	0.053 (2.79)	0.062 (4.52)	0.268 (17.53)	0.107 (5.75)	0.066 (3.49)	0.062 (3.35)	-0.003 (-0.15)	0.044 (2.29)	0.107 (5.64)
5	0.178 (10.74)	0.163 (9.50)	0.046 (4.62)	0.099 (5.609)	0.072 (3.86)	0.065 (3.48)	0.255 (16.42)	0.051 (2.58)	0.094 (5.13)	0.046 (2.48)	0.027 (1.41)	0.052 (2.77)	0.104 (5.55)
6	0.204 (12.72)	0.138 (7.80)	0.093 (5.03)	0.091 (5.09)	0.032 (1.62)	0.072 (3.93)	0.238 (15.01)	0.046 (2.20)	0.082 (4.41)	0.040 (2.10)	0.004 (0.19)	0.050 (2.62)	0.113 (6.03)
7	0.184 (11.23)	0.133 (7.49)	0.083 (4.43)	0.111 (6.34)	0.087 (4.74)	0.066 (3.57)	0.264 (17.23)	0.067 (3.46)	0.088 (4.74)	0.048 (2.58)	0.019 (0.07)	0.39 (2.05)	0.087 (4.49)
8	0.193 (11.91)	0.116 (6.35)	0.065 (3.41)	0.102 (5.76)	0.075 (4.03)	0.043 (2.28)	0.249 (15.86)	0.065 (3.34)	0.073 (3.88)	0.045 (2.37)	0.010 (0.49)	0.044 (2.18)	0.969 (3.51)
9	0.173 (10.41)	0.133 (7.45)	0.075 (3.95)	0.093 (5.25)	0.079 (4.28)	0.039 (2.04)	0.266 (17.38)	0.053 (2.68)	0.051 (2.66)	0.053 (2.88)	0.002 (0.09)	0.039 (2.05)	0.093 (4.87)
10	0.173 (10.41)	0.132 (7.39)	0.065 (3.38)	0.003 (5.20)	0.051 (2.65)	0.022 (1.16)	0.253 (16.23)	0.038 (1.89)	0.055 (2.89)	0.064 (3.49)	-0.017 (-0.82)	0.043 (2.24)	0.093 (4.84)
Linear Forecasts	0.156 (9.18)	0.103 (5.59)	0.126 (7.07)	0.112 (6.42)	0.047 (2.46)	-0.087 (-4.82)	0.3026 (20.81)	0.052 (2.64)	-0.071 (-3.78)	-0.021 (-1.08)	-0.106 (-5.68)	0.001 (0.05)	0.037 (1.79)

Note: A nearest neighbor algorithm was used to compute the nonparametric forecasts recursively, using a window of the last 500 observations. The linear forecasts were computed recursively from an AR(10) modern, again using a window of 500 observations. For each stock index the first column gives the correlation between the predicted values and the realized values of the daily stock returns, and the second column gives the associated t-values for this correlation (in brackets). N is the embedding dimension.

To facilitate a direct comparison between the nonparametric and the linear forecasts, we computed recursive linear forecasts based on moving windows of 500 observations.[9] In all cases, the daily returns were regressed on a constant and the 10 most recent lagged values of itself, and the sample over which the forecasts were computed was identical to the sample used for the nonparametric forecasts. The second part of Table 17.4 gives the correlation between the recursive forecasts from the linear model and the realized values of the daily stock returns. Only in the cases of France and Spain are the correlations between predicted and realized daily price changes higher for the linear model than for the best set of nonparametric forecasts. The picture emerging from a comparison of the nonparametric and the linear forecasts of daily stock returns is that the nonparametric forecasts tend to be better than the linear forecasts, and may be worth the extra efforts that the computations entail. Although, for some values of the embedding dimension, the nonparametric forecasts produced a negative correlation with the realized values of the daily returns, only positive correlation coefficients were statistically significant at the 5 percent critical level. In contrast, in the case of the recursive linear forecasts, some of the correlations between the relized and the predicted series took on a significantly negative value.

Note also that the daily returns on the World Index are not more predictable than the most predictable of the national-returns series. The World Index is a weighted measure of the national indexes and should therefore emphasize the common, or international, component in stock prices. Our results give no reason to believe that averaging across the national-returns series gives rise to stronger evidence of detectable nonlinear components.[10]

5   Economic significance of the predictability of daily returns: Some trading results

We have already analyzed the statistical significance of the predictability of daily returns. It is not clear, however, to which extent the statistically significant evidence of predictable components in daily returns translates into profitmaking possibilities for investors in the markets. It is important to analyze this issue; Jensen (1978) defined an efficient market this way: "A market is efficient with respect to information set Ω_t if it is impossible to make economic profits by

---

[9] It would be misleading to compare the nonparametric predictions to the fitted values from an ordinary least squares regression that used the entire sample of observations. Such a regression would not account for the fact that, at the point in time when the linear regressions are computed, only the preceding observations are known to the investors.

[10] Work by Granger (1991) suggests that although nonlinear components may be important to individual series, linear aggregation across such series may cause the evidence of nonlinearities to decline.

trading on the basis of information set Ω_t." Clearly, application of the forecasts in a trading strategy provides additional information to the statistical analysis.

As the final step in our analysis, we used the predicted daily returns on the 13 stock indexes in an investment strategy built on the following principle: If next day's stock return is predicted to be positive, hold the stock index, otherwise hold cash.[11] This is known as a switching strategy because it switches the portfolio between the two funds (the stock index and cash), and has previously been analyzed by, among others, Pesaran and Timmermann (1992a). We assume that the investor starts with funds worth $100 in cash and follows the switching rule thereafter. We chose to focus on the switching strategy for a number of reasons. First, because the investor is not allowed to go short, there is no risk of bankruptcy associated with the switching portfolio. Second, because no leverage is used in the investment strategy, it is straightforward to compare the payoffs on the switching portfolio to those of the market portfolio in a mean-variance sense.

Although trading results based on the stock indexes provide essential information about the economic value of the forecasts, it should be emphasized that the stock indexes are not directly tradable. This is in contrast to futures indexes which, however, have not existed for a sufficiently long period to provide data for an international comparison of nonlinear components in daily returns. To deal with the problem that some of the constituents of the national indexes may not be traded on a daily basis, the trading results from the recursive linear predictions can be regarded as a benchmark that reflects the problem associated with nonsynchronous trading.

To compute the forecasts for each country, we applied the embedding dimension that produced the highest correlation between predicted and realized daily returns (cf. Table 17.4). This procedure recognizes the difficulty of predicting in a nonlinear dynamic system on the basis of a small data sample. For all of the stock indexes, Table 17.5 gives statistical information about payoffs from three portfolios: the buy-and-hold strategy in the market index, a switching strategy based on recursive one-step-ahead forecasts from a linear autoregressive model, and a switching strategy that uses the nonparametric forecasts, again computed recursively. Apart from the case of the recursive linear forecasts for the daily returns in the United States and Germany the mean returns of the market indexes are smaller than the mean returns of the two switching portfolios. In the case of the switching portfolios that use nonparametric forecasts, the mean returns

[11] By holding cash rather than investing the money in the overnight money market, we are not getting the maximum payoff on the switching portfolio. However, using cash as the only alternative to the stock index allows us to interpret the excess return on the switching portfolios relative to the market portfolios as being exclusively due to the market timing skills of the adopted forecasting procedure applied to the stock returns (as opposed to the excess returns on stocks over and above returns on an overnight account).

Table 17.5 Economic value of predictions of daily price changes (1980–92)

	Belgium	Denmark	France	Italy	Japan	Norway	Spain	Sweden	Switzerland	UK	USA	West Germany	World
Market Index													
Mean	0.000506	0.000519	0.000682	0.000443	0.000351	0.000739	0.000686	0.000824	0.00031	0.000547	0.000506	0.000412	0.000463
Std. dev.	0.008378	0.008905	0.010435	0.012429	0.011772	0.014443	0.01108	0.01197	0.009658	0.008994	0.010996	0.012401	0.008389
End wealth	320	311	451	258	201	501	422	570	191	373	312	233	261
Linear Forecasts													
Mean	0.000921	0.000722	0.000939	0.001102	0.000546	0.000876	0.001618	0.000980	0.000360	0.000664	0.000355	0.000087	0.000661
Std. dev.	0.005911	0.006899	0.007422	0.009208	0.008181	0.009826	0.007567	0.008878	0.007237	0.006686	0.007872	0.009679	0.006265
Switching frequency	0.38	0.36	0.40	0.48	0.39	0.38	0.42	0.42	0.41	0.40	0.47	0.45	0.44
Break-even transaction costs	0.0011	0.0006	0.0006	0.0014	0.0005	0.0004	0.0022	0.0004	0.0001	0.0003	−0.0003	−0.007	0.0005
End wealth	929	522	892	1557	356	823	3853	881	225	529	230	110	421
Sign proportion (SN)	58.8	55.4	55.8	57.2	53.4	54.9	60.7	57.2	53.5	54.5	50.2	51.1	56.3
(SN)	7.74	4.38	4.55	7.13	2.14	4.07	10.08	5.38	2.84	3.03	−0.57	0.39	5.41
Non parametric													
Mean	0.001001	0.000964	0.000818	0.000829	0.000598	0.001410	0.001725	0.001040	0.000561	0.000560	0.000553	0.000491	0.000611
Std. dev.	0.006027	0.006595	0.007612	0.009304	0.007714	0.009660	0.007956	0.008480	0.007051	0.007073	0.007631	0.009720	0.005626
Switching frequency	0.42	0.47	0.44	0.45	0.44	0.44	0.40	0.47	0.43	0.45	0.48	0.49	0.44
Break-even transition costs	0.0011	0.0010	0.0003	0.0009	0.0006	0.0016	0.0025	0.0005	0.0006	0.0002	0.0001	0.0001	0.0004
End wealth	1129	932	664	766	409	3236	4894	1021	370	440	383	306	380
Sign proportion (SN)	59.7	57.7	55.4	54.6	53.7	57.3	62.6	55.5	54.4	53.6	51.6	51.9	54.0
(SN)	9.14	7.11	4.25	4.47	3.06	6.98	12.03	4.59	3.86	2.49	1.32	1.48	3.32

Note: End wealth gives the finalperiod value of investing $ 100 in the portfolios, assuming zero transaction costs. Switching frequency gives the proportion periods where a portfolio switch occurs. Break-even transaction costs are the levels of transaction costs that imply that the mean of the market index equals the mean of the switching portfolio. Sign proportion gives the proportion of correctly predicted signs of the daily changes in stock prices, and $S(N)$ gives the value of the predictive failure test statistics proposed by Pesaran and Timmermann (1992b). The data sets are described in the Appendix.

are between 2 and 250 percent higher than the mean returns on the respective buy-and-hold portfolios. As far as the standard deviations of the returns on the portfolios are concerned, the market indexes have a considerably higher standard deviation than the daily returns on the switching portfolios.

For 7 of our 13 portfolios, the standard deviation of the switching portfolios that use nonparametric forecasts is smaller than the standard deviation of the returns on the switching portfolios based on recursive linear forecasts. Assuming zero transaction costs, both sets of switching portfolios' mean variance dominate the market indexes in almost all of the countries investigated. No such ranking follows in the comparison between the two sets of switching portfolios. However, the switching portfolio based on recursive nonparametric forecasts' mean variance dominate the switching portfolio based on recursive linear forecasts in Denmark, Japan, Norway, Sweden, Switzerland, and the United States, whereas the opposite result holds for France, Italy, and the United Kingdom.

The above analysis assumed that no transaction costs are incurred when the portfolio switches between a stock-market index and cash. This should, of course, only be considered as an approximation but it may apply to the case where a large investors trades in a futures index because transaction costs typically are small for this type of trade. Alternatively, the investors may use leverage to decrease the proportional transaction costs. This idea could also be pursued in a trading strategy based on options.

Transaction costs particularly matter for switching portfolios based on daily signals because the turnover on such portfolios tends to be very high. Thus, even with small transaction costs, the predicitability of stock returns may not be worthwhile to exploit. The sort of problems associated with high-frequency trading is well explained by Fama and Blume (1966) who explored the use of a filter rule in daily trading. The filter rule is based on the belief that short-run trends may be present in the level of stock prices. Let x be the size of the filter. Then, investors following a filter rule are instructed to go long in a portfolio when the price of the portfolio increases by at least x percent from a previous low, and to go short if the price falls by at least x percent from its previous maximum. Fama and Blume found that the filter sizes that paid the highest mean returns either used a very small filter, resulting in very frequent trading, or used a very large filter, in which case the invested funds were out of the market most of the time.

To get an estimate of the importance of transaction costs, we computed the break-even transaction costs that, if incurred when switching between cash and an index, will give the same mean return on the switching portfolios and the market index. If transaction costs are this high, then the returns on the market index will be a mean-preserving spread of the returns on the switching portfolio. Because the switching portfolios change the asset allocation between 35 and 50 percent of all periods, transaction costs can only be between 0.01 and 0.22

percent for the switching portfolios based on linear forecasts and between 0.01 and 0.25 percent for the switching portfolios that use nonparametric nearest-neighbor forecasts.[12]

The final funds in the portfolios based on the three investment strategies are also reported in Table 17.5. Accounting for the size of the initial library used to compute the forecasts, the funds were invested over a period slightly shorter than 10 years. It is clear that the final wealth of the switching portfolios based on the nonparametric forecasts was between 15 and 1,200 percent larger than the final wealth of the market index. As can be seen from the case of the portfolios invested in the indexes in the United States and Germany, the final wealth of the switching portfolios based on recursive linear predictions is not always larger than the final wealth of the market index. Only in the case of France, Italy, the United Kingdom, and the World Index was the final wealth of the switching portfolio based on the recursive linear forecasts higher than the final wealth of the switching portfolio based on nonparametric forecasts.

For many investment strategies, the essential information contained in a set of forecasts is the sign of the forecast rather than the actual values of the forecast. Indeed, signals are often generated that only tell the investor whether markets are predicted to go up or down. Table 17.5 gives the proportion of correctly predicted signs and the value of the nonparametric market timing test recently proposed by Pesaran and Timmermann (1992b), which we briefly introduce. Consider an $n \times n$ contingency table with realized values tabulated along the rows (i) and predicted values tabulated along the columns (j), such that n represents the number of categories. Let P_{ij} denote the probability of a realization in the cell of the ith row and the jth column of the contingency table and let P_{i0} be the probability of cells in the ith row, and let P_{0i} be the probability of cells in the ith column. The nonparametric statistic tests the null hypothesis of no market timing, which formally is

$$H_0 : \sum_{i=1}^{n} (P_{ii} - P_{i0} P_{0i}) = 0 \tag{17.12}$$

This null hypothesis (H_0) asserts that the proportion of correct predictions (the diagonal elements in the contingency table) equals the proportion that can be expected, provided that independence between the distribution of realized and predicted values holds. Also define $P' = (P_{11}, P_{12}, \ldots, P_{1n}; P_{21}, P_{22}, \ldots; P_{n1}, \ldots, P_{nn})$, and Ψ_0 as the $n^2 \times n^2$ diagonal matrix that has P_0 as its diagonal

---

[12] As mentioned earlier, we assume that investors do not hold their cash in an overnight account when they are out of the stock index. Overnight interest is, however, unlikely to alter our conclusion: With the funds out of the index (roughly) half of the time, an overnight rate of, say, 10% per annum will be equivalent to 0.01 percent on a daily basis. In comparison with most of the break-even transaction costs, this is a small number.

elements (P_0 being the true value of P). Then, the nonparametric market timing test is given by

$$s_n = \sqrt{n} V_n^{-1/2} S_n, \tag{17.13}$$

where

$$S_n = \sum_{i=1}^{n} \left(\hat{P}_{ii} - \hat{P}_{i0} \hat{P}_{0i} \right), \ \hat{P}_{ij} = \frac{n_{ij}}{n},$$

$$V_n = \left[\frac{\partial f(P_0)}{\partial P} \right]' (\Psi - P_0 P_0') \left[\frac{\partial f(P_0)}{\partial P} \right] \text{ (evaluated at } P_0 = (\hat{P}), \tag{17.14}$$

and

$$\frac{\partial f(P)}{\partial P_{ij}} = 1 - P_{0i} - P_{i0} \quad \text{for} \quad i = j,$$

$$- P_{j0} - P_{0i} \quad \text{for} \quad i \neq j. \tag{17.15}$$

This test statistic asymptotically distributed as a normal $N(0, 1)$ variate. In our case, we categorize the daily returns according to their sign, so that n is 2. For this case, it can be shown (Pesaran and Timmermann 1992c) that the above market timing test statistic is asymptotically identical to the nonparametric Henriksson-Merton test (Henriksson and Merton 1981).

For the nonparametric forecasts of the daily stock returns, it is only in the case of the daily returns in the United States and Germany that the values of the nonparametric test statistically were insignificant at the 5 percent level. Furthermore, only in 5 of 13 cases (France, Italy, Sweden, the United Kingdom, World Index), was the value of the market timing test statistic higher for the recursive linear forecasts than for the recursive nonparametric forecasts. Hence, these results also support the broad conclusion that nonparametric predictions may be worthwhile to undertake.

5.1 Predictability of daily stock returns and transaction costs: International comparisons

We next investigated whether the evidence of predictable components in daily stock returns can be explained by the presence of transaction costs. Estimates for transaction costs in the markets under consideration were obtained from Beckers (1992) and are shown in Table 17.6. Initially, we computed the correlation between the total transaction cost estimates given in Table 17.6 and the first-order autocorrelation coefficients in Table 17.1.[13] The correlation between the

[13] In these and the following computations the total transaction costs were set equal to 38 basis points for the United States and 40 basis points for the United Kingdom because the calculations are based on the average transaction costs incurred from buying and selling.

Table 17.6. *Some estimates of commission and duty/taxes for institutional size trades.*

Country	Commission	Taxes/Duty	Total
Belgium	30	19.5	50
Denmark	20	—	20
France	20	15	35
Italy	30	10	40
Japan	20	30	50
Norway	20	—	20
Spain	37	30	67
Sweden	20	—	20
Switzerland	20	9	29
UK	15	50	15–65
USA			30–45
Germany	19	6	25

Note: The Table is reproduced from Beckers (1992).

two sets of estimates was 0.58. Furthermore, in a regression of the first-order autocorrelation coefficients of returns in the 12 countries on a constant and the total transaction cost estimates, we obtained a coefficient of the total cost variable of 0.33 with a t-value of 2.24. Thus, at the 5 percent critical level, we can reject the null hypothesis that the coefficient of total transaction costs is zero in this regression. It appears that transaction costs explain a large proportion of the serial correlation in daily returns.

Transaction costs constitute a reasonable intuitive explanation of serial correlation in the indexes. The intuition is that serial correlation in rates of return may not be removed by arbitrage if transaction costs are high and many shares do not trade at close every single day. This is particularly important if the considered stock index is broadly defined and contains many small and illiquid shares.

From a comparison of the estimates of transaction costs from Table 17.6 to the break-even transaction costs of the switching portfolios based on the non-parametric forecasts (from Table 17.5), it is clear that the estimated transaction costs are higher than their respective break-even levels. Thus, although the difference in the final wealth levels between some of the switching portfolios and their corresponding market portfolios is quite large, the massive portfolio turnover generated by the daily signals appears to rule out profit opportunities for investors who face institutional-size transaction costs.

6   Conclusion

Our comparison of patterns in 13-daily-stock-returns series over the period 1980–92 showed that although there is evidence that returns are not independent and identically distributed, the evidence of chaotic components in daily returns is rather inconclusive. Given this uncertainty, we argued for the use of a nonparametric nearest-neighbor algorithm that can identify nonlinear patterns both of a stochastic and of a chaotic nature. A comparison of the correlation between predicted and realized values of daily returns indicated that the recursive nonparametric nearest-neighbor forecasts dominate the recursive lienar forecasts for most of the analyzed series. Also, the use of the forecasts in a simple investment strategy gave evidence that these nonparametric forecasts may have a higher economic value to an investor than the linear forecasts do.

Although our trading results indicated that the returns of the switching portfolios based on nonparametric forecasts' mean variance dominate returns on the market indexes, the difference in returns between the two sets of portfolios is of a magnitude that most likely can be explained by transaction costs in the markets under consideration. Furthermore, even assuming very small transaction costs on cannot conclude from the trading results that the financial markets are in any way inefficient because our results are bound to be joint test of the model generating expected returns and the efficient market hypothesis (see Fama 1991).

7   Appendix

We analyzed 12 national stock indexes and Morgan Stanley's World Index using daily price changes over the period Jan. 1, to April 30, 1992. The investigated series were downloaded from DataStream, and we considered the following data:

Belgium (2,984 observations): the index was the Brussels Stock Exchange General Index (DataStream mnemo BRUSIDX).

Denmark (2,886 observations): Copenhagen Stock Index (CHAGENI).

France (2,918 observations): Paris CAC General Index (PARCACG).

Italy (3,109 observations): DataStream Total Market Index (TOTMKIT).

Japan (2,995 observations): Nikkei Dow Jones average Index (225) (JAP-DOWA).

Norway (3,068 observations): Oslo Stock Exchange Index for the Industry (OSLOSEI)

Spain (2,816 observations): Madrid Stock Exchange (MADRIDI)

Sweden (2,831 observations): Stockholm, Jacobson & Ponsbach Industrial (SHOLMSE).

Switzerland (2,960 observations): Credit Suisse General Index (KRSGENR).

United Kingdom (3,116 observations): FT ALL-Share Index (FTALLSH).

United States (3,080 observations): Standard & Poor's Composite Index (S & PCOMP).

West Germany (3,047 observations): Commerzbank Index (FURTCOM).

Morgan Stanley World Index (2,758 observations): Capital International Index (WRLDCAP).

Dividends were ignored in our computations first, because we studied the daily changes in some weighted market indexes and, second, because of the absence of a published time series showing the daily dividends as they actually occurred over the period. To avoid including returns for days where the markets were closed, we excluded data points when the stock price was identical on two consecutive days.

REFERENCES

Atchison, M. D., Butler, K. C., and Simonds, R. R. (1987). Nonsynchronous security trading and market index autocorrelation, *J. Finance*, **42**, 111–18.

Beckers, S. (1992). Trade execution analytics in european equity markets, BARRA Int. Ltd.,

Blattberg, R., and Gonedes, N. (1974). A comparison of the stable and student distributions as statistical models for stock prices, *J. Business*, **47**, 244–80.

Brock, W. (1986). Distinguishing random and deterministic systems: Abridged version, *J. Econ. Theory*, **40**, 168–95.

Brock, W. A., Dehert, W. D., and Scheinkman, J. (1986). A test for independence based on the correlation dimension. University of Wisconsin at Madison.

Brock, W., Hsieh, D. A., and LeBaron, B. (1991). *Nonlinear Dynamics, Chaos, and Instability: Statistical Theory and Economic Evidence*. MIT Press, Cambridge, MA.

Diebold, F. X. (1986). Testing for serial correlation in the presence of ARCH, unpublished manuscript, University of Pennsylvania.

Diebold, F. X., and Nason, J. A. (1990). Nonparametric exchange rate prediction? *J. Int. Econ.* **28**, 315–32.

Fama, E. F. (1964). Mandelbrot and the stable paretian hypothesis. In *The Random Character of Stock Prices*, ed. P. Cootner, MIT Press, Cambridge, MA.

(1991). Efficient capital markets: II, *J. Finance*, **46**, 1575–1617.

Fama, E. F., and Blume, M. E. (1966). Filter Rules and Stock Market Trading, *J. Business*, **39**, 226–41.

Frank, M., Gencay, R., and Stengos, T. (1988). International chaos? *Eur. Econ. Rev.*, **32**, 1569–84.

Frank, M. Z., and Stengos, T. (1988). Some evidence concerning macroeconomic chaos, *J. Monetary Econ.*, **22**, 423–38.

Granger, C. W. J. (1991). Developments in the nonlinear analysis of economic series, *Scand. J. Econ.*, **93**, 263–76.

Grassberger, P., and Procaccia, F. (1983). Measuring the strangeness of strange attractors, *Phys.*, **D 9**, 189–208.

Henriksson, R. D., and Merton, R. C. (1981). On market timing and investment performance II. statistical procedures for evaluating forecasting skills, *J. Business.*, **54**, 513–33.

Hsieh, D. A. (1989). Testing for non-linearity in daily foreign exchange rate changes, *J. Business*, 339–68.

(1991). Chaos and non-linear dynamics: Applications to financial markets, *J. Finance*, **46**, 1839–77.

Kon, S. J. (1984). Models ôf stock returns–a comparison, *J. Finance*, **39**, 147–65.

Linden, N., Satchell, S. E., and Yoon, Y. (1993). Predicting British financial indices. An approach based on chaotic theory, *Struct. Change Econ. Dyn.*, **4**, 145–62.

Mandelbrot, B. (1964). The variation of certain speculative prices. In *The Random Character of Stock Prices*, ed. P. Cootner, MIT Press, Cambridge, MA.

Pesaran, M. H., and Timmermann, A. (1992a). Forecasting stock returns, *J. Forecasting*,
    (1992b). A simple non-parametric test of predictive performance, *J. Bus. Econ. Stat.*, **10**, 461–65.
    (1992c). A generalisation of the non-parametric Henriksson-Merton test of market timing, *Eco. Lett.*,

Ramsey, J. B., Sayers, C. L., and Rothman, P. (1990). The statistical properties of dimension calculations using small data sets: Some economic applications, *Int. Econ. Rev.*, **31**, 991–1020.

Satchell, S. E., and Yoon, Y. (1992). Misspecification in measurement of the correlation dimension, Mimeo, University of Cambridge, Cambridge, England.

Scheinkman, J. A., and LeBaron, B. (1989). Non-linear dynamics and stock returns, *J. Business*, **62**, 311–37.

Sugihara, G., and May, R. M. (1990). Non-linear forecasting as a way of distinguishing chaos from measurement errors in times series, *Nature*, **344**, 734–41.

Takens, F. (1981). Detecting strange attractors in turbulence. In *Dynamical Systems and Turbulence*, eds. D. Rand and L. Young, Springer-Verlag, Berlin.

Takens, F. (1984). On the numerical determination of the dimension of an attractor. In *Dynamical Systems and Bifurcations*, Vol. 1125, Lecture Notes in Mathematics, Springer-Verlag, Berlin, pp. 99–106.

Theiler, J. (1990). Statistical precision of dimension estimators, *Phys. Rev.*, **41**, 3038–51.

Wolff, R. (1990). A note on the behaviour of the correlation integral in the presence of a time series, *Biometrica*, **77**, 689–697.

CHAPTER 18

Nonparametric forecasts of gold rates of return

Thanasis Stengos

In this paper we attempt to forecast nonparametrically the rates of return of a daily gold series. We find ourselves unable to successfully produce out-of-sample forecasts for the above series. To evaluate further the lack of forecastability, we also perform a number of simulations where we produce out-of-sample forecasts of artificially generated series of known complexity, as measured by the largest Lyapunov exponent. The nonparametric methods seem to work sufficiently well on some simple systems for which traditional models do not work. However, the data requirements rise quite sharply as the true complexity of the underlying data-generating process rises. This may account for our inability to successfully forecast the gold rates-of-return series.

1   Introduction

The hypothesis of market efficiency suggests that asset prices are determined by the interaction of rational agents. In addition, one usually also requires that publicly available information cannot be used to construct profitable trading rules. In other words, market efficiency has come to be associated with the notion that information acquisition by individuals is a futile activity. Underlying the above notion of efficiency, the martingale model allows for a particular equilibrium that specifies precisely how information is reflected in prices. Lucas (1978) explores the underlying assumptions of the martingale model that include constant and common time preferences, common probabilities, and risk neutrality or the absence of aggregate risk, and has been incorporated into textbooks such as Brealy and Myers (1984). Leroy (1989) provides an excellent survey of the

The paper is a revised version of an earlier draft entitled "Nonparametric forecasts of precious metal rates of return." The author wishes to acknowledge the financial support from Social Sciences and Humanities Research Council of Canada. I want to thank participants at seminars at Brock University, Indiana University, LSE, University College London, and Wilfrid Laurier University for helpful comments.

martingale hypothesis, its relation to the more restrictive random-walk model, and its empirical success (or lack of it).

Recently, there have been a number of papers in economics that use tools that were developed in the area of nonlinear dynamics to test for the presence of nonlinear structure in various economic time series (see Barnett and Chen 1988; Frank and Stengos 1988; and Lorenz 1989). In financial series, a number of recent studies have found nonlinear structure (see Frank and Stengos 1989; Hsieh 1989; Scheinkman and LeBaron 1989). These findings raise the possibility that systematic and usable nonlinear structure in the rates of return has yet to be accounted for. Brock (1988) discusses from a theoretical point of view some of the issues associated with the presence of nonlinearities in finance. White (1988) has pointed to bounded rationality as an explanation of why such potentially useful information has remained uncovered. He employs neural networks to investigate the nonlinear structure of IBM daily stock returns.

Following Frank and Stengos (1989) we conduct a thorough investigation of the behavior of gold rates of return. Because of the diversity of gold uses (store of value, medium of exchange, value in production, and aesthetic value) and its importance in society both historically and present, the question of efficiency in the gold market is an important one; see Jastram (1977) for a historical perspective. With new supply and demand for gold accounting for only approximately 1 percent of its existing stock annually, its current price is therefore heavily influenced by future spot price expectations. Thus, possible sales of large holdings of government-owned gold only add to the economic uncertainty and hence will cause expectations to be more unstable than is usually the case (see Fama and French 1988). The implied price instability of gold prices puts the study of market efficiency in the gold market on a different footing than the study of market efficiency for other assets and raises the possibility of nonlinearities that could be potentially exploitable.

Prediction is central in both econometrics and in other sciences. In the physical sciences, where the systems under investigation are often simpler, there is less of a problem than in economics, where the theoretical models are either overly simplified, and hence quite incomplete to render accurate forecasts, or they are too complicated to handle analytically. One can sometimes carefully measure the initial conditions and then use the equations of the model to produce forecasts, but, without a set of equations well founded in economic theory, this method cannot work satisfactorily. Alternatively, one may resort to ad hoc statistical models. Predictions are generated by assuming that the future is a parametric stochastic function of the past. Recently, the troubling nature of the functional-form assumptions have received increased attention (see Gallant and White 1988).

One usually employs a statistical model in place of a theoretical model because of an absence of well-established knowledge about the system. Accordingly, one would like to impose little prior structure because of the uncertainty that surrounds the nature of this structure. It is therefore the lack of well-established prior knowledge that necessitates the use of ad hoc methods. Such methods are then assessed according to how well they work in practice.

We evaluate a simple approach to forecasting using nonparametric regression techniques. We apply kernel methods and nearest-neighbor methods to estimate the regression function (conditional mean) of the variables that we want to forecast and then we forecast out of sample. Kernel methods have been extensively used in econometric applications; see Ullah (1988) for a survey. Applications of nearest-neighbor methods include the work of Robinson (1987) in a regression context as well as the work of Farmer and Sidorowich (1987, 1988a, 1988b) in a forecasting context.[1]

Apart from a natural desire for riches by beating the market, there are additional reasons why one would like to pursue this question. Farmer and Sidorowich (1987, 1988b) report some success in using this approach to forecast simple chaotic systems. Given the results of Scheinkman and LeBaron (1989) and Frank and Stengos (1989), one might conjecture that such methods could potentially aid in forecasting financial rates of return.

LeBaron (1988) reports the results of similar tests for some financial indices – the tent map, and the Mackey-Glass map – after he fit an autoregressive process of dimension 10, AR(10). On the value of weighted Center for Research in Security Prices (CRSP) index between July 1962 and March 1974, a very limited degree of forecastability was found. On other indexes and during other periods, no forecastability was found. The tent map was readily forecasted; the Mackey-Glass data were also forecastable, but to a lesser degree.

More recently, Frank and Stengos (1990), Prescott and Stengos (1990), and Diebold and Nasan (1990) all have found lack of out-of-sample forecastability in gold rates of return and exchange rates. The present study is more general in scope than the studies of Frank and Stengos (1990) and Prescott and Stengos (1990) because we use daily rates for return for the period January 1976 to April 1993, whereas they only used data for the period January 1976 to June 1986. We also employed a variety of nonparametric filters, whereas they only employed a single nearest-neighbor and kernel filter, respectively.

The paper is organized as follows: Section 2 provides a statement of the problem. Section 3 presents an overview of the nonparametric filters that we used to produce the out-of-sample forecasts. Section 4 describes the data and reports the empirical forecasts for daily gold rates of return. Both traditional linear methods and nonparametric methods fail to forecast out of sample. Section 5 attempts to calibrate the findings of the previous section by conducting

---

[1] To derive the properties of the nonparametric forecasts, one has to assume that the process is stationary, ergodic, and Markovian. These assumptions are commonly employed in asset pricing theory. In fact, the Markovian structure of asset prices is central in the development of the Lucas (1978) model.

a number of simulations with artificially generated data of known complexity. In Section 6, we conclude.

2   Estimation problem

The true system takes the following form: $X_{t+1} = \mathbf{F}(X_t)$, $F : R^n \to R^n$. The law of motion for the system X_t is represented by F. Our information set is assumed to be restricted to a time series of scalar observations $\{x_t\}_{t=1}^T$, with $X_t = h(X_t)$, $h : R^n \to R$. An empirical model for the system takes the form:

$$x_t = g(x_{t-1}, x_{t-2}, \ldots, x_0) \tag{18.1}$$

A statistical model is a set of assumptions concerning $g(\cdot)$. Commonly, $g(\cdot)$ is assumed decomposable into signal and error components. For example, in the case of the popular autoregressive (AR) and autoregressive moving-average (ARMA) models, $g(\cdot)$ assumes a particular linear form. In the case of an ARMA(k, l) model, we have

$$x_t = \sum_{i=1}^{k} \alpha_i x_{t-1} + \sum_{j=1}^{l} \beta_j \varepsilon_{t-j} + \varepsilon_t \tag{18.2}$$

Let $E(\cdot)$ denote mathematical expectation. The noise component is assumed to satisfy $E(\varepsilon_t) = 0$, $E(\varepsilon_t^2) = \sigma_\varepsilon^2$ and $E(\varepsilon_s \varepsilon_t) = 0$ for all s and t, such that $t \neq s$. Forecasting, then, requires selection of values for k and l followed by statistical estimation of the α_i and β_j values. Note that if the ε_t are assumed to be independent, the ordinary least squares (OLS) forecasts will be optimal in the class of all forecasts, linear and nonlinear. However, if the errors are only uncorrelated, then the OLS forecasts from equation (18.2) will only be the best linear forecasts [in the mean squared error (MSE) sense]. It is the independence-of-the-errors assumption that is used commonly to justify the linearity of the functional form in equation (18.2) that is troubling.

Nonparametric techniques simply allow for an unspecified conditional mean. In other words, we have that

$$x_t = E(x_t | x_{t-1}, x_{t-2}, \ldots, x_{t-k}) + \varepsilon_t. \tag{18.3}$$

In the above case, we assume the ε to be well behaved, allowing for the possibility of weak dependence but requiring weak stationarity (see Robinson 1990). Then, kernel methods imply that $E(x_t | x_{t-1}, x_{t-2}, \ldots, x_{t-k})$ in equation (18.3) can be estimated by $\hat{E}(x_t | x_{t-1}, x_{t-2}, \ldots, x_{t-k})$, where

$$\hat{E}(x_t | x_{t-1}, x_{t-2}, \ldots, x_{t-k}) = \sum_t r_t x_t, \tag{18.4}$$

where the r_t are the kernel weights to be described below. Similarly, one can obtain other types of weights to form an estimate of the regression function, such as nearest-neighbor weights.

3   Estimating the regression function nonparametrically

Silverman (1986) presents a general introduction to nonparametric density estimation, while Ullah (1988) focuses on nonparametric estimation of econometric
functionals. The conditional mean of a random variable x, given a vector of
conditioning variables w, can be written as $E(x|w) = M(w)$. In parametric
estimation, $M(w)$ is typically assumed to be linear in w, but in the nonparametric approach, $M(w)$ remains a general functional form. The conditional mean
of x can be expressed as

$$E(x|w) = M(w) = \int x[f(x, w)/f_1(w)]dx, \tag{18.5}$$

where $f_1(w)$ is the marginal density of w. In the nonparametric framework,
forecasts of x conditional on w are calculated directly by constructing an empirical counterpart to equation (18.5).

The approach can be illustrated by considering the problem of estimating a
univariate density function $f(z)$ using the random sample $z_1, \ldots, z_n$ (see, e.g.,
Silverman 1986). Let $\hat{F}(z)$ be the empirical cumulative distribution function
defined as the proportion of the sample values that are less than or equal to z.
An estimate of the density function $f(z)$ can be obtained from

$$\hat{f}(z) = \frac{\hat{F}(z + h/2) - \hat{F}(z - h/2)}{h}$$

for small values of h, or

$$\hat{f}(z) = (hn)^{-1} \sum_{1}^{n} I\left(\frac{z - z_t}{h}\right) \tag{18.6}$$

where $I(\cdot)$ is the usual indicator function. The estimate $\hat{f}(z)$ described by
equation (18.6) has the significant deficiency that it is not smooth. Spikes and
potholes are likely to characterize $\hat{f}(z)$, especially where the data are sparse.
The family of kernel estimators, introduced by Rosenblatt (1956), attempts to
correct this problem:

$$\hat{f}(z) = (nh)^{-1} \sum_{1}^{n} K\left(\frac{z - z_t}{h}\right) \tag{18.7}$$

where the kernel function K satisfies certain conditions, including

$$K(z^*) \geq 0, \int K(z^*)dz^* = 1, \quad \text{for} \quad z^* = (z - z_t)/h. \tag{18.8}$$

Certain kernels, such as the normal density function used in this paper, also
satisfy $\int z^* K(z^*)dz^* = 0$. Because it is possible to choose the function K so
that it is continuous, the resulting kernel estimator of the density function also

will be continuous. In the present paper, the kernel is chosen to be the standard multivariate normal density function, which assigns a positive weight to every observation in the sample when estimating the point $f(z)$. The largest weights are attached to the observations closest to the point z. Unlike the histogram estimator (18.6), the kernel estimator (18.7) uses the information on each side of a spike or a pothole to flatten spikes and fill in potholes. Clearly, the choice of kernel and the window width, h, determine the degree of smoothness imposed on $\hat{f}(z)$. If the kernel function is very flat, then all data points in the sample receive similar weights in the estimation of $f(z)$, and this imposes a high degree of smoothing. Similarly, if the window width h is large, the estimation of $f(z)$ draws in distant data points, and this also has a smoothing effect.

Consider now the time-series process $\{x_t\}$ and, in particular, the problem of estimating the mean of x_t conditional on $(x_{t-1}, \ldots, x_{t-p})$. Robinson (1983) has discussed the nonparametric estimation of the joint density of the time-series data-generating process (DGP) of (x_t, y_t) and of the conditional mean of x_t, given $(x_{t-1}, \ldots, x_{t-p}, y_t, \ldots, y_{t-p})$. Central limit theorems are established, and Robinson obtains results for the rate at which consistency is achieved.

Let $f(z)$ be the multivariate DGP of the $p + 1$ dimensional random vector z, which we write as $z = (x_t, w_t)$, where $w_t = (x_{t-1}, \ldots, x_{t-p})$. The kernel estimator of the joint density is

$$\hat{f}(x_1, w) = n^{-1}h^{-(p+1)} \sum_1^n K\left(\frac{x - x_t}{h}, \frac{w - w_t}{h}\right).$$

Similarly, the estimator for the marginal distribution of w is

$$\hat{f}(w) = n^{-1}h^{-p} \sum_1^n K_2\left(\frac{w - w_t}{h}\right),$$

where $K_2(w^*) = \int K(x^*, w^*)dx^*$. Again, the asterisk denotes the transformation $x^* = (x - x_t)/h$, where x_t is considered fixed. Similar transformations apply to the elements of w. Given equation (18.5), above, which defines the conditional expectation of x given w, and some algebraic manipulations, one can derive the nonparametric estimator of the regression function as

$$\hat{E}(x|w) = \sum_1^n x_t r_t \tag{18.9}$$

where

$$r_t = K_2\left(\frac{w - w_t}{h}\right) \bigg/ \sum_{t=1}^n K_2\left(\frac{w - w_t}{h}\right).$$

Expression (18.9) can be evaluated at any value of w to yield the nonparametric estimator of the regression function. Clearly, out-of-sample forecasts, conditional on a set of known w values, can be calculated using expression (18.9); see, for example, Moschini, Prescott, and Stengos (1988). The choice of h can be made using cross-validation techniques (see Härdle 1990) in such a way as to minimize the overall mean squared error. We follow this approach in the in-sample estimation to select the appropriate h, and then we use it in the out-of-sample forecasting experiments.

The nearest-neighbor method can be intuitively explained in the following way. Take the time series $\{x_t\}_{t=1}^{T}$ and convert it into a series vector of **k** components each denoted as $x_t^k = (x_t, x_{t-1}, \ldots, x_{t-k+1})$. In the context of estimating chaotic systems, the above **k** vectors are known as k histories. In that context, for k sufficiently long, there is a diffeomorphism between the DGP that cannot be observed and the observed collection of these **k** vectors or k histories (see Takens 1981). Therefore, reconstruction of the dynamics of the system can rely on this collection of k histories, because the DGP itself is unknown.

Now, for the nearest-neighbor forecasting problem, one takes the most recent history available and searches over the set of all k histories to find the K nearest neighbors. For instance, if one wants to forecast x_t from the information available at $t-1$, one computes the distance of the vector x_{t-1}^k defined as $x_{t-1}^k = (x_{t-1}, x_{t-2}, \ldots, x_{t-k})$ and its K nearest neighbors to form an alternative estimator of $E(x_t | x_{t-1}, x_{t-2}, \ldots, x_{t-k})$. Typically, one uses the Euclidean distance. For a more thorough discussion of the weighting schemes that are available for the construction of the above distance, see Robinson (1987). From a computational point of view, uniform weights are the most popular in the literature (see Härdle 1990). Also, the choice of weights will only affect the bias and variance contribution terms to the MSE upto a proportionality factor. Hence, asymptotically, the choice of weights is not important, although there may be small sample effects. Hence, in the present application, we used uniform weights to weigh the contribution of the K nearest neighbors in the overall estimate of the regression function $E(x_t | x_{t-1}, x_{t-2}, \ldots, x_{t-k})$.

4   Empirical results

We consider daily time series of gold prices traded on the London exchange[2] from the beginning of January 1975 to the end of April 1993. The gold price is denominated as U.S.\$ per fine ounce. If the original prices are denoted as P_t, then the daily rate of return is $x_t = \log(P_t) - \log(P_{t-1})$. We tested for a unit root in both the $\log(P_t)$ and the x_t series, because the nonparametric filters that we use require stationary data. The augmented Dickey-Fuller test for the levels is -1.5815 and for the first differences is -33.6120. Therefore, the hypothesis that the x_t series is integrated of order one $[I(1)]$ is strongly rejected in favor

---

[2] The data are from I.P. Sharp commodities data base comdaily.

of the rates-of-return series. As it can be seen, there is a strong evidence for kurtosis in the series, although not so much for skewness. We proceeded to obtain the in-sample nonparametric estimates of the regression function, after having first eliminated any day-of-the-week effect from the series by regressing it on daily dummies.

We then obtained 250 out-of-sample one-step-ahead forecasts by parametric AR and nonparametric methods. We evaluated these forecasts by running the regression of the x_t^1 (actual) on the x_t^1 (forecasted). The coefficient of the independent variable should be close to unity if these forecasts are unbiased, and also, the R^2 from this regression should be high if the signal dominates the noise. However, a cautionary note is in order. The above measure of forecastability is a linear one. If the underlying DGP is nonlinear, then other information about the quality of the forecasts may be useful, such as the sign of the deviation of the actual value from its predicted value. Alternatively, one could devise measures that are based on robust regression techniques to assess the unbiasedness hypothesis of the forecasts (see Huber 1981).

In Table 18.1, we also report the results of these forecast evaluations. As it can be seen, these results are clearly disappointing, using the linear measure of forecast performance described above. Previously, (Frank and Stengos 1989), the dimension estimates for gold and silver rates of return were close to six. Hence, we chose the parametric and nonparametric benchmarks to include six lags, even though, at least for the parametric case, in-sample diagnostics suggested that a more parsimonious AR process might have been a better choice. The nonparametric forecasts are quite similar. The choice of the number of nearest neighbors did not seem to affect the results. We report the results with $K = T^{1/2}$, approximately 55, using uniform weights. From a computational point of view, the choice of uniform weights is very convenient (see Härdle 1990). Also, the kernel forecasts were based on a choice of a cross-validated value of h that is selected in the in-sample estimation of the regression function. Then, the chosen h is used to compute the forecasts out-of-sample. The above evidence suggests that the gold rates of return are not forecastable with these methods for the given sample size.

5   Simulation experiments[3]

Our inability to find any forecastable structure in these rates of return calls into question the findings of previous studies that have suggested that there is evidence of nonlinear structure in the rates of return of these precious metals as well as in the rates of return of certain stock-market indexes (see, Frank and Stengos 1989, Scheinkman and LeBaron 1989). In this section we will attempt

---

[3] This section draws from material reported by Frank and Stengos (1990).

Table 18.1. *Summary statistics for gold rates of return*

Number of obs	Mean	Std. Dev.	Minimum	Maximum	Skewness	Kurtosis
4765	0.00024	0.01432	−0.13235	0.13315	0.31753	11.13008

Forecast accuracy for gold rates of return

Forecast variable	Nearest neighbor	Kernel method	ARMA (3,3)
$\hat{\beta}$	−0.1215	−0.1494	−1.2152
Std. error	−0.1291	−0.1521	−1.5127
R^2	0.0001	0.0001	1.0001
M	6	6	–

Note: The results above are based on the regression of the rates of return, x_t, on a constant and its forecasted one-step-ahead value x_t^f using the estimation method indicated. These regression results are based on 250 pairs of actual and forecasted values. $\hat{\beta}$ = estimated coefficient of x_t^f; Std. error = standard error of $\hat{\beta}$; R^2 = coefficient of determination of the above regression (we use it as a measure of forecastibility); M = number of lags used to estimate the regression functions (embedding dimension).

to address that question. With real world rates of return as is the case with precious metals, the true DGP is not observable. Therefore, we conducted a number of simulations on known DGPs. We analyzed two sorts of systems: iterated tent maps and a mock martingale based on the tent map.

The tent map is represented by $x_t = F^1(x_{t-1})$, where x_0 is given and where

$$F^1(x_{t-1}) = \begin{cases} 2x_{t-1} & \text{if} \quad 0 < x_{t-1} < 1/2 \\ 2(1 - x_{t-1}) & \text{if} \quad 1/2 \le x_{t-1} < 1 \end{cases}$$

The function $F^2 \equiv F^1[F^1(x)]$ and, in general, the Nth iterated tent map is created as $F^N(x) \equiv F^1[F^{N-1}(x)]$. Therefore, by using the iterations, more complex systems can be created in a natural and systematic way. Let the one-time-iterated map be denoted by

$$x_t = F^1[F^1(x_{t-1})]$$

$$= \text{constant} \pm (2^2)x_{t-2}.$$

The constant appears because x_t may be on either side of the boundary point 1/2. Given T observations, the Lyapunov exponent of the one-time-iterated tent map is given as

$$\lambda = (1/T) \sum_{t=1}^{T} [\log(|\partial x_t / \partial x_{t-2}|)]$$

$$= (1/T) \sum_{t=1}^{T} [\log(2^2)]$$

$$= 2\log(2).$$

Because the Lyapunov exponent of the tent map is $\log(2)$, in effect, one iteration means that the positive Lyapunov exponent for the generated series has doubled from before. It is easy to see that, in the case of a series generated from N iterations, the exponent is increased by an N-fold. Farmer and Sidorovich (1987) refer to such iterations as the extrapolation time. Note that the same argument does not apply for the correlation dimension. Given that the attractor of the one-dimensional tent map is closed and bounded, the distance between points in the attractor will be the same asymptotically for any iterated tent map as it is for the simple tent map. In other words, the dimension estimates in this case should be the same. Even though for one- and tow-times-iterated systems, one-step-ahead forecasting can be successful with limited sample sizes, the data requirements seem to rise exponentially in the number of iterations or extrapolation time (see Farmer and Sidorowich 1987).

To illustrate some of the issues in chaos, Frank, and Stengos (1988) used the logistic map to create data reminiscent of financial time series. The mock martingale is given as

$$P_{t+1} = P_t + x_t - 0.5$$

$$x_{t+1} = 4x_t(1 - x_t)$$

where x_0 is taken to be a value in $(0,1)$. The examples were used to create both the data set as well as the data to forecast. Only observations prior to data t are used in an attempt to forecast x_t. Given that the evidence with the real-world data showed that the kernel and the nearest-neighbor-method estimates were quite similar, and because the length of the simulated series was quite large, to reduce the computation costs, we only used one nearest-neighbor method to obtain nonparametric forecasts. We also used parametric AR specifications to produce forecasts for the purpose of comparison.

The basic findings from the simulations are set out in Tables 18.2 and 18.3. Linear time-series models such as $AR(k)$ and $ARMA(k, l)$ have no success in forecasting these nonlinear systems. This is to be expected because they assume functional forms that are not valid. The inability of familiar parametric models to forecast does not mean that the systems are lacking in predictable structure. Among the results, the most interesting finding is the performance of the nonparametric techniques. They work well in simple systems, because the mock martingale was readily forecastable even from fairly small data sets. If N denotes the extrapolation time, once- and twice-iterated tent maps ($N = 1, 2$) also are readily forecasted. When $N = 3$, the data requirements rise rather

Table 18.2. *Nearest-neighbor forecast quality on the mock martingale*

| Forecast | Mock martingale | | | |
	P_t	P_t	ΔP_t	ΔP_t
$\hat{\beta}$	0.9971	0.9989	0.9913	1.0085
t-statistic	212.5110	348.2032	251.1720	333.6721
R^2	0.9531	0.9716	0.9731	0.9987
T	500	1,000	500	1,000
M	3	3	3	3

Note: The same explanations apply as in Table 18.1 with the addition that T denotes the number of observations that were generated and used to estimate the regression function in-sample. Then, the 250 observations that are used to assess the forecastibility of the system were computed as in the case of the precious-metal rates-of-return series using the rolling estimation method.

abruptly. When $N = 4$, even using a data set of 60,000 observations only led to an R^2 of 0.52 from regressing the actual on the forecast value. Computer limitations prevented us from trying the case of $N = 5$. However, it is suspected that it would require at least 10^6 observations to work in a satisfactory manner. Data requirements seem to rise sharply in the extrapolation time. This finding seems consistent with that of Farmer and Sidorowich (1987).

The above simulations suggest that complex nonlinear systems can display forecastability only for extremely large data sets. These data sets are not available for real-life economic applications, although recently, with the computerization of stock-market trading, the collection of intradaily observations will contribute to the creation of very large data sets. In that case, it would be interesting to see the forecastability that would be present in these series.

6   Conclusions

The main conclusion is that the nonparametric methods seem to work sufficiently well on some simple systems for which traditional models do not work. However, the data requirements rise quite sharply as the true complexity of the underlying DGP rises. This may account for our inability to successfully forecast the gold rates of return. Hopefully, longer data series will enable us in the future to determine whether forecastability is indeed possible in these nonlinear processes, or whether the nonlinearities that have been found to be present in these data are so complex that, for all intents and purposes, they are not exploitable.

Table 18.3. *Forecast accuracy on iterated tent map*

Forecast technique	N = 1		
	Nearest neighbor	AR (1)	ARMA (1, 1)
$\hat{\beta}$	1.0021	0.9785	1.0015
t-statistic	128.1300	18.7820	18.5800
R^2	0.9744	0.0041	0.0037
T	500	2,500	2,500
M	2		
	N = 2		
	Nearest neighbor	AR (2)	ARMA (1,1)
$\hat{\beta}$	1.0417	0.9996	0.8841
t-statistic	87.0821	18.7420	17.3510
R^2	0.9227	0.0009	0.0006
T	500	2,500	2,500
M	2		
	N = 3		
	Nearest neighbor	Nearest neighbor	Nearest neighbor
$\hat{\beta}$	0.9352	1.0051	1.0139
t-statistic	20.1671	38.2631	38.4710
R^2	0.1420	0.6431	0.7393
T	500	2,500	5,000
M	3	3	3
	N = 3		
	Nearest neighbor	AR (3)	ARMA (1,1)
$\hat{\beta}$	1.0116	1.0053	1.0031
t-statistic	102.5700	16.7320	16.5410
R^2	0.9591	0.0021	0.0001
T	15,000	2,500	2,500
M	3		
	N = 4		
	Nearest neighbor	Nearest neighbor	Nearest neighbor
$\hat{\beta}$	0.9124	0.9824	0.9178
t-statistic	15.5300	16.3531	17.1710
R^2	0.0001	0.0031	0.0042
T	5,000	7,500	15,000
M	4	4	4

Table 18.3. *(cont.)*

	N = 4		
	Nearest neighbor	AR (4)	ARMA (2, 2)
$\hat{\beta}$	1.0035	0.9931	1.0081
t-statistic	26.2510	18.5410	17.5430
R^2	0.5173	0.0071	0.0001
T	60,000	2,500	2,500
M	4		

Note : N = The degree of iteration of the tent map, i.e., $F^N(x)$, as explained in the text.

REFERENCES

Barnett, W., and Chen, P. (1988). The aggregation-theoretic monetary aggregates are chaotic and have strange attractors. In *Dynamic Econometric Modelling*, eds. W. Barnett, E. Berndt, and H. White, Cambridge Uniersity Press, New York.

Brealy, R., and Myers, S. (1984). *Principles of Corporate Finance*, 2nd ed., McGraw-Hill, New York.

Brock, W. A. (1988). Nonlinearity and complex dynamics in economics and finance. In *The Economy as an Evolving Complex System*, eds. P. Anderson, K. Arrow, and D. Pines, Addison-Wesley, Reading, MA.

Diebold, F. X., and Nason, J. M. (1989). Nonparametric exchange rate prediction?, *J. Int. Econ.* **28**, 315–32.

Fama, E., and French, K. (1988). Business cycles and the behavior of metals prices, *J. Finance*, **43**(5), 1075–93.

Farmer, J. D., and Sidorowich, J. J. (1987). Predicting chaotic time series, *Phys. Rev. Lett.*, **59**, 845–8.

  (1988a). Can new approaches to nonlinear modelling improve economic forecasts? In *The Economy as an Evolving Complex System*, eds. P. Anderson, K. Arrow, and D. Pines, Addison-Wesley, Reading, MA.

  (1988b). Exploiting chaos to predict the future and reduce noise, Technical Report LA-UR-88-901, Theoretical Division and Center for Nonlinear Studies, Los Alamos National Laboratory.

Frank, M. Z., and Stengos, T. (1988). Chaotic dynamics in economic time series, *J. Econ. Surv.* **2**(2), 103–33.

  (1989). Measuring the strangeness of gold and silver rates of return, *Rev. Econ. Stud.*, **56**, 553–68.

  (1990). Nearest neighbor forecasts of precious metal rates of return, Department of Economics, mimeo, University of Guelph.

Gallant, A. R., and White, H. (1988). *A Unified Theory of Estimation and Inference for Nonlinear Dynamic Models*, Basil Blackwell, Oxford Publ.

Härdle, W. (1990). *Applied Nonparametric Regression*, Cambridge University Press, New York.

Hsieh, D. A. (1989). Testing for nonlinear dependence in foreign exchange rates: 1974–1983, *J. Business*, **62**, 339–68.

Huber, P. J. (1981). *Robust Statistics*, Wiley, New York.

Jastram, R. W. (1977). *The Golden Constant: The English and American Experience 1560–1976*, Wiley, New York.

LeBaron, B. (1988). Stock return nonlinearities: Some initial tests and findings, Unpublished Ph.D. dissertation, Department of Economics, University of Chicago.

LeRoy, S. F. (1989). Efficient capital markets and martingales, *J. Econ. Lit.*, **XXVII**, 1583–1621.

Lorenz, H. W. (1989). *Nonlinear Dynamical Economics and Chaotic Motion*, Springer-Verlag, Berlin.

Lucas, R. E., Jr. (1978). Asset prices in an exchange economy, *Econometrica*, **46**, 1426–45.

Moschini, G., Prescott, D. M., and Stengos, T. (1988). Nonparametric forecasting: An application to the US hog supply, *Empirical Econ.*, **13**, 141–54.

Prescott, D. M., and Stengos, T. (1990). Testing for Forecastable Nonlinear Dependence in Weekly Gold Rates of Return, Working Paper, Economics No. 91/31, European University Institute.

Robinson, P. M. (1983). Nonparametric estimators for time series, *J. Time-Ser. Anal.*, **4**, 185–208.

  (1987). Asymptotically efficient estimation in the presence of heteroskedasticity of unknown form, *Econometrica*, **55**, 875–91.

  (1990). Time series with strong dependence, paper presented at the 6th World Congress of the Econometric Society, Barcelona, Spain.

Rosenblatt, M. (1956). Remarks on some nonparametric estimates of a density function, *Ann. Math. Stat.*, **27**, 832–37.

Scheinkman, J. A., and LeBaron, B. (1989). Nonlinear dynamics and stock returns, *J. Business*, **62**, 311–37.

Silverman, B. W. (1986). *Density Estimation for Statistics and Data Analysis*, Chapman and Hall, London.

Takens, F. (1981). Detecting strange attractors in turbulence, In *Dynamical Systems and Turbulence*, eds. D. Rand and L. Young, Springer-Verlag, Berlin.

Ullah, A. (1988). Nonparametric estimation of econometric functionals, *Can. J. Economics*, **XXI**, 625–58.

White, H. (1988). Economic prediction using neural networks: The case of IBM daily stock returns, Discussion Paper No. 88–20, Department of Economics, University of California at San Diego.

For EU product safety concerns, contact us at Calle de José Abascal, 56–1°,
28003 Madrid, Spain or eugpsr@cambridge.org.

www.ingramcontent.com/pod-product-compliance
Ingram Content Group UK Ltd.
Pitfield, Milton Keynes, MK11 3LW, UK
UKHW042316180425
457623UK00005B/17